"In our day when the evil of anti-Semitism is rising, Christians need to know they stand on a Jewish foundation and are part of a Jewish story. Jay Phelan tells that story down to our own time and draws attention to the questions and efforts Jews made to live in alien cultures, particularly regarding theological issues such as the role of the law, particularity, and the land of Israel. In doing so he draws parallels to similar questions and dynamics in the Christian faith. This is a helpful contribution and will assist Jewish-Christian dialogue."

— Klyne R. Snodgrass
author of *Stories with Intent: A Comprehensive Guide to the Parables of Jesus*

"In a climate of religious and political polarity, John Phelan's book is a welcome and timely contribution to the evangelical world and beyond. His insights clearly emerge not only from careful scholarship but also from faithful relationships with Jewish brothers and sisters. I learned much reading his book, and I recommend it for all who seek to reflect the handiwork of the creator in the diversity of peoples!"

— Michelle A. Clifton-Soderstrom
North Park Theological Seminary

Separated Siblings

An Evangelical Understanding of Jews and Judaism

John E. Phelan Jr.

William B. Eerdmans Publishing Company
Grand Rapids, Michigan

Wm. B. Eerdmans Publishing Co.
4035 Park East Court SE, Grand Rapids, Michigan 49546
www.eerdmans.com

Published 2020
Printed in the United States of America

26 25 24 23 22 21 20 1 2 3 4 5 6 7

ISBN 978-0-8028-7455-9

Library of Congress Cataloging-in-Publication Data

Names: Phelan, John E., Jr., author.
Title: Separated siblings : an evangelical understanding of Jews and Judaism / John E. Phelan, Jr.
Description: Grand Rapids, Michigan : William B. Eerdmans Publishing Company, 2020. | Includes bibliographical references and index. | Summary: "A concise introduction to Judaism—including its history, beliefs, and practices—geared toward an American evangelical audience"—Provided by publisher.
Identifiers: LCCN 2020015362 | ISBN 9780802874559 (paperback)
Subjects: LCSH: Judaism—Relations—Evangelicalism. | Evangelicalism—Relations—Judaism. | Evangelicalism—United States.
Classification: LCC BR1641.J83 P44 2020 | DDC 261.2/6—dc23
LC record available at https://lccn.loc.gov/2020015362

Unless otherwise noted, quotations of the Hebrew Scriptures are taken from the JPS Hebrew-English Tanakh (Philadelphia: Jewish Publication Society, 2000).

Unless otherwise noted, quotations of the New Testament are taken from the Today's New International Version (TNIV).

To the memory of Chana Tova Poupko,
beloved granddaughter of Rabbi Yehiel Poupko,
and in thanksgiving for my grandson,
Kjell Nathaniel Nelson-Phelan

CONTENTS

FOREWORD

When the twentieth century began, little, if anything, had changed in the attitude and theology of Christianity and its representative churches to Judaism and the Jewish people. In their view, the Jewish people had committed the most heinous of crimes: not mere homicide, the murder of a person, but deicide, the murder of a god. This sin was compounded by the fact that they who knew the Father at Sinai should have been the first to recognize the son, born out of their very flesh, at Calvary. Augustine taught that Israel would wander the earth homeless in an abased and despicable state as punishment for that crime in order to testify to the truth of Jesus Christ, to the consequences of rejecting him. To be sure, Augustine never imagined the annihilation or the murder of any Jews. Invoking Psalm 59, Augustine declared, "Slay them not!"

> Slay them not, lest my people be unmindful;
> with Your power make wanderers of them;
> bring them low, O our shield, the Lord. (Ps 59:12 [11])

The very life of the Jewish people was to be preserved as a lesson in the wages of sin.

The classic Christian teaching of contempt, the *adversus Iudaeos* tradition, was an absolutely necessary condition for the destruction of European Jewry. At the same time, it was wholly insufficient. When World War II ended, Christian churches looked at themselves, at Europe, at Christendom itself, in horror and shame. The churches took note of the perpetrators and the collaborators and the bystanders who stood with folded arms, most of whom were baptized. Christianity, especially the Roman Catholic Church and the Reformation churches, realized the consequence of their teaching.

Thus, one of the greatest, if not the greatest, theological change in Christian thinking took place. In the wake of the destruction of European Jewry, the Roman Catholic Church and some Protestant denominations affirmed that the Jewish people were not guilty of the crime of deicide, that the promise God made to Abraham and Sarah and the contract God and Israel entered into at Sinai were still in force and efficacious, for the gifts of God are irrevocable. In practice, these churches no longer seek to bring Israel to Christ.

The destruction of European Jewry is a far, far greater challenge to Christian faith than it is to Judaism. In the twentieth century, the two greatest forces of evil in human history were arrayed against the Jewish people. Lenin and Stalin, in their way, and the unmentionable one, along with his German people, declared, "Let us wipe them out as a nation; Israel's name will be remembered no more" (Ps 83:5 [4]). No two greater forces in history have ever been arrayed against God's chosen. God kept the promise. We emerged from these tyrannies to build two great Jewish civilizations. We left Europe through its chimneys, leaving behind our ashes and millions of collaborators and bystanders who were only too happy to see us leave. We reestablished Jewish sovereignty in our ancient homeland, and we built a great Jewish civilization in the United States of America. God did not abandon us. Christians did.

The Roman Catholic Church, the Lutheran Church, other Reformed churches, and some churches not implicated in the destruction of European Jewry understood that they were all heirs to the Christian teaching of contempt for Judaism and the Jewish people. And so, in the United States of America, that rare Western country with no history of government oppression of the Jews, where all believers are free to pursue their beliefs and to develop the institutions that express their faith, it was possible for the first time in two thousand years for Christians to develop a productive and respectful relationship with the Jewish people and with Judaism. The Roman Catholic Church pursued this with warmth, friendship, repentance, commitment, and great scholarship that nourished profound theological change and set a powerful example for the Protestant churches. To significantly lesser degrees some of the Protestant churches did the same. Thus, the American Jewish community has, since World War II, enjoyed excellent developing relationships with the various Christian churches. Nevertheless, it is still the case that some Christian thinkers have extended the classic Christian teaching of contempt from Judaism and the Jewish people to Zionism and the State of Israel.

It is in this historic American and Christian context that the evangelical-Jewish relationship has developed. It is the youngest of the relationships between the Jewish people and Christian churches in the United States, for two reasons. First, for all practical purposes, unlike the Roman Catholic and Protestant churches, evangelicalism has essentially no institutional antecedents in Europe, no forebears who oppressed the Jewish people and took part in the destruction of European Jewry. Second, for the most part, American Jews and American evangelicals do not live in the same places in the United States. While a few scholarly conferences took place between evangelical and Jewish scholars in the late 1970s and early 1980s, it is only more recently that the relationship has begun.

Some years ago, I met Dr. John Phelan, past president of North Park Theological Seminary. I asked him for a gift of two priceless commodities: time and knowledge. I asked him to teach me the New Testament. I should know it. After all, the New Testament is a Jewish book! It was written by Jews, by and large for Jewish people. It is about the Torah. It is about Judaism. In fact, if I may put it this way, the New Testament, the source of our Jewish dilemma, is really for the most part a series of internal family letters that then went public to all the gentiles!

Storytelling is a tradition of the Torah. Faithful Jews and Christians are challenged to identify the concepts inherent in the narratives. As a genre of Jewish literature, the Gospels are no different. Continuing the literary precedent of the Torah, the critical concepts and beliefs of the Gospels emerge in encounters between Jesus, his followers, many Jews, and, on one or two occasions, a gentile. Therefore, it makes sense to continue this tradition.

How has the evangelical-Jewish relationship grown in the past two decades? It is really quite simple. I woke up one morning and realized that only one hour's drive from the offices of the Jewish Federation of Metropolitan Chicago are the offices of *Christianity Today*. And like someone discovering fire or the wheel, I realized that hardly anyone in the Jewish community knew this. I picked up the phone. I called David Neff, then editor in chief of *Christianity Today*. I said, "I'd like to meet with you." We had a remarkable meeting. He asked what I was seeking. I said, "Two things. First, that you talk *with* us before talking *about* us; second, that you fulfill the Roman Catholic teaching in the notes to *Nostra Aetate*, that is, that you come to know Judaism and the Jewish people as we know ourselves."

David and I developed a wonderful relationship over the years. At one point we looked at each other and said, "We need to expand this." Out of this was birthed the National Evangelical-Jewish Conference, which for the first time brought together national leadership from the Jewish community—its various national organizations and synagogue denominations, as well as rabbis and scholars—with their counterparts in a variety of national evangelical communal institutions, academic institutions, and seminaries. Jay Phelan, who has taught me what little I know about the New Testament, is a participant in this annual conference and serves as a co-chair. One of the greatest benefits of Dr. Phelan's becoming a deep and trusted friend of the Jewish people is this very book. Dr. Phelan wants evangelicals to come to know Judaism and the Jewish people as Judaism and the Jewish people know themselves.

This book is the product of an enormous amount of research, scholarship, and authorial skill. It is also the product of many friendships that Dr. Phelan enjoys in and with the Jewish community. Wisely, he circulated the manuscript to a variety of friends and colleagues in the Conservative, Orthodox, and Reform Jewish traditions. Everyone who has read various chapters of the book says one thing: "When I read what Dr. Phelan writes about Judaism and the Jewish people, I recognize the Jewish people. I recognize the American Jewish community. I recognize Israel. I recognize myself." In this book, Jay Phelan presents Judaism and the Jewish people to evangelical Christians as Judaism and the Jewish people understand themselves. As such, in years to come, this work will come to be seen as a watershed moment that brought about mutual understanding between evangelical Christians and Jews.

Rabbi Yehiel Poupko
Rabbinic Scholar
Jewish United Fund/Jewish Federation of Metropolitan Chicago

PREFACE

Why would a Christian write a book on Jews and Judaism? Are there not good introductions to the topic written by Jews? Is not this project a bit presumptuous? There are, in fact, excellent introductions to Jewish belief and practice written by Jews for the general reader. Norman Solomon's *Judaism: A Very Short Introduction* is just one of several excellent examples.[1] In fact, the number of books written by Jews about the various aspects of their culture, community, traditions, and prospects is overwhelming. Judaism has from its beginning been a literate, text-based culture. Studying and reflecting upon Torah has been central to clarifying and passing on Jewish ethics, worship, and identity. And for Jews this has never been merely "religious." The study of Torah is the study of *everything*—not just "theology" or "religion." Torah (a term defined further in the first chapter) involves every aspect of Jewish life: what one eats, how one dresses, where and how one lives, whom one marries, and how one raises children.

For a Christian to venture into this thicket of history and practice is perilous indeed. The peril is not least the result of the historically brutal and dismissive ways Christians have treated Jews and read their texts. This sad and sorry history will be discussed in later chapters. But suffice it to say, that Jews have the right to be skeptical about Christians and their motives for speaking of Jews. And yet, I believe this is a valuable exercise and fully worth the risk. I am at best an amateur when it comes to Judaism. One can never know someone else's tradition from the "inside." But I trust I am an amateur in the sense of one who loves the object of his work, study, or play.

1. Norman Solomon, *Judaism: A Very Short Introduction* (Oxford: Oxford University Press, 1996). For a more comprehensive account see Dan Cohn-Sherbok, *Judaism: History, Belief and Practice* (London: Routledge, 2003).

Having said that, I trust that my education, research, and teaching have, at least in part, prepared me for this task. But there were other, perhaps more important and surprising opportunities and relationships that encouraged me to do this work.

For more than a decade I have been privileged to be friends with Rabbi Yehiel Poupko, the Judaic scholar for the Jewish Federation of Chicago, one of the most important Jewish charitable and advocacy organizations in the United States. When we met each other Yehiel and I discovered that with all our differences we shared significant similarities. We were both deeply committed to our own traditions and sacred texts. We both loved studying and arguing about those texts. And we both loved the give-and-take of scholarly investigation. Yehiel suggested that we study the New Testament together. He was particularly interested in the book of Romans, having heard how crucial that letter is for Christian thought and practice. I readily agreed.

For more than five years we worked our way through Romans. Early on Yehiel said something that I was to hear over and over again: "With my Jewish eyes the text seems to be saying . . ." He came to the New Testament with an angle of vision not entirely available to me. His extensive knowledge of the Jewish sacred texts and traditions enabled him to raise questions and make observations that would not have occurred to me. It was wonderful. Over and over during our study of Romans Paul delighted and exasperated him (and still does!). It took us five years to get through Romans and another five on 1 Corinthians. We had arrived at chapter 14 before I moved to Minnesota (Yehiel has yet to forgive me for this lapse in judgment). I kept hoping to persuade him to read some Torah with me, but he kept insisting on reading Paul. Seeing Paul "through Jewish eyes" was a powerful and revealing experience.

In recent decades, many Jewish scholars have written insightful and helpful books on Christianity (in particular on Jesus and Paul).[2] The results have been important and impressive. In 2011 *The Jewish Annotated New Testament* appeared.[3] Edited by Amy-Jill Levine and Marc Zvi Brettler, it

2. See Daniel Boyarin, *A Radical Jew: Paul and the Politics of Identity* (Berkeley: University of California Press, 1994); Alan Segal, *Paul the Convert: Apostate and Apostasy of Paul the Pharisee* (New Haven: Yale University Press, 1990); Daniel R. Langton, *The Apostle Paul in the Jewish Imagination* (Cambridge: Cambridge University Press, 2010); Amy-Jill Levine, *The Misunderstood Jew: The Church and the Scandal of the Jewish Jesus* (San Francisco: HarperCollins, 2007); Jacob Neusner, *A Rabbi Talks with Jesus* (Montreal: McGill-Queen's University Press, 2000).

3. Amy-Jill Levine and Marc Zvi Brettler, eds., *The Jewish Annotated New Testament* (Oxford: Oxford University Press, 2011). A second edition appeared in 2017.

includes brief commentaries on every book of the New Testament and a series of articles on historical, theological, and cultural issues crucial to understanding the New Testament. Outstanding Jewish scholars penned every commentary and article. Studying the New Testament with Yehiel or reading Jewish scholars' assessments of the New Testament and early Christianity has not always been easy. Sometimes tough, even painful questions are raised. Sometimes cherished interpretations are challenged. And always there is the reminder that we have mutual disagreements that we dare not paste over. But interreligious dialogue worth the name does not entail setting aside one's beloved beliefs and practices for the sake of a temporary feeling of solidarity. It is not only fair but necessary to ask hard questions and raise difficult issues with each other.

Nevertheless, a Christian student of the Jewish tradition clearly has to be very careful. Christians have in the past, and, tragically, in the present, willfully misunderstood and caricatured both Jews and Judaism. Frequently Jewish sacred texts and traditions have been studied by Christians not for the sake of understanding, but of refutation. Apologetics have frequently trumped understanding. Having said all this, I still insist that it is as important to explore Jews and Judaism "with Christian eyes" as it is for Christians to see their own sacred texts and traditions "through Jewish eyes." I trust that what follows will be an exercise in mutual respect and appreciation for a tradition and people I love. But I also trust it will not be a bland exercise in mutual admiration, but a *critical* appreciation. In our years together, as I have suggested, Yehiel and I have never tried to pretend we had no differences and disagreements. Ours has not been, to say the least, an exercise in religious relativism. Jews and Christians share a common text, the Old Testament for Christians and Tanakh for Jews. We both worship the God of Abraham, Isaac, and Jacob. But we read our common text and understand the person and accomplishments of Jesus of Nazareth very differently.

There is a second reason for viewing Jews and Judaism "with Christian eyes." I am convinced that many, if not most, Christians have only the vaguest understanding of Jews and Judaism. However valuable those volumes I cited earlier, these Christians are not likely to pick them up and read them. I trust of course that they *will* read a book about Jews and Judaism written by a Christian. Many Christians learned all they think they know about Jews and Judaism in Sunday School classes or through sermons. In many of these classes and sermons the "Pharisees" were the foil for the preacher or teacher. And the "Pharisees" were always hypocritical, legalistic, hostile to Jesus, and generally unattractive. For most Christian traditions to call someone a "Pharisee" is to insult them. I will argue that although some Pharisees clearly conflicted with Jesus, in the end he was closer to them than any other group in first-century Judaism. And although early scholarship dismissed Pharisaism as legalistic and "sterile," it was the Pharisees whose courage and creativity enabled Judaism to survive.

I fear that for many Christians their understanding of Jews and Judaism is limited to this caricature of the first-century Pharisees, scraps of texts from the prophets, and fragments of the stories of Abraham, David, and Daniel. And even this fragmentary understanding ends with the death of Jesus or the destruction of the temple in 70 CE and only picks up with the Shoah and the foundation of the state of Israel. Most of the history of the Jews, I suspect, is unknown and unappreciated by most Christians. It is, admittedly, a difficult and daunting history. It is the story of a vulnerable people living at the sufferance of others under the constant threat of extinction. But it is also the story of a remarkable intellectual and spiritual flourishing under these most difficult circumstances. Frederick the Great in 1779 famously asked the Marquis D'Argens, "Can you give me one single irrefutable proof of God?" D'Argens replied, "Yes, your Majesty, the Jews."[4] It was a pretty good answer.

It is important to understand and appreciate the history, traditions, and texts of the Jews, lest we fall prey to anti-Jewish or even anti-Semitic sentiments. The Jews are not simply an ancient people walking around dusty Palestine at the time of Jesus. They are a living, vital, contemporary people, but still vulnerable and still under threat. But there is an additional reason such study is important. Studying with Jews and exploring Jewish texts has enriched my own faith. Jews like Yehiel, Rabbi David Sandmel, and Yossi Klein Halevi, who have loved their own tradition and respected mine, have, perhaps ironically, helped me become a better Christian. The differences between us are large and undeniable. But we still worship together the God of Abraham, Isaac, and Jacob and seek to do his will. And many of us await the coming of the Messiah—some of us for the first time, others for the second.

4. This anecdote has been repeated numerous times and credited to different rulers and may, in fact, be apocryphal. I found this form of the tale in a review of Paul Johnson's *A History of the Jews* written by Jonathan Sarna in the September 1987 issue of *Moment Magazine*, a publication associated with Brandeis University.

ACKNOWLEDGMENTS

I want to thank the many Jewish friends and collaborators who have helped me understand their tradition. None of them is responsible for the errors and misunderstandings in the chapters that follow. Pride of place goes to Rabbi Yehiel Poupko for a friendship and collaboration of many years. Other Jewish conversation partners have included Rabbi David Sandmel, Dr. Amy-Jill Levine, Yossi Klein Halevi, Dr. Marcie Lenk, and Ethan Felson. I have learned a great deal over the years from Jewish members of the evangelical-Jewish dialogue group. Among them, Dr. Ruth Langer, Rabbi Harold Berman, Rabbi David Saperstein, Rabbi Steve Gutow, and Dr. Adam Gregerman. I am especially thankful for the opportunity to participate in the activities of the Shalom Hartman Institute in Jerusalem. I am grateful for the friendship and support of its president, Rabbi Donniel Hartman. I am also thankful to my colleagues at North Park Theological Seminary, especially Dr. Stephen Chester, Dr. Klyne Snodgrass, and Dr. James Bruckner, for many years of conversation on this and many other topics. I also want to thank Dr. James D. Ernest, editor-in-chief at Eerdmans, and my editor Dr. Andrew Knapp and the staff of Eerdmans for their patience and encouragement. And, as always, I am thankful to my wife Dawn for putting up with years of stacks of books and papers. You, beloved, make it all possible.

CHAPTER 1

Introducing Judaism

The Lord said to Abram: "Go forth from your native land and from your father's house to the land that I will show you.

I will make of you a great nation,
And I will bless you:
I will make your name great,
And you shall be a blessing.
I will bless those who bless you
And curse those who curse you;
And all the families of the earth
Shall bless themselves by you."

—Genesis 12:1–3

Hath not a Jew eyes? Hath not a Jew hands, organs, dimensions, senses, affections, passions! Fed with the same food, hurt with the same weapons, subject to the same diseases, healed by the same means, warmed and cooled by the same winter and summer, as a Christian is. If you prick us, do we not bleed?

—William Shakespeare, *The Merchant of Venice*

"Woman," Jesus replied, "believe me, a time is coming when you will worship the Father neither on this mountain nor in Jerusalem. You Samaritans worship what you do not know; we worship what we do know, for salvation is from the Jews."

—John 4:21–22

Who or what is a Jew anyway? This question perplexes many non-Jews and, not surprisingly, some Jews as well. Is Judaism a *religion* like Christianity and Islam? Is Jewishness a *racial* or *ethnic* marker? Are Jews part of a *people*, citizens of a *nation*, whether or not they happen to live in the land of Israel? Scripture itself uses various terms to refer to the Jews. According to Rabbi Hayim Donin, "The Bible refers to Abraham as Ibri (Hebrew), probably because he migrated from the other side (east) of the Euphrates River and Ibri means 'from the other side.'"[1] This is an *ethnic* identifier. Later in the Genesis narrative, Jacob, Abraham's grandson, was famously renamed "Israel" after his wrestling match with God (Gen 32:22–32). This was, or at least became, a *national* identifier, the name of the land and the people. The word "Jew" came from the name for the Southern Kingdom of Israel, named after the one of the sons of Jacob and later ruled by the descendants of David: Judah. It was also the name for the Roman province of Judea. It was this term, Donin suggests, that came to link the people and their faith: "the people are called Jewish, their faith Judaism, their language Hebrew, and their land Israel."[2] Judaism, then, has an *ethnic*, *national*, and *religious* character. All three are key to understanding Judaism today.

What Is Judaism?

Classic Judaism developed in the wake of the destruction of the Second Temple (70 CE). The great postwar rabbis developed and consolidated a way of Jewish life that endures to this day. For centuries this rabbinic tradition demonstrated a remarkable consistency. Throughout history there were certainly "apostate" Jews or Jews with different ideas of the precise nature of Judaism. There were Jews who converted to Christianity or Islam. There were Jews who rejected the ways their ancient rabbis had interpreted the Jewish tradition and lived the Jewish life. And there were Jews who did not take their obligations to Torah seriously. But for the vast majority of Jews, whether they lived in Palestine or Babylon, northern Europe or North Africa, it was quite clear what it meant to live and worship as a Jew. And it was no less clear to the Christian and Muslim officials who ruled over them. As

1. Hayim Halevy Donin, *To Be a Jew: A Guide to Jewish Observance in Contemporary Life* (New York: HarperCollins, 1972), 7.
2. Donin, *To Be a Jew*, 7.

my friend Rabbi Yehiel Poupko likes to say, "My grandfather did not have a Jewish identity; he was just Jewish."

What bound these diverse groups of Jews together? Two key *covenants* framed Jewish self-understanding in the Bible and well into the modern era. The *covenant with Abraham* established a *people* chosen by God to bless and be a blessing. It also promised them the *land* of Israel as a place to live and serve God. The *covenant with Moses* called them to a way of life rooted in God's Torah, God's teaching or instruction. Throughout the history of the Jewish people, to be a Jew has meant to be a *people* that lived in accordance with God's commandments as revealed in Torah. Historically, for most Jews, this Torah has included not only the five books of Moses, but the traditional rabbinic interpretations and applications of this Torah from Sinai. In the aftermath of the twin disasters of the destruction of the temple in 70 CE and the disastrous Bar Kokhba rebellion (132–135 CE), for the next fifteen hundred years, this rabbinic tradition flourished. The ancient rabbis and their heirs enabled the survival of the Jewish people. But in eighteenth-century Europe new movements brought significant changes to Judaism as well as Christianity.

New Challenges

The Enlightenment

The arrival of the Enlightenment, the explosion of "secular" learning, and the rise of the nation-state in Europe heralded these changes. The sixteenth-century Reformation had perforated the "sacred canopy" in Europe. No longer would Europe be connected by a common religious tradition. The Christian church was fragmenting into various denominations and cults. Roman Catholics, Lutherans, Reformed, Baptists, and Mennonites all had different understandings of the nature of Christianity and the way to serve God. These divisions contributed to a vicious war—the Thirty Years' War—fought early in the seventeenth century. The conflict left Europe weary of sectarian strife and brought with it a call for religious tolerance and freedom of conscience. Then, as now, "religion" was often seen to be *the* problem. As a result, individual loyalties and identities began to shift. No longer did people find their identity primarily in religion or ethnicity but in being a citizen of one of the emerging nation-states of Europe. Increasingly one was a citizen first and a believer second. While Christianity in both its Roman Catholic and various Protestant forms remained dominant, there were now more and more options for both belief and, increasingly, unbelief.

All of this obviously had a significant impact on the Jews of Europe. Jews in the eighteenth and nineteenth centuries were increasingly able to participate in the wider society of Europe and the United States. They could, depending on the country, attend university, participate in politics, grow successful businesses, and contribute to the arts and sciences in ways that were closed to them before. Some doors, in some places, still remained closed. One of the great questions in Europe would be the "emancipation" of the Jews. That is, could Jews now be full citizens of their countries, members of European society, active in every aspect of national and cultural life, or were there areas of life forbidden to them? Were the Jews capable of being citizens first and Jews second? Different countries answered these questions in different ways—as we will see.

This meant that for Jews the question of "Jewish identity" was raised, if not for the first time, certainly now in a new way. For centuries, obedience to the strictures of Torah as interpreted by the rabbis had determined the boundaries of the Jewish community. But following the food laws and the Jewish calendar made full integration into the societies of Europe difficult. If Jews remained strictly Torah observant, did this mean their participation in European society was limited? Some Jews reasoned that this was a new era and that there needed to be a reform of the old practices to permit Jews to participate fully in their various societies. If the sacred canopy of Christianity was pierced in the sixteenth century, perhaps one could say the sacred canopy of Judaism was pierced in the eighteenth and especially the nineteenth century. What did it now mean to be a Jew when following the Jewish law was deemed by some to be optional? And what did it mean to be a Jew when someone like Karl Marx, raised as a Jew, could reject belief in God entirely?

Modern Jews faced agonizing questions: Could the "peculiar" practices of the Jews—the food laws and calendar, the strange rituals, and, in some cases, odd clothing—be laid aside for the sake of participating in European society? Would Jews be accepted into the wider world if the Jewish *religion* continued to be practiced, even if shorn of some of its more "alien" characteristics? Could the national aspirations of the Jews coexist with the growing nationalism of the various European nation-states? Could the Jews truly be patriotic citizens of Germany or France if they were waiting for the coming messiah? But if these things were all laid aside, what would it mean to be a Jew? And even if they were laid aside, would Europe finally accept them?

Tragically, European Jews would find that, whatever they did, their efforts to fit in would be resisted—sometimes violently.

Ongoing Conflicts

In spite of the nineteenth-century process of emancipation, Europeans continued to distrust the Jews. British citizens, for example, could accept that a Baptist or Methodist or Anglican could be a loyal citizen of their country. But, they wondered, could a Jew or, for that matter, a Roman Catholic really be a loyal citizen? Both Jews and Roman Catholics were deemed to have "divided loyalties" (and sometimes still are). They were loyal to another "nation," the Jewish people in the case of the Jews; the Pope in the case of the Roman Catholics. Could Judaism be just one more "religion" among many? Could Jews put aside their national aspirations and odd sense of "chosenness" and be loyal citizens of Great Britain, France, or Germany? Could Judaism be "just" a religion and not a nation or a people?

Some Jews sought to disconnect Judaism from national aspirations and preserve the "religious" aspects of Judaism without all of its alienating "peculiarities." They hoped by displaying their national loyalty and patriotism to secure a place in the political, economic, and social worlds of their individual nations. At the same time, by preserving certain elements of their ancestral faith and discarding others, they hoped to preserve their Jewishness. Other Jews, however, thought this was an abandonment of what it meant to be Jewish. As the nineteenth century wore on, even these accommodating strategies failed. The reasons for this failure are not difficult to discover.

The Rise of Racism

For many in Europe and the United States, whatever the Jews thought, Judaism was not merely a nation or religion; it was a *race*. Although the terms are often used interchangeably, "race" is not the same thing as "ethnicity." The latter refers to people who share a common language, social and cultural practices, and ancestral and national experiences. Ethnicity is a *sociological* construct. The developing pseudoscience of "race," however, sought to classify human beings in the same way zoologists classified animals. It was a *biological* construct: "Large groups could be identified by skin color and then divided into subspecies by head shape, hair structure, and other quantifiable characteristics. With the chemistry of life still poorly understood, it was thought that the features of each given human subspecies were transmitted through one's blood."[3]

For the "racist" the problem with "others," whether Jews, Africans, or Asians, was not cultural or even religious but *biological.* They had "bad blood." Aristocrats everywhere sneered, "Blood will out," when evaluating the behavior of their "inferiors." One could change one's religion, one's language, one's cultural associations, but not one's "blood." The brutal effects of "racial science" were seen in the lynching of African Americans in the American South and, ultimately, in Hitler's death camps. Being a sophisticated, educated, urbane, patriotic German Jew did not matter if you had Jewish "blood." Throughout much of Europe in the late nineteenth century and well into the twentieth, Jews were not permitted to be "merely" a religion among others. They were an "alien" race in the body politic to be marginalized and ultimately eliminated.

Zionism and Secularism

As a result of this ongoing hostility, in the late nineteenth century some Jews began to argue that, given the oppression and insecurity of Jews in Europe, they would be safe only if they had their own land, their own nation, where they could defend themselves effectively. This movement, called Zionism, will be the subject of a subsequent chapter. Zionism was, from the beginning, controversial. Many of the early Zionists were not at all religious. Their reasons for wanting a nation were entirely "secular." Many religious Jews, both "liberal" and "conservative," scoffed at the idea of a Jewish nation—particularly in their ancient homeland of Israel. Some more liberal Jews feared this would undermine the places they had secured in the various European states. Some Jews, now called "Orthodox" for their preservation of traditional ways of Jewish life and practice, insisted that Israel would be reestablished as a nation only when the messiah came. The establishment of the State of Israel in the wake of World War II became a source of pride, identity, and not inconsiderable anxiety for Jews of the "Diaspora"—Jews living outside of the land of Israel. What did it now mean for Israel to be a nation for a Jew in New York or Paris or Moscow? This is still a very live question.

3. Eugene B. Borowitz, *Liberal Judaism* (New York: Union of American Hebrew Congregations, 1984), 28.

Judaism Today: A People

Today there are "secular" Jews who do not identify with Jewish religious practices or care particularly about the State of Israel. There are also "secular" Jews who very much identify with the Jewish cultural practices, their heritage and history, and care deeply about the State of Israel. They may hold a Passover Seder or attend synagogue on holidays even if they no longer believe in God. Then there are Jews that believe in and are committed to the God of Israel and practice certain parts of their traditional religion—but not others. They believe that Judaism needs to change and adapt to speak to Jews in a modern world and that certain practices of the past may be safely set aside. And, of course, there are Jews who believe the entirety of God's law was handed down at Sinai as an eternal and enduring covenant and that Jews are still bound by God's commands as they were understood and taught by the ancient rabbis. If their understanding of and practice of their religious traditions are so different, in what sense are all these people still Jews? This is a subject of ongoing controversy among Jews today.[4]

If Judaism was merely a *religion*, traditional Jews would probably deny that more liberal and secular Jews were really Jews. Among Christians, it is not uncommon for one denomination of Christians to deny that another is "really" Christian. If being a Christian entails assenting to a certain set of beliefs, then those who do not assent to my particular set of beliefs are not really "believers."

For the most part, however, Jews have not looked at it this way, as Judaism for most Jews is not just a religion, it is still in spite of everything a *people*. If you go to Israel, to Jerusalem or Tel Aviv, and sit with a coffee at an outdoor café you will see that Jews come from every nation, tongue, and tribe. There are Ethiopian Jews; Jews from Morocco, Egypt, and Iran; Jews from Russia, the Balkans, and Brooklyn. They vary radically in appearance, language, and demeanor. Some are scrupulous in their practice of Torah; some are not. And yet, most Jews would consider this variety one people, even one "ethnicity," regardless of their religious practice.

According to Orthodox Jewish law a person is a Jew if they are born to a Jewish mother. Some traditions of Judaism now expand that to include children born to Jewish fathers. Even if someone never knew their mother was Jewish, in the eyes of Torah, that person is still Jewish. They may repudiate their place in the Jewish people, but were they ever to decide to

4. See Donniel Hartman, *The Boundaries of Judaism* (London: Continuum, 2007).

identify with the Jewish people, and follow the Jewish law, they would be received as a Jew. Furthermore, converts to Judaism do not merely adopt a new set of religious beliefs and practices; they become Jews, a part of the Jewish people, regardless of their ethnic heritage. To be a Jew is not simply to agree to a set of beliefs or even to behave in a certain way, but to be part of a *people*. But this raises a critical question: If a person is still a Jew even if he or she does not practice Judaism, follow Torah in any sense, are the Jewish *people* sustainable? Is there a Jewish people without the practice of Torah?

In his book *Future Tense*, Rabbi Jonathan Sacks cites the famous American Rabbi Joseph Soloveitchik, who said in 1956 there were two covenants in Jewish life, "a covenant of fate" and "a covenant of faith or destiny."[5] The "covenant of fate" recalls the slavery in Egypt and all the exile, misery, and suffering endured by the Jewish people throughout history. The "covenant of faith" was formed by the covenant at Sinai. The "covenant of fate," Sacks argues, contributes to the "collective consciousness" of the Jews. "When one Jew suffers, all feel pain."[6] Whereas Christians are frequently indifferent to the suffering of their coreligionists around the world, Jews will leap to aid even a single Jew who is suffering and in need. The "covenant of fate" meant that it did not matter to anti-Semites in Europe whether you were "racially" a Jew, you followed Torah, or you were an atheist. Torah scholars and Jewish communists were both murdered side by side by the Nazis. This mutual hatred sustained Jewish identity. This was the "covenant of fate."

Sacks wonders, however, whether this "covenant of fate," so strong and binding both before and after the Holocaust (or Shoah), is enough to enable the long-term survival of the Jewish people. In the long run, doesn't being a Jew *require* Judaism in order for there to be a Jewish *people*? Sacks would not want to argue that "secular Jews" are no longer Jews. As an Orthodox rabbi he would certainly affirm that the child of a Jewish mother, however alienated from her Judaism, is still a Jew. And he would be first in line to support Jews, even irreligious Jews, who are suffering because of their Jewishness. But for the Jewish *people* to survive, he argues, you need more than the "covenant of fate." He writes, "*without the covenant of faith, there is no covenant of fate. Without religion, there is no global nation.*"[7] Jewish faith, one might say, may not be integral to being a Jew, but it is integral to there being a Jewish *people*. Without the practices associated with the covenants with

5. Jonathan Sacks, *Future Tense: A Vision for Jews and Judaism in the Global Culture* (London: Hodder and Stoughton, 2009), 37.

6. Sacks, *Future Tense*, 37.

7. Sacks, *Future Tense*, 38; emphasis his.

Abraham and Moses, however they are understood within the various Jewish denominations, there is no "covenant of faith." Sacks concludes, "*Only* the covenant of faith sustained a covenant of fate. And only such faith will, in the long run, keep Jews together in a bond of mutual responsibility."[8]

Jews are a *people*, then, sustained by a covenant of faith. While anti-Semitism is very much alive and well, Jews, particularly in the United States, no longer require the hostility of others to sustain their identity—they no longer need "the covenant of fate." This, according to Sacks and many others, requires a reaffirmation and recommitment to the covenant of faith. Jews will argue, as they always have, over what that covenant of faith entails and how it is to be practiced. In a sense, Jews in America and, for that matter, in Europe and even Israel have been victims of their own success. In the United States they found the liberation they longed for in Europe. But rampant rates of intermarriage between Jews and non-Jews and the growing secularism among younger Jews raise concerns among many Jewish leaders. If Jewish parents no longer form a Jewish home, if their children no longer know or care that they are Jews, if a large percentage of Jews no longer even minimally practice their faith, how many generations will the Jewish people in any meaningful sense survive? How long will there be a "covenant of faith"? Many Christians are raising the very same questions about the fate of Christianity in Europe and the United States.

In a poignant passage of his book *What Can a Modern Jew Believe?*, my friend Rabbi Gilbert Rosenthal writes,

> We are a small people; we number perhaps 13 million in the world. Salo W. Baron estimated that there should have been at least 100 million Jews in the world had it not been for persecutions, pogroms, massacres, forced conversions, and expulsions. Sergio della Pergola calculates that had the *Shoah* (Holocaust) not annihilated six million Jews, we should number 32 million by natural growth. So our numbers are shrinking; we have fewer and fewer Jews on whom we may count to live up to the standards laid down for us in the Torah and by the Divine charge. And that worries me most profoundly.[9]

Is there a Jewish people if there is no longer a Jewish faith? Is there a Jewish people if Jews no longer observe God's commands? Does it matter? It is one

8. Sacks, *Future Tense*, 45.

9. Gilbert S. Rosenthal, *What Can a Modern Jew Believe?* (Eugene, OR: Wipf and Stock, 2007), xv.

of the burdens of this book to argue that this ought to matter to Christians as well as Jews. However great the differences between us—and they should not be glossed over—according to the apostle Paul we are bound together by a common root (Rom 11:17–32) and a shared set of promises. Christianity itself depends on there being a Jewish people who live out the covenants with Abraham and Moses, who live by Torah and worship the one God. Paul insisted that God had not rejected or abandoned his people (Rom 11:1). He also insisted that both the followers of Jesus and the people of Israel will share God's salvation. Paul continued to see a critical role for the faith and the people of Israel. While the apostle Paul and Rabbi Sacks would disagree about many things, they would agree fully about the "covenant of faith."

Key Texts and Terms

Sacred Texts

While Jews and Christians share a common text, they read and understand the nature of that text very differently. What Christians call the Old Testament Jews call Tanakh.[10] The word is a combination of three Hebrew words: Torah, Nevi'im, and Ketuvim. Torah refers to the five books of Moses: Genesis, Exodus, Leviticus, Numbers, and Deuteronomy. Although the entire Tanakh is from God, the Torah is primary and foundational. For traditional Jews, no doctrine can be affirmed unless it is found in the Torah. The five books of Moses are called the "Written Torah." For traditional Jews, the "Oral Torah," the traditional rabbinical interpretations of the Written Torah, is equally important. The second division, Nevi'im, means "prophets." This includes not only the major and minor prophets from Isaiah to Malachi (excluding Daniel), but also books Christians normally think of as "historical": Joshua, Judges, 1–2 Samuel, and 1–2 Kings. The third division, Ketuvim or "writings," includes Psalms, Proverbs, Job, the Song of Songs, Ruth, Lamentations, Ecclesiastes, Esther, Daniel, Ezra, Nehemiah, and 1–2 Chronicles. Again, books Christians would locate among the prophets (Daniel) or history (Ezra, Nehemiah, 1–2 Chronicles) are found elsewhere in the divisions of Tanakh. Some have suggested that the late dates and/or unusual character of some of these works relegated them to the "writings" rather than the "prophets."

10. For the standard English translation see *JPS Hebrew-English Tanakh.*

For Jews, the category Torah is not exhausted by the content of the five books of Moses. Traditional Jews believe that God handed on not only the Written Torah to Moses but also the "Oral Torah." "We believe," writes Rabbi Donin, "that God's will was also made manifest in the Oral Tradition or Oral Torah which also had its source at Sinai, revealed to Moses and then taught by him to the religious heads of Israel."[11] According to the Mishnah, the great rabbinic compilation of the oral tradition, "Moses received the Law from Sinai and committed it to Joshua, and Joshua to the elders, and the elders to the Prophets; and the Prophets committed it to the men of the Great Synagogue. They said three things: Be deliberate in judgment, raise up many disciples, and make a fence around the Law."[12] This clearly refers to the Oral Torah. With Donin, "this Oral Torah . . . clarifies and provides the details for many of the commandments contained in the Written Torah."[13] The Oral Torah clarifies, for example, what it does and does not mean to "work" on the Sabbath. About this, and many other issues, the Written Torah is rather vague.

This "Oral Torah" was not written down until the late second/early third century CE. The rules and interpretive moves of the Oral Torah were incorporated into the Mishnah. For traditional Jews, like Donin, this is a compilation of the Oral Torah given by God to Moses to share with the elders of Israel. Michael Fishbane describes the Mishnah "as the written digest of the hitherto exclusively oral traditions of the Tannaim (the Pharisaic sages c. 200 B.C.E.–200 C.E.). . . . The abstract formulations and topical structure of the *Mishnah* resembles contemporary Roman codes, and in its content projects the code of behavior . . . the sages sought to impose on the people at large."[14] The compiler of the Mishnah was Rabbi Judah the Prince, a leader of the Jewish community in the land of Israel. The rulings of renowned rabbis of the previous centuries, like Hillel or Gamaliel, are juxtaposed and sometimes critiqued by their contemporaries and disciples. Every aspect of religious, social, familial, and moral life is minutely examined.

The compilation of the Mishnah, however, did not end, but only began the conversation. In the following centuries, the rabbis who followed the Tannaim had their own discussions and arguments about the application of

11. Donin, *To Be a Jew*, 24–25.

12. *m. Avot* 1:1. English translations of the Mishnah, unless otherwise noted, are taken from *The Mishnah*, trans. Herbert Danby (Oxford: Oxford University Press, 1933).

13. Donin, *To Be a Jew*, 25.

14. Michael A. Fishbane, *Judaism* (New York: HarperCollins, 1987), 41.

the rulings in the Mishnah. These discussions were brought together in the Gemara, or "compilation." The rabbis of the Gemara are called the Amoraim. Finally the rulings of the Tannaim in the Mishnah and the discussion of the Amoraim in the Gemara were brought together in the Talmud. The Talmud exists in two forms, the Jerusalem Talmud, produced in the land of Israel in the mid-fourth century, and the Babylonian Talmud, put into final form in the fifth century. "These two great collections from the two prominent centers of Jewish life and scholarship form the next foundation document of developing Judaism."[15]

Tanakh, Mishnah, and Talmud are all considered Torah by Jews. "In the broadest sense . . . the study of Torah refers not only to the Scriptures and the Oral Torah, but also to the entire body of rabbinic legislation and interpretation based upon the Torah that developed over the centuries."[16] For a traditional Jew, all of it is Torah and all of it is from God. Christians read the Old Testament through the life, ministry, death, and resurrection of Jesus of Nazareth. They read his story as compiled by the evangelists and explicated by the apostles. Jews read the five books of Moses and the rest of Tanakh through the lenses of the rabbis and the enduring oral tradition that informed their interpretations and rulings. But the sacred and authoritative texts of the Jews did not end with the publication of the Talmud. We now turn to midrash.

The rabbis did more than wrestle with intricate legal texts; they did more than argue with each other. They were not only concerned with raising up disciples to further their own work. They were concerned to communicate the significance of the Torah to ordinary Jews. If ordinary Jews failed to follow God's will laid down in both Written and Oral Torah, their work was pointless. Midrash reflects the efforts of the rabbis to read and exposit Torah so as to communicate its commands to Jews who were merchants and mothers, farmers and butchers. The word "midrash" means "exposition" or "inquiry." It was an inquiry "into the language, ideas, and narratives of the *Torah*. . . . Its two major divisions are legal *midrash* (or *midrash halakha*) and nonlegal *midrash* (or *midrash aggadah*; this includes grammatical explications, theology, ethics and legends)."[17]

Fishbane argues that midrash haggadah reflects "a more personal spirit of application and performance. . . . Coming from the same Tannaitic and

15. Fishbane, *Judaism*, 42.
16. Donin, *To Be a Jew*, 27.
17. Fishbane, *Judaism*, 145.

Amoraic academies as the legal teachings, that aggadic spirit reflects the theological quests and concerns of the rabbis as reflective interchanges among themselves and as highly stylized sermons delivered to the people on Sabbath and holidays."[18] The midrash haggadah introduces us to the rabbis as exegetes and storytellers. It "is a more playful style of interpretation. It uses parable, legend, or other creative methods. In this method the rabbis answer questions about the text by telling a story that explains why it is so."[19] These narratives often provide the "back story" for stories in the Tanakh. We learn from a midrashic story that Abraham was already a monotheist before God called him. His father had set up shop selling idols and Abraham not only thwarted his efforts to sell the idols but destroyed them entirely.[20]

Some of the narratives and reflections are gathered into larger commentaries focused on a single book: *Genesis Rabbah* or *Leviticus Rabbah.* Other examples include more topical compilations like the midrash on Exodus entitled *Mekilta de-Rabbi Ishmael* and the collection of homilies for Sabbaths and feast days entitled *Pesikta de-Rab Kahana.*[21] Rabbi Ishmael, the author or compiler of the *Mekilta*, was thought to be a contemporary of the famous second-century Rabbi Akiva. This collection deals more with legal matters, that is, halakah rather than haggadah, or narrative. The *Pesikta de-Rab Kahana* has a storied history: "It remained well known and studied from the end of the fifth century until it disappeared sometime in the sixteenth century."[22] It was rediscovered and republished only in the nineteenth century. There are far too many examples of midrash to cite in this brief introduction. But for Jews these exegetical explorations and narrative explications are authoritative and sacred texts. To study them is to study Torah.

A final important text should be mentioned: the prayer book. The Jewish prayer book is called a siddur. The word comes from the Hebrew word for "order." "It presents all the prayers to be recited at the various daily and

18. Fishbane, *Judaism*, 45–46.

19. Sara E. Karesh and Mitchell M. Hurvitz, "Aggadah," *Encyclopedia of Judaism* (New York: Infobase Publishing, 2005), 5.

20. *Gen. Rab.* 38:10.

21. *Pesikta de-Rab Kahana*, trans. William G. Baude and Israel J. Kapstein (Philadelphia: Jewish Publication Society, 2002). *Mekilta de-Rabbi Ishmael*, 3 vols., trans. Jacob Z. Lauterbach (Philadelphia: Jewish Publication Society, 1935).

22. Yehiel E. Poupko, introduction to the new edition of *Pesikta de-Rab Kahana*, trans. Baude and Kapstein, xi.

Sabbath . . . worship services in their proper order according to the traditions of the community that printed it."[23] Like the Mishnah, Gemara, and midrash, the prayer book was an oral product until compiled in written form by Saadia Gaon in the ninth century. Saadia Gaon was the head of a renowned rabbinic academy in Sura, Babylonia.[24] Over the centuries, various rabbis and communities developed their own versions of the prayer book. In the United States, the various Jewish denominations have produced prayer books reflecting the nature of their communities and commitments. A recent English version of the prayer book is *The Koren Siddur*, translated and commented on by Rabbi Jonathan Sacks.[25]

A Few Important Terms

Already I have introduced a number of terms unfamiliar to most Christians. Words such as "Mishnah," "Gemara," "Talmud," and "midrash" are for the most part completely unfamiliar or only vaguely understood. In the chapters that follow the reader may encounter many other unfamiliar terms and concepts. There will be a glossary of such terms at the end of this volume, but it will perhaps be helpful to introduce some of them here. I note here that the transliteration of Hebrew words is not consistent. Although I will strive for consistency, you will find, for example, various writers transliterating the word for Jewish law as "halakha," "halakah," and "halacah."

- *Berith*: several times we will have occasion to explore the *covenant* between God and Israel. Fishbane defines a covenant as "the religious bond between God and Israel contracted at Sinai with the giving of the Torah. For Judaism it refers to the eternal bond between God and the people of Israel grounded in the nation's obedience to the divine commandments. It is a major theological concept, expressive of divine grace and concern for the Jews and their reciprocal obligations to God."[26]

23. Karesh and Hurvitz, "Siddur," *Encyclopedia of Judaism*, 478–79.

24. Karesh and Hurvitz, "Saadia Gaon," *Encyclopedia of Judaism*, 440–41.

25. *The Koren Siddur*, introduction, translation, and commentary by Jonathan Sacks (Jerusalem: Koren, 2006). See also *The Expanded ArtScroll Siddur*, trans. Nosson Scheerman, 3rd ed. (Brooklyn: Mesorah, 2016).

26. Fishbane, *Judaism*, 143.

- Halakah: this is a term already introduced in this chapter. It refers to any normative Jewish law, custom, or practice. It is also used to refer to the "entire complex" of law, custom, or practice.[27]
- *Mitzvah/mitzvot* (pl.): a Hebrew word meaning "commandment(s)." According to Jewish tradition there are 613 of them, 365 negative and 248 positive. From these basic commandments "Judaism actually evolved thousands of commandments," mostly developed by the rabbis in their continuing explication and exploration of Torah. The term "mitzvah" is perhaps best known to Christians in the Bar Mitzvah, the service by which a young Jewish male becomes a "son of the commandments" and officially responsible to obey them.[28]
- *Kashrut*/kosher: Traditional Jews follow a complex set of dietary laws that instruct them on what they may or may not eat and in what combination. The word "kosher" means "fit" and indicates that something is permitted to a traditional Jew. The word "treif" (literally "torn") refers to something that is not kosher and should be avoided.[29]
- Shema: Literally, "hear," the word normally refers to the prayer recited daily by religious Jews. It is a combination of portions from Deuteronomy 6:4–9, 11:13–21, and Numbers 15:37–41. According to Rabbi Adin Steinsaltz, "it contains the main principles of Jewish faith and forms the basis of our individual and collective relationship with the Almighty."[30]
- *Tefillah*: the Hebrew word for "prayer." "Prayer," writes Rabbi Steinsaltz, "is a direct and unequivocal act of relating to God. In whatever way it is performed, and in whatever manner it is uttered, prayer is essentially one thing: an explicit addressing by the human 'I' to the Divine 'Thou.' In the most essential sense, prayer is direct speech, in which man confronts and addresses his Creator."[31] A traditional Jewish life is one of both personal and communal prayer.
- *Teshuva*: repentance, turning back to God. "It is a central theme of the Days of Awe, the 10 days in between *Rosh Hashanah* [Jewish New Year] and *Yom Kippur* [the Day of Atonement], when repentance, prayer, and charity can mitigate one's deserved punishments for the upcoming year

27. Fishbane, *Judaism*, 143.
28. Karesh and Hurvitz, "mitzvah," *Encyclopedia of Judaism*, 333–34.
29. Karesh and Hurvitz, "kashrut," *Encyclopedia of Judaism*, 267–69.
30. Adin Steinsaltz, *A Guide to Jewish Prayer* (New York: Schocken Books, 2000), 404.
31. Steinsaltz, *Guide to Jewish Prayer*, 8.

and ensure a good year."[32] The Day of Atonement deals with sins against God. For sins against another person the penitent must ask forgiveness and seek reconciliation with the one wronged.

Additional significant terms will be discussed in the proper context. The final section of this chapter introduces the various Jewish "denominations" that will figure in the subsequent narrative.

Jewish Denominations

Subsequent to the destruction of the Second Temple in 70 CE, the rabbis took a fragmented and distressed people and formed them into a coherent community. Over the centuries there were certainly varied trends and sects within Judaism; but outside of the Karaites, a medieval group that rejected the Oral Law of the rabbis and sought to follow the Written Torah, there was remarkable unanimity among Jews.[33] Jews in northern and central Europe (called Ashkenazim, a term originally applied to German Jews) and those in Spain and North Africa (called Sephardim) had different traditions and practices. The Ashkenazim lived under Christian rule while the Sephardim lived under Muslim rule. Their surrounding cultures impacted their perspectives and practices. But they held in common a commitment to both the Written and Oral Torah as expounded in Tanakh, Mishnah, Talmud, and midrash. It was only as a result of the Enlightenment that clear denominations emerged. Today in the United States there are four distinct denominations among Jews.

Orthodox Judaism: Orthodox Jews are those who continue to live their lives in strict obedience to halakah. About 12 percent of American Jews are Orthodox. They continue to live by the traditions of the ancient rabbis as did their forebears. Orthodoxy, like Reform Judaism, is a nineteenth-century phenomenon, the former arising in response to the latter. Today Orthodox Judaism is roughly divided between Modern Orthodox, Orthodox, and Heredim or "ultra-Orthodox" Jews. Modern Orthodox Jews are scrupulous in their observance of the *mitzvot* but insist that living a fully Jewish life and living in the modern world is possible. The more conservative Orthodox and Heredim (the fearful or Godfearers) view modern life as a distraction

32. Karesh and Hurvitz, "teschuva," *Encyclopedia of Judaism*, 518.
33. Karesh and Hurvitz, "Karaites," *Encyclopedia of Judaism*, 267.

from the strict life of Torah study and religious observance they think is required by Judaism and take various steps to protect themselves from the impingements of modernity.[34]

Reform Judaism: The eighteenth and nineteenth centuries saw educated European Jews finding greater success and acceptance within their respective countries. For many of these Jews it meant leaving their Jewish lives and practices behind. Some, like the German/Jewish writer Heinrich Heine, for convenience' sake converted to Christianity. Others began to argue that a modified Jewish life would render Jews acceptable to European society and preserve Judaism itself. The reformers valued both Jewish and secular education. They argued for prayers in the vernacular and rejected messianism. They denied the divine authorship of the Torah and engaged in historical criticism of their sacred texts. "They considered themselves bound by only those Jewish laws . . . that concerned ethics."[35] Today Reform Judaism is the largest of the Jewish denominations in the United States. About 40 percent of American Jews are Reform. In Christian terms, it would be considered the "mainline" Jewish denomination.

Conservative Judaism: Conservative Judaism traditionally maintains a middle ground between Orthodox and Reform Judaism. Less than 30 percent of American Jews are Conservative. "Conservative Jews stress that Judaism has evolved historically to meet the changing needs of the Jewish people in various eras and circumstances. They believe that Jewish law should continue to evolve in the present and future. Nevertheless, Conservative Judaism maintains the traditional view that Jews must obey and observe the will of God through the commandments."[36] Conservative Jewish scholars, like Reform Jewish scholars, tend to use historical/critical methods to study their ancient texts. While Orthodox Jews insist the Torah is of divine origin and Reform Jews generally believe it is not strictly of divine origin, Conservative Jews emphasize divine inspiration rather than divine authorship.

Reconstructionist Judaism: Reconstructionist Judaism is an American phenomenon. Mordecai Kaplan, the father of Reconstructionist Judaism, "sought to develop his idea that Judaism was not only a religion, but also a civilization, complete with its own language, land, music, art, folkways, and culture."[37] Unlike the other denominations, "Reconstructionism explains

34. Karesh and Hurvitz, "Orthodox Judaism," *Encyclopedia of Judaism*, 368–71.
35. Karesh and Hurvitz, "Reform Judaism," *Encyclopedia of Judaism*, 419–22.
36. Karesh and Hurvitz, "Conservative Judaism," *Encyclopedia of Judaism*, 98–100.
37. Karesh and Hurvitz, "Reconstructionist Judaism," *Encyclopedia of Judaism*, 416–18.

that Judaism grew out of the social and historical experience of the Jewish people. . . . It does not insist upon a belief in a supernatural God, divine intervention." The notion of Jewish *peoplehood* and involvement in social justice activism are both critical for Reconstructionist synagogues and individuals. Reconstructionist Judaism is the smallest of the denominations.

QUESTIONS FOR DISCUSSION

1. To what extent is a Jew/Judaism an ethnic group, a religion, a national identity? What difference does it make?
2. How are the Jewish "denominations" similar to and different from Christian denominations?
3. How is the Jewish understanding of the canon of sacred Scripture similar to and different from that of Christians?

FURTHER READING

Elazar, Daniel J., and Rela Mintz Geffen. *The Conservative Movement in Judaism: Dilemmas and Opportunities.* Albany: State University of New York Press, 2000.

Fishbane, Michael A. *Judaism: Revelation and Tradition.* New York: HarperCollins, 1987.

Kaplan, Dana Evan. *American Reform Judaism: An Introduction.* Piscataway, NJ: Rutgers University Press, 2003.

Solomon, Norman. *Judaism: A Very Short Introduction.* 2nd ed. Oxford: Oxford University Press, 2014.

CHAPTER 2

God of Abraham

Listen, Israel: the Lord is our God, the Lord is one.

—*Koren Siddur*

And the Lord spake unto Moses, saying: "Speak unto the children of Israel, and say unto them, I am the Lord your God" . . . that is, "I am the Lord who spoke, and the world was; I am the Judge; I am full of compassion. I am the Judge who punishes; I am faithful to give a full reward."

—*Sifra* 85c

Who is He who trails me steadily, uninvited and unwanted, like an everlasting shadow, and vanishes into the recesses of transcendence the very instant I turn around to confront this numinous, awesome, and mysterious "He"?

—Rabbi Joseph Soloveitchik

Every day, often several times, religious Jews recite the Shema. It is at the same time a confession and a commitment. Words from Deuteronomy 6:4–9 call Jews to acknowledge the unity, singularity, and particularity of their God; they call Israel to love and obey the God who delivered them from Egypt and gave them his Torah. In these words they express what sort of God this is and their commitment to serving him.

The God of Israel

Words from Deuteronomy 11:13–21 warn Jews that worshiping other gods will bring dire consequences; God's word, God's will, is to be firmly fixed in their minds and the minds of their children. Words from Numbers 15:37–41 call them to use even their attire as a reminder of the commands of their God: "Speak to the Israelites and tell them to make tassels on the corners of their garments. . . . This shall be your tassel, and you shall see it and remember all the LORD's commands and keep them."[1]

The God of Israel, then, is *a God who engages.* This is not the god of the deist who creates the world and leaves it to its own devices. No, this is a God who *pursues* his people. As Rabbi Abraham Joshua Heschel suggests, the Bible is not simply the story of the human search for God, but God's pursuit of humanity: "The incidents recorded in the Bible to the discerning eye are episodes of one great drama: the quest of God for man; His search for man, and man's flight from him."[2] Adam and Eve are hiding in the garden and God calls, "Where are you?" (Gen 3:9). Abram is minding his own business and the Lord says, "Go forth from your native land, your people and your father's house to the land I will show you" (Gen 12:1). Jacob is running away when God declares, "I am the LORD, the God of your father Abraham and the God of Isaac: the ground on which you are lying I will assign to you and your offspring" (Gen 28:13). And, of course, Moses is tending sheep when God speaks to him out of the bush: "Moses, Moses!" (Exod 3:4). None of them is looking for God, seeking a call from God, but God is looking for *them*, pursuing *them*, calling *them*.

The God of Israel is also a *particular* God. He is not a philosophical abstraction. He is not an "unmoved mover" or a "god beyond god." He has a

1. *Koren Siddur* (Jonathan Sacks's translation), 100.

2. Abraham Joshua Heschel, *God in Search of Man* (New York: Farrar, Straus and Giroux, 1955), 197.

name. In most English Bibles the divine name, represented by the so-called Tetragrammaton YHWH, is rendered as "the LORD." Religious Jews never pronounce the name of God. They use circumlocutions like "the Lord" or "Hashem" (the name). When Moses encountered God he wondered what he would tell the Israelite slaves about this God in the burning bush: "When I come to the Israelites and say to them, 'The God of your fathers has sent me to you,' and they ask me, 'What is His name?' what shall I say to them?" (Exod 3:13). Not just any god will do. And God responds: "God said to Moses, 'I am that I am.' Thus you shall say to the Israelites, 'I Am sent me to you'" (Exod 3:14 marginal reading).

The God of Israel is a *singular* God. There is only one God. He has no consort; no competition; no equal. The constant temptation for Israel was idolatry. The first commands were "to have no other gods besides me" and "not make for yourself a sculptured image or any likeness of what is in the heavens above or on the earth below" (Exod 20:3–4). The gods and goddesses of the Egyptians, the Canaanites, the Babylonians, the Persians, the Greeks, and the Romans would be seductive—they were immediate, tactile. They must be resisted. The rabbis thought idolatry the most serious sin of all: "He who commits idolatry denies the Ten Commandments, and all that was commanded to Moses, to the Prophets and to the Patriarchs."[3] Even to say there was "another power" alongside the God of Israel was forbidden. "The Holy One, blessed be He, said, 'I am the first' . . . for I have no father; 'and I am the last' for I have no brother; 'and beside me there is no God' for I have no son."[4]

The God of Israel is also a *relational* God. Israel is commanded to "Love the LORD your God with all your heart and with all your soul and with all your might" (Deut 6:5). It is difficult to imagine loving the "unmoved mover" or the "first principle of the universe." But the God of Israel, the God of the Bible is not only a remote figure obscured by glory. The God of Israel is both *transcendent* and *intimate* (rather than simply immanent). He is, on the one hand, familiar to humans because they are created in his image (Gen 1:27). He meets them in gardens (Gen 3:8), under trees (Gen 18:1), and in flaming bushes (Exod 3:1–5). On the other hand, God is a source of awe, fear, and even terror. Consider Mt. Sinai, ablaze with lightning, obscured by smoke and clouds when God spoke to Israel. But "when the people saw it, they fell

3. *Sifre Num.* Shelah, 111 in C. G. Montefiore and H. Loewe, *A Rabbinic Anthology* (Philadelphia: The Jewish Publication Society, 1960), 253.

4. *Ex. Rab.* 40:4–5.

back and stood at a distance" (Exod 20:18). In fact they were quite sure they had heard enough from God himself. To be in intimate relation with the God of Israel is not a trivial thing.

Finally, the God of Israel is a *covenanting* God. He establishes a covenant with Abraham and promises land and offspring. He establishes a covenant with his people Israel and gives them his Torah. The Torah is more than a set of dos and don'ts. It is a way of forming an individual and communal identity. It is a means of making a *people.* For the Jew the Torah is a constant source of joy, delight, and challenge. To maintain their identity as the people of God Israel had to maintain their commitment and obedience to Torah. The temptations to forget God would be myriad: in their success they could forget God (Deut 6:10–13); in their sin they could replace God (Deut 6:14, 15); in their disobedience they could test God (Deut 6:16–18). They were made a people by the gracious call of God. They were maintained as a people by their obedience to and love of Torah. In the rest of this chapter we will explore further this God: a God who *creates, calls, and covenants.*

The God Who Creates

The story of creation is not simply about how the world began. It is not even in principle a story about *human* beginnings. It is a story about *God.* Genesis not only introduces the reader to the world of darkness and light, fish and fowl, and man and woman. It introduces us to God. As Michael Wyschogrod puts it, "The God of the Bible is a person. He is one of the characters who appears in the stories told in the Bible. He has a personality that undergoes developments in the course of the story. He creates man with certain expectations, which are apparently disappointed, and he is then sorry that he has created him. He is subject to the emotions of anger and jealousy, among others. He is also filled with burning love, particularly toward Abraham and his descendants."[5] Later Jewish and Christian interpreters would find this passionate depiction of God uncomfortable and argue the descriptions were accommodations to human weakness or extended metaphors.[6] None of these efforts has ever succeeded in purging either the Jewish or Christian imaginations of the passionate God of the Bible.

5. Michael Wyschogrod, *The Body of Faith: God in the People Israel* (New York: Seabury, 1983), 84.

6. Rosenthal, *What Can a Modern Jew Believe?*, 28.

In the Greco-Roman period a few Jewish thinkers were significantly attracted to Hellenistic philosophy. Perhaps most famously, Philo of Alexandria was at the same time a faithful Jew and an ardent student of Plato. For Philo it was impossible for God to "repent" or change his mind. Human beings can repent and change their minds, but not God. "Do you doubt," he wrote, "whether the imperishable, and everlasting and blessed God, the Being endowed with all the virtues, and with all perfection, and with all happiness is unchangeable in his counsels and whether he abides by the designs which he originally formed, without changing any of them?"[7] The answer Philo clearly expects from his reader is "No!" As we will see, later Jewish and Christian thinkers would follow Philo down this same road—and, for that matter, still do.

But the early rabbis were not entirely convinced by Philo and his peers. "It cannot be maintained," writes Wyschogrod, "that the rabbinic enterprise constitutes a demythologization of the encounter with the biblical God. There are too many rabbinic texts in which God thinks and hopes, plans and fails, and sometimes succeeds, in which his emotions influence his conduct. The rabbis were not philosophers and were not particularly upset by the anthropomorphisms of the Bible."[8] By creating the world the God of the Bible thoroughly entangled himself with his creation. By creating the world he made himself a part of the story—a story of human failure and divine frustration. And yet, it was a story of hope. From the very beginning God was concerned with the destiny of the man and woman, created in his image. They were driven from the garden because of their disobedience, but that was not the end of the story.

The failure of God's creation was not simply the failure of Adam and Eve. It eventually entailed the failure of the entire human race. So great was this failure that "the LORD regretted that he had made man on the earth and His heart was saddened" (Gen 6:6). God famously decided to destroy the world and start over with one family—the family of Noah. But, given the behavior of Noah's son, this second beginning was no more successful than the first (Gen 9:18–28). More than once God seeks the advice of or shares his frustrations and plans with one of his creatures, his partner in creation and redemption. Later in the book of Genesis God asks, "Shall I hide from Abraham what I am about to do?" (Gen 18:17). What he is about to do is

7. Philo, *On the Unchangeableness of God* 6, in *The Works of Philo*, new updated version, trans. C. D. Yonge (Peabody, MA: Hendrickson, 1993), 160.

8. Wyschogrod, *Body of Faith*, 85.

destroy Sodom, and Abraham tries, unsuccessfully as it turns out, to talk him out of it. Moses has more success when he convinces God not to destroy the people of Israel and start over with him (Num 14:10–25). This love and anger, passion and frustration, is what Abraham Joshua Heschel called the divine "pathos." However philosophically abstract and existentially remote both Jewish and Christian thinkers at times try to make the God of Israel, this "pathos" keeps bursting through.[9]

The Hebrew Scriptures are, in fact, the account of the God of Israel's passionate, ongoing, and frustrating efforts to form a people who will love and obey him. God calls Abraham and promises him a posterity that cannot be counted. He rescues Israel from Egypt and through Moses gives them Torah and makes a covenant with them. He anoints David and promises him an eternal kingdom. Throughout the vicissitudes of Israel's life with God he remains a faithful, if often frustrated, lover of his people. They fail, stumble, and rebel. He rebukes, punishes, and exiles. They weep and repent. He relents and restores. But he remains faithful not simply to his people but to his creation. The God who creates is the God who re-creates. The God who wounds is the God who heals. The God who judges is the God who redeems.

In the aftermath of the destruction of the First Temple and the exile of God's people, Israel's prophets looked forward to more than the restoration of Israel to the land. "For behold! I am creating a new heaven and a new earth. The former things shall not be remembered, they shall never come to mind. Be glad, then, and rejoice forever in what I am creating. For I shall create Jerusalem as a joy and her people as a delight. And I will rejoice in Jerusalem and delight in her people. Never again shall be heard there the sounds of weeping and wailing" (Isa 65:17–19). God's "new creation" would be a restoration of the "old creation" without the dangers and disappointments present in the old: "They shall not build for others to dwell in, or plant for others to enjoy. . . . They shall not toil to no purpose; they shall not bear children for terror, but they shall be a people blessed by the LORD, and their offspring will remain with them" (Isa 65:22–23). Ezekiel says that when God restores Israel's fortunes, they shall no longer "defile themselves by their fetishes and their abhorrent things and by their other transgressions. I will save them in all their settlements where they sinned, and I will cleanse them" (Ezek 37:23). In fact, "they shall follow My rules and faithfully obey My law" (Ezek 37:24b).

9. See Abraham Joshua Heschel, *The Prophets* (San Francisco: Harper, 2001).

When the temple had been destroyed, the city leveled, and the people killed or carried away into exile, the presence of God had departed (see Ezek 10). But now, "I will make a covenant of friendship with them—it shall be an everlasting covenant with them—I will establish them and multiply them and I will place My Sanctuary among them forever. My Presence shall rest over them; I will be their God and they shall be My people. And when My Sanctuary abides among them forever, the nations shall know that I the LORD do sanctify Israel" (Ezek 37:26–28). Over the centuries, God had seemed to abandon his people and his creation more than once. From the garden, to the flood, to enslavement in Egypt, to exile in Babylon, Israel had reason to wonder if now at last they were on their own. But in the end, the prophets insist, God has abandoned neither Israel nor his creation. There was a time when Adam and Eve were driven away from the face of God. There will be a time, say the prophets, when God's people will return not simply to the garden, but to God's presence: "'Not like this world is the world to come.' In the world to come there is neither eating nor drinking; no procreation of children or business transactions; no envy or hatred or rivalry; but the righteous sit enthroned, their crowns on their heads, and enjoy the lustre of the Shechinah."[10] In the end as in the beginning, the people of God, God's creation, bask in the glory of God's presence. The God of creation is the God who is *present* to his people. Not an unmoved mover, not a god beyond god, not the first principle of the universe. This God, Israel's God, is the God who made heaven and earth and called Abraham to an unknown destination.

The God Who Calls

Abraham is a figure who looms large in the imaginations of three great world religions. Although you will hear Judaism, Christianity, and Islam called "Abrahamic" faiths, Jon D. Levenson warns, "Historically, Abraham has functioned much more as a point of differentiation among the three religious communities than as a node of commonality."[11] Judaism, Christianity, and Islam each has their own "Abraham." Their interpretations of the significance of his life differ in significant and telling ways. "Although interreligious concord," Levenson writes, "is devoutly to be desired, the patriarch is less

10. *b. Ber.* 17a, in Montefiore and Loewe, *Anthology*, 607.
11. Jon D. Levenson, *Inheriting Abraham* (Princeton: Princeton University Press, 2012), 9.

useful to that end than many think."[12] Judaism, Christianity, and Islam are similarly called "people of the book"—a statement that leaves unanswered the question "Which book?" Be that as it may, the story we tell here is of Israel's Abraham and Abraham's God.

There is something quite odd about the call of Abraham. Genesis 12 records the call of God: "Go forth from your native land, and from your father's house to the land that I will show you" (Gen 12:1). But the reader is not told *why* God called Abraham. No backstory is supplied to explain why, out of all the people available, God selected this particular man and his family to start over again after the disasters of the flood and the Tower of Babel (Gen 6–11). We are not told that Abraham was earnestly seeking God or even piously waiting on God. In fact, according to Michael Wyschogrod, "In the Bible, it is not Abraham who moves toward God, but God who turns to Abraham with an election that is not explained because it is an act of love that requires no explanation."[13] God calls Abraham simply because he "falls in love with him."

Wyschogrod notes that this explanation did not satisfy the rabbis. In a famous story in *Genesis Rabbah* 38 Abraham's father Terah is depicted as a seller of idols. He assigns his son the role of salesman in his shop. Abraham turns out to be the worst salesman of idols in history. He not only talks every customer out of purchasing one of Terah's creations, he smashes up most of his stock. The Abraham of *Genesis Rabbah* 38 is an ardent monotheist.[14] The rabbis also believed that Abraham faithfully observed the Torah long before Moses delivered it to the people from God at Mount Sinai. As the Mishnah reports, "We find that Abraham our father had performed the whole Law before it was given."[15] So far as the rabbis were concerned, God chose Abraham for good reasons: he opposed idolatry, worshiped the one God, and followed Torah faithfully.

But the biblical account has none of this. Only later in Genesis do we find that God expects Abraham to "instruct his children and his posterity to keep the way of the Lord by doing what is just and right" (Gen 18:19). After Abraham's death, God tells Isaac, his son, "Abraham obeyed Me and kept My charge: My commandments, My laws, and My teachings" (Gen 26:5). But in Genesis 12 this is all in the future. "God's relationship with Abraham," writes

12. Levenson, *Inheriting Abraham*, 9.
13. Wyschogrod, *Body of Faith*, 64.
14. *Gen. Rab.* 38:12–13.
15. *m. Qidd.* 4:14.

Wyschogrod, "is truly a falling in love."[16] But this love affair is from the beginning a bit rocky. In a way Abraham "pre-enacts the experience of the Jewish people."[17] He is faithful to God's call, but he struggles to remain faithful. He risks his future line when he lies about his wife first to Pharaoh and then to Abimelek (Gen 12; 18). He permits Sarah's servant Hagar, pregnant with his son Ishmael, to be driven away (Gen 16). For even the rabbis such actions are not above criticism: "Did not Abraham our father show lack of faith?"[18]

But in the midst of these struggles and failures, Abraham demonstrates courage and faithfulness. He rescues his nephew Lot and refuses to be enriched by the plunder of Sodom (Gen 14). He circumcises the males of his household in keeping with the command of God, establishing the covenant with God in his own ancient body (Gen 17). He pleads with God over the fate of Sodom (Gen 18). He prays for the healing of Abimelek (Gen 20). And perhaps most controversially, he obeys God's command to sacrifice his son Isaac only to have God rescue him at the last moment (Gen 22).[19] His struggles, his failings, distinguish him

> radically from other putative founder figures, like the Buddha, Confucius, Jesus and Muhammad. Genesis, like the entire Jewish Bible, is extraordinarily reticent about providing editorial evaluations of Abraham. The same reticence also partly accounts for the occasional willingness of the Jewish tradition to find serious fault with Abraham. In this, too, Judaism seems radically different from the way most religious traditions treat their founders, who are regarded as models for emulation and, in the case of orthodox Christianity, as the very incarnation of God himself.[20]

But Abraham's struggles also tell us something about Israel's God. The God who calls is not only the God who loves, but the God who continues to love when Abraham, and later Israel, falter. In Exodus 32 when God, furious with his people, tells Moses that he intends to destroy them and start over with him, Moses reminds God of his call of Abraham: "Remember Your servants Abraham, Isaac, and Israel, how You swore to them by Your

16. Wyschogrod, *Body of Faith*, 64.

17. Levenson, *Inheriting Abraham*, 4.

18. *Tanh.*, Wayiggash, 2, f. 67b in Montefiore and Loewe, *Anthology*, 519.

19. For a view of the sacrifice of Isaac that contrasts with that of Levenson, see Donniel Hartman, *Putting God Second* (Boston: Beacon Press, 2016), 46–48. Hartman suggests the sacrifice was a form of "God intoxication."

20. Levenson, *Inheriting Abraham*, 4.

Self and said to them 'I will make your offspring as numerous as the stars of heaven, and I will give to your offspring this whole land of which I spoke, to possess forever'" (Exod 32:13). Moses's intercession, as mentioned above, is successful where Abraham's failed. Moses had reminded God that he was not only a God who *called*, but a God who *covenanted* with his people. He had made promises and he was bound to keep those promises. While the Torah given by Moses was ringed with warnings and conditions, God's covenant with Abraham was *unconditional.* And, as Paul would later tell the Roman followers of Jesus, "God's gifts and his call are irrevocable" (Rom 11:29).

The God Who Covenants

In Genesis 12 God promises Abraham that he will become a great nation and commands him to leave his family for an undisclosed destination. When Abraham arrives in Canaan, God tells him, "I will assign this land to your offspring" (Gen 12:7). The problem, of course, is that Abraham famously has no offspring. And both Abraham (at this point Abram) and his wife Sarah (at this point Sarai) are old. When God reiterates his promise in Genesis 15, Abraham quite reasonably asks, "O Lord God, what can you give me seeing that I shall die childless and the one in charge of my household is Dammesek Eliezer!" (15:2). God insists that Eliezer, like Lot before him and Ishmael after him, will not be Abraham's heir; "none but your very own issue shall be your heir" (v. 4). God goes on to promise the possession of the land, but Abraham is still not convinced: "O Lord God, how shall I know that I am to possess it?" (v. 8). A startling ceremony follows Abraham's question.

God tells Abraham to produce a heifer, a ram, a goat, a dove, and a young pigeon. Genesis tells us, Abraham "cut them in two, placing each half opposite the other; but he did not cut up the birds" (v. 10). Abraham falls into a deep sleep and God reiterates his promise, warning of the difficulties ahead for his offspring. "A smoking oven and a flaming torch passed between those pieces" (v. 17). We are told "on that day the Lord made a covenant with Abram" (v. 18). This clearly is something more than a promise. According to John Goldingay, "covenants and oaths are even more formalized and explicit commitments [than promises], made with ceremony and solemnity, [and] even more self-binding."[21] Levenson writes, "The parallels from Mesopotamia and

21. John Goldingay, *Old Testament Theology*, vol. 1, *Israel's God* (Downers Grove, IL: IVP, 2003), 197.

in Jeremiah 34:17–22 suggest that the ritual is one of self-cursing: the one who passes between the cut-up pieces is solemnly affirming that if he violates the covenant he will be like them—dead. . . . The covenant, then, is strictly promissory. No obligations are imposed on the human partner. God, as it were, curses himself should he fail to grant the land to Abram's future offspring."[22]

Once again Abraham has to wait. And once again God returns with his promises: Abraham will become the father of many nations and will possess the entire land of Canaan (Gen 17:4–8). On this occasion a "sign" of the covenant is added: circumcision. Every male heir of Abraham is to be circumcised on the eighth day. And once again, Abraham wonders about all this. He, in fact, falls down laughing at the idea that he and Sarah could become parents at their advanced ages (v. 17). God seems unperturbed by Abraham's display of mirth and once more states his promise that Sarah will bear a son. But this time he sets a deadline: by next year (v. 21). So Abraham, whatever his doubts, obediently endures circumcision himself and sees to the circumcision of every male in his household, including his son Ishmael.

According to Levenson, "Both versions of the Abrahamic covenant present it as unconditional. That is, the existence of the pact and the promises it makes to the human partner and his descendants . . . are not dependent on the fulfillment of any conditions. God pledges to carry out his promises regardless of the conduct of the human partners."[23] Abraham endured long years of disappointment, questions, and, perhaps in the end, cynicism. But in spite of it all, he obeyed—he was *faithful.* James Kugel cites several texts that demonstrate the importance of Abraham's faithfulness to ancient Jewish thinkers:

> He established His covenant in his flesh, and when tested he was found faithful. (Sir. 44:20)

> The LORD knew that Abraham was faithful in the midst of his affliction. . . . And in everything in which He had tested him he was found faithful, and his soul was not impatient, yet he was not slow to act for he was faithful and a lover of God. (Jub. 17:17–18)

> Abraham was found faithful to [G]o[d] for favor. (4QPseudo-Jubilees b fragment 7:1–2)[24]

22. Levenson, *Inheriting Abraham*, 44.
23. Levenson, *Inheriting Abraham*, 55.
24. James L. Kugel, *How to Read the Bible* (New York: Free Press, 2007), 132.

Kugel notes that in Greek there is a close relationship between the notion of faithfulness and *faith.* To be faithful to God one needs to have faith in God.[25] Genesis 15:6 explicitly declares, "Abraham believed the LORD and he credited it to him for righteousness" (TNIV). The English version of the Tanakh produced by the Jewish Publication Society puts the verse this way: "And because he put his trust in the LORD, He reckoned it to his merit." Paul would cite this verse to indicate that Abraham, the man of faith, was the forebear of all who had faith, whether Jew or gentile: "So also Abraham 'believed God and it was credited to him as righteousness.' Understand, then, that those who have faith are children of Abraham" (Gal 3:6–7). Levenson puts it this way: "Like Paul, the rabbis of the Talmudic period, too, would quote Genesis 15:6. . . . But for them it provided evidence that the Jewish people are 'people of faith and the descendants of people of faith.' The difference between their theology and Paul's does not lie in the question of whether faith is or is not important; it is highly important in both theologies. The essential difference, rather, lies in the question, faith in what?"[26]

Christians have often misunderstood the nature of faith and faithfulness not only within Judaism but within their own tradition. Trusting God, having faith in God, meant for Abraham believing the promises God made, however unlikely they appeared. And these promises were not dependent on Abraham's faithfulness, Abraham's "works." As we have seen, the promises to Abraham were unconditional: "By myself I swear, the LORD declares" (Gen 22:16). But however important his belief in God, it was Abraham's *responses* to God that demonstrated his faith in God: he left his home, he circumcised the males of his household, he even agreed to sacrifice his son. He was faithful in *response* to the promises of God. He was not faithful in order to *acquire* the promises of God.

Paul's Abraham

Some Christian Reflections

As Levenson suggested above, although Jews and Christians both look to Abraham as a forefather in faith, they understand the role of Abraham very differently. N. T. Wright argues that Paul is constantly rereading and reimag-

25. Kugel, *How to Read*, 122–23.
26. Levenson, *Inheriting Abraham*, 27.

ining Judaism in light of the death and resurrection of Christ.[27] Israel's story is not repudiated as much as reframed. God, so far as Paul is concerned, is not doing something new. He has not planted a new "tree." The old "olive tree" of Israel remains intact. Some branches have been removed, some branches added, but it is the same tree (Rom 11:17–21). Abraham is still a model of faith and faithfulness for Paul as he was for the rabbis. But Paul insists in Romans 4 that Abraham is now not only the father in faith of the "circumcised," but of the "uncircumcised" since his faith was credited *before* he was circumcised (Rom 4:9–12). In Galatians he makes the same point about the law of Moses. God made promises to Abraham and his "seed" long before the Torah was given to Moses. "The law, introduced 430 years later, does not set aside the covenant previously established by God and thus do away with the promise" (Gal 3:17). Neither the covenant requirement of circumcision nor the community-forming commitment of Torah nullifies the promise that was made to Abraham before either appeared.

Why is this important to Paul? He is arguing that the promises made to Abraham are *inclusive* rather than *exclusive* (not *universal* rather than *particularistic*). They extend to his gentile converts every bit as much as his Jewish confreres. For Wright, this means that Paul is redefining election:

> Abraham is thus "the father of us all": the stone that some exegetical builders have refused is in fact the climax, the head of the corner, the answer to the questions of [Romans] 4:1. We do not have to regard Abraham as our "forefather according to the flesh," Paul is concluding, because he is the father of us all, Jew and Gentile alike, in accordance with the promise of Genesis 17:5 which made him "the father of many nations." . . . This is the way the one God always intended to work (and this is what Abraham always believed that he would do) in order to include Gentiles in his "seed."[28]

For Wright's Paul, then, God *always* intended to include the gentiles in the promises made to Abraham and, ultimately, to Israel. Paul, reading the Hebrew Scriptures through his understanding of the death and resurrection of Jesus, describes a very different Abraham than the rabbis. Paul's Abraham is not simply the first Jew, but the first *believer.*

27. For Wright's exhaustive discussion of the theology of Paul see *Paul and the Faithfulness of God*, 2 vols. (Minneapolis: Fortress, 2013).

28. Wright, *Paul and the Faithfulness*, 1006.

Levenson's Response

Levenson notes Paul's "ambivalence about Jews who did not become Christians."[29] This ambivalence is clear in Romans 9–11, a passage we will explore thoroughly in a subsequent chapter. Paul is distressed that his fellow Jews have by and large refused to acknowledge Jesus as Lord. He does not conclude, however, that this means God has finally and completely rejected his people. Quite the contrary: "Did God reject his people? By no means!" (Rom 11:1). He seems to see their rejection as only temporary. Their disobedience, Paul thinks, has given the gospel an opportunity to spread to the gentiles. But there will come a time when "all Israel will be saved" (Rom 11:25). Paul sees in the rejection of Israel a larger divine plan that will lead to their salvation.

So far as Paul is concerned, then, Israel has not been *replaced* by the church. Rather the members of the new band of gentile Jesus followers are being added to the ancient community of Israel. So was Paul a "supersessionist"? Did he believe that the new community, the church of Jesus Christ, has superseded or replaced the old community of Israel? The answer has to be both yes and no. On the one hand, it is impossible to deny that for Paul something new and final had occurred in Jesus of Nazareth. On the other hand, it is equally certain that Paul never imagined that Jews as Jews or Israel as Israel had been utterly rejected and thrust aside by God. God's covenant with his people endures.

Those who followed Paul, Levenson argues, were not always as careful or "ambivalent" about the Jews. In fact,

> in much of the classical Christian tradition, Abram and the Jews were only instrumental to the emergence of the gospel and its exportation to all the nations of the world. For the classical Jewish tradition (and many contemporary Christians), Abram and the people who descend from him have full importance in their own right: their election, God's mysterious singling out of them from among all the families of the earth, is not canceled when they fail at the lofty ethical and theological mission that comes to be associated with their first father. The promises endure, despite appearances to the contrary.[30]

29. Levenson, *Inheriting Abraham*, 29.
30. Levenson, *Inheriting Abraham*, 35.

Paul would largely agree with Levenson. Even the rejection of Jesus as messiah does not lead to the final rejection of the Jews. Paul holds out hope for Israel, convinced that God's promises endure in spite of appearances to the contrary. Abraham remains the "first Jew" and the forefather of all those grafted into the ancient olive tree—gentiles included. Is this Paul attempting to "square the circle"? Is it a blatant contradiction in terms? I think not, and I will make my case for this assertion later in this book.

The God of Abraham

So who is the God of Abraham? He is the creator God who made the world and all that is in it. He is the God who calls his people to mercy and justice and judges them when they fail. He is the God of mercy who pursues the fearful and fallen and seeks a relationship with them. He is the God who calls Abraham out of Harran and makes his family a "demonstration plot" of God's righteousness. He is the God who makes a covenant with his people—an unconditional covenant of love with Abraham and then a covenant with Moses that makes a *people* from a motley collection of slaves. According to Paul, this is a blessed people: "Theirs is the adoption, theirs the divine glory, the covenants, the receiving of the law, the temple worship, and the promises. Theirs are the patriarchs, and from them is traced the human ancestry of the messiah, who is God over all, forever praised! Amen" (Rom 9:4–5). It would be disingenuous and dishonest to suggest that the differences between Jews and Christians are not significant or don't matter. We read the story of Abraham's God very differently. We understand the identity and accomplishments of Jesus of Nazareth very differently. We pray and worship very differently. And yet our common stories, however fraught at times, are stories of people of faith seeking to live out faithfully the legacy of "our father Abraham."

QUESTIONS FOR DISCUSSION

1. Both Jews and Christians use the term "covenant" to refer to the commitment of the God of Israel to his relationship with his people. How do the Jewish and Christian understandings of covenant differ?
2. Philosophically minded Jewish thinkers struggled with the actions of God in

the Hebrew Scriptures. What is at risk for both Jews and Christians if God is distanced from creation?

3. Abraham is important for both Jews and Christians for different reasons. Why is Abraham important for Jews? Why is he important for Christians?

FURTHER READING

Heschel, Abraham Joshua. *God in Search of Man: A Philosophy of Judaism.* New York: Farrar, Straus and Giroux, 1955.

Levenson, Jon D. *Inheriting Abraham: The Legacy of the Patriarch in Judaism, Christianity and Islam.* Princeton: Princeton University Press, 2012.

Wyschogrod, Michael. *The Body of Faith: God in the People Israel.* New York: Seabury, 1983.

CHAPTER 3

God of Moses

The eighth fundamental principle is that the Torah came from God. We are to believe that the whole Torah was given through Moses our teacher entirely from God.

—Maimonides

Moses received the Law from Sinai and committed it to Joshua, and Joshua to the elders, and the elders to the Prophets; and the Prophets committed it to the men of the Great Synagogue. They said three things: Be deliberate in judgment, raise up many disciples, and make a fence around the Law.

—*m. Avot* 1:1

A Jew without Torah is obsolete.

—Abraham Joshua Heschel

Of all the principles of faith none presents so many difficulties to modern Jews as the eighth.

—Louis Jacobs

The last chapter argued that the God of the Bible is a God who seeks out and communicates his will to his creatures. This chapter will examine the way in which God reveals himself to his creatures.

The God Who Reveals

Judaism, Christianity, and Islam all believe God has revealed himself. The agency and outcome of these revelations differ, of course, but their sacred texts both describe and, in one sense or another, contain this revelation. For Jews the most profound revelation of God's person and purposes was at Sinai.

The God of the Torah

Exodus 19 describes the elaborate preparations required for the encounter between God and his people. The people were to wash their clothing, rope off the mountain to avoid the destruction of both people and animals, and abstain from sexual relations (Exod 19:10–15). When God speaks, the scene is dramatic and terrifying: earthquake, fire, smoke, and a loud trumpet blast.

What God spoke, of course, was the Ten Commandments—the foundational moral and spiritual document of both Jews and Christians and, for that matter, much of the western world, religious or otherwise (Exod 20:1–17). In this incident God spoke not to an individual—to Abraham, Isaac, or Jacob, but to a whole people. He was not making an agreement with an individual or a family, but with a *nation*. The arc of revelation had moved to its pinnacle. But for the people it was all too much: "All the people witnessed the thunder and lightning, the blare of the horn and the mountain smoking; and when the people saw it, they fell back and stood at a distance. 'You speak to us,' they said to Moses, 'and we will obey, but let not God speak to us, lest we die'" (Exod 20:18–19). The rest of the revelation of God's will would be through Moses. Perhaps, the rabbis thought, it was all too much of a good thing.

When God revealed his presence to the Israelites, he did not show forth "all His goodness at once, because they could not have borne so much good; for had He revealed His goodness to them at one time they would have died. Thus, when Joseph made himself known to his brethren, they were unable to answer him because they were astonished by him (Gen. XLV, 3). If *God* were to reveal Himself all at once, how much more powerful would be the effect. So He shows Himself little by little."[1] It would, in fact, take God a significant amount of time to reveal his entire will to Moses and the people of Israel.

The Problem of Revelation

Revelation would seem a simple thing: God speaks, people hear and understand. But in fact, it has never been that easy—even with something as evidently simple and direct as the Ten Commandments. Consider the first command that God gives to humans in the garden of Eden: "Of every tree of the garden you are free to eat; but as for the tree of knowledge of good and bad, you must not eat of it; for as soon as you eat of it, you shall die" (Gen 2:16–17). The serpent shows himself to be the first exegete—"the shrewdest of all the wild beasts that the Lord God had made" (Gen 3:1). "Did God *really* say, 'You shall not eat of any tree in the garden'?" (Gen 3:2). The serpent turns God's statement around, implying that the entire garden was off-limits to them. Eve corrects him, saying that only the one tree in the middle of the garden was off-limits. After this misdirection the serpent suggests that the real reason for God's prohibition is selfish—eating the fruit would make Adam and Eve God's equals. Thus God's commandment is nullified. The rest, as they say, is history. Even straightforward commands can be difficult.

The Ten Commandments, like the command in the garden, seem pretty straightforward. But they still raise all kinds of questions. How does one *practice* these commandments? What constitutes "idolatry"? What does it mean to "misuse the name of God"? If one is to refrain from "work" on the Sabbath, how does one define "work"? How does one "honor" one's father and mother? Even such apparently straightforward commandments regarding murder, adultery, theft, false testimony, and coveting raise questions of application and implication. And this is as true for Christians as it is for Jews. *Possessing* the commandments is not enough. They are not merely to be inscribed on plaques; they are meant to be *lived*. But how? A vast literature developed over the millennia within Judaism to address this very question:

1. *Tanh.*, Debrahim, 1a in Montefiore and Loewe, *Rabbinic Anthology*, 130.

How does one obey, live, and love the commandments of God, God's revelation, God's Torah? Such questions continue to motivate religious Jews to this very day: How is God's will to be lived *today*?

The Nature of Torah

As we saw in the first chapter, you will often hear a Jew speaking of "studying Torah." Christians tend to think immediately of the five books of Moses, the Torah par excellence. Of course, Jews can also speak of these books as Torah—the Torah from Sinai. But when Jews speak of *studying* Torah they mean much more than the five books of Moses. Torah (instruction) can be used to refer to the entire Hebrew Bible, the so-called Oral Torah, collected in the Mishnah, the Jerusalem and Babylonian Talmuds, various collections of midrash, and other ancient Jewish literature. Much of this vast literature has canonical status within Judaism. The five books of Moses, however, are the font from which everything else springs. The ancient rabbis insisted that every doctrine must first be located within the Torah from Sinai.

The Ten Commandments, of course, were just the first of the laws given to Israel at Sinai. Moses entered "the thick cloud where God was" (Exod 20:18). He came out of the darkness with a whole collection of divine commands addressing communal and social relationships, food and clothing, the worship of God, regulations for the Sabbath, and much else. For traditional Jews this further revelation of the will and purposes of God to Moses extended through Exodus to Leviticus, Numbers, and Deuteronomy. They believe in fact, that the Pentateuch in its entirety was delivered to Moses on Sinai. But this is not all. They also believe that the aforementioned Oral Torah, rabbinic interpretations and applications of the Written Torah, was also given orally to Moses at Sinai and passed down from generation to generation of kings, prophets, and scholars: "God gave the Israelites the two Laws, the Written Law and the Oral Law. He gave them the Written Law with its 613 ordinances to fill them with Commandments, and to cause them to become virtuous. . . . And He gave them the Oral Law to make them distinguished from the other nations."[2]

This Oral Torah was not written down until well after the beginning of the so-called "common era." The Mishnah (repetition or teaching) was compiled by Rabbi Judah the Prince around 200 CE and includes "a collection of

2. *Num Rab.*, Naso, 14:10 in Montefiore and Loewe, *Rabbinic Anthology*, 159.

rulings about matters of practice, ritual and law. The rulings are sometimes presented anonymously, sometimes ascribed to named individuals" and often "present two or more conflicting rulings on the same question."[3] How ancient these oral traditions are is a matter of debate. Some, as indicated, would have them go back to Mt. Sinai. Others would locate their origins in the Second Temple or postexilic period.[4] Whatever the case, following the Oral Torah is the mark of a traditional Jew to this day.

Some have argued that the Pharisees, so prominent in the New Testament, were precursors to the early rabbis and developers of the rabbinic tradition enshrined in the Mishnah. Jesus famously debated points of the Torah with the Pharisees and even conflicted with them over "the traditions of the elders" (Mark 7:1–23). Is he here referring to the Oral Torah or what would become the Oral Torah? Some have thought so. Shaye J. D. Cohen is not so sure: "The common scholarly view that mishnaic law is somehow Pharisaic is not baseless but cannot be sustained." He argues that there is clearly a link between the Pharisees of the New Testament and the rabbis of later centuries, but "this hardly means that all Pharisees became rabbis or that all rabbis were latter-day Pharisees. . . . No doubt some of the laws of the Mishnah derived from the Pharisees of the Second Temple period, but mishnaic law cannot be regarded *tout court* as Pharisaic."[5] It cannot be doubted that the destruction of the temple in 70 CE and the failure of the Bar Kokhba rebellion in 135 CE changed everything. The loss of key institutions and key leadership required fresh thinking. The Pharisees, no doubt, provided the foundation but their courageous disciples innovated to enable the survival of the Jewish people.

Whatever the case, the Mishnah and the Talmud reflect the ongoing necessity to interpret and apply God's revelation at Sinai to an ever-changing situation. Jews faced different challenges to faithfulness when they moved from being a wandering horde of former slaves to a settled agricultural community, to an established kingdom with king, temple, and priesthood, to a devastated community bereft of all three. The growing legal tradition reflected in the Mishnah also reflected the challenge of being scattered throughout the Mediterranean and eastern worlds—from Rome in the west

3. Shaye J. D. Cohen, "Mishnah," in *The Eerdmans Dictionary of Early Judaism*, ed. John J. Collins and Daniel C. Harlow (Grand Rapids: Eerdmans, 2010), 960–61.

4. Adin Steinsaltz, *The Essential Talmud*, trans. Chaya Galai (New York: Basic Books, 2006), 36–42.

5. Cohen, "Mishnah," in Collins and Harlow, *Eerdmans Dictionary of Early Judaism*, 960–61.

to Babylonia in the east, from Greece and Asia Minor in the north to Egypt and North Africa in the south. An agricultural people became an urban people. Shepherds, farmers, and carpenters became merchants, physicians, and scholars. A once insular people were confronted with the learning of Persia, Greece, Egypt, and Rome.

To study and apply God's Torah became the abiding passion of the Jewish people and especially of the rabbinic community. The history and development of the Jewish community after the destruction of the temple in 70 CE and the failure of the Bar Kokhba rebellion in 135 CE will be discussed later in this book. But suffice it to say at this point that the near collapse of the Jewish community in the wake of these twin disasters required a Herculean spiritual and intellectual effort to enable its survival. This effort is reflected in the Mishnah and in the extended set of commentaries and reflections on the Mishnah called the Talmud. There are two versions of the Talmud, the Jerusalem and the Babylonian. It is no exaggeration to say that without the effort to study, reflect, argue about, and teach the traditions reflected in the Mishnah and the Talmud, Judaism would not have survived the various tragedies and assaults it has endured to the present day. Judaism today owes a great deal to the Pharisees and their heirs. Some Christians have in the past suggested that the religion and faith of the Pharisees was "sterile." Given the outcome of their work, this assessment could not be more mistaken.

Moses

Before God could address the people at Sinai, however, he had to address Moses. It is hard to overestimate the importance of Moses in Jewish thought and life. His beginning was both auspicious and inauspicious: he was a child of a slave who became the heir of a king; he was a leader of his people who fled them as a murderer; he was a poor shepherd *in* the wilderness chosen to shepherd Israel *through* the wilderness; he was an inarticulate spokesperson and unwilling prophet. Throughout his years of leadership he was harried and harassed by a recalcitrant people and a dangerous God. He faced constant complaints from the people and yet interceded for them when God had determined finally in exasperation to destroy them (see Num 14:13–19). And yet at one point, during an earlier rebellion, Moses had clearly had it: "I cannot carry all of this people by myself, for it is too much for me. If You would deal thus with me, kill me rather, I beg You, and let me see no more of my wretchedness" (Num 11:14–15).

Moses, towering figure that he is, remains fully human. His greatness is measured not so much by his ability as by his willingness to pay attention to God—the God who revealed himself, perhaps most famously, at the burning bush. God calls Moses as he had Abraham, Isaac, and Jacob. And yet there was something unique about the call of Moses. In one sense Moses is just another in a string of unlikely heroes called by God: Abraham, a childless octogenarian, founds a people; Jacob, a shifty scoundrel, gives them his name; Joseph, an insufferably arrogant dreamer, saves them from starvation; and now Moses, a man with a past and a speech impediment, becomes their leader and lawgiver. But Moses will receive more from God than had any before him.

God's Intimacy with Moses

The voice out of the bush tells Moses, "I am . . . the God of your father, the God of Abraham, the God of Isaac, and the God of Jacob" (Exod 3:6). God goes on to tell a terrified Moses that he is to confront the all-powerful Pharaoh and liberate his people from slavery. Moses, it soon becomes clear, doesn't want the job. But God is persistent. James Kugel describes the next scene as follows:

> In his initial casting about for an excuse, Moses hits upon the fact that he himself does not know the specific name of this God. . . . Of course, Moses is curious about the name, but he is also playing for time; he is frightened, but also intrigued. Who *is* this God, and what is happening to me? So he presents the question not as a real question but as an objection. "If I tell the Israelites that You appeared to me, the first thing they will ask is: 'What was his name?' Since I do not know the answer to that, I cannot possibly accept this mission."[6]

God's answer is famously obscure and, perhaps, not particularly helpful. The TNIV, and many other English translations, render the Hebrew: "I AM WHO I AM" (Exod 3:14). But that is not the only way to read the words. The English version of the Tanakh of the Jewish Publication Society basically punts and transliterates the Hebrew: *Ehyeh-Asher-Ehyeh.* A footnote informs the reader that the Hebrew is uncertain and can be rendered, "I am that I am"

6. Kugel, *How to Read*, 211.

or "I am who I am" or "I will be what I will be." Moses is still understandably confused, so in the end "God then explains in the next sentence, 'This is what you will tell the Israelites, 'The Lord [that is YHWH] . . . has sent me to you.' Moses thus does get the answer he is looking for, and eventually he even accepts the mission."[7]

Much could be said about this encounter and the revelation to Moses of God's name.[8] Suffice it to say that this incident makes it plain that Moses has been granted unprecedented intimacy with God. Not only has God called him, God has revealed the divine name to him. This name, represented by four Hebrew letters and rendered in English as YHWH, is not, as we have seen, pronounced aloud by religious Jews but represented by words like "Lord" or "Hashem" (the name). And Moses's intimacy with God only grows. Moses encounters God like no one before him. In the wake of the crisis of the golden calf, Moses, evidently shaken by recent events, wants to make sure God is still with him. God assures him, "you have truly gained My favor and I have singled you out by name" (Exod 33:17). God and Moses are on a first-name basis—but even this is not enough for Moses: "O let me behold Your presence," he asks. And, sheltered in a rock, Moses sees the glory of God as it moves away from him (Exod 33:19–23). Throughout the Torah, Moses is God's constant conversation partner: "The LORD would speak to Moses face to face, as one man speaks to another" (Exod 33:11). When the people are too frightened to hear directly from God, Moses relays his commands and expectations to them.

The Enduring Importance of Moses

Moses's stature grew throughout the Second Temple (or postexilic) period. Writing around 180 BCE, Ben Sira declared, God made Moses "equal in glory to the holy ones, and made him great to the terror of his enemies. By his words he performed swift miracles; the Lord glorified him in the presence of kings. He gave him commandments for his people, and revealed to him his glory. For his faithfulness and meekness he consecrated him, choosing him out of all humankind. He allowed him to hear his voice and let him into the dark cloud, and gave him the commandments face to face, the law of life and knowledge."[9]

7. Kugel, *How to Read*, 211.
8. See Kugel, *How to Read*, 209–16.
9. Sir. 45:1–5 NRSV.

A few decades later the book of Jubilees depicts Moses as a prophet, lawgiver, and intercessor. God not only gives Moses the law and responds to his prayers on behalf of disobedient Israel, he shows him what is ahead for Israel: "I shall send to them witnesses so that I might witness to them, but they will not hear. And they will even kill the witnesses. And they will persecute those who search out the Law, and they will neglect everything and begin to do evil in my sight. And I shall hide my face from them, and I shall give them over to the power of the nations to be captive, and for plunder, and to be devoured."[10]

Philo of Alexandria, a contemporary of Jesus, and Josephus, the first-century CE historian and revolutionary, both present Moses in terms that would appeal to a more sophisticated and educated crowd—both Jewish and Roman. "In his *Life of Moses*, Philo presents Moses as the 'greatest and most perfect of men' (1:1–2) who combined in his character the ideal king, legislator, high priest and prophet (2:1–7 . . .). He was a philosopher, a living embodiment of law and justice, an interpreter of sacred mysteries, and a mystic who underwent heavenly ascent and deification. Moses was not only beyond all others, his qualities were superhuman."[11] Josephus also "emphasizes Moses as the most ancient legislator, a brilliant general, a philosopher, teacher, an incomparable prophet, and a poet who invented a musical instrument."[12]

For the rabbis who rebuilt Judaism following the disasters of 70 and 135 CE, Moses was the teacher par excellence. He was the source not only of the five canonical books of the Written Torah, but of the Oral Torah and other Jewish traditions. The authority of the rabbis was the authority of Moses, antecedent to the temple and the kingship and stretching all the way from Sinai to the land of Israel and, latterly, to Babylonia. However different and even odd their work may seem to outsiders, the rabbis insisted that it *continued the work of revelation* that began with the burning bush in the wilderness, continued in the rumbles and thunders of Sinai, was sustained by prophets and priests in the land of Israel, and was now entrusted to them and their successors.

A story in the Talmud describes a bewildered Moses visiting the famous school of Rabbi Akiva:

10. Jub. 1:12–13, *The Old Testament Pseudepigrapha*, vol. 2, ed. James H. Charlesworth, trans. O. S. Wintermute (Garden City, NY: Doubleday, 1985), 53.

11. Daniel K. Falk, "Moses," in Collins and Harlow, *Eerdmans Dictionary of Early Judaism*, 969.

12. Falk, "Moses."

> When Moses ascended on high [to receive the Torah], he found the Holy One, blessed be He, sitting and tying knots on the letters. [Moses] said to Him: "Lord of the Universe, what are those for?" He replied, "After many generations a man will be born Aqiva ben Joseph; he will infer stacks of laws from each of these marks. [Moses] said to Him, "Lord of the Universe, show him to me!" He said, "Move back!" [Moses] went and sat in the eighth row [of Aqiva's school], but could not make sense of what they were talking about, and grew faint. When [the disciples] reached a certain point [in the discussion], they asked [Aqiva], "Master, on what do you base this?" He replied, "It is Torah [received by] Moses at Sinai." Moses was reassured.[13]

Even though Moses could not understand the abstruse discussion in Akiva's classroom, he was reassured when he understood that the great rabbi's work was an extension of his own, so much so that it could be considered "Torah received by Moses at Sinai."

Torah as Revelation Today

But what does all this mean for contemporary Jews and, for that matter, contemporary Christians? In what sense are the five books of Moses, in the Tanakh for Jews and in the Old Testament for Christians, still *revelation*? In what sense are Mishnah, Talmud, and midrash revelation for contemporary Jews? How would the New Testament be considered *revelation* for Christians? And in what sense for both communities does God continue to reveal himself? For both communities and their various denominational divisions, this is a vexed set of questions for more than one reason.

I began this chapter with a comment from Rabbi Louis Jacobs: "Of all the principles of faith none presents so many difficulties to modern Jews as the eighth."[14] The "principles of faith" he refers to are the famous Thirteen Principles of the great medieval scholar Maimonides (Moses ben Maimon, also call Rambam). Maimonides was born in Cordoba, Spain, but when the city fell to a fanatical Muslim tribe his family was forced to

13. *b. Menah.* 3:28b in *The Talmud: A Selection*, ed. and trans. Norman Solomon (London: Penguin Books, 2009), 591.

14. Louis Jacobs, *Principles of the Jewish Faith* (New York: Basic Books, 1964), 218.

flee.[15] The family settled in Fez, Morocco, in 1160. Maimonides eventually found his way to Alexandria in Egypt where he served as both physician and scholar. His most famous works are the "*Mishnah Torah* (1178), the first commentary to codify halakah in a logical system; *The Guide to the Perplexed* (1185–90), which attempted to reconcile Judaism and Aristotelian thought; and *Thirteen Principles of Faith*, a treatise outlining Maimonides' interpretation of the basic theological beliefs of Judaism."[16]

A poetic hymn based on the Thirteen Principles is found at the end of the morning service in most Jewish prayer books.[17] In the *Koren Siddur*, translated into English by Rabbi Jonathan Sacks, the Eighth Principle reads as follows:

> I believe with perfect faith:
> That the entire Torah now in our hands
> is the same one that was given to Moses our teacher,
> peace be upon him.[18]

This assertion of Maimonides finds its authority from the words of the Mishnah. In *Sanhedrin* 10:1 the rabbis declare, "All Israelites have a share in the world to come." But there are some exceptions. "These are those that have no share in the world to come: he that says there is no resurrection of the dead prescribed in the Law, and [he that says] that the Law is not from heaven and an Epicurean." For the rabbis, as for the Pharisees (and Jesus), the resurrection of the dead was a foundational doctrine. The Epicurean, Herbert Danby notes, is not a philosophically minded Jew but someone "free from restraint" and "licentious and skeptical."[19] But it was perhaps most serious for a Jew to deny that the "Law is from heaven." That was to deny that Israel has heard from God—that Israel had a revelation. Why is this such a problem for Jacobs's "modern Jews" and, for that matter, for modern Christians? How are both modern Jews and modern Christians to understand the nature of *revelation*?

15. Karesh and Hurvitz, "Maimonides," *Encyclopedia of Judaism*, 305–7.

16. Karesh and Hurvitz, "Maimonides," 305–7.

17. Hayim Halevy Donin, *To Pray as a Jew: A Guide to the Prayer Book and the Synagogue Service* (New York: Basic Books, 1980), 200–201.

18. Sacks, *Koren Siddur*, 204.

19. Danby, *Mishnah*, 397.

The Rise of Historical Criticism

In the seventeenth century, philosophers and theologians began to raise questions about the historical reliability of the Bible. Jewish thinker Baruch Spinoza was famously excommunicated by the Jews of Amsterdam "for denying that the Torah was literally true and given by God . . . and that the soul is immortal. Spinoza rejected the idea of a personal God. He believed that God or nature is the force that sustains the universe; consequently everything in it is an aspect of God."[20] For his pains Spinoza was also condemned by Christians. His work was only at the beginning of a process that would see the sacred writings of both Christians and Jews subjected to analysis by skeptical scholars who saw them as merely human documents and not in any sense "inspired" or "revealed." By the nineteenth century modern scholars would assert that the Torah was not delivered to Moses at Sinai but developed over many centuries and only consolidated during the Babylonian exile. But not all who read the sacred texts "critically" were skeptics. Some, while agreeing that these texts needed to be read in their historical and cultural contexts, argued that, however human and culturally conditioned they were, they still were in some sense inspired and from God—a *revelation.*

In his book *Liberal Judaism*, the late Reform Jewish scholar Eugene Borowitz asks how the "modern Jew" understands God's revelation.[21] Unlike Orthodox Jews, and for that matter many traditional Christians, Borowitz and other liberal Jews do not believe "God communicates words."[22] That is to say, God communicates, God reveals, but not through the concrete literal words of the biblical and rabbinic texts. The words of the sacred text perhaps bear witness to revelation, give insight into revelation, but are not themselves revelation. In this case the ancient texts themselves can become a treasured historical document describing the experience of a people, but are not entirely binding on Jews (or Christians) today. Many more "liberal" Christians would say something very similar.

For many Jews and Christians, both "conservative" and "liberal," this is simply not enough. If God has not spoken in some sense through these texts to our forebears, for many they are little more than antiquarian documents that perhaps offer moral and spiritual "suggestions," but nothing truly authoritative. Given the reigning individualism and subjectivity within the

20. Karesh and Hurvitz, "Spinoza, Baruch," *Encyclopedia of Judaism*, 494–95.

21. Borowitz, *Liberal Judaism*, 256–70.

22. Borowitz, *Liberal Judaism*, 269.

wider society, many traditionalists fear that a modern person may choose to follow the paths recommended in the sacred texts or not, may select what they like and ignore what they find inconvenient. Such individualism, traditionalists argue, strikes the foundation of communal formation and corporate self-understanding.

Nevertheless, however committed Jews or Christians may be to their sacred texts, modern questions cannot be ignored. And for many liberal, and for that matter traditional, Jews and Christians, the biblical text poses conundrums. How is one to understand the commands to destroy the Canaanites down to the last man, woman, and child (Deut 20:16–19)? How is one to make sense of God commanding Abraham to sacrifice his son Isaac (Gen 22)? How is it that God appears on some occasions to be so cruel and unsparing? Are these accounts truly the very words of God? Is everything in our sacred texts to be accepted without question and without critique? Are all of these accounts still *revelation*? Such difficult passages, of course, could be multiplied.

Confronting Religion's Autoimmune Disease

The problem is more than the texts themselves. In his provocative book *Putting God Second*, Rabbi Donniel Hartman, speaking out of the Orthodox Jewish tradition, argues that readers of our sacred texts can suffer from what he calls "God intoxication" and "God manipulation."[23] For the God-intoxicated person, Hartman suggests, "the awareness of living in the presence of the one transcendent God demands an all-consuming attention that can exhaust one's ability to see the needs of other human beings. This religious personality is defined by strict non-indifference to God. The more we walk with God, the less room we have to be aware of the human condition in general, and consequently our moral sensibilities become attenuated" (46).

Hartman argues that even a figure like Abraham can be an example of God intoxication. When God commands Abraham to sacrifice his son, he appears, shockingly, to agree without hesitation. Abraham had not always behaved this way. When God had proposed the complete destruction of Sodom, Abraham argued against it (Gen 18:16–33). But now, "Abraham's personality—his desires, values, and commitments—disappears the moment

23. Hartman, *Putting God Second*, 43–66. Hereafter, page references are given in parentheses in the text.

the word of God penetrates his consciousness. His intoxication with the divine eclipses all human concerns" (47).[24] God intoxication, of course, is very much a contemporary problem, as Hartman amply illustrates. The God-intoxicated person is so absorbed in his or her vision of the transcendent that human obligations become secondary and human justice uninteresting. Intoxication with God can ironically lead to a person ignoring God's will rather than following it.

The second example of "religion's autoimmune disease" is God manipulation. This happens when individuals

> align the identity and will of the One with the interests and agendas of those who lay claim to God's special love. Antithetical to God intoxication, in which God's transcendence shifts our vision away from humanity toward the transcendent One, here the passionate yearning to be loved by the transcendent One unleashes a sinful impulse to control the transcendent. In a paradoxical manner, monotheism, which sought to uproot idolatry, gives birth to perhaps the greatest idolatry of all, the idolatry of human self-intoxication, an idolatry in which God is drafted in the service of human self-interest. (46)

Hartman argues that the notion of holy war presents a classic example of God manipulation. Faced with an enemy other standing in the way of prosperity and safety, "God manipulation" uses God to justify the destruction of the other. Since these are God's enemies as well as yours, the thinking goes, they may be destroyed without compunction or pity. "Through the disease of God manipulation," Hartman argues, "the standards of justice are set aside, and the God who is supposed to be served through righteousness to all, and who is characterized as the judge of the whole earth, is suddenly transformed into a God who blinds people to their moral responsibility" (62).

Our sacred texts, our *revelation*, Hartman insists, call us to follow a God of love, justice, and truth. But what are we to do when we see God or one of our heroes within those sacred texts apparently acting or commanding people to act in ways that seem contrary to God's own love, justice, and truth? If we believe that God reveals himself and his truth in the sacred texts, we must be willing to engage deeply the questions, conflicts, and difficulties raised by those texts. Jews have never believed the Bible stands alone. It must be read, interpreted, and *lived*. The ancient rabbis were fully aware of the questions and

24. For a very different view see Levenson, *Inheriting Abraham*.

conflicts the text raised and at their best did not flinch in the face of the painful dilemmas Torah sometimes raised. They never doubted that God's revelation was present in the Torah. But they insisted that discerning the implications of that revelation was a long, ongoing, communal exercise. The Jewish tradition joins the ancients and the moderns in wrestling with the question, What does God command *now*? The process of reading and rereading is unending and full of dangers. Individuals can lose themselves and their moral compass in their eagerness to love and serve God. This is one reason, at least, for the communal process of Torah study and ethical reflection among Jews.

Ongoing Revelation

However important the ongoing study and reflection on Torah, God's revelation, the rabbis were skeptical about *ongoing* revelation. They were wary of those who claimed to be modern prophets or speaking on behalf of God. They knew their work to be important and even a continuation, in some sense, of the work of Moses. But they did not imagine that they were experiencing divine revelation in the same way as Moses or the prophets. In a famous story in the Babylonian Talmud, Rabbi Eliezer is arguing a point of halakah with a number of colleagues. When they disagree with his interpretation he calls on the miraculous to establish his point. He makes a carob tree uproot itself and move. He forces a stream to run backwards. He nearly collapses the schoolhouse walls to prove he is right. His colleagues are not impressed. Finally he declares,

> If the law accords with my opinion, let Heaven [itself] declare than I am right! [At this,] a heavenly voice proclaimed, Why do you challenge Rabbi Eliezer, for the *halakha* accords with him in all matters! Rabbi Joshua arose to his feet, and declared, It is not in heaven (Deuteronomy 30:12). What does It is not in heaven mean? Rabbi Yirmiya said, Now that the Torah has been given on Mount Sinai we no longer pay attention to any heavenly voice, for at Mount Sinai the words Follow the majority (Exodus 23:2) were written in the Torah. Rabbi Nathan met [the prophet] Elijah and asked What did the Holy One, blessed be He, do when that happened? [Elijah] replied, He laughed, and said, My children have outvoted Me, my children have outvoted Me![25]

25. *b. Metz.* 4:59b in Solomon, *The Talmud*, 469–70.

This process of communal *discernment* is clearly subject to both "God intoxication" and "God manipulation," as Rabbi Hartman argues.[26] But readings unchecked by tradition or community can become self-serving and destructive. Judaism provides a rich and enduring source of readings and rereadings of its sacred texts deeply rooted in long and ardent arguments about the meaning and application of Torah. These arguments continue to this day because the task of discerning the will of God never ends. For Jews, God no longer makes his will known through prophets, but still speaks when God's people seek to understand and, especially, obey his Torah. There is safety and joy in the communal process as well as dangers and frustrations.

The Revelation of God

Torah does more than reveal the word of God. It reveals in a profound sense *God's self*. For Abraham Joshua Heschel, in the prophets of Israel one encounters the "divine pathos." The God of Israel is not the God of the Stoics or the "unmoved mover" of Aristotle. When we read the Bible we are not merely encountering the words of an ancient people. Nor should we imagine we are hearing the unfiltered words of God. According to Maimonides: "When we are told that God addressed the Prophets and spoke to them our minds are merely to receive a notion that there is a Divine knowledge to which the Prophets attain; we are to be impressed with the idea that the things which the Prophets communicate to us come from that Lord and are not altogether the products of their own conceptions and ideas. . . . [But] we must not suppose that in speaking God employed voice or sound."[27]

Maimonides, of course, would disagree with Heschel's notion of "divine pathos"—the notion of God experiencing human emotion would be distasteful to him. But Maimonides's restrictions on the human perception of God's communication appeal to Heschel. "Vain would be any attempt to reconstruct the hidden circumstances under which a word of God alarmed a prophet's soul. Who could uncover the divine data or piece together the strange perception of a Moses?" We were not on the mountain with Moses. We did not hear the "still small voice" heard by Elijah.[28] "All we have," says

26. Hartman, *Putting God Second*, 19–66.

27. Moses Maimonides, *The Guide for the Perplexed*, trans. M. Friedlander (New York: Dover Press, 1956), 97.

28. See 1 Kgs 20:19.

Heschel, "is a Book, and all we can do is to try to sense the unworded across its words."[29] While this may sound similar to Borowitz's assertion that "God does not use words," something else is meant here.

Every Jew and Christian, liberal or conservative, who believes God speaks, *reveals* himself in our sacred texts, faces this conundrum. God may speak through the agency of the prophets, but we are not prophets. God's revelation, even if it comes in "words," does not come to us unfiltered. Perhaps that is a good thing, or otherwise, as the Israelites feared, if God speaks to us we will die.[30] But this requires us to exercise humility when we read and interpret our texts. It requires us to listen to our traditions, something Jews and Roman Catholics are much better at doing than Protestants, and perhaps especially than evangelicals. It also requires us to stand in awe before the mystery of both God and his revelation. As Heschel so eloquently puts it,

> Some of us approach the Bible stalking on the stilts of a definition. But who are we to speak of the mystery without knowledge and to state what it means that His spirit burst forth from its hiddenness? Who has fathomed the depth of the Bible? Have we entered the springs of its wisdom or walked in the recesses of its innermost meaning? Have the gates of its holiness ever been open to us, and have we ever comprehended the expanse of its world? Where were we when the word was set as a limit and God said: "Thus far shall my wisdom be disclosed and no further." Souls are not introduced to a range of mountains through the courtesy of a definition. Our goal, then, must not be to find a definition, but to learn how to sense, how to intuit the will of God in the words. The essence of intuition is not in grasping what is describable but in sensing what is ineffable. The goal is to train the reason for the appreciation of what is beyond reason. It is only through the ineffable that we may intuit the mystery of revelation.[31]

Not every Jew, of course, would agree with Heschel. Borowitz, for one, while respecting Heschel, worried that this approach failed to "make clear how he would resolve a direct clash between a prophetic revelation (most particularly those of Moses) and an ethical imperative."[32] Perhaps Rabbi Hartman would raise a similar concern. Borowitz also worried that Heschel

29. Heschel, *God in Search*, 188.

30. Exod 20:19.

31. Heschel, *God in Search*, 189.

32. Borowitz, *Liberal Judaism*, 264.

"unqualifiedly cloaked the rabbinic tradition with the authority of prophetic revelation." He concludes, "in the face of such traditionalist consequences liberals have generally not looked to Heschel for a modern understanding of revelation."[33] Perhaps not, but it strikes me that Heschel's attempt to hold both the tradition and the mystery together offers both "traditionalists" and "progressives" a way to navigate the hard questions raised by "God intoxication" and "God manipulation" while not abandoning either the notion of "God's revelation" or the human responsibility represented in the tradition to continue reading, interpreting, and living the Torah. We will have occasions in the chapters that follow to return to the questions raised in this one and to explore further the meaning in Judaism that there is a God who reveals.

QUESTIONS FOR DISCUSSION

1. What do Jews mean by Torah? What do Christians mean by *law*? What can Christians learn about Torah from Jews?
2. Why is Moses such a towering figure in Judaism?
3. The Torah from Sinai has been interpreted, reinterpreted, and applied for millennia. It is a living text. How is the way Jews read and interpret Torah similar or different from the way Christians read their sacred texts?

FURTHER READING

Buber, Martin. *Moses: The Revelation and the Covenant.* New York: Harper & Row, 1958.

Hartman, Donniel. *Putting God Second: How to Save Religion from Itself.* Boston: Beacon, 2016.

Jacobs, Louis. *A Jewish Theology.* Springfield, NJ: Behrman House, 1973.

Soloveitchik, Joseph R. *Halakhic Man.* Translated by Lawrence Kaplan. Philadelphia: Jewish Publication Society, 1983.

33. Borowitz, *Liberal Judaism*, 264.

CHAPTER 4

God of the Commandments

Moses went and repeated to the people all the commands of the LORD and all the rules; and all the people answered with one voice, saying, "All the things the LORD has commanded we will do!" And Moses wrote down all the commands of the LORD.

—Exodus 24:3–4

So then, the law is holy, and the commandment is holy, righteous and good.

—Romans 7:12

These are things whose fruits a man enjoys in this world while the capital is laid up for him in the world to come: honoring father and mother, deeds of loving-kindness, making peace between a man and his fellow; and the study of the Law is equal to them all.

—*m. Pe'ah* 1:1

Judaism without halakhah is no longer Judaism. It is an anarchical system of several loosely held beliefs.

—Gilbert Rosenthal

The only reason that a devout Jew needs for the observance of any of the commandments . . . is that they reflect the will of God.

—Hayim Halevy Donin

Liberals insist on the freedom to determine for themselves which aspects of their inherited faith they will continue to observe and what in their belief now requires the creation of new forms.

—Eugene Borowitz

Exodus shows the Jewish people at the moment of their formation as a people. God their deliverer through Moses their leader has presented all the "commands" and "rules" that would constitute his covenant with them. And they have agreed to abide by "all the things the LORD has commanded." After a solemn ceremony of confirmation and commitment, the path of God's people is set before them.

God's Commandments and God's People

To be a Jew, now as then, is to be confronted with the commandments of God in all their glory and complexity. The Hebrew Scriptures are a record of that confrontation: accounts of faithfulness and failure, of resistance and repentance. But however strained the relationship between God, his people, and his law, the commandments of God were not seen as a burden or imposition. Quite the contrary, Torah was a means of showing and living in love: "Love the LORD your God with all your heart and with all your soul and with all your strength" (Deut 6:5). "Love your neighbor as yourself" (Lev 19:18; see also Mark 12:29–31). "Jewish law," according to Elliot Dorff, "should be seen as an expression of *love* between the people of Israel and God, among the people Israel as a community, and between the people of Israel and the rest of humanity."[1] God's commands were not simply a means of control but a method of love.

For the last two thousand years the commandments of God have been a battleground between Jews and Christians. The harsh critique of the Pharisees in the Gospels and Paul's apparent dismissal of the "law" in his letters have convinced many Jews that the early Christians did not really understand the role of the commandments in Jewish life. Paul's views have been particularly perplexing for both Jews and, for that matter, Christians. Sometimes he seems to affirm the holiness and goodness of the "law" (as in Rom 7, an epigraph at the start of this chapter) and at other times he appears to see the "law" as passé. I would suggest that both Jews *and* Christians have frequently misunderstood Paul's teaching on the "law." But in fairness to Paul's readers, both ancient and modern, he has *not* made it easy for them. He does at times seem to be, if not contradictory, at least attempting to sustain a difficult tension.

1. Elliot N. Dorff, *For the Love of God and People: A Philosophy of Jewish Law* (Philadelphia: Jewish Publication Society, 2007), xiv.

For millennia, the vast majority of Jews agreed that following God's commandments was the most appropriate way to live as a Jew and serve God (even if some of them didn't strictly always do so). There were (and are), of course, many arguments about what God's commandments required in any given situation. The vast rabbinic literature is focused on addressing just these questions, providing precedents and arguments for their successors to this very day. But, as we saw in the previous chapter, with the arrival of the Enlightenment, Jews, especially in Europe and the United States, began to wonder if there were elements of the commandments that were no longer useful in and applicable to the modern world. Were the commandments regarding food, the Sabbath, and purity still viable and useful? Were not the message of the prophets and the "ethical" commands of the Bible the true beating heart of Judaism? Many Jews within the Reform movement within the United States thought so.

Nevertheless, many Jews and Christians would continue to insist that God's commandments are *still* viable and important—but *which* commandments? All would perhaps quote the prophet Micah:

> With what shall I approach the LORD, do homage to our God on high? Shall I approach Him with burnt offerings, with calves a year old? Would the LORD be pleased with thousands of rams, with myriad of streams of oil? Shall I give my first-born for my transgression, the fruit of my body for my sins? He has told you, O man, what is good, and what the LORD requires of you: only to do justice and love goodness, and to walk modestly with your God. (Mic 6:6–8)

The final line is especially stirring, but it raises a key question: What does it mean in any *concrete* situation to "do justice, to love goodness, and to walk modestly [or humbly] with your God"? A traditional Jew would say the commandments of God and the extended rabbinic reflections on them are intended to address exactly that question. Without the ability to address the *particular*, the *general*, however lovely, is vague and impractical. A person needs not only to know what to think, but how to *live*.

What Are God's Commands?

Jews refer to any commandment of God as a *mitzvah* (*mitzvot*, pl.). In popular speech a *mitzvah* is simply a good or charitable act. While *mitzvah* entails an individual act, "*halakha* is the overall term for Jewish law; it refers also to the final authoritative decision on any specific question."[2] Literally halakah refers to a way of going: "*Halakha* is concerned with the proper application of the commandments (*mitzvoth*) to every situation and circumstances."[3] The commandments of God touch on every area of life: what one eats, what one wears, how one spends time, and how one worships; they are concerned with human sexuality, child rearing, business dealings, and communal relationships. In spite of their pervasiveness, the commandments do not intend to impose but to *form*. They do not simply seek to enforce, but to *reveal*:

> It is in *deeds* that man becomes aware of what his life really is, of his power to harm and to hurt, to wreck and to ruin; of his ability to derive joy and to bestow it upon others; to relieve and to increase his own and other people's tensions. It is in the employment of his will, not in reflection, that he meets his own self as it is; not as he should like it to be. In his deeds man exposes his immanent as well as his suppressed desires, spelling even that which he cannot apprehend. What he may not dare to think, he often utters in deeds. The heart is revealed in the deeds.[4]

According to Jewish tradition God revealed 613 commandments to Moses at Sinai: 365 prohibitions and 248 positive commands. According to Dan Cohn-Sherbok, "these prescriptions . . . are classified in two major categories: (1) statutes concerned with ritual performance characterized as obligations between human beings and God; and (2) judgments consisting of ritual laws that would have been adopted by society even if they had not been decreed by God (such as laws regarding murder and theft)."[5] Cohn-Sherbok provides a list of all 613 commands as compiled by Moses Maimonides.[6] This may seem to be quite enough, but, as we have seen, the commands raised many questions that needed to be answered. If one is not to work on the Sabbath, for example, what constitutes work? Changed circumstances also

2. Donin, *To Be a Jew*, 29.

3. Donin, *To Be a Jew*, 29.

4. Abraham J. Heschel, *Between God and Man: An Interpretation of Judaism*, ed. Fritz A. Rothschild (New York: Free Press, 1997), 82. This book is an anthology of Heschel's works. Heschel uses "man" generically throughout his work. It is difficult to adjust without at times damaging the beauty and rhythm of his language.

5. Dan Cohn-Sherbok, *Judaism: History, Belief, and Practice* (London: Routledge, 2003), 397.

6. Cohn-Sherbok, *Judaism*, 404–18.

raised questions: How does one obey the commands regarding offerings and worship when the temple has been destroyed? These were, and are, questions that the ancient and modern rabbis sought and continue to seek to answer.

As we have seen, traditional Judaism argued that in addition to the "Written Law," God passed on the "Oral Law" to Moses. This Oral Law was finally written down as the Mishnah. The Mishnah supplied "teachers and judges with an authoritative guide to the Jewish legal tradition."[7] The Talmud contains further glosses, interpretations, and reflections on the Mishnah. But according to *Numbers Rabbah*, Naso, 14:10, the Oral Law served another purpose:

> God gave the Israelites two Laws, the Written Law and the Oral Law. He gave them the Written Law with its 613 ordinances to fill them with commandments and to cause them to become virtuous. . . . And He gave them the Oral Law to make them distinguished from the other nations. It was not given in writing so that the nations could not falsify it, as they have done with the Written Law, and say they are the true Israel.[8]

When Christians claimed the Hebrew Scriptures, the Old Testament, as their own and also laid claim to the story of Israel, Jews could point to the Oral Law as a unique gift from God, a distinguishing mark not colonized by the church. When Christians read the Old Testament through the lenses of the "Christ event," Jews read and continue to read the Torah through the Oral Law, the Talmud, and the ongoing reflections of the rabbis. This literature is theirs alone.

Why Keep Them?

The Bible is an ancient book. While many of the commandments continue to make sense to modern people, both believers and nonbelievers, other commandments may appear absurd or even oppressive. Few people would quibble over the prohibition of murder and theft. Most would agree that committing adultery is harmful. But where is the harm in eating pork? Why would it matter to God that we mix meat and cheese or get a tattoo? Are

7. Cohn-Sherbok, *Judaism*, 397.
8. *Num. Rab.*, Naso, 14.10 in Montefiore and Loewe, *Rabbinic Anthology*, 159.

such things really the commands of God, or do they represent the attempt of an ancient people to create and sustain a distinct culture and preserve a unique people? Is the Torah unchanging divine revelation or merely a human attempt to hear and respond to God or the Divine? If the former, it may not be abrogated. If the latter, it may, indeed must, be adjusted as God's people continue to look for God's presence and purpose in the present moment.

Both Jews and Christians have struggled with these questions. Did God really speak to Moses? To the prophets? To Jesus? To the evangelists? Does God still speak to us? How do believers hear and respond to the voice of God today? Christians and Jews, liberal and conservative, traditional and "progressive," will have very different ways of answering these questions. But they are enduring ones—and complex ones. In his book *A Jewish Theology*, Louis Jacobs helpfully describes how various groups of Jews have sought to answer the question of the continuing authority of Torah and the *mitzvot*. The approaches he outlines are not very different from those used by Christians to describe the authority of the Scriptures.

Jacobs begins rather uncharitably and unhelpfully with a category he calls "fundamentalism." By this he means the viewpoint of traditional Judaism. For this group, with all its diversity, the Torah is still divine revelation. For the traditionalist, the will of God for the Jewish people has not changed. While the law must, as always, reckon with the challenges of modern life, it has not fundamentally changed. Jews must continue to obey the commandments of God regardless of the changes in culture, because *God commanded them to do so.* According to one of the historic defenders of this position, Rabbi Samson Rafael Hirsch,

> Let us not deceive ourselves. The whole question is simply this. Is the statement "And God spoke to Moses saying," with which all the laws of the Jewish Bible commence, true or not true? Do we really believe that God, the Omnipotent and Holy, spoke thus to Moses? Do we speak the truth when in front of our brethren we lay our hand on the scroll containing these words and say that God has given us this Torah, that His Torah, the Torah of truth and with it of eternal life, is planted in our midst? If this is to be no mere lip-service, no mere rhetorical flourish, then we must keep and carry out this Torah without omission and without carping, in all circumstances and at all times.[9]

9. Louis Jacobs, *A Jewish Theology* (Springfield, NJ: Behrman House, 1973), 216.

Traditional Christians would say similar things about the Bible and its authority. For both traditional Jews and Christians, this does not mean that there aren't enduring questions of meaning and significance. This does not mean there are no significant questions of application. The ancient rabbis would never deny the authority of Torah, but even they recognized that sometimes the Torah needed to be adapted and reread to reflect a very different place and time. Not even for the traditionalist, either Jew or Christian, is the Bible a bee trapped in amber. If God is a living God then this text continues to be a living text as God's people are a living people.

At the other end of the Jewish spectrum is what Jacobs calls the "Classical Reform" view. On this view Judaism is not a religion of ritual laws and traditions, but "an ethical religion, a prophetic religion."[10] In the Pittsburgh Platform of 1885 Reform Jews declared,

> We recognize in the Mosaic legislation a system of training the Jewish people for its mission during its national life in Palestine, and today we accept as binding only its moral laws, and maintain only such ceremonies as elevate and sanctify our lives, but reject all such as are not adapted to the views and habits of modern civilization. We hold that all such Mosaic and Rabbinical Laws as regulate diet, priestly purity, and dress originated in ages and under the influence of ideas utterly foreign to our present mental and spiritual state.[11]

This was, of course, an era flush with confidence in human reason, modern progress and the triumph of western civilization. Modernity offered a way out of the hoary and discredited customs of the past, whether they were religious or cultural. This modern confidence affected the Christian world as well as the Jewish. The educated individual was deemed capable of taking charge of his or her own religious and moral life.

One of Reform Judaism's most influential thinkers, Rabbi Eugene Borowitz, offers a chastened view of this modern (over)confidence:

> Liberal religion, which had as good as deified the self, ascribing to human consciousness or ethics a certainty it denied to God and revelation, lost much of its credibility as the self became discredited as its own savior. After all we have seen of human failure, individual and social, its optimistic

10. Jacobs, *A Jewish Theology*, 218.
11. Jacobs, *A Jewish Theology*, 218.

> humanism seemed shallow compared with the old religious paradigms of reality. They, at least, had unambiguous worthy standards by which persons, families, communities and nations could direct their randy freedom, whereas liberals had such openness and tolerance that they could hardly ever tell us when we must say no to a new possibility.[12]

This should not be taken to suggest that Borowitz was considering a return to Orthodoxy, but that he recognized that the old liberal project as it was conceived, while providing a great deal of freedom for the individual, was largely a failure at providing a coherent structure for a family, a community, or a nation. Individual freedom became individualism; liberty became license; community lost coherence. This has required both Liberal Judaism and, for that matter, Liberal Christianity to begin to reimagine their respective traditions.

But how might those traditions be reimagined? Was there an approach that valued and preserved the tradition and accepted the critiques and questions of modernity? The key problem for many late nineteenth-century Christians and Jews was the emergence of historical criticism. Throughout the nineteenth century, scholars, especially in Germany, raised questions about the historical reliability of the Bible. Did God really create the world in six days? Did Moses really part the Red Sea? Did Jesus really heal the sick and raise the dead? Perhaps most critical for Jews was the question of whether Moses really received the law of God at Sinai. Did Moses hear the law from God on the mountain or was the law developed and codified over many centuries and only finalized during the Babylonian captivity? The words of Hirsch cited above are directly addressed to this question. For both Jews and Christians the question was not simply a question of history, but of reliability and authority. Could their sacred texts be trusted? Could their *God* be trusted?

Between the traditionalist and liberal stances there were several mediating positions. There were Jews in the late nineteenth century who believed that ultimately it didn't matter whether the Sinai event was strictly historical. Obedience to the commandments was incumbent upon Jews regardless. Unlike the "classic Reform" position, they did not reject the traditions that offended modern sensibilities. Rabbi Elliot Dorff, for example, writes, "modern biblical scholarship has convinced me that the Torah originally consisted

12. Eugene B. Borowitz, *Renewing the Covenant: A Theology for the Postmodern Jew* (Philadelphia: Jewish Publication Society, 1991), 24.

of oral traditions that were only later written down at different time periods. The text of Torah is thus for me a human document."[13] This does not mean that for Dorff the Torah lacks authority for the Jew. Nor does it mean that the Torah is not in some sense a *revelation*. For Dorff, "what marks an event as a revelation of God is not that the event itself is of a special character but that it is interpreted as such by a human community."[14]

Torah, then, for these Jews is not a direct revelation of God to Moses at Sinai, nor is it merely a human document developed over centuries by the ancients and incumbent on no one. Rather: "Jewish law . . . is of human authorship, a human, communal response to events that the Jewish community accepts as revealing God or God's will for us. The law is divine because of its internal wisdom (its soundness as a way of living as demonstrated by experience), its moral goodness and its durability (strength). Here, as usual, wisdom, morality, and power are characteristics that we call divine. The authority of Jewish law for the Jew is then a function of both its communal acceptance and its divinity."[15]

For Dorff, the authority of Torah is not that it was given by God to Moses, but that the Jewish people accepted it as a divine document, as revelation. It is surely true that such a document as the Torah, or the New Testament, or any sacred text requires a community to accept it as authoritative. Without such acceptance such a text becomes an antiquarian curiosity. But surely this also raises the question of to what extent the text holds authority over the community and to what extent the community holds authority over the text.

All this raises other questions: Which community? Are such decisions regarding the authority of our sacred texts made by a vote of the majority? By experts? By scholars? By our most pious members? Must nothing change? Must everything change? Jaroslav Pelikan famously describes this tension: "Tradition is the living faith of the dead; traditionalism is the dead faith of the living. Tradition lives in conversation with the past, while remembering where we are and when we are and that it is we who have to decide. Traditionalism supposes that nothing should ever be done for the first time so all that is needed to solve any problem is to arrive at the supposedly unanimous testimony of this homogenized tradition."[16] For Pelikan, unlike many Americans, *tradition* is not a bad word. Tradition becomes "traditionalism," how-

13. Dorff, *For the Love*, 29.

14. Dorff, *For the Love*, 29.

15. Dorff, *For the Love*, 30.

16. Jaroslav Pelikan, *The Vindication of Tradition* (New Haven: Yale University Press, 1984), 65.

ever, when the conversation with the past ends. This can happen in two ways. The meaning and practice of the sacred text can become frozen in time, at some ideal point in the past. A certain authoritative voice or set of voices can be made the *only* voice(s). No other voice(s) is deemed worthy of a hearing. Second, the meaning and practice of the text can be limited to simply what my particular group does. Nothing must change. No questions may be raised. In either case the tradition ceases to be a *living* tradition and sinks into traditionalism and irrelevance. This can happen at either end of the religious spectrum.

Given these options (and there are, of course, others), how are modern Jews trying to negotiate the extremes? How is the Torah, the tradition, to be preserved as a living tradition, a lively text? Why should Jews, in spite of all the modern historical, theological, and spiritual questions, continue to live out of their ancient law, their ancient traditions? One of the twentieth century's greatest religious thinkers and spiritual guides attempted to answer these questions. Abraham Joshua Heschel, it may appear, was trying to square the circle. Whether or not either side of the historical, critical, and spiritual divide was satisfied with his attempt is ultimately not important. His efforts said, and continue to say, something profound about Judaism, God, Torah, and the Jewish people. His reflections, as far as I am concerned, are no less important for Christians.

Abraham Joshua Heschel and the People of God

Rabbi Abraham Joshua Heschel was born in Warsaw in 1907. He was "a descendent of a long line of outstanding leaders of the Hasidim. . . . At the age of ten he was at home in the world of the Bible, he had acquired competence in the subtle dialectic of the Talmud, and had also been introduced to the world of Jewish mysticism, the *Kabbalah*."[17] At the age of 20 he left this closed world and began studies at the University of Berlin, concentrating on Semitics and philosophy. "His life and work can perhaps be understood as an attempt to achieve a creative viable synthesis between the traditional piety and learning of Eastern European Jewry and the philosophy and scholarship of Western civilization."[18] It is fair to say that Jewish scholars and thinkers are invested in that task to this very day, as, in their own way, are Christian thinkers and scholars.[19] But Heschel took a unique path.

17. Heschel, *Between God and Man*, 7.
18. Heschel, *Between God and Man*, 7.
19. See, for example, Borowitz, *Renewing the Covenant.*

During his years in Berlin he experienced a crisis of faith and practice. He left off dressing as a Hasid. He expanded his social and intellectual world to include people and ideas that were new and challenging to his former understanding and practice of Judaism. He later wrote that during an evening stroll in Berlin it struck him that

> I had forgotten God—I had forgotten Sinai—I had forgotten that sunset is my business—that my task is "to restore the world to the kingship of God." So I began to utter the words of the evening prayer. *Blessed art thou, Lord our God, King of the universe, who by his words brings on the evenings*. . . . On that evening in the streets of Berlin, I was not in a mood to pray. My heart was heavy, my soul was sad. It was difficult for the lofty words of prayer to break through the dark clouds of my inner life.[20]

How is a modern Jew to remember God? How is a modern Jew to recall Sinai? And how is such a Jew to live faithfully in the modern western world? These were questions that would pursue Heschel throughout his life. You cannot, even in the modern world, he would argue, separate God from Sinai. You cannot have the knowledge of God or the fear of God, without the will of God. "The way to God is a way of God," he would write.[21]

For Heschel, to experience God was to know wonder, awe, and radical amazement. But this wonder, this awe, was not the exclusive privilege of the mystic exalted in prayer. It was available to the ordinary Jew who was obedient and faithful:

> The presence of God is a majestic expectation, to be sensed and retained and, when lost, to be regained and resumed. Time is the presence of God in the world. Every moment is His subtle arrival, and man's task is *to be present*. His presence is retained in moments in which *God is not alone*, in which we try to be present in His presence, to let Him enter our daily deeds, in which we coin our thoughts in the mint of eternity. The presence is not one realm and the sacred deed another; the sacred deed is the divine in disguise.[22]

20. Samuel H. Dresner, *Heschel, Hasidism, and Halakha* (New York: Fordham University Press, 2002), 9.

21. Heschel, *Between God and Man*, 80.

22. Heschel, *Between God and Man*, 80.

For a Jew, knowing the presence of God does not require a "leap of faith" or a "leap of thought" but "a leap of action."[23] It is in obedience that we "walk humbly with our God." The apostle James would agree: "Show me your faith without deeds, and I will show you my faith by what I do" (Jas 2:18b). Sacred deeds were, however, not simply a way of showing the faith of the obedient individual. "Sacred acts," says Heschel, "*mitzvoth*, do not only imitate, they represent the divine."[24]

Eugene Borowitz considers Heschel a "precursor of Jewish postmodernity."[25] His Judaism was "modernized but quite traditional." His Berlin education prepared him to address the modern intellectual and spiritual tradition, a tradition Borowitz suggests Heschel found "shallow" in comparison to the "depth of traditional belief."[26] The human experience of God and the world was important to Heschel. But unlike modernity he did not *begin* with the human experience but with God's revelation. The human experience *of* God was confirmed by human obedience *to* God. Borowitz writes, "By pressing an unwavering theocentricity on the Jewish community, Heschel attempted to move it to what we now can see was a characteristic postmodern stance: an openness to God as a present lived reality."[27] But this "present lived reality" was not individualistic, solipsistic—merely self-referential. It was a part of a communal experience with deep roots in Israel's past.

Samuel Dresner argues that Heschel found fault with both the left and right sides of American Judaism. After escaping Europe for the United States, Heschel landed at Hebrew Union College in Cincinnati where he would teach philosophy and rabbinic studies.[28] Hebrew Union College is the school of the Reform movement in the United States. In 1945 Heschel relocated to the Jewish Theological Seminary of America in New York. There he was "Professor of Jewish Ethics and Mysticism."[29] After his move to the Jewish Theological Seminary he was invited to return to Hebrew Union and address a convention of Reform rabbis. He told them,

> There can be no Jewish holiness without Jewish law, at least the essence of Jewish law. Jewish theology and tefillin go together.... Why are you afraid

23. Heschel, *Between God and Man*, 81.
24. Heschel, *Between God and Man*, 85.
25. Borowitz, *Renewing the Covenant*, 27.
26. Borowitz, *Renewing the Covenant*, 27.
27. Borowitz, *Renewing the Covenant*, 27.
28. Heschel, *Between God and Man*, 8.
29. Heschel, *Between God and Man*, 8–9.

> of wearing talis and tefillin every morning, my friends? There was a time when our adjustment to Western civilization was our supreme problem. . . . By now we are well adjusted. . . . Our task today is to adjust Western civilization to Judaism. America, for example, needs Shabbos. What is wrong with Shabbos, with saying a *brokho* (blessing) every time we eat, with regularity of prayer? What is wrong with spiritual discipline?[30]

The Reform rabbis were concerned with getting their thinking correct, their theology right—their haggadah. But Heschel would insist in the same address that "there is no aggadah without halakha. There can be no Jewish holiness without Jewish law" (92).

However, the reverse was also true. Heschel was just as concerned about the kind of rigid Jewish practice that was so "halakhocentric" it seemed to minimize piety and engagement of the divine. Just as there was no "aggadah without halakha," "halakha alone is not enough. The Law guides, but it needs the heart to guide also. Halakha is an *answer* to a question, namely: What does God ask of me? The moment the question dies in the heart, the answer becomes meaningless. The question, however, is agadic, spontaneous, personal. . . . The task of religious teaching is to be a midwife and bring about the birth of the question" (92). For Heschel the life of a Jew requires both wonder and obedience, knowledge of God and knowledge of Torah: haggadah and halakah. Judaism, Heschel argued, was more than "religious behaviorism," more than "sacred physics" (104). "Halacha must not be observed for its own sake but for the sake of God. The law must not be idolized. It is a part, not all, of the Torah. We live and die for the sake of God rather than for the sake of the law" (106–7).

No Jew would deny the importance of Torah. No Jew would deny that *mitzvot* are crucial to Jewish identity. But are the commandments contained only in the great ethical assertions of the Ten Commandments and the thunderous proclamations of the prophets? Are they not also found in the intricate expectations of halakah as exposited by the rabbis? Why do these matter today? Perhaps the question is answered by the passage from *Numbers Rabbah* cited earlier. They set the Jews apart. A major concern of Borowitz's *Renewing the Covenant* is that when liberal Jews reduced the concern of Judaism to the *ethical* they inadvertently undermined the Jewish sense of particularity. If the ethical commands are *universal,* why does one

30. Dresner, *Heschel,* 92–93. Hereafter, page references to this work are given in parentheses in the text.

need a *Jewish people*? In fact, why does one need religion or, for that matter, God at all?[31] And yet it does not seem that Borowitz can bring himself to insist that every Jew should return to the strictures of rabbinic practice—at least not completely.

The problem for both Jews and Christians is that Pandora's box has been opened. We have, as Heschel suggests, adjusted to modernity quite well. However strong our communal structures and expectations in the western world, we now have choices. The sanctions of church and synagogue do not prevent either Jews or Christians from walking away from their respective faiths. Even the most Orthodox or fundamentalist traditions cannot ultimately (at least legally) prevent apostasy. Whether we like it or not, our churches and synagogues are all now "voluntary organizations." A Jew living centuries ago in a small village in Eastern Europe or an urban ghetto in London, Rome, or Paris had little choice in the matter. A Christian in medieval England or France was in a similar position. In both cases it was much easier for the community to sanction inappropriate behavior and enforce compliance.

All of this means that for both Jews and Christians the practice of one's faith is increasingly *voluntary*—a conscious act. And perhaps more than ever the practice of one's faith is a mark of identity—a boundary marker. Obedience to the commandments for a religious Jew means more than "ethical behavior." Increasingly, even among Reform Jews, it means engaging in activities that identify oneself as a Jew: keeping kosher, keeping the Sabbath, circumcising sons, engaging in ritual prayer. Jews will continue to debate, as they always have, which commandments are to be obeyed and in what manner. But perhaps the modern world that has done so much to undermine the *mitzvot* has now demonstrated the clearest reasons for their practice. It has perhaps demonstrated that the covenant and the *mitzvot* are indispensable if Judaism is to survive.

Some Christian Reflections

Protestant Christians in general and evangelical Christians in particular have had a difficult time with "commandments." Most would acknowledge, of course, that the Ten Commandments (excluding, perhaps, the Sabbath) are binding on everyone. But "good works," or, in Jewish terms, *mitzvot*, have

31. See Borowitz, *Renewing the Covenant*, 64–65.

been more of a problem. Luther's exposition of "justification by faith" suggested to many Protestants that it was dangerous to focus on "good works" because that could lead to "works righteousness." Wrongly believing that Jews imagined they were "saved" by keeping the law, by "good works," most Protestants looked askance at "legalism" and leaned toward, if not falling into, antinomianism. Many Protestants found their justification for this position in the apostle Paul. But I would suggest that the Protestant tradition has often seriously underestimated the importance of obedience to God's commands in the New Testament in general and in Paul's letters in particular.

In Paul's great letter to the Romans he insists on "justification by faith." This justification comes "apart from the works of the law."[32] But, to the consternation of many, just a few verses earlier Paul had written, "All who sin apart from the law will also perish apart from the law, and all who sin under the law will be judged by the law. For it is not those who hear the law who are righteous in God's sight, but it is those who obey the law who will be declared righteous" (Rom 2:12–13). Various unsuccessful attempts have been made to explain this passage away. One commentator on Romans went so far as to ignore chapter 2 altogether. But one has to assume that Paul was not intending to be blatantly contradictory. Perhaps Paul meant two different things by the word "law" in these two passages. Be that as it may, the important point is that Paul, along, by the way, with Jesus, clearly expected that to be a follower of Jesus was to be obedient to the law of God. Gentiles would not be required to take on the "identity markers" of the Jews, but *both Jewish followers of Jesus and gentile followers of Jesus would demonstrate their righteousness by obedience.*

The great danger of Protestantism is what the young German martyr Dietrich Bonhoeffer called "cheap grace." He argued this was the mortal enemy of the church: "Cheap grace is preaching forgiveness without repentance; it is baptism without the discipline of community; it is the Lord's supper without confession of sin; it is absolution without personal confession. Cheap grace is grace without discipleship; grace without the cross; grace without the living incarnate Jesus Christ."[33] He would say that only those who believe are obedient, and only those who are obedient believe. He can say such a thing on good authority: "Not everyone who says to me, 'Lord, Lord,' will enter the kingdom of heaven, but only those who do the will of

32. Rom 3:28, author's trans.

33. Dietrich Bonhoeffer, *Discipleship*, trans. Barbara Green and Reinhard Krauss (Minneapolis: Fortress, 2001), 44.

my Father who is in heaven" (Matt 7:21). Any follower of Jesus who imagines obedience to the will of God is not important presumes on the grace of God. Such grace is "cheap grace."

Heschel would suggest to both Jews and Christians that knowledge of God and obedience to God are intimately connected. God is known and experienced in obedience to the divine command. For Jews you cannot have haggadah without halakah. For Christians you cannot have grace without obedience. Jesus was once asked, "Of all the commandments which is the most important?" He answered, "The most important one . . . is this: 'Hear, O Israel: The Lord our God, the Lord is one. Love the Lord your God with all your heart and with all your soul and with all your mind and with all your strength.' The second is this: 'Love your neighbor as yourself.' There is no commandment greater than these" (Mark 12:29–31). And so it is.

QUESTIONS FOR DISCUSSION

1. What is the "Oral Torah" and how does it enable Jews to continue to be obedient to God's commandments?
2. What is meant by God's "revelation"? How are traditional Jews and Christians similar or different in their understanding of revelation?
3. How are Jews constituted as a *people* by their obedience to Torah?

FURTHER READING

Borowitz, Eugene B. *Liberal Judaism.* New York: Union of American Hebrew Congregations, 1984.

———. *Renewing the Covenant: A Theology for the Postmodern Jew.* Philadelphia: Jewish Publication Society, 1991.

Donin, Hayim Halevy. *To Be a Jew: A Guide to Jewish Observance in Contemporary Life.* New York: HarperCollins, 1991.

Dorff, Elliot N. *For the Love of God and People: A Philosophy of Jewish Law.* Philadelphia: Jewish Publication Society, 2007.

CHAPTER 5

Israel

The LORD said to Abram, "Go forth from your native land and from your father's house to the land that I will show you."

—Genesis 12:1

If I forget you, O Jerusalem, may my right hand wither; let my tongue stick to my palate if I cease to think of you, if I do not keep Jerusalem in memory even at my happiest hour.

—Psalm 137:5–6

All may be compelled to go up to the land of Israel, but none may be compelled to leave it. All may be compelled to go up to Jerusalem but none may be compelled to leave it, whether they be man or woman.

—*m. Ketubbot* 12:11

My heart is in the East
And I am at the edge of the West.
How can I possibly taste what I eat?
How could it please me?
I'd gladly leave behind me
all the pleasures of Spain
if only I might see
the dust and ruins of your Shrine.

—Judah Halevi

There is hardly a major passage in the Five Books of Moses which fails to reflect and to reiterate the promise that God made to Abraham, that the land of Canaan would be his inheritance and that of his descendants.

—Arthur Hertzberg

Sometime during the years 1088–89, a precocious Jewish teenager arrived in Granada to begin what he hoped would be a life of poetry and pleasure in this more tolerant region of Muslim Spain.[1] But it was not to be. A new Islamic warrior caste arrived in Granada and made life intolerable for its Jews as well as for many of its Muslim inhabitants. They were "ascetic, militant, hostile to laxness and luxury" (280). Judah Halevi was forced to flee from one Spanish city to another, always seeking a place where he could write his poetry and practice his faith without threat from either Christians or Muslims. But it seemed that in the late eleventh and early twelfth centuries there was no safe place for Jews in either Europe or North Africa.

Even though Halevi settled in Toledo, married, and had children, misery pursued him. Two of his three children died, and an outbreak of violence against the Jews of Toledo brought him to the point of despair. His poetry changed and became intensely spiritual. He produced a spirited defense of Judaism entitled *The Kuzari: An Argument for the Faith of Israel.*[2] It is depicted as a dialogue between a learned rabbi and a Khazar king who is eventually converted to Judaism. Simon Schama suggests, "it is impossible to read the *Kuzari* without feeling that Halevi is writing as much for his own self-clarification as for the enlightenment of others" (284).

For Halevi, Jewish learning and literature, religion and tradition, could not be separated from the land itself: from Israel, from Jerusalem. "The critical moment" in the *Kuzari*, Schama writes, "comes when Halevi describes exile from Zion as a kind of sleep; an awakening would happen when the Jews returned to the land where the covenant was made, the laws were received and the prophets opened to vision" (285). The rabbi tells the king that it is better to live in the Holy Land than any town occupied by heathen. The king responds, "If this be so thou fallest short of the duty laid down in the law by not endeavoring to reach that place and make it thy abode in this life and death although thou sayest, 'Have mercy on Zion for it is the house of our life'" (286). It seems clear that this is an argument the king is not just putting to the rabbi, but to Halevi himself.

By this time Halevi was by the standards of the time an old man in his mid-60s. He longed to go "east" as the poem in the epigraph illustrates, but the journey from Spain to the Holy Land was long, dangerous, and un-

1. The following narrative is drawn largely from Simon Schama, *The Story of the Jews*, vol. 1, *Finding the Words, 1000 BC–1492 AD* (New York: HarperCollins, 2013). Hereafter, page references to this work are given in parentheses in the text.

2. The *Kuzari* is readily available in English from, among others, Schocken Books.

comfortable. At the time the Crusaders were in control of the land and the status of Jews was as perilous there as in Spain. The land was full of violent men, both Christian and Muslim. But finally he could bear it no longer. He left behind his beloved grandchild and made his way east. After a miserable journey, he made it to Egypt, where the Jews of Alexandria received him as a celebrity. After a couple of false starts he finally left for Acre by ship and disappeared from history. No one knows whether he made it to the Holy Land or up to Jerusalem. According to one rumor he finally got to the gates of Jerusalem only to be trampled to death by an Arab rider's horse (291). Such an end seems tragically apropos.

Judah Halevi longed for the Holy Land, for Jerusalem, for the same reasons that Jews before and after him did. This was the land of their forebears; the land of Abraham and Sarah, Isaac and Rebekah, Jacob, Rachel, and Leah. It was land God had promised them and given them. It was land they had gained, lost, regained, lost, gained, and then apparently lost irretrievably. And yet however long it was lost, however remote it was in time and distance, longing for its very dust remained central to Jewish self-identity and hope. It was the place of longing, hope, and memory. It was the one place where the Jews could freely and perfectly practice their faith. *All* God's commands could only be fulfilled in the Holy Land. Finally, it was the place where they could be safe and whole both spiritually and physically. The more miserable and perilous their lives, the more poignant and powerful their longing to be restored to their land. Judah Halevi's life abundantly illustrates both the longing and, if the legends be true, the peril.

Longing, Hope, and Promise

The land is promised and given before anything else. God calls Abraham and promises him the land before circumcision, before Sinai, and before David's royal house. The promise of the land antedates every other promise. While the Canaanites were still in the land God told Abraham, "To your offspring I will give this land" (Gen 12:7). As Arthur Hertzberg notes in the epigraph, there is hardly an important passage in Torah that does not in some sense reiterate this promise. It is reiterated in connection with circumcision in Genesis 17:8: "The whole land of Canaan, where you now reside as a foreigner, I will give as an everlasting possession to you and to your descendants after you." It is reiterated in connection with Sinai. Deuteronomy 30 insists that even if they were driven out of the land by disobedience God would eventually bring them back to the land and establish them permanently:

> When all these things befall you—the blessing and the curse that I have set before you—and you take them to heart amidst the various nations to which the LORD your God has banished you; and you return to the LORD your God, and you and your children heed His command with all your heart and soul, just as I enjoin upon you this day, then the LORD your God will restore your fortunes and take you back in love. He will bring you together again from all the peoples where the LORD your God has scattered you. Even if your outcasts are at the ends of the world, from there the LORD your God will gather you, from there He will fetch you to the land that your fathers possessed, and you shall possess it; and He will make you more prosperous and more numerous than your fathers. (Deut. 30:1–5)

The great crises of the late seventh and early sixth centuries BCE saw the already tiny Kingdom of Judah reduced even further as the Babylonians carried groups of artisans and intellectuals into exile. Among those early exiles was the prophet Ezekiel, a visionary who saw the *shekinah*, God's glory, leaving Solomon's Temple (Ezek 10:18–19). God tells the prophet that because of the evil committed by the leaders and the people, the city and the land will be lost. At the end of chapter 11 the prophet sees "the glory of the LORD" leave the city and pause above the mountains east of the city, as if waiting to see if there is any response to the fearful warnings of the prophecy. And then Ezekiel is returned to his place of exile in Babylonia (Ezek 11:22–24).

Ezekiel was also a prophet of hope. Even in the fearful vision of chapter 11 God promises, "I will gather you from the peoples and assemble you out of the countries where you have been scattered and I will give you the land of Israel" (11:17). Ezekiel famously describes the restoration of Israel as the resurrection of an army of bleached bones in the desert (Ezek 37:1–14). This is, of course, consistent with Deuteronomy 30 and with the rest of the exilic and postexilic prophets. The land may be lost, but the loss will not be permanent. God will eventually bring the people back and restore the land and grant them peace. At that point "nor shall they ever again defile themselves by their fetishes and abhorrent things, and by their other transgressions. I will save them in all their settlements where they sinned, and I will cleanse them. They shall be my people and I will be their God" (Ezek 37:23).

The great prophet of return and restoration was Isaiah. The book of Isaiah included prophecies both preceding and following the exile. It spoke to Jews toiling in distant Babylonia, to those straggling back to the land, and to returnees struggling to make a life in a blighted landscape. Whatever their situation, there was hope.

> Arise, shine for your light has dawned; the Presence of the LORD has shone upon you! Behold! Darkness shall cover the earth, and thick clouds the people; but upon you the LORD will shine, and His Presence be seen over you. And nations will walk by your light, kings by your shining radiance. Raise your eyes and look about: they have all gathered and come to you, your sons shall be brought from afar, your daughters like babes on shoulders. (Isa 60:1–4)

Isaiah adds here a universal element to this return. "Nations will walk by your light." The return of God's people would mean that not only would *they* worship and obey the God of Israel, but their gentile oppressors would be subject to God as well.

Isaiah, of course, was not alone in saying this. A later postexilic prophet would insist that "the LORD will be king over all the earth; in that day there shall be one LORD with one name" (Zech 14:9). The survivors of God's great victory over the nations will come year by year to worship God, celebrating the Festival of Tabernacles—or else (14:16–19). The land, the city of Jerusalem, thus becomes not only an object of longing, hope, and promise for Israel, but, as far as the prophets are concerned, for the whole earth. No matter how one understands and describes the development of Jewish monotheism, by the time of the great exilic and postexilic prophets God is Lord not just of the land and people of Israel, but of the entire earth and all its people.

It is understandable, then, that for the rabbis, many of them residing in Babylon, the land of Israel was still the center of the universe:

> Just as the navel is found at the center of a human being, so the Land of Israel is found at the center of the world, as it is stated: "Who dwell at the center of the earth" [Ezek 38:12], and it is the foundation of the world. Jerusalem is at the center of the Land of Israel, the Temple at the center of Jerusalem, the Holy of Holies is at the center of the Temple, the Ark is at the center of the Holy of Holies and the Foundation Stone is in front of the Ark, which point is the foundation of the world. (*Tanhuma, Kedoshim*)[3]

3. As cited in Arthur Hertzberg, *Judaism: The Key Spiritual Writings of the Jewish Tradition* (New York: Simon and Schuster, 1991), 205.

The Mishnah famously says that the land of Israel is, indeed, holier than any other. But within Israel, the closer you get to Jerusalem and its temple, the holier things get. According to *m. Kelim* 1:6–9 there are varying degrees of holiness in the world:

1. The land of Israel is holier than any other land.
2. The walled cities of the land are still more holy.
3. Jerusalem is still more holy.
4. The Temple Mount is still more holy.
5. The rampart is still more holy.
6. The court of women is still more holy.
7. The court of the Israelites is still more holy.
8. The court of the priests is still more holy.
9. Between the porch and the altar is still more holy.
10. The sanctuary is still more holy.
11. The holy of holies is still more holy.

In fact, "the rabbis never missed an opportunity to extol the land, to praise its soil and climate, to laud its special spirituality and sanctity. Israel is the holiest of lands and higher in elevation than any other land (*m. Kelim* 1:6ff; *Qidd.* 49b). Rabbi Shimon ben Yochai preached in a sermon 'God tested all of the lands and could find not a single place worthy of the Children of Israel except the Land of Israel' (*Lev. Rab.* 13:2)."[4]

To Jews in exile, whether in Babylon or Egypt or, later, in Europe and America, the land was a dream and an aspiration. During the long years of powerlessness and oppression the hopes of the prophets sustained many in their misery. The land became an object of longing, as it was for Judah Halevi, in spite of the dangers on the way and the dangers once you arrived. As Zechariah shouted to a scattered people, "'Away, away! Flee from the land of the north'—says the LORD—'though I swept you [there] like the four winds of heaven'—declares the LORD. 'Away, escape, O Zion, you who dwell in Fair Babylon!'" (Zech 2:6–7). Here, finally, Jews would be able to be fully Jews, to follow Torah completely, and be safe from their enemies.

4. Rosenthal, *What Can a Modern Jew Believe?*, 137.

Fulfilling All the *Mitzvot*

Rabbi Gilbert Rosenthal argues that for the rabbis the land of Israel was not simply the place where Jews belonged, nor was it simply the holiest place on earth: "The sages noted that only in the land of Israel could a Jew perform all the *mitzvot*, notably agricultural laws that are not observed in the Diaspora."[5] The rabbis of the Talmud would insist that any Jew living outside of the land was missing something:

> One should live in the Land of Israel, even in a city the majority of whose people are not Jews, rather than live outside the Land, even in a city the majority of whose people are Jews. Whoever lives in the Land of Israel is considered to be a believer in God. . . . Whoever lives outside of the Land is considered to be in the category of one who worships idols. . . . Whoever lives in the Land of Israel lives a sinless life, as it is written, "The people who dwell there will be forgiven of their iniquity" [Isa 33:24]. Whoever is buried in the Land of Israel is considered as though he were buried beneath the Altar. . . . Whoever walks a distance of four cubits in the Land of Israel is assured of a place in the world to come. (*b. Ketub.* 110b–111a)[6]

But that is not all:

> Living in the land of Israel equals in import the performance of all the commandments of the Torah. (*Lev. Rab.* 34)
>
> Rabbi Zeira said: Even the conversation of those who are living in the land of Israel is Torah. (*b. Qidd.* 49b)
>
> The atmosphere of the Land of Israel makes men wise. (*b. B. Bat.* 158b)
>
> The Holy One, praised be He, said: A small group of men in the Land of Israel is dearer to Me than the great Sanhedrin outside of the land. (*y. Ned.* 6:8)[7]

The land of Israel was the place to study Torah perfectly, follow the *mitzvot* fully, and to flourish as a Jew. In spite of all the obstacles put in their

5. Rosenthal, *What Can a Modern Jew Believe?*, 137.
6. Cited in Hertzberg, *Judaism*, 205–6.
7. Cited in Hertzberg, *Judaism*, 206.

way, through the Roman, Byzantine, and Muslim eras Jews continued to make their way to the land. Hertzberg cites the example of a seventeenth-century Talmudist named Isaiah Hurwitz who made his way from Prague to the land of Israel. He wrote back to his followers in Europe that although Jerusalem was a ruin, "it is still the glory of the whole earth." He was hoping more Jews would return to the land and the city. He considered the revival of the city and the land a sign of the coming deliverance. He hoped to "develop a wonderful activity for the study of Torah" and to be "a faithful shepherd to those who would study our sacred Law." Everyone, he declared, should move to the city of Jerusalem. "It is particularly holy and the gate of heaven. I have firm confidence that the Lord will let much knowledge of Torah spread through me, so that the word may be fulfilled that out of Zion shall go forth the Law."[8]

When European Jews experienced the Enlightenment and emancipation, Jews from the Reform tradition argued it was time to drop the connection between Jews and the land. They poured scorn on the early Zionists who aspired to reclaim the land and national existence of Israel. But traditional Jews continued to hope for the restoration promised by the prophets. Renowned twentieth-century rabbi Joseph Soloveitchik argued that "Jewish destiny is linked with this land; we have no other. Only in this land, our Sages say, does the *Shekinah* dwell and only there does prophecy flourish. This *segulah* [singular] attribute of the land is no more rationally explicable that the *segulah* of the people."[9] In fact, "the union of the people of Israel with the land of Israel is comparable to a marriage. The crossing of the Jordan river involved more than geographic movement; it represented a marriage between the people and the land; a union of rocky hills and sandy trails and a people whose future destiny is to this day bound up with the state and welfare of the land."[10]

For the secular Zionists the land was not important for its sacredness. Rather it was a place where Jews could escape persecution and protect themselves. But for religious Jews like the sages, such as Isaiah Hurwitz and Rabbi Soloveitchik, it was much more. It is difficult, Soloveitchik writes, "for non-Jews to understand the depth of attachment which the Jew, to this day,

8. Cited in Hertzberg, *Judaism*, 207.

9. Joseph B. Soloveitchik and Abraham R. Besdin, *Reflections of the Rav: Lessons in Jewish Thought Adapted from Lectures of Rabbi Joseph B. Soloveitchik* (Jerusalem: Department of Torah Education and Culture in the Diaspora of the World Zionist Organization in Jerusalem, 1979), 120.

10. Soloveitchik and Besdin, *Reflections of the Rav*, 120–21.

has to this land. They view this bond solely in secular, nationalistic terms." But this misses the point: "The intense, passionate involvement of Jews today throughout the world with the Land of Israel testifies to an identification which transcends normal devotion and, instead, reflects a fusion of identities, the *segulah* [singular] dimension."[11] Standing in Jerusalem as the Sabbath arrives, as candles are lit, and as silence falls over the city, it is not difficult to understand this.

A Place to Be Safe

The Persian king Cyrus permitted the exiled Jews to return to their land after his conquest of Babylon. For Isaiah this was the work of God. The prophet has God tell the king, "For the sake of Jacob My servant, Israel My chosen one, I call you by name, I hail you by title, though you have not known Me" (Isa 45:4). Cyrus is even called God's "anointed," his "messiah" (Isa 45:1). All the evidence suggests the return to the land was difficult. The struggling community found it difficult to complete the work on the Second Temple. And when it was completed many thought it rather unimpressive in comparison to the magnificent Temple of Solomon destroyed by the Babylonians (see Ezra 3:7–13). The books of Ezra and Nehemiah describe how political and religious life were restored and a coherent community was formed around the study of Torah and the rituals of the temple. Although the Jews were under foreign domination, they were back in the land. They could worship their God, study his Torah, and live a fully Jewish life more or less in safety.

Their trials, of course, were far from over. Alexander the Great swept away the Persians and at his death his generals divided up his conquests. The Jews were impacted especially by the dynasties of Syria and Egypt: the Seleucid and the Ptolemaic. Antiochus IV of the Seleucid dynasty, for reasons that are debated to this day, sought to fully integrate the Jews into his kingdom. The story of his offenses and the resulting revolt by the Maccabees is described in 1 Maccabees. The outcome of the conflict was the establishment of Jewish sovereignty in the land under the leadership of the so-called Hasmonean dynasty. When members of that dynasty fell to squabbling among themselves in the first century BCE, the Roman general Pompey took control of Israel and effective Jewish sovereignty was ended. For the next two

11. Soloveitchik and Besdin, *Reflections of the Rav*, 125.

millennia Jewish presence in the land waxed and waned but never quite disappeared—and neither did Jewish longing.

Two great cataclysmic events during the late first and early second centuries of the common era dramatically changed the nature of Judaism and its relationship with the land. A revolt broke out against the Romans in 66 CE that saw Jewish rebels capture Jerusalem and the temple. The Romans responded quickly. The Roman general Vespasian seized the Galilee by 67 and drove the rebels to Jerusalem where they squabbled among themselves. While the Romans were outside of the walls of the city, a civil war between the various rebel factions was going on within the city.

> By Passover of 70 CE Titus [Vespasian's son and future Roman emperor] had massed a large force around Jerusalem while Jewish factions inside the city were killing one another. As Titus' battering rams began to strike, the factions finally came together. One by one the Romans breached the walls of the city, gaining control of the entire city except for the Temple area. By building siege ramparts, Titus was finally able to take the Temple Mount itself. According to Josephus, Titus planned to spare the Temple from destruction, but it was nevertheless engulfed in a conflagration and could not be saved. The ensuing slaughter of men, women, and children and the leveling of the city which followed dealt a lasting blow to Jewish life in the Land of Israel.[12]

A new way of being Jewish was needed. There was no longer a temple. There were no longer sacrifices. The power of the high priestly elite was shattered. It was up to the Pharisees to rebuild a coherent Jewish life.

Unfortunately, this did not end the violence and strife in the land. Some sixty years after the destruction of Herod's Temple another revolt wracked the land. The Roman emperor Hadrian evidently decided to rebuild the city of Jerusalem as a pagan city called Aelia Capitolina. "Aelia" was drawn from the emperor Hadrian's surname and "Capitolina" indicated that the city was dedicated to "Jupiter Capitolinus." The city came complete with a temple to that deity and this proved too much for Jewish patriots. The result was the so-called Bar Kokhba revolt. The leader of the revolt was a charismatic figure named Simeon Ben Kosiba. "Bar Kokhba" is apparently a play on his name meaning "Son of a Star" and alluding to

12. Lawrence H. Schiffman, *From Text to Tradition: A History of Second Temple and Rabbinic Judaism* (Hoboken, NJ: Ktav, 1991), 161.

Numbers 24:17.[13] Very little is known of the revolt, but it was evidently enough of a threat that the Romans sent as many as 50,000 troops to put it down.[14] Hadrian celebrated the victory on coins and with a triumphal arch.[15] Changes in Judaism that had begun after 70 CE were solidified and finalized following 135 CE:

> After the Bar Kokhba war there was little left of the Jewish peasantry in the south. The city of Aelia Capitolina, on the site of Jerusalem, was officially prohibited to Jews; Hadrian outlawed Judaism throughout the holy land, and the sages who supported Bar Kokhba were executed. Rabbi Akiva and other scholars tortured to death by the Romans became hallowed prototypes of the Jewish martyr in the liturgical poetry and other medieval writings on this theme.[16]

The center of rabbinic and intellectual life in the land shifted north to the Galilee. The revolt "set the stage for a more pacific and conciliatory policy of the Jewish authorities toward the Romans and for the resumption of the rapid development in rabbinic Judaism."[17] Things had well and truly changed. There would be no more revolts. The Romans had taught the rabbis a grim lesson. Resorting to violence against their imperial masters was suicidal. "All the suffering and fervent yearnings for redemption had culminated not in a messianic state, but in a collection of traditions which set forth the dreams and aspirations for the perfect holiness that state was to engender. As prayer had replaced sacrifice, Torah, in the form of the *Mishnah*, had now replaced messianism. A different kind of redemption was now at hand."[18]

Thus began the longest and bitterest exile. Jews continued to live in the land, although most were spread around the Mediterranean and Europe: the Diaspora. They were vulnerable to the whims of first pagan, then Christian and then Muslim overlords. They had no army, no military force. They were limited to certain professions and particular areas within states and cities. Even if they acquired wealth and power, they were vulnerable to the

13. For more on the Bar Kokhba rebellion see Hanan Eschel, "Bar Kokhba Revolt," in Collins and Harlow, *Eerdmans Dictionary of Early Judaism*, 421–25.

14. Eschel, "Bar Kokhba Revolt," 424.

15. Eschel, "Bar Kokhba Revolt," 424.

16. Robert M. Seltzer, *Jewish People, Jewish Thought: The Jewish Experience in History* (New York: Macmillan, 1980), 249.

17. Seltzer, *Jewish People*, 249.

18. Schiffman, *From Text*, 176.

envy and abuse of the more powerful. They were alien, other, despised, and distrusted. In times of threat they were often scapegoats. In the wake of a fourteenth-century plague one Gillaume de Machaut wrote,

> After that came a false, treacherous and contemptible swine; this was shameful Israel, the wicked and disloyal who hated good, and loved everything evil, who gave so much gold and silver and promises to Christians, who poisoned several rivers and fountains that had been clear and pure so that many lost their lives; for whoever used them died suddenly. Certainly ten times one hundred thousand died from it in country and in city. Then finally this mortal calamity was noticed. He who sits on high and sees far, who governs and provides for everything did not want this treachery to remain hidden; he revealed it and made it so generally known that they lost their lives and possessions. Then every Jew was destroyed, some hanged, others burned; some were drowned, others beheaded with an ax, or sword. And many Christians died together with them in shame.[19]

Such scenes were repeated with grim regularity throughout Europe into the modern era and beyond.[20] This is the background for Judah Halevi's despair in Spain and longing for Israel.

The European Enlightenment brought with it the hope that Jews could be treated not as a dangerously alien people, but as full citizens of their respective countries. Thus was born what Rabbi Jonathan Sacks calls "the Adjectival Jew." "For the first time, Jewishness was no longer the primary mode of identity. Where once there had been Jews who happened to live in England, France, or Germany, there were now Englishmen, Frenchmen and Germans who happened to be Jews."[21] But there was pushback. The nineteenth century saw the rise of classic "anti-Semitism." The term itself was coined during the century to replace the more prosaic "Jew hatred." But by the end of the nineteenth century, many Jews, both secular and religious, despaired of ever being safe in Europe. This led to the creation of Zionism.

A young Hungarian Jew named Theodor Herzl went to Paris as a journalist to cover the trial of Captain Alfred Dreyfus, a French Jewish army officer

19. In René Girard, *The Scapegoat*, trans. Yvonne Freccero (Baltimore: Johns Hopkins University Press, 1986), 2.

20. See David Nirenberg, *Anti-Judaism: The Western Tradition* (New York: W. W. Norton, 2013).

21. Jonathan Sacks, *One People: Tradition, Modernity, and Jewish Identity* (London: The Littman Library of Jewish Civilization, 1993), 27.

accused of treason. Herzl "was profoundly affected by the false accusations leveled against [Dreyfus] and by the popular anti-Semitism that accompanied Dreyfus' trial and disgrace."[22] This led to the creation of "political Zionism," which sought a Jewish homeland in Palestine. Herzl himself was not religious. His goals were nationalistic rather than theological. In August of 1897 he convened the first World Zionist Congress and created the World Zionist Organization with the goal "to create for the Jewish people a home in Palestine secured by public law."[23] At the end of the meeting Herzl made this startlingly prescient prediction: "Were I to sum up the Basel Congress in a word . . . it would be this: At Basel I founded the Jewish state. If I said that out loud today, I would be answered by universal laughter. Perhaps in five years, and certainly in fifty, everyone will know it."[24]

The Zionist movement was hardly universally popular among Jews. Liberal Jews seeking a place in the cultural and intellectual lives of their respective countries were scandalized. Many traditional Jews were equally outraged: "The Reform movement opposed Zionism as a betrayal of the universal mission of Israel. In fact, the first conference was supposed to have been held in Munich, but the Munich rabbis protested and forced its removal to Basel. . . . Many in the Orthodox Jewish world were equally negative on Zionism, arguing that only the messiah could bring Jews back to their ancient home."[25] The Arab residents of Palestine were also not happy about the growing waves of Jewish immigrants making their way back to the land. The outcome of the Zionist movement was, in the wake of World War II and the Shoah, the foundation of the State of Israel. This facilitated the return of millions of Jews to the land.

What does the land mean to Jews? What does the State of Israel with all of its accomplishments and ambiguities mean to Jews? Different Jews would answer that question differently, of course, but as Rabbi Soloveitchik, cited earlier in this chapter, suggested, in spite of the history of war, exile, persecution, and genocide, "Jewish destiny is linked to the land."[26] Rabbi Jonathan Sacks illustrates this with his own story. Coming from a pious Jew-

22. Bernard Reich, "The Founding of the Modern State of Israel and the Arab-Israeli Conflict," in *The Cambridge Guide to Jewish History, Religion and Culture*, ed. Judith R. Baskin and Kenneth Seeskin (Cambridge: Cambridge University Press, 2010), 259. On the rise of modern anti-Semitism see Seltzer, *Jewish People*, 626–42.

23. Reich, "The Founding," 260.

24. Reich, "The Founding," 260.

25. Rosenthal, *What Can a Modern Jew Believe?*, 143.

26. Soloveitchik and Besdin, *Reflections of the Rav*, 120.

ish home in Britain, the young Sacks arrived at Cambridge University in the late 1960s. "Cambridge," he writes, "was like a revelation. Here for the first time I could feel the lure of another history, the siren call of a different culture. Everything about it was dazzling: the river, the lawns, the college buildings dating back to medieval times, the gowns, the bicycles, the dons, the whole rich texture of a world of stunning beauty that was not my own."[27]

In the late spring of 1967, rumbling came out of the Middle East. The Arab states, it seemed, were gearing up for an attack on Israel. It appeared to Sacks and many other Jews that a tragedy was in the making, perhaps even a second Holocaust. He recalls that "it was then that an extraordinary thing began to happen. Throughout the university Jews suddenly became visible. Day after day they crowded the little synagogue in the center of town. Students and dons who had never before publicly identified as Jews could be found there praying. Others began collecting money. Everyone wanted to help in some way, to express their solidarity, their identification with Israel's fate."[28] This was, of course, the Six Day War. Israel won a startling and complete victory in a matter of six days. It was a victory that shaped the destiny of the country for better and for worse to this very day.[29]

Life for Sacks went back to normal, "but not completely. For I had witnessed something in those days and weeks that didn't make sense in the rest of my world."[30] The threat to Israel, to the state, to the land, had galvanized Jews around the world. Whether they were secular or religious, wealthy or poor, educated or uneducated, the threat to Israel had changed them: "Collectively the Jewish people had looked in the mirror and said, We are still Jews. And by that they meant more than a private declaration of faith, 'religion' in the conventional sense of the word. It meant they felt part of a people, involved in its fate, implicated by its destiny, caught up in its tragedy, exhilarated by its survival. I had felt it. So had every other Jew I knew."[31]

It took a threat to the land and the people to remind Sacks, dazzled as he was by the possibilities of a Cambridge University education, what it meant

27. Jonathan Sacks, *A Letter in the Scroll: Understanding Our Jewish Identity and Exploring the Legacy of the World's Oldest Religion* (New York: Free Press, 2000), 26.

28. Sacks, *A Letter*, 28.

29. On the war and its political, social, and moral outcomes see Yossi Klein Halevi, *Like Dreamers: The Story of the Israeli Paratroopers Who Reunited Jerusalem and Divided a Nation* (New York: HarperCollins, 2013).

30. Sacks, *A Letter*, 28.

31. Sacks, *A Letter*, 28.

to be a Jew. For *Israel* means both land and people. And throughout its long and bitter history, to be part of one was to be part of, or at least long for, the other. *Israel mattered.*

Christian Reflections

One of the great differences between Christianity and Judaism is that from the beginning Christianity aspired to be a *universal* faith. Paul made this explicit in Galatians 3:26–29: "So in Christ Jesus you are all children of God through faith, for all of you who were baptized into Christ have clothed yourselves with Christ. There is neither Jew nor Gentile, neither slave nor free, neither male nor female, for you are all one in Christ Jesus. If you belong to Christ, then you are Abraham's seed, and heirs according to the promise." Although the prophets spoke of the universal worship of God, Judaism has never claimed that the God of Israel wanted everyone to convert to Judaism. Quite the contrary. Converts are accepted but, in most cases, with some reluctance. Judaism, in spite of its universal God, is not a universal tradition but a *particular* one. It has a particular calling, a particular set of rites, a particular covenant, a particular literature, and a particular land. This particularity, this "chosenness," is both its blessing and its burden. To return to Rabbi Soloveitchik, "The word 'singular' means 'being only one,' 'exceptional,' 'extraordinary' and 'separate.' The word *segulah* in Hebrew similarly connotes singularity. In Exodus (19:5), the Torah enunciates the doctrine of the election of Israel as a cardinal tenet of our faith. 'And you shall be to Me *segulah* from all other peoples.' The word *segulah* is interpreted by Rashi as referring to 'a cherished treasure, comparable to costly vessels and precious stones for which a king has a special regard.'"[32] This "singularity," Soloveitchik insists, "involves no denigration of other nations. It is a specialness—a nation, one of its kind, which God has designated to preserve and disseminate His Divine teachings. This is singularity."[33]

How are Christians to respond to this? This was one of the great questions of the early church and especially of the apostle Paul. How could he make sense of the ongoing "singularity" of Israel, both people and land, and

32. Soloveitchik and Besdin, *Reflections of the Rav*, 119.

33. Soloveitchik and Besdin, *Reflections of the Rav*, 120.

the new thing that had occurred in the death and resurrection of Messiah Jesus? Paul will ask, "Did God reject his people?" Had Israel been "superseded," replaced? Are the Jews no longer the people of God? Is their covenant, their calling, no longer operative? Paul's answer is "By no means!" In chapters 9–11 of Romans Paul struggles to understand Israel's rejection of Messiah Jesus and to sustain a place for Israel as Israel in God's loving intention. He will go so far as to say, "all Israel will be saved" (Rom 11:26). God was by no means finished with the Jews.

It is one of the burdens of this book to struggle with the issue of the universal and the particular, the God of Abraham, Isaac, and Jacob, the God of all the earth and, for Christians, the God and Father of our Lord Jesus Christ. For Paul, in spite of the universality of his Christian gospel, it remained important to preserve Jewish particularity. This raised, both then and now, many difficult questions, not the least of which is how a modern Christian understands the ongoing claim of Jews upon the land of Israel itself. The Jews, I think this chapter has made clear, come by this claim honestly. The entire Torah is suffused with promise, longing, and hope for the land—as is Jewish history. But what do such claims mean both theologically and politically in this politically volatile and theologically divided world? This is an enduring and profoundly challenging question.

QUESTIONS FOR DISCUSSION

1. Why is the land of Israel so important to most Jews? Why is it not important for some Jews?
2. The rabbis insisted that a fully Jewish life could only ultimately be lived in the land of Israel. Why?
3. What did/does the return to the land and the establishment of the State of Israel mean to Jews? To Christians?

FURTHER READING

Cohn-Sherbok, Dan. "The Promised Land." Pages 432–37 in *Judaism: History, Belief and Practice.* London: Routledge, 2003.

Gilbert, Martin. *Israel: A History*. Rev. and updated ed. New York: Harper Perennial, 2008.

Halevi, Yossi Klein. *Like Dreamers: The Story of the Israeli Paratroopers Who Reunited Jerusalem and Divided a Nation.* New York: HarperCollins, 2013.

Sacks, Jonathan. *A Letter in the Scroll: Understanding Our Jewish Identity and Exploring the Legacy of the World's Oldest Religion.* New York: Free Press, 2000.

Wyschogrod, Michael. *The Body of Faith: God in the People Israel.* New York: Seabury, 1983.

CHAPTER 6

God of Prayer

Rabbi Eliezer says: He that makes his prayer a fixed task, his prayer is no supplication.

—*m. Berakhot* 4:4

Prayer without devotion is no prayer at all . . . So before starting to pray, a person ought to stop everything for a little while in order to get into a prayerful mood. Then one should prayer quietly and with feeling, not like somebody who carries a burden and finally drops it, quite refreshed. Even after prayer one ought to sit quietly for a few minutes and then go on one's way.

—Maimonides

In the palace of the king there are many rooms and there is a key for each room. An axe, however, is the passkey of passkeys, for with it one can break through all the doors and the gates. Each prayer has its own proper meaning and it is there for the specific key to a door in the Divine Palace, but a broken heart is an axe which opens all the gates.

—Baal Shem Tov

The words [of prayer] must not fall off our lips like dead leaves in the autumn. They must rise like birds out of the heart into the vast expanse of eternity.

—Abraham Joshua Heschel

No other mitzva is quite like *tefila*, the obligation to acknowledge God as Creator and consummate benefactor, the obligation to seek one's needs and the needs of the Jewish people and humanity from God, the obligation to acknowledge that all goodness comes from God.

—Yehiel Poupko

When the temple was destroyed, the Jewish way of worshiping God through its sacrifices and offerings came abruptly and finally to an end. Prayer had always been critical to the daily life of Jews, but now it assumed a much greater role. Now, rather than morning and evening sacrifices, there were morning and evening prayers. But Jewish prayer as it developed over the centuries would speak to every aspect of Jewish life, both public and private. Jewish life to this day is a life of communal and individual prayer.

Models of Prayer

The Pray-er

First Samuel begins with a poignant story of a childless, desperate woman pleading her case with God. Barren women are not uncommon in the Hebrew Scriptures. Perhaps most famous is Sarah, the wife of Abraham. Although promised a son, it is many decades before, much to her amusement, she finally bears Isaac, although she is by then an octogenarian (Gen 21:1–7). Rebekah, Isaac's wife, is also childless before Isaac intercedes with God for her (Gen 25:21). She produces twins, Jacob and Esau. In turn the patriarch Jacob's favorite wife, Rachel, is also childless—and angry. "Give me children, or I shall die," she shouts at a frustrated Jacob (Gen 30:1). Finally, "God remembered Rachel; God heeded her and opened her womb" (Gen 30:22). The result of this pregnancy was Joseph. The mother of Samson could be added to this painful sisterhood (see Judg 13). But the story of Hannah is unique.

Hannah, like Rachel, is the preferred wife, the most beloved. Her rival Peninnah, like Leah, envious of this, "provokes" and "irritates" Hannah until she exhausts herself weeping and refuses to eat (1 Sam 1:7). On their yearly visit to Shiloh to worship and sacrifice at the Tabernacle, the *Mishkan*, she leaves her family to offer desperate prayers in the sanctuary: "in her wretchedness, she prayed to the LORD, weeping all the while" (1 Sam 1:10). She makes a vow that if God gives her a son, she will return him to the Lord. So intense is her prayer that "only her lips moved but her voice could not be heard" (1:13). This was because "Hannah was praying in her heart" (1:13). This verse would become crucial to the rabbis. The High Priest Eli famously misinterpreted Hannah's intensity as drunkenness and rebuked her. But in the end Hannah's prayers were heard, and Samuel, the great prophet and judge of Israel, was born (1 Sam 1:19–20).

For the rabbis, the most important aspect of this story was not Hannah's barrenness, Eli's obtuseness, or even Samuel's birth. Most important was Hannah the pray-er, the model of prayer: "Chana exemplifies the ideal devotional women and Jew at prayer. She is the *isha hamitpalelet*, the prayerful woman, bar none. Chana is the only person in TaNaKh whose request in prayer is both recorded and granted; and who then returns to God to offer thanksgiving in a *shir*, epic song. Her *tefilot* and *shir*, requests and thanksgiving, make her the most prayerfully active figure in TaNaKh."[1] For the rabbis and pious Jews life is woven together by prayer. What one prays, when one prays, and how one prays are all important. But *who* one is during prayer makes all the difference. Hannah became a model pray-er because her prayer was an *avoda shebalev*, a prayer of the heart.

For Jews there is something different about the command, the *mitzvah*, to pray. As Rabbi Poupko points out, "the overwhelming majority of the *mitzvuot* are behavioral, fulfilled in deeds and actions. The intent does not much matter as long as the mitzva is done."[2] One could argue that *most* of the commandments of God in Torah are done as a matter of routine, without thinking at all. For a pious believer they become second nature and do not require conscious thought or reflection. But this is not the case with prayer. "During *tefila*, a person brings the fullness of his or her self into active relationship with the Kadosh Barukh Hu [The Holy One, Blessed be He]."[3] This is the "service of the heart" seen in the story of Hannah who was "praying in her heart" (1 Sam 1:13). This focused intention in prayer is also called *kavvanah*.

"Prayer," writes Rabbi Adin Steinsaltz, "which is the speech addressed by man to his Creator, loses its essential quality when it becomes solely the recitation of words, without inward attention to the meaning of the words being spoken."[4] Prayer requires *kavvanah*, "a complex term [meaning] among other things, intention, attention, purpose, devotion, and concentration of thought during prayer or in the performance of religious commandments."[5] In his chapter on *kavvanah* Rabbi Steinsaltz goes on to argue for four levels of *kavvanah* from simple comprehension

1. Yehiel Poupko, *Chana: A Life in Prayer* (Great Neck, NY: Arthur Kurzweil, 2017), xxxii. For Hannah's song see 1 Sam 2:1–10. Compare this with Mary's song, Luke 1:46–56.

2. Poupko, *Chana*, 31.

3. Poupko, *Chana*, 31.

4. Adin Steinsaltz, *A Guide to Jewish Prayer*, trans. Rebecca Toueg (New York: Schocken Books, 2000), 34.

5. Steinsaltz, *Guide to Jewish Prayer*, 34.

of the words read or recited to mystical exaltations. But a pray-er is not required to be a great mystic or saint: "As one of the Tosaphists said, 'I pray with the mind of a little child'—that is with the absolute simplicity and innocence of a child. Since talmudic times, eminent sages have always asserted that prayer that comes from the depths of the heart, with earnest inward desire, reaches a higher level than that attained through the most sophisticated *Kavvanah.*"[6] And for that Hannah was, for the rabbis, the most outstanding model. She was no saint or mystic, but a simple Israelite women praying from her heart for a child. The Jewish pray-ers are asked today to bring this simplicity, this intention, this focus to the daily round of prayers that bind their lives individually and their community corporately to God.

Hannah's prayer was simple, intensely personal, and passionately felt. She was not praying on behalf of some great national cause: the defeat of Israel's enemies or the coming of messiah. She was not a priest or a rabbi or other learned figure leading the community to pray. She was an ordinary, desperate woman yearning for a child. Hannah showed Israel *how* to pray but in the wake of soul-crushing disasters the rabbis who gave us the Mishnah had the task of telling a dispirited and battered people *what* to pray. Their actions and decisions, forged by disaster, shape Jewish prayer to this very day.

The Prayer

How does one pray after an unthinkable tragedy? How does one worship after the place of worship has been destroyed? How does one pray when "the house of prayer for all nations" (Isa 56:7) is a smoldering ruin? In the wake of the great Jewish revolt of 66–70 CE, there was no longer a temple, sacrifice, or priesthood. The rabbis who had survived the conflagration were confronted with a daunting task: to rebuild the worship of the Jewish people without Israel's key institutions, foundational practices, or hereditary leadership. Centuries of Jewish worship practice had been swept away. If the rabbis had been unsuccessful in this task, it is unlikely that the Jewish people would have survived. It was the genius of the rabbis to substitute individual and communal prayer for the worship of the temple. Prayer, both individual and communal, was now the key to Jewish survival.

6. Steinsaltz, *Guide to Jewish Prayer*, 38.

> Rabbi Isaac said: We have now no prophet or priest or sacrifices or Temple, or altar which can make atonement for us: from the day whereon the Temple was laid waste, nought was left to us but prayer. Therefore, O God, hearken and forgive.[7]

> The congregation of Israel says, "We are poor; we have no sacrifices to bring as a sin offering." God replies, "I need only words," as it says, "Take with your words (Hos. XIV,2). 'Words' mean 'words of the Law.'" The congregation says, "We do not know anything [we are not learned]." God replies, "Weep and pray and I will receive you."[8]

Although there was a rich tradition of prayer within the Hebrew Bible and the temple ritual, for the rabbis *the* prayer was the Amidah (standing) or the *Shemoneh Esrei*, the Eighteen (Benedictions). This prayer to this day is "the heart of every service. It contains the basic components of prayer: praising God, petitioning Him, and thanking Him. Whenever the Talmud refers to *tefilah* ('prayer') it means the *Shemoneh Esrei*, and not any other blessing, supplication or psalm. It is The Prayer."[9] The Prayer even replaced the sacrifices: "Its times were correlated to the times for the Temple's perpetual offerings, and it now functioned as Israel's covenantal worship of God. These prayers required no particular setting, but whenever possible, they were to be recited while standing erect, facing Jerusalem, and its ruined Temple."[10] Already the Mishnah considers the daily repetition of this prayer as essential to Jewish life: "Rabban Gamaliel says: A man should pray the Eighteen [Benedictions] every day."[11]

Traditional Jews date the basic formula of the Amidah to "the 120 Men of the Great Assembly in the fifth century BCE," but agree that "shortly after the destruction of the Second Temple in the first century CE, the form and order of these blessings were crystallized by Simon Ha-Pakuli in Yavneh at the request of Rabbi Gamliel."[12] Yavneh, a village northwest of Jerusalem near the Mediterranean coast, was where Rabbi Yohanan Ben Zakkai, a survivor of the destruction of Jerusalem in 70 CE, established a center for

7. *Midr. Ps.* 5:4 (27a #7), in Montefiore and Loewe, *Rabbinic Anthology*, 342.

8. *Ex. Rab.* Tezawweh, 38:4, cited in Montefiore and Loewe, *Rabbinic Anthology*, 343.

9. Donin, *To Pray*, 69.

10. Ruth Langer, "Jewish Worship and Liturgy," in Baskin and Seeskin, *The Cambridge Guide*, 341.

11. *m. Ber.* 4:3.

12. Donin, *To Pray*, 69.

Jewish learning. This rabbinic academy eventually moved to Tiberias in the Galilee and became crucial to the compilation of what would become the Mishnah. The very first tractate of the Mishnah, *Berekoth*, or "blessings," describes the ways Jews are required to pray. For the rabbis, nothing was more important:

> Just as a sacrifice required precision to be acceptable, so did this new worship. Its eighteen separate paragraph-length benedictions needed to be recited in order. Its language, ideally, was Hebrew, the cultic language of the Bible and the Temple, not a vernacular like Greek or Aramaic. To facilitate its recitation, the Rabbis decreed that when the prayer was recited in a community, defined as a minimum of ten adult males (a *minyan*), one person would serve as the community's representative before God (*sheliah tzibbur*), reciting the prayers aloud while the others fulfilled their obligations by responding "amen."[13]

Jews around the world say this prayer every day, multiple times a day. Its blessings are adapted according to the day of the week and the particular season of the year. It is the superstructure around which the rest of the Jewish prayer life is constructed.[14]

When to Pray

The Prayers: Daily, Weekly, Sabbath

The Amidah is at the heart of nearly every daily, weekly, and Sabbath service. Its content varies according to the day and the season but it is an essential part of the prayer life of every praying Jew. Rabbi Donin divides the prayer into three sections: "three blessings wherein we praise God, a middle section of thirteen blessings wherein we petition Him to satisfy various needs, and a closing section of three blessings wherein we thank God and take leave of Him."[15] He has good precedent for this division: "A person should never petition for his requirements in the first three blessings or in the last three.

13. Langer, "Jewish Worship," 341.

14. For the full forms of these and other Jewish prayers in English translation see the previously mentioned *The Expanded ArtScroll Siddur* or Rabbi Sacks's *The Koren Siddur.*

15. Donin, *To Pray*, 73.

For Rabbi Hanina taught: 'In the first blessings one resembles a servant who praises his master, in the middle ones, one resembles a servant requesting some gifts from his master, and in the last ones, one resembles a servant who has received his gift and takes his leave.'"[16]

The first section praises God. The final section thanks God. The middle section asks God. It addresses six personal needs and six communal needs: the needs of the individual Jew and of the Jewish people. Donin provides the Hebrew and English text of each blessing as well as a brief commentary.[17] The complete *Shemoneh Esrei* may also be found in an English Siddur.

The first blessing praises God's power and recalls God's gracious blessings of Israel through the Patriarchs:

> Blessed are You HASHEM [the Name], our God and the God of our forefathers, the God of Abraham, the God of Isaac, and God of Jacob; the great, mighty, and awesome God, the supreme God, Who bestows beneficial kindnesses and creates everything, Who recalls the kindnesses of the Patriarchs and brings a Redeemer to their children's children, for His Name's sake, with love. O King, Helper, Savior, and Shield. Blessed are You HASHEM, Shield of Abraham.[18]

For Rabbi Donin, this blessing establishes at the beginning of the prayer the relationship between God and those praying. It asserts a "family lineage" and historical relationship with the God who made promises to the patriarchs and matriarchs of Israel.[19] This section establishes the right of the praying Jew to intercede with God.

The second section of the prayer moves from praising God to interceding with God. The pray-ers ask for wisdom, seek forgiveness for sins, and pray for health and prosperity in the days to come. Several of the blessings have a distinctive eschatological element. There is a prayer for the return of the exiles, the so-called Diaspora; there is a prayer for the restoration of judges and the direct reign of God over Israel and for the rebuilding of Jerusalem; and, perhaps most famously, the following prayer: "The offspring of Your servant David may You speedily cause to

16. Donin, *To Pray*, 73.
17. Donin, *To Pray*, 76–113.
18. *ArtScroll Siddur*, 235.
19. Donin, *To Pray*, 77.

flourish and raise his glory through Your salvation, for we hope for Your salvation all day long. Blessed are You HASHEM, Who causes the glory of salvation to flourish."[20]

This blessing illustrates one of the contemporary challenges for modern Jews. Today's Jews use different prayer books. While traditional Jews use the prayer books their forebears used for many centuries, Jews impacted by the Reform movement developed their own traditions and texts of prayer. Although pious and traditional Jews continued to hope for the coming of messiah, this blessing from the Amidah became controversial within the emerging Reform movement in nineteenth-century Germany. These Jews were not expecting or hoping for messiah and a return to the land of Israel, but for acceptance and "emancipation" in their European homelands:

> German Jews['] . . . hope was to integrate further into German society; they did not want to ask God to restore them to Palestine. They wanted their liturgy to reflect their desire for full social and political emancipation. The Reform movement made such changes to the traditional liturgy, excising the hope for the speedy ingathering of the exiles from the Diaspora and substituting a prayer for the building of a universal messianic era.[21]

Reform Jews had been equally uncomfortable with the notion of the resurrection of the dead, mentioned in the second blessing. This too was eliminated. But in the 2007 publication *Mishkan T'filah: A Reform Siddur*, a reference to God's raising the dead was restored as an option—to some controversy.[22] This move by some members of the Reform movement in the United States toward more traditional forms of prayer and worship is part of a larger reclamation of more traditional forms of Jewish life—much to the chagrin of many within Reform Judaism. The struggle over the nature of the prayer book and worship practices within contemporary Reform Judaism is a key part of a process that some fear may further fragment the movement.[23] Conservative Judaism has had its own struggles over the content of

20. *ArtScroll Siddur*, 243.

21. Dana Evan Kaplan, *American Reform Judaism: An Introduction* (New Brunswick, NJ: Rutgers University Press, 2003), 82.

22. Dana Evan Kaplan, *The New Reform Judaism* (Philadelphia: Jewish Publication Society, 2013), 153–57.

23. Kaplan, *New Reform*, 153–57.

the prayers and the character of the liturgy.[24] Modern Jews, then, like modern Christians, have found themselves engaged in "worship wars": debates over the nature and significance of prayer, the structure of worship, the role of preaching, and the function of music within worship.

The final section of the Amidah contains prayers of thanksgiving to God:

> We gratefully thank You, for it is You who are HASHEM, our God and the God of our forefathers for all eternity, Rock of our lives, Shield of our salvation are You from generation to generation. We shall thank You and relate Your praise—for our lives, which are committed to Your power and for our souls that are entrusted to You; for Your miracles that are with us every day; and for Your wonders and favors in every season—evening, morning, and afternoon. The Beneficent One, for Your compassions were never exhausted, and the Compassionate One, for Your kindnesses never ended—we have always placed our hope in You.[25]

Rabbi Donin suggests that "one of the basic virtues that Judaism always encouraged in people is to be grateful, to be appreciative, to say thank you." Ingratitude, for Donin, is not simply a moral flaw but "the very essence of heresy."[26] When one leaves the presence of God, thanksgiving is always called for.[27]

In addition to the Amidah, two additional crucial prayers should at least be mentioned. The first is the Kaddish. Like the Amidah, it is part of every Jewish worship service. There are various forms of the Kaddish. The full form is prayed at the end of the Amidah.[28] It begins "May His great Name grow exalted and sanctified (Cong.—Amen.) in the world that He created as He willed. May He give reign to His kingship in your lifetime and in your days, and in the lifetime of the entire Family of Israel swiftly and soon. Now respond: Amen."[29] According to Donin, "no prayer in all of Jewish liturgy

24. Daniel J. Elazar and Rela Mintz Geffen, *The Conservative Movement in Judaism* (Albany: State University of New York Press, 2000), 56–64.

25. *ArtScroll Siddur*, 245.

26. Donin, *To Pray*, 100.

27. For a complete discussion of the various prayers of the Jewish people the reader is directed to Donin's more popular *To Pray as a Jew* and Steinsaltz's more comprehensive *A Guide to Jewish Prayer.* Many popular guides to the various aspects of Jewish prayer are readily available.

28. *ArtScroll Siddur*, 253.

29. *ArtScroll Siddur*, 253.

arouses greater emotion than *Kaddish*."[30] To pray the Kaddish is to "sanctify the name of God publicly." "The simplest form of Kaddish HaShem," he continues, "is a public declaration of our belief that God is great and holy, which elicits from others the response. . . . 'May his great Name be blessed forever and ever.'"[31] Confronted with martyrdom, Jews have continued to declare their faithfulness to this one God.

A third daily element of Jewish prayer is the Shema. It is recited in the morning and evening prayers. The Shema consists largely of citations from Deuteronomy and Numbers and functions as a confession, "a declaration of faith, a pledge of allegiance to One God, an affirmation of Judaism."[32] It famously begins, "Hear, O Israel, the Lord our God, the Lord is One." The title for the prayer comes from the first word in Hebrew: *shema*, hear. The affirmation continues with the command from Deuteronomy 6 to "Love the Lord your God with all your heart, with all your soul, with all your means." This prayer is to be said seated, rather than standing, and with great concentration and focus—especially during the recitation of the first section of the prayer.[33] So important is the Shema that it is to be prayed at the point of death as a kind of coda on a life of piety and faithfulness.

The Times of Prayer

When do Jews pray? There are three daily services: *shaharit* (morning), *minhah* (afternoon), and *ma'ariv* or *arvit* (evening). According to Rabbi Steinsaltz, the morning service "is the longest and most complete of the daily prayers. The most basic reason for its length and complexity is that this is the prayer with which one begins the new day."[34] Steinsaltz compares the prayer to going up to worship God in the temple. The praying Jew moves through the "world of action" (the women's courtyard) to the "world of formation" (the men's courtyard), to the "world of creation" (the priestly court and the holy place), to the "world of emanation" (the holy of holies). Steinsaltz is here reflecting the four worlds of kabalistic lore, the Jewish mystical tradition (87). This framework also reflects the conviction that prayer

30. Donin, *To Pray*, 217.
31. Donin, *To Pray*, 217.
32. Donin, *To Pray*, 144.
33. Donin, *To Pray*, 147.
34. Steinsaltz, *Guide to Jewish Prayer*, 86. Hereafter, page references to this work are given in parentheses in the text.

is now the means by which one approaches God, rather than by means of a physical structure in Jerusalem or elsewhere. Prayer is an interior temple, a verbal holy place.

The *minhah* service "was established to correspond to the *Tamid* (daily) sacrifice offered at dusk" (96). The actual time of the service is between noon and sunset. Praying Jews are normally in the midst of their normal occupations and step out of the flow of their day to remember who they are and what God requires of them. The *ma'ariv* or evening prayer service is to be prayed "from the appearance of the stars until midnight." "*Ma'ariv* is the nighttime prayer, an aspect stressed in its Shema benedictions, both with regard to the general course of human life—with everyone completing their daily tasks and preparing for rest and repose—and with regard to the significance of the time of day: i.e. the descent of darkness and the surrounding gloom. In Jewish tradition darkness symbolizes descent, gloom, the inability to see properly, and is always accompanied to some extent by 'fear of the night'" (98–99). During every part of the day praying Jews recall their place as individuals within a particular tradition, community, and people and affirm their love of and dependence on the God of Israel.

Holidays and Festivals

In addition to the daily prayers and their weekly adaptations, there are significant *seasonal* prayers. Every fall in the west, Jews celebrate a season of festivals and services called the "Days of Awe." Included are Rosh Hashanah, the Jewish New Year, and Yom Kippur, the Day of Atonement. On Rosh Hashanah Jews recall the past year and anticipate the year to come. They are reminded of their sins and failures to be sure, but, "from the halakhic viewpoint, Rosh ha-Shana is one of the days on which neither *Tahanun*—'Supplication'—nor *Vidduy*—'Confessions of Sins'—is recited. The focus is rather on resolving to do better in the coming year, and the request that God reveal His glory to the world, so as to make it easier for us to fulfill his commands" (180).

On Yom Kippur, the Day of Atonement, Jews spend the day in self-denial, prayer, and repentance. There are five services, beginning on the eve of Yom Kippur with the prayer called the Kol Nidre. "The dramatic prayer is usually attended by the largest number of worshippers of the year. . . . For the ceremony, Torah scrolls are taken from the ark and held by the leaders of the congregation standing as a solemn court. The Cantor asks permission from the heavenly and earthly courts to pray among sinners, and then chants the Kol Nidre, which is a legal proclamation annulling vows. The idea is to prevent punishment because of vows one might have forgotten."[35] "Each service" of the Day of Atonement, Dan Cohn-Sherbok writes, "has its own characteristic liturgy. In all of them, however, the confession of sins (*viddui*) is pronounced—shorter confessions as well as longer ones are in the first person plural to emphasize collective responsibility. In some liturgies there are also confessions of personal transgressions."[36]

The completion of the solemnities of the Day of Atonement leads Jews into the construction of the *sukkot*, temporary shelters, to celebrate the "Festival of Booths," commemorating the wilderness wanderings of the Jewish people when they lived in temporary structures or booths. Sukkot is also a harvest festival. "It is a requirement to rejoice on Sukkot, possibly because it coincides with the grape harvest, suggesting an abundance of wine. It also marks the end of the period of judgment; by Sukkot, one has passed through the trials of Rosh Ha-Shanah and Yom Kippur and has come through unscathed."[37] Modern Jews who celebrate Sukkot spend part of every day in the shelters and eat meals there as well. There are, as in all the festivals, special prayers, readings, and recitations for Sukkot in addition to the normal prayers.[38]

While there are many more days of celebration, mourning, and remembrance, I will touch on one final critical day of prayer and memory: Pesach or Passover. Passover recalls God's deliverance of the people of Israel from Egyptian bondage. Unlike Rosh Hashanah and Yom Kippur, Pesach is based in the home rather than the synagogue. The Passover meal, called the Seder, includes a ritual recited at the dinner table with family and friends as a part of a meal. The most important part of the ritual is the telling of the story of the exodus—the reading of the haggadah, the "telling" or "narration" of the exodus story. Although "the essential nature of the Pesah *Seder* has remained almost unchanged since the end of the Second Temple period," Rabbi Stensaltz acknowledges that "there is a great variety of customs among the diverse Jewish communities regarding the details of the *Seder*. . . . Some of these customs are particular to a congregation, and some are practiced by individual families."[39]

35. Karesh and Hurwitz, "Kol Nidre," *Encyclopedia of Judaism*, 277–78.

36. Cohn-Sherbok, *Judaism*, 517.

37. Karesh and Hurwitz, "Sukkot," *Encyclopedia of Judaism*, 502–3.

38. Steinsaltz, *Guide to Jewish Prayer*, 177ff.

39. Steinsaltz, *Guide to Jewish Prayer*, 159–60. See also Karesh and Hurwitz, "Passover (Pesach)," *Encyclopedia of Judaism*, 380–81.

Through daily patterns of prayer and yearly patterns of celebration and mourning, Jews pray their way into a common identity. Praying Jews are reminded of every aspect of God's nature and purpose: God as creator, redeemer, lawgiver, and judge. They are also reminded of their own privileges and failings. They repent of their sins, anticipate God's deliverance, and pray for God's assistance in the large and small realities of life. For a pious, praying Jew every single day is framed with prayer. The Amidah and Shema remind Jews of God's love and care for them and God's expectations of them both individually and corporately. God's gracious call to Abraham and his deliverance through Moses made the Jews a people. It is through their prayers and obedience to Torah, through *tefillah* and *mitzvot*, that they keep their identity intact.

Women and Prayer in Judaism

On the one hand, in Judaism "women are obligated to pray."[40] On the other hand, within traditional Judaism, women were not required to participate in the daily round of prayers described above. They were not counted as a part of the *minyan* or even required to attend synagogue. Many traditional synagogues to this day have a women's gallery where women may observe but not officially participate in the prayers of the men. "The Mishnah," writes Ruth Langer, "exempted women from mandatory participation in the recitation of the *shema*, but required them to participate in the grace after meals and 'prayer.'" The rabbis debated whether this reference to "prayer" meant *the* prayer, the Amidah, or more informal, personal prayers.[41] This did not prohibit Jewish women from developing their own prayer traditions within both the domestic sphere and the synagogue. Some women even developed the skill to lead other women in the traditional prayers.

Within the modern era the Reform, Reconstructionist, and Conservative movements have significantly expanded the roles and participation of women in worship and adapted their prayer books to include women and their concerns.[42] "In a traditional synagogue," Langer writes, "women's participation is entirely peripheral. Women never lead any element of

40. Steinsaltz, *Guide to Jewish Prayer*, 26.

41. Langer, "Jewish Worship," 354.

42. See Kaplan, *American Reform Judaism*, 186–208; and Elazer and Geffen, *Conservative Movement*, 56–58.

the service and never count toward the worshipping community's quorum necessary for public prayer."[43] Increasingly in non-Orthodox communities women are called to read Torah, to lead prayers, and finally to lead their communities as rabbis. This, of course, has not happened without controversy. The first woman to be ordained as a rabbi was Regina Jonas. She was ordained in Germany in 1935 and later murdered by the Nazis.[44]

The first Reform woman rabbi was ordained in 1972 and the first Conservative woman rabbi was ordained in 1983. Orthodox women "have yet to produce a prayer book, largely because as Orthodox Jews, they accept the authority of and pray with the received Hebrew text. But over the last few decades, some Orthodox feminists have been gathering as women's prayer groups, worshiping together and reading from the Torah, though not as in a formal *minyan*."[45] To this day the prayers of women are restricted at the Western Wall in Jerusalem, to some considerable controversy.

A Christian Response

The evangelical wing of Christianity has tended to look askance at fixed prayers, preferring prayers to be spontaneous rather than prepared and assigned by religious authorities. In the Sermon on the Mount Jesus had warned about "babbling like pagans, for they think they will be heard because of their many words" (Matt 6:7). Fixed prayers and settled liturgies have often been considered "vain repetition" assiduously to be avoided. It should be clear from what was written above that the rabbis also recognized the dangers of "vain repetition" and "babbling like pagans." The set prayers that bind Jews together to this day were to be done with deep intention, with the service of the heart, with *kavvanah*. At the same time, however simple or learned the pray-er, the words of the great prayers of the Jewish prayer book, the *Siddur*, were deemed to possess inexhaustible depths. Repeated day after day, year after year, as labors of love, as labors of the heart, they were not emptied of meaning, but expanded, enriched.

The earliest Christian patterns of prayer were not unlike those of the Jewish tradition. According to Paul Bradshaw, "the evidence appears to

43. Langer, "Jewish Worship," 354.
44. Langer, "Jewish Worship," 354.
45. Langer, "Jewish Worship," 355.

suggest that the oldest practice was . . . to pray three times a day (*Didache* 8:3), which has a parallel in a threefold practice of daily prayer in Judaism that may well be its origin, even if the precise hours ended up being a little different."[46] Eventually, according to what came to be called "Cathedral prayer," the times of prayer were morning and evening and celebrated in churches. Bradshaw suggests these forms were quite simple, including praises and intercessions. "The core of the praise in the morning was made up of Psa. 148–150, repeated daily to which local traditions might add other elements, such as Psa. 63 or the canticle Gloria in excelsis."[47] The evening prayers included the hymn *Phos hilarion*, "Hail, gladdening light," and Psalm 141. As time went on, the monastic communities added services of prayer, some of them quite short, until there were as many as nine services of prayer a day.

Spontaneity and novelty are perhaps overrated. Today many Christians are finding value in reclaiming the prayers and practices of the past. Many Protestant Christians are "praying the hours" using prayer books like *The Divine Hours* by Phyllis Tickle.[48] Others use the Episcopal *Book of Common Prayer* or similar prayer books to frame their hours, days, and years with prayer.[49] There is something powerful in joining one's voice and heart with millions of others to, as Rabbi Poupko puts it, "acknowledge God as Creator and consummate benefactor, . . . to seek one's needs and the needs of the Jewish people and humanity from God."[50] This is "a presumptuous act," a mere human "dar[ing] to stand before the Almighty Creator."[51] And yet it is constituent to being part of God's people and necessary to forming God's people individually and corporately. These are the gift of the Hebrew Scriptures to all God's people: from its prayers who wrestle with God, Abraham, Jacob, Moses, and Hannah, to the prayers in the book of Psalms that have formed Jewish and Christian devotion for millennia.

46. Paul F. Bradshaw, "'The Early Church' under 'Daily Prayer,'" *The New Westminster Dictionary of Liturgy and Worship*, ed. Paul Bradshaw (Louisville: Westminster John Knox, 2002), 140–41.

47. Bradshaw, "The Early Church," 141.

48. See, for example, Phyllis Tickle, *The Divine Hours: Prayers for Summertime* (New York: Doubleday, 2000).

49. See *The Book of Common Prayer* (New York: Church Hymnal Corporation, 1979).

50. Poupko, *Chana*, 31.

51. Poupko, *Chana*, 34.

QUESTIONS FOR DISCUSSION

1. Why is Hannah a model of prayer?
2. How did prayer take the place of worship in the temple after it was destroyed in 70 CE? What does this suggest?
3. The Jewish prayer book contains daily prayers as well as prayers for holy days and other sacred occasions. Within the Christian tradition many denominations have prayer books and regular times of prayer. What are the advantages of such structures for spiritual and communal life?

FURTHER READING

Donin, Hayim Halevy. *To Pray as a Jew: A Guide to the Prayer Book and the Synagogue Service*. New York: Basic Books, 1980.

The Koren Siddur. Translated with commentary by Jonathan Sacks. Jerusalem: Koren Publishers, 2006.

Poupko, Yehiel E. *Chana: A Life in Prayer*. Great Neck, NY: Arthur Kurzweil, 2017.

Steinsaltz, Adin. *A Guide to Jewish Prayer*. Translated by Rebecca Toueg. New York: Schocken Books, 2000.

CHAPTER 7

God of Righteousness

You shall be holy, for I, the LORD your God, am holy.

—Leviticus 19:2b

Justice, justice shall you pursue, that you may thrive and occupy the land that the LORD your God is giving you.

—Deuteronomy 16:20

The righteous man is rewarded with life for his fidelity.

—Habakkuk 2:4

The just shall live by his faith.

—Habakkuk 2:4 (KJV)

For I tell you that unless your righteousness surpasses that of the Pharisees and the teachers of the law, you will certainly not enter the kingdom of heaven.

—Matthew 5:20

R. Johanan said: Come and see how great is the power of righteousness, for it is placed in the right hand of God, as it is said, "Thy right hand is full of righteousness" (Psa. XLVIII, 10). Great is righteousness, for God is praised with it in the hour when He brings salvation to Israel, as it is said, "I that speak with righteousness, mighty to save" (Isa. LXIII, 1). Great is righteousness for it brings honour and life to those who practice it, as it is said, "He that follows after righteousness shall find righteousness and honour" (Prov. XXI, 21).

—*Midrash Proverbs*

One cannot understand Judaism and one cannot live Judaism without its goal of holiness. If one separates its ethics of righteousness and justice from its disciplines of kashrut and Sabbath, if one separates compassion and mercy for humanity from the disciplines of religious family life, one does not understand nor live Judaism.

—Hayim Halevy Donin, *To Be a Jew*

It was not the hope of bliss in a future life but the establishment of the kingdom of justice and peace that was central to the Jewish faith.

—Dan Cohn-Sherbok, *Judaism*

What is justice? How is one to be righteous? What *is* God's will for both individuals and nations? These are arguably the foundational questions of both the Hebrew Scriptures and the New Testament: How am I individually, how are we communally, to be righteous, to act justly? And, perhaps ironically, outside of the question of the identity of Jesus of Nazareth, this is the most contentious question between Jews and Christians.

What Does It Mean to Be Righteous?

It is actually pretty simple. A righteous person does what is right. To do what is right is to do what comports with God's will for an individual. A righteous people, a just community, does what is right, what comports with God's will corporately. Righteousness, justice (*tzedakah*) is what God wants for and from both individuals and nations: "Justice, justice you shall pursue" (Deut 16:20).

Before outlining what has been called "the Holiness Code," in Leviticus 19 God tells Moses, "Speak to the entire assembly of Israel and say to them: 'Be holy because I, the LORD your God, am holy" (Lev 19:1). "Holiness," writes Solomon Schechter, "is the highest achievement of the Law and the deepest experience as well as the realization of righteousness."[1] In being called to holiness Israel was being called to the *imitatio Dei*, the imitation of God. The ancient rabbis argued that Israel as God's family, God's bride, was to imitate the ways of God.[2]

> Holiness, according to Abba Saul, is identical with the Imitation of God. The nature of this imitation is defined by him thus: "*I and he*, that is like unto him (God). As he is merciful and gracious, so be thou (man) merciful and gracious." The Scriptural phrases "walking in the ways of God" (Deut. 11:23), and "being called by the name of God" (Joel 3:5), are again explained to mean "As God is called merciful and gracious, so be thou merciful and gracious; as God is called righteous, so be thou righteous; as God is called holy, so be thou holy."[3]

1. Solomon Schechter, *Aspects of Rabbinic Theology* (New York: Schocken Books, 1961), 199.
2. Schechter, *Aspects*, 200.
3. Schechter, *Aspects*, 201–2.

To be holy one must be righteous. To be righteous one must imitate God and obey his commands.

There is nothing abstract about this righteousness. It is decidedly concrete. It entails actual human behaviors that are consistent with God's will and reflective of God's person. For Jews these behaviors are described in the books of Moses and explored, applied, and made relevant in the vast rabbinical conversation that continues to this day. God's will covers every aspect of a Jew's life—from how one prays to what one eats and whom one marries. To act in accordance with God's commands is to act righteously. Righteous acts lead to holiness. Unrighteous or sinful acts, however, lead to God's judgment. It is difficult to read the Hebrew Scriptures without encountering this. But it is certainly not unique to what Christians call the Old Testament.

The same views of righteousness and holiness are found in the New Testament. Jesus himself makes obedience to God central to his teaching. He also argues that the *imitatio Dei* is critical for his followers: "Be perfect, therefore, as your heavenly Father is perfect" (Matt 5:48).[4] At the end of Matthew's Sermon on the Mount, Jesus warns that the person who does not put his words into practice is foolish while those who do are wise (Matt 7:24–27). Perhaps surprisingly, even Paul, the apostle of grace, would warn, "for we must all appear before the judgment seat of Christ, that everyone may receive what is due them for the things done while in the body, whether good or bad" (2 Cor 5:10). His letters are full of his expectations and commands to his churches. They are also full of his exasperation with those who do not obey the commands of God.

However Paul understood the relationship between Israel's Torah and the new work God was doing among the gentiles, he was no antinomian. He was clear that obedience to God's will was as important to him as it was to any Jewish rabbi of his time or later. His gentile converts were to be righteous, holy, and obedient. Some see contradiction between James and Paul, but I think Paul would actually have agreed with James: "Do not merely listen to the word, and so deceive yourselves. Do what it says" (Jas 1:22). Perhaps Paul would even have agreed that "faith, by itself, if it is not accompanied by action, is dead" (Jas 2:17).

Nevertheless, the relationship between obedience to Torah and human righteousness was a bone of contention between Jews and Jesus's followers in the early centuries of emerging Christianity and remains so to this day. Especially troubling was the question of obedience to the Torah and "sal-

4. Luke 6:36 has "be merciful."

vation." Both Jews and Christians talk about "salvation," but tend to mean different things by the term. To make a broad generalization, although concerned for the "salvation" of individuals, Jews have tended to talk about the salvation of Israel as a people; Christians more often think about the salvation of individual sinners. In both communities obedience to the will of God leads to righteous individuals and righteous communities. In both communities the outcome of righteousness is salvation. But the means of the salvation and the content of the salvation are both overlapping and contradictory.

Righteousness and the Rabbis

Rabbi Hama ben Rabbi Hanina (third century CE) argued that God himself provided a model for the righteous person. God *clothed the naked*, making skins for Adam and Eve. He *visited the sick*, appearing to Abraham when he was recovering from circumcision. He *comforted mourners*, blessing Isaac after the death of his father Abraham. He *buried the dead*, burying Moses in his unknown grave. As imitators of God his people should also clothe the naked, visit the sick, comfort mourners, and bury the dead.[5] Such concrete righteousness was critical for the rabbis. Through the righteous actions of the righteous both Israel and the wider world would be blessed:

> It is the righteous, for whose sake blessing comes to the world. It is a Sanctification of the Name that when the righteous are in the world, blessing comes to the world; when [or, if] the righteous are removed from the world, blessing leaves the world. The house of Obed-Edom was blessed because of the Ark (II Sam. VI, 10). If because of the Ark, which could receive neither reward nor punishment, blessing came to a household, how much more does blessing come because of the righteous for whose sake the world was created.[6]

Because of the righteous, the naked, the sick, the mourners, and the dead are blessed. And because of the righteous, God blesses the entire creation. The righteous are in effect an ark of blessing for the world. "When Israel does

5. Cited in Arthur Hertzberg, *Judaism: The Classic Introduction to One of the Great Religions of the Modern World*, rev. ed. (New York: Simon and Schuster, 1991), 243.

6. *Sifre Deut.* 'Ekeb. 38.77b, Montefiore and Loewe, *Rabbinic Anthology*, 86–87.

the will of God, they are as stars, but if they do not do it, they are as dust."[7] The righteous participate through their obedience in what would come to be called the *tikkun olam*, the healing of the world.

What righteousness entailed at a very practical and even mundane level is seen in the medieval and early modern "ethical wills." These "wills" were written by a father for his son, instructing him on the practical content of righteousness. In addition to the typical activities of visiting the sick, burying the dead, comforting mourners, and giving to the poor, one finds strikingly specific instructions in the way of faithfulness. Judah ibn Tibbon, a twelfth-century physician and scholar, addressed his son Samuel with the following advice: he should study both "religion" and "science"; he should clothe himself decently, "for it is unbecoming for any one . . . to go shabbily dressed." Samuel was to demonstrate good morals and courteous behavior; he should "take fees from the rich, [but] heal the poor gratuitously." He was to take care of his library, arranging it in "fair order, so as to avoid wearying yourself in searching for the book you need." He was to "make it a fixed rule in your home to read the Scriptures and to peruse grammatical works on Sabbaths and festivals."[8]

The famed scholar Nachmanides advised his son to speak gently, avoiding anger; to pursue humility and remember that he would give account to God: "In all your actions, words and thoughts, and at all times, think of yourself as standing before God, with his *Shekinah* resting upon you for his glory fills the universe" (246). His son was to "read the Torah regularly, so you will be able to fulfill its precepts." He was to "examine your deeds in the morning and in the evening, and thus all your day will be spent in repentance" (246–47). When he prayed, he was to "remove all worldly matters from your heart. Set your heart right before God. Cleanse your thoughts and meditate before uttering a word." In this way he would avoid sin. "All your deeds" will be "upright, and your prayer pure, clean, devout and accepted before God" (247).

Righteousness, the *imitatio Dei*, entailed a set of practices spelled out in Torah and applicable to every mode and station of life. For the ancient rabbis, the medieval mystics and philosophers, the Hasids and Kabbalists, and Jews to this day, this *imitatio* requires "that we live every waking moment in the awareness that we are never alone, for God is always present" (242). For

7. *Sifre Deut.* 'Ekeb. 38.77b, Montefiore and Loewe, *Rabbinic Anthology*, 87.

8. Hertzberg, *Judaism*, 245–46. Hereafter, page references to this work are given in parentheses in the text.

practicing Jews, both ancient and modern, righteousness entails conformity to God's commands in Torah. And those commands touch on every aspect of human life. And human life, however mundane or exhilarating, is lived before the God who is always present and who both judges and forgives.

The Evil Inclination

But there was a problem. The Hebrew Scriptures make it clear that Israel, however called by God and gifted with the law, was not always faithful either individually or corporately. In spite of all the warnings of the prophets and divine punishments, the people and their rulers persisted in disobedience and folly. The rabbis argued that working against the individual and communal pursuit of righteousness and holiness was the "evil inclination," the *yetzer ha-ra*. A good deal of rabbinic writing is taken up with the problems and possibilities of the *yetzer ha-ra*.

Genesis tells us that human beings were created good—very good, in fact (Gen 1:31). And yet, within a very short time the man and the woman created by God disobeyed God's command and fell into shame and sin. How could this be? If God created them good, how could they in turn do evil? The rabbis explained this through the presence of the *yetzer ha-ra*. To call it the "evil inclination" is, in one sense, to distort its purpose. It "might be better described as the personal impetus to fulfill a certain desire, whether it be pleasure, security, or material acquisition."[9] Rabbi Nahman b. Samuel would argue, "Were it not for the urge-to-evil a man would not build a house, take a wife, beget a child, or engage in business; as it is written [in Eccl 4:4], 'All effort and excelling in work comes only of a man's rivalry with his neighbor'" (*Gen. Rab.* 9:7).[10] "Without the driving force of the *yetzer ha-ra*," writes Louis Jacobs, "life would no doubt be good but it would be a colourless, uncreative, pallid kind of good."[11]

The *yetzer ha-ra* cannot be, indeed must not be, destroyed. Its destruction would mean the destruction of life itself. But it must be channeled and controlled. This is done through obedience to God's commands and rigorous attention to God's Torah. God himself had warned Cain, "if you do right, there is uplift. But if you do not do right, sin crouches at the door;

9. Karesh and Hurwitz, "yetzer ha-tov/yetzer ha-rah," *Encyclopedia of Judaism*, 563–64.
10. Borowitz, *Liberal Judaism*, 358–59.
11. Jacobs, *A Jewish Theology*, 244.

its urge is toward you, yet you can be its master" (Gen 4:7). Even Cain, the murderer of his brother, was not powerless before the *yetzer ha-ra*. However powerful the evil inclination, human beings have the power to fight back, to resist evil. Maimonides would famously write: "Give no credence to the idea expressed by foolish heathens and thoughtless Jews that when a person is born God decrees whether he is to be just or wicked. Not so. Every human being may become righteous like Moses our teacher or wicked like King Jeroboam; wise or foolish, merciful or cruel, niggardly or generous, and so with all other qualities. No one coerces him or decrees what he must do or draws him to either of the two ways. Every person turns to the way he desires."[12]

This does not mean that the rabbis were optimistic about human beings' capacity to resist the evil inclination. They did not underestimate its power and were often despairing at the failures of even the wisest to resist it. But God had provided the rabbis the means by which the *yetzer ha-ra* might be managed and controlled. Human beings could obey; they could "choose life." They were not powerless before the blandishments of sin:

> Raba said: Though God created the *Yetzer ha-Ra*, He created the Law, as an antidote [lit. spice] against it.[13]

> God said to the Israelites, "I created within you the evil *yetzer*, but I created the Law as a drug. As long as you occupy yourself with the Law, the *yetzer* will not rule over you. But if you do not occupy yourselves with the Torah, then you will be delivered into the power of the *yetzer*, and all its activity will be against you."[14]

Throughout a person's life the *yetzer ha-ra* assaults, tempts, and drives human beings. But the rabbis insist that God is there to aid flagging humans to resist their own worst impulses:

> R. Simeon b. Levi said: The evil *yetzer* of a man waxes strong against him day by day and seeks to kill him, and if God did not help him, man cold not prevail against it.[15]

12. Borowitz, *Liberal Judaism*, 356.
13. *b. B. Bat.* 16a, Montefiore and Loewe, *Rabbinic Anthology*, 295.
14. *b. Quidd.* 30b, Montefiore and Loewe, *Rabbinic Anthology*, 296.
15. *b. Quidd.* 30b, Montefiore and Loewe, *Rabbinic Anthology*, 295.

> There is no brigand stronger than the Evil Inclination. But God delivers Israel from the Evil Inclination.[16]

It should be clear that the Jewish understanding of the "evil inclination" and the human vulnerability to it is not the same as the Christian notion of "original sin" as it is popularly understood. It should also be clear that many, if not most, Christians understand human freedom in a different way than Jews. There is some overlap, of course. Both the Jewish understanding of the evil inclination and the Christian notion of original sin entail the recognition of human weakness in the face of temptation to disobedience. But for Jews this does not mean human beings are inherently incapable of obedience to God's will. For some, but not all, Christians, this is exactly what original sin entails. And some, but not all, Christians would also react against the Jewish notion of human freedom outlined by Maimonides. Especially since the controversies of Augustine and Pelagius in the late fourth/early fifth century, Christians have struggled with the conflict between divine predestination and human freedom.[17]

Repentance

What is to be done? God demands righteousness, obedience to his commands. Human beings frequently if not invariably fail to live up to God's exact standards and face divine judgment. God's will must be obeyed. Failure to obey puts both individuals and entire communities at risk of God's judgment. In the Torah, the world of Noah, the city of Sodom, and the generation of the exodus demonstrated what happens to both individuals and communities who persist in violating God's will. It is important here to remember that Jews did not and do not think they are "saved" by "keeping the law." They are rather "saved" by God's gracious choice of Israel. Even using the term "saved" with regard to Judaism is probably a category error. Jews keep the law to maintain the covenant with God and their place "in the world to come." Even the most disobedient and recalcitrant Jew could repent and turn to God and be received by God and the community.

The Torah provided a means of repentance and atonement for individuals and the community through the sacrificial system of the taberna-

16. *Pesiq. Rab.* 32b, Montefiore and Loewe, *Rabbinic Anthology*, 295.

17. See John E. Phelan Jr., "The Long Shadow of Augustine," *ExAud* 30 (2014): 1–21.

cle/temple. The solemn Day of Atonement with its prayers and sacrifices enabled Israel as a whole to reflect on their sins and renew their relationship with God. All of this was possible when there was still a temple and a priesthood. But what was to be done when the temple was a ruin and the priests slaughtered or dispersed? How were Israelites corporately and individually to be restored to God? This was one of the major challenges facing the ancient rabbis. For them, the answer was repentance—*teshuvah*, turning.

There is almost nothing the rabbis are more passionate and more eloquent about than repentance. For the rabbis, Montefiore argues, "the compassion of God is much more often insisted on than His severity. The attribution of lovingkindness is more powerful than the attribute of justice."[18] Louis Jacobs cites a striking passage from the Jerusalem Talmud: "They asked of wisdom: What is the punishment of the sinner? Wisdom replied: 'Evil pursueth sinners' (Prov. 13:21). They asked of prophecy: What is the punishment of the sinner? Prophecy replied: 'The soul that sinneth it shall die' (Ezek. 18:4). They asked of the Holy One, blessed be He: What is the punishment of the sinner? He replied: 'Let him repent and he will find atonement.'"[19] Jacobs comments, "God in His infinite mercy, so the passage implies, forgives the repentant sinner, disregarding, as it were, the rigor of the philosopher and the moral condemnation of the prophet."[20]

The rabbis argue that no one is beyond the power of repentance. Both Cain, the murderer of his brother, and Manasseh, Israel's most wicked king, were capable of repenting and being forgiven by God:

> "And Cain went out" (Gen. IV.16). On his way Cain met Adam who said to him, "What has happened as regards the judgment passed upon you?" Cain replied, "I repented, and I am pardoned." When Adam heard that, he smote his face and said, "Is the power of repentance as great as that? I did not know it was so."[21]

> If a man were to come and say that God does not receive the penitent, Manasseh would come and testify against him, for there was never a man

18. Montefiore and Loewe, *Rabbinic Anthology*, 315.
19. Jacobs, *Jewish Theology*, 247–48.
20. Jacobs, *Jewish Theology*, 248.
21. *Lev. Rab.* Zaw. 10:5, Montefiore and Loewe, *Rabbinic Anthology*, 316.

> more wicked than he, and yet, in the hour of his repentance, God received him, as it is said, "He prayed unto God, and God was entreated of him" (II Chron. XXXIII, 13).[22]

The rabbis were not naïve. They knew that "repentance" could be insincere. A true penitent was one who genuinely "turns": "'Who is the penitent man?' R. Judah said: The man who, when the same opportunity for sin occurs once or twice, refrains from sinning."[23]

Teshuvah, Eugene Borowitz insists, "denotes action rather than feeling. It points to a need to change one's direction (from a false to a true way)."[24] It involves, he argues, four steps:

> First, we ought to feel proper remorse for what we did. The rabbis do not consider a bad act a triviality. . . . Second, we must now do what we can to remedy the effects of our wrongdoing. Ideally we must sincerely ask the pardon of those whom we have offended (and, by Jewish law, they must grant it to us), make good their loss, and give up our sinful gains. . . . Third, we should confess our guilt to God. Doing evil estranges us from God even as violating an understanding with a friend changes our relationship. . . . Fourth, facing God, we need to resolve, as genuinely as we can, not to repeat this evil.[25]

Borowitz cites the beautiful words of Rabbi Samuel ben Nahmen, who insisted that "the gates of prayer are sometimes open and sometimes closed—but the gates of repentance are always open."[26] There is both rigor and grace in this call to repentance. It does not take our failings lightly, but it makes clear God's willingness to always receive the truly repentant.

A rabbinic parable in some ways strikingly similar to Jesus's parable of the Prodigal Son illustrates God's willingness to receive the penitent: "A king had a son who had gone astray from his father a journey of a hundred days; his friends said to him, 'Return to your father'; he said, 'I cannot.' Then his father sent to say, 'Return as far as *you* can, and I will come to you the rest of the way.' So God says, 'Return to me and I will return to you.'"[27]

22. *Num. Rab.* Naso, 14:1, Montefiore and Loewe, *Rabbinic Anthology*, 317.
23. *b. Yoma*, 86b, Montefiore and Loewe, *Rabbinic Anthology*, 317.
24. Borowitz, *Liberal Judaism*, 359.
25. Borowitz, *Liberal Judaism*, 359–60.
26. Borowitz, *Liberal Judaism*, 360.
27. *Pesiq. Rab.* 185a, Montefiore and Loewe, *Rabbinic Anthology*, 321.

For Jews the way back to God, to righteousness, is through repentance, turning. God in his infinite mercy promises to receive penitents even if they are as wicked as Cain or Manasseh: "God says, 'My hands are stretched out towards the penitent; I reject no creature who gives me his heart in penitence. Therefore it says, 'Peace, peace to the far and to the near. To all who draw near to me I draw near, and I heal them.'"[28] One can always turn from sin to righteousness.

The Day of Atonement

Repentance is always available, but there is a special day for Jews to fast, mourn, reflect, and repent of the sins of the previous year. This is Yom Kippur, the Day of Atonement: "the LORD spoke to Moses, saying: Mark, the tenth day of this seventh month is the Day of Atonement. It shall be a sacred occasion for you: you shall practice self-denial, and you shall do no work throughout that day. For it is a Day of Atonement, on which expiation is made on your behalf before the LORD your God" (Lev 23:26–28).

In the Mishnah, considerable space is given to a description of the rites associated with the Day of Atonement. In *Yoma*, the temple rituals are described in some detail before the rabbis turn to the behavior of individuals on that most holy day: "On the Day of Atonement, eating, drinking, washing, anointing, putting on sandals, and marital intercourse are forbidden."[29] After describing compassionate exceptions to these strictures the rabbis describe the nature and effect of the Day of Atonement: "Repentance effects atonement for lesser transgressions against both positive and negative commands in the Law; while for greater transgressions it suspends punishment until the Day of Atonement comes and effects atonement."[30]

Ironically, the Day of Atonement is effective only for transgressions against God. "For transgressions that are between a man and his fellow the Day of Atonement effects atonement only if he has appeased his fellow."[31] Jews are encouraged to seek to be reconciled with those they have wronged or sinned against—the wronged person must accept their repentance and restitution and forgive them. A Christian is reminded of the words of Jesus in the Sermon

28. *Midr. Ps.* 120:7 (235a #7), Montefiore and Loewe, *Rabbinic Anthology*, 323.

29. *m. Yoma* 8:1.

30. *m. Yoma* 8:9.

31. *m. Yoma* 8:9.

on the Mount: "If you are offering your gift at the altar and there remember that your brother or sister has something against you, leave your gift at the altar and be reconciled to that person and come offer your gift" (Matt 5:23–24).

There was nothing automatic about this. "If a man said, 'I will sin and repent, and sin again and repent,' he will be given no chance to repent. [If he said,] I will sin and the Day of Atonement will effect atonement, then the Day of Atonement effects no atonement."[32] The rituals of the Day of Atonement do not function *ex opere operato.*

> You might think that the Day of Atonement does not atone without the sacrifices and the goat: it does, because it says, "It is the Day of Atonement, to make an atonement for you" (Lev. XXIII, 28); or you may think that the Day of Atonement atones for the penitent and the impenitent alike, since both sacrifices and the Day of Atonement are efficacious in obtaining atonement. But just as sin offerings and trespass offerings atone only for those who repent, so, too, the Day of Atonement atones only for those who repent.[33]

Neither the sacrifices nor the Day of Atonement were magical. God demanded genuine repentance from Israel: "For I desire goodness, not sacrifice; obedience to God rather than burnt offerings" (Hos 6:6).

That judgment follows sin is unambiguously declared in Torah. How can a sinful person, a sinful people, be restored to righteousness in light of the violation of God's law, God's holiness? Rabbi Adin Steinsaltz puts it this way:

> The concept of crime and punishment is primarily based upon the assumption that they have a cause-and-effect relationship, and that, as the biblical verse says, "Evil shall slay the wicked" (Psalm 34:21). Forgiveness, therefore, is not only a change or reversal of the Supreme Law that defines good and evil, but a violation of the laws of causality, an elimination and cancellation of the past. . . . The pardoning of sins is not like removing a stain, which leaves a faint mark, but like a wind dispersing the clouds, leaving no sign of their having been there before. Forgiveness becomes, then, the actual creation of a new temporal order in which it is as if the sin never existed. . . . Since Yom Kippur is the day of Divine pardon and forgiveness, it is the revelation of a Supreme Essence that transcends the limits of the whole world.[34]

32. *m. Yoma* 8:9.
33. *Sifra* 102a, Montefiore and Loewe, *Rabbinic Anthology*, 238.
34. Steinsaltz, *Guide to Jewish Prayer*, 196.

The Day of Atonement effects a new creation for Israel, for the individual Jews, and, for that matter, the entire created order. In Christian terms it is perhaps fair to say that the rabbinic doctrine of repentance is an example of the grace of God.

Christian Reflections

In *Liberal Judaism*, Eugene Borowitz contrasts the Jewish view of *teshuvah*/ repentance with that of Christianity. In Judaism, "God continually gives people another chance so as never to foreclose the opportunity for them to become righteous. And, since it is free human righteousness that God seeks, the sovereign God freely forgives."[35] However important the Day of Atonement, Borowitz insists that every Jew should perform *teshuvah* and needs "no rabbi, no rite, no synagogue" to do so (362). He suggests that such access to God, human freedom, and genuine repentance are more problematic for Christians. Because of the Christian notion of original sin, "no matter what you might do, you cannot overcome the iniquity which estranges you from God. . . . God is so holy, and pure that sinful humans cannot stand in intimate relationship with the Divine" (362–63).

Here Borowitz enters one of the most complex and controversial areas of Christian theology: atonement theory. For Christian thinkers, he argues, "Only an extraordinary act of forgiving love by God can bridge the terrifying gap between humanity and God. In the classic version, God, as one of the three persons of the Trinity, enters history in the God-man person of Jesus of Nazareth. Because Jesus as God need not suffer and die, his willingly doing so makes restitution for humankind's primal iniquity. He thus saves people from God's judgment and restores them to God's favor" (363).

He goes on to discuss the Protestant Christian need for "faith" and the Roman Catholic Christian need for the sacraments to seal one's salvation. He concludes that "repentance has value in Christianity but it cannot by itself effectuate that supreme forgiveness which is available only through Christ and his church. Judaism teaches that God is so loving and close that God immediately responds to anyone who performs genuine *teshuvah*" (363).

It is undeniable that a major stream of Christian theology views the effects of Jesus's death in just such a manner. But however important, this

35. Borowitz, *Liberal Judaism*, 361. Hereafter, page references to this work are given in parentheses in the text.

is only one stream, and even within it are many and varied ebbs and flows. Borowitz here reverses the normal Marcionite claim that the God of the "Old Testament" is a fierce God of judgment and the God of the New Testament a loving Father. For Borowitz, the God of Judaism is a loving Father eager to forgive his children while the God of Christianity "is so holy and pure that the sinful human being cannot stand in intimate relationship with the divine" (362–63). Perhaps it is more just to suggest that both holiness and intimacy, judgment and forgiveness, are credited to Israel's God in both the "Old Testament" and the New Testament.

Borowitz is certainly right that there are significant differences in the Christian notion of "original sin" and the Jewish notion of the *yetzer ha-ra*. At the same time, many Christians would argue today that the doctrine of original sin is not found in the New Testament itself but is a later theological development especially credited to (or blamed upon) St. Augustine. Theologian James McClendon baldly states, "'original sin,' the view that the pervasive presence of sin in the human species is caused by the first sin of the first human pair, is not the teaching of Scripture. It rests upon historic but mistaken readings."[36]

McClendon rightly sets the origin of the doctrine in the contest between the monk Pelagius and bishop Augustine. Pelagius insisted human beings were capable of obeying the will of God and living righteous, holy, and, especially, chaste lives. Augustine was alarmed by this because it appeared to undercut the need for the grace of God. In response,

> Augustine produced a series of controversial writings (411–20) that solidified a new doctrine of inherited sinfulness. It attributed total inability to all the children of Adam "in whom all sinned" . . . as Augustine read Romans 5:12 in his Vulgate Latin Bible (*De pecc. Orig.* II, 35). As a consequence of their participation in Adam's original act, all had sinned, so that at birth all were already guilty, all were depraved, and all deserved eternal punishment. Pelagius stoutly denied these theses.[37]

In short, Augustine argued that humans contributed nothing to their salvation. Even their repentance was predestined by God's solemn decision. His views were controversial. The monastic community in particular found them

36. James W. McClendon Jr., *Systematic Theology*, vol. 2, *Doctrine* (Nashville: Abingdon, 1994), 325.

37. McClendon, *Doctrine*, 325.

hard to swallow. Were all their prayers and disciplines essentially meaningless? And even when the Roman Catholic Church in council had affirmed Augustine's views in theory, in practice priests often ignored their rather unpalatable implications.[38]

It was roughly a thousand years after the death of Christ that the more complete form of the doctrine cited by Borowitz was developed by Anselm of Canterbury (1033–1109). Anselm's renowned book *Cur Deus Homo*, "Why a God-Man," famously framed the atonement in legal terms. Human beings were, as Augustine suggested, helpless, locked in sin and guilt. This has produced a debt that is so large that only God can deal with it. But there is a problem:

> None can satisfy the "debt" of sin but God, yet none should satisfy it but those who have incurred it, that is, ourselves (*homo*). To Anselm . . . the human condition presented itself as self-evident to any thinker: Our guilt cannot be self-healed. He thought he saw a necessary remedy that could be seen quite apart from our scriptural and churchly knowledge of Christ. . . . The solution, logically compelling even apart from what is in fact known of Christ, is that there be a God-man, the *Deus-homo*. . . . As the God-man, though himself without sin, he *ought* to make Satisfaction; and as God he *can* do so.[39]

The reformer John Calvin developed this further. He moved from the notion of the satisfaction of a debt to the harsher notion of "punishment." Jesus's death did not merely entail settling our accounts with God. Rather Jesus was punished for sin on our behalf: "It was expedient at the same time for him [Christ] to undergo the severity of God's vengeance, to appease his wrath and satisfy his just judgment. For this reason, he must also grapple hand to hand with the armies of hell and the dread of everlasting death. . . . He suffered the death that God in his wrath had inflicted upon the wicked! . . . 'My God, my God, why hast thou forsaken me?'" (*Inst.* 2.16.10–11).[40] However popular the "penal substitutionary atonement" is among traditional Calvinists, Lutherans, and, especially, American evangelicals, it is a fairly recent theological development and has never been universally accepted or affirmed.

In his section "The Biblical Teaching of Atonement," McClendon rightly notes that in the New Testament one finds not a settled doctrine of the atone-

38. See Phelan, "Long Shadow."
39. McClendon, *Doctrine*, 204.
40. McClendon, *Doctrine*, 206.

ment, but a series of metaphors. There are certainly metaphors of justice and judgment, punishment and substitution, but these are not the only metaphors and, according to McClendon, "there is no New Testament example of a courtroom metaphor in which God is the righteous judge, Christ the defendant, and the cross a penalty paid. At the least," he wryly concludes, "this brings out the creative novelty of the Latin-atonement teaching!"[41]

There are other significant metaphors—military victory, defeat of the "powers and authorities"; metaphors of kinship and redemption, Christ as our "kinsman redeemer"; metaphors of sacrifice used to restore the relationship between a person and God. But in the New Testament the sacrifice is not so much to placate God as it is to appeal to human beings: "All this is from God, who reconciled us to himself through Christ and gave us the ministry of reconciliation: that God was reconciling the world to himself in Christ, not counting people's sins against them. And he has committed to us the message of reconciliation" (2 Cor 5:18, 19). McClendon concludes: "In no ordinary sense of the words was Jesus put to death as a religious sacrifice: priests did not slaughter him; accepted biblical ritual did not require but rather forbade anything of the sort. No sacral words were spoken at his slaying; no altar smoke curled skyward to please the nostrils of a primitive God."[42] Jesus, in other words, was not sacrificed *to* God as a ritual human sacrifice to appease an intractable deity. This is simply not the view of the New Testament.[43]

I would suggest that the differences between the God of Tanakh and the God of the New Testament are not as large as Borowitz (and many Christians) would suggest. The New Testament shows a God seeking intimacy with his people and eager for their repentance and restoration. The barrier between God and his people in both Tanakh and the New Testament is their sin and disobedience. Through his prophets and messengers God pursues reconciliation and restoration. *God* is not the one who needs to be reconciled, as Paul insists in 2 Corinthians 5:18–19, but us. Whoever else he was, Jesus of Nazareth was a prophet of God's love and longing. He sought "the lost sheep of the house of Israel" to bring them home to God. Through him, to allude to Abraham Joshua Heschel's famous book, God was in search of humanity.[44] Adam, where are you?

41. McClendon, *Doctrine*, 219.

42. McClendon, *Doctrine*, 225.

43. For a fuller discussion of these issues see McClendon, *Doctrine*, 199–237.

44. Heschel, *God in Search of Man*.

This is not to say there is no difference between what Jews and Christians think about repentance, reconciliation, atonement, and salvation. The differences are significant. Christians experience the presence, power, and love of God in Jesus of Nazareth who is the Son of God, the Word, the Second Adam, possessing "the name above every name" (Phil 2:9). Christians believe through Jesus's death and resurrection that both they and the world are being made new. And for Christians faith in Jesus is not simply believing certain things about him, but entrusting themselves to his forgiving and renewing mercy demonstrated on the cross. Jews, of course, disagree with all of this. Nevertheless, the very real differences should not obscure the fact that both Jews and Christians worship a God who longs for us to be righteous, individually and corporately; a God eager to respond to our repentance, eager to forgive, eager to love, and eager to save. Both believe, as the New Testament puts it, "God is not willing that any should perish but all come to repentance" (2 Pet 3:9).

QUESTIONS FOR DISCUSSION

1. How do Jews and Christians differ with regard to "righteousness" and "salvation"? Where are there similarities?
2. Jews speak of "the evil inclination." Christians refer to "original sin." How are these different or similar?
3. What do "repentance" and "atonement" mean to Jews?

FURTHER READING

Cohn-Sherbok, Dan. "Sin and Repentance." Pages 420–25 in *Judaism: History, Belief and Practice.* London: Routledge, 2003.

Sacks, Jonathan. *To Heal a Fractured World: The Ethics of Responsibility.* New York: Schocken Books, 2005.

Soloveitchik, Joseph B. *The Lonely Man of Faith.* Foreword by David Shatz. New York: Doubleday, 2006.

———. *On Repentance.* Edited and adapted by Pinchas H. Peli. Jerusalem: Maggid Books, 2017.

CHAPTER 8

Exile and Restoration

On the seventh day of the fifth month—that was the nineteenth year of King Nebuchadnezzar of Babylon—Nebuzaradan, the chief of the guards, an officer of the king of Babylon, came to Jerusalem. He burned the House of the LORD, the king's palace, and all the houses of Jerusalem; he burned down the house of every notable person. The entire Chaldean force that was with the chief of the guard tore down the walls of Jerusalem on every side.

—2 Kings 25:8–10

When the builders had laid the foundation of the Temple of the LORD, priests in the vestments with trumpets, and Levites sons of Asaph with cymbals were stationed to give praise to the LORD, as King David of Israel had ordained. . . . All the people raised a great shout extolling the LORD because the foundation of the House of the LORD had been laid. Many of the priests and Levites and the chiefs of the clans, the old men who had seen the first house, wept loudly at the sight of the founding of this house.

—Ezra 3:10–12

For you see that our sanctuary has been laid waste, our altar thrown down, our temple destroyed; our harp has been laid low, our song has been silenced, and our rejoicing has ended; the light of our lampstand has been put out, the ark of our covenant has been plundered, our holy things have been polluted, and the name by which we have been called has been profaned; our free men have suffered abuse, our priests have been burned to death, our Levites have gone into captivity, our virgins have been defiled and our wives have been ravished; our righteous men have been carried off, our little ones cast out, our young men have been enslaved and our strong men made powerless.

—4 Ezra 10:21–23

It happened that R. Johanan b. Zakkai went out from Jerusalem, and R. Joshua followed him, and he saw the burnt ruins of the Temple, and he said, "Woe is it that the place, where the sins of Israel find atonement, is laid waste." Then said R. Johanan, "Grieve not, we have an atonement equal to the Temple, the doing of loving deeds" as it is said, "I desire mercy not sacrifice."

—Avot of Rabbi Nathan 4:11a

Every year, traditional Jews commemorate Tisha B'Av, the ninth day of the month of Av. This is one of the two major fast days in Judaism. Jews recall with grief the destruction of two temples: Solomon's Temple, destroyed by the Babylonians in 586 BCE, and the Second Temple, Herod's Temple, destroyed by the Romans in 70 CE. Mishnah *Ta'anit* 4 declares that five things befell Israel on the ninth of Av: "It was decreed against our fathers that they should not enter the Land [of Israel], and the Temple was destroyed the first and second time, and Beth-Tor was captured and the City was ploughed up. When Ab comes in, gladness must be diminished."[1] The references to the destruction of the Second Temple, the fall of Beth-Tor, and the ploughing of the city refer to the brutal outcomes of the "first" and "second" Jewish rebellions, the final being the so-called Bar Kokhba revolt.

The Mishnah goes on to give instructions for the fast:

> In the week wherein falls the 9th of Ab it is forbidden to cut the hair or wash the clothes; but it is permitted on the Thursday because of the honour due to the Sabbath. On the eve of the 9th of Ab let none eat of two cooked dishes, let none eat flesh and let none drink wine. Rabban Simeon b. Gamaliel says: A man need but make some difference [that is, eat somewhat less than his custom]. R. Judah says: A man must turn up his couch [that is, sleep on the ground]. But the sages did not agree with him.[2]

Rabbi Adin Steinsaltz describes a variety of mourning customs, some common to all Jews, some unique to particular communities: no eating or drinking, washing, wearing any kind of leather footwear, sexual relations, giving greetings, even the study of Torah since it "gladdens the heart."[3] People will sit on the floor rather than a chair, and some will take up the strictures of R. Judah and sleep on the floor. "Few lights are lit (even in the synagogue), and one tries to avoid any kind of amusement or frivolity, so as to keep one's mind focused on mourning."[4]

The destruction of the First Temple destroyed not only the original place of worship for the kingdom of Israel, it reflected the destruction of the Jewish commonwealth and marked a change in the very nature of Judaism. Jews were now dispersed into Egypt and Babylon and within a few

1. *m. Ta'anit* 4:6.
2. *m. Ta'anit* 4:7.
3. Steinsaltz, *Guide to Jewish Prayer*, 230.
4. Steinsaltz, *Guide to Jewish Prayer*, 231.

centuries were found in significant numbers throughout the Mediterranean basin. The decades following the destruction of the First Temple were called "the Exile." The Exile officially ended when the Persian king Cyrus permitted Jews to return to their ancestral land and restore their community and their temple. This process is described in the so-called postexilic prophets and the books of Ezra and Nehemiah. A Second Temple was built and the worship of God was restored to the city of Jerusalem. But the people of Israel were forever changed. Many Jews never returned to the land from exile. They had built new lives in Babylon, Egypt, and elsewhere. They had followed the advice of the prophet Jeremiah who had told them,

> Thus said the LORD of Hosts, the God of Israel, to the whole community which I exiled from Jerusalem to Babylon: Build houses and live in them, plant gardens and eat their fruit. Take wives and beget sons and daughters and take wives for your sons, and give your daughters to husbands, that they may bear sons and daughters. Multiply there, do not decrease. And seek the welfare of the city to which I have exiled you and pray to the LORD in its behalf; for in its prosperity you shall prosper. (Jer 29:4–7)

Many of them were prosperous and settled, with no particular desire to take the long dangerous trip to an uncertain future in a devastated land. These Jews of Babylon, Egypt, Greece, and eventually Rome came to be known as the "Diaspora."

This meant that the older patterns of Jewish life and worship in the land had to change. New institutions and forms of worship needed to be created. New texts needed to be composed and new traditions needed to be forged. The next seven hundred years or so, from the destruction of the First Temple to the destruction of the second, were among the most creative, controversial, and consequential, not simply in the history of the Jewish people, but in the history of the world. Although for the Jewish people this era began and ended in grief and loss, in between the Judaism we know today was being formed. And in the latter part of the period it gave birth to a troublesome younger brother—Christianity. This is the Second Temple period: the seedbed of the modern world.

The German philosopher Karl Jaspers calls this era part of "the Axial age."[5] According to Karen Armstrong,

5. See Karl Jaspers, *The Origin and Goal of History*, trans. Michael Bullock (New Haven: Yale University Press, 1952; repr. Westport, CT: Greenwood Press, 1976).

> From about 900 to 200 BCE, in four distinct regions, the great world traditions that have continued to nourish humanity came into being: Confucianism and Daoism in China; Hinduism and Buddhism in India; monotheism in Israel; and philosophical rationalism in Greece. This was the period of the Buddha, Socrates, Confucius, and Jeremiah, the mystic of the Upanishads, Mencius, and Euripides. . . . The Axial Age was one of the most seminal periods of intellectual, psychological, philosophical, and religious change in recorded history; there would be nothing comparable until the Great Western Transformation, which created our own scientific and technological modernity.[6]

Jaspers himself grandly claims, "What is new about this age, in all three areas of the world is that man [*sic*] becomes conscious of Being as a whole, of himself and his limitations. He experiences the terror of the world and his own powerlessness. He asks radical questions. Face to face with the void he strives for liberation and redemption. By consciously recognizing his limits he sets himself the highest goals. He experiences absoluteness in the depths of selfhood and in the lucidity of transcendence."[7] It was an age of *reflection*, he argues, where disaster and change had shattered one era, causing prophets, philosophers, scribes, and poets to ask how what *is* may be connected to what *was* and what *will be*.[8]

The notion of an "Axial Age" has been criticized, but it is certainly true that the destruction of the Kingdom of Judah and the scattering of the Jews brought Jewish prophets and sages into greater contact with this larger world. It forced them to contemplate what it might mean to be faithful to the God of Israel when it was not possible to offer sacrifices in Jerusalem. It required them to engage with Persian sages, Greek philosophers, and, eventually, Roman jurists. While Israel had always been a tiny land surrounded by larger kingdoms and imperial powers, now it appeared that, without land, king, and temple, Jews were particularly vulnerable. How could Israel's past be integrated with the Jews' present? What would their future be?

Throughout Jewish history it has seemed that the Jews are always just about to disappear. Constantly threatened by hostile forces, whether military, political, cultural, or religious, it has appeared, not least to Jews, that both the Jews and Judaism might melt away. Whether through conquest,

6. Karen Armstrong, *The Great Transformation* (New York: Alfred A. Knopf, 2006), xii.
7. Jaspers, *Origin and Goal*, 2.
8. Jaspers, *Origin and Goal*, 1–21.

assimilation, conversions, pogroms, or outright murder the Jews have always seemed to be at risk. But they have survived and, perhaps ironically, the Second Temple period laid the groundwork for their survival. Shaye J. D. Cohen argues several shifts occurred during the Second Temple period: the leadership of the people went from the king to the priests; prophets gave way to scribes; revelation gave way to erudition.[9] Each move would enable the post-70 CE rabbis to take up and assure the task of Jewish survival, Jewish flourishing.

The Canonization of Scripture

At the center of this was the creation of the Jewish canon of Scriptures and the publication of the Hebrew Bible. Cohen writes, "Second Temple Judaism is a 'book religion.' At its heart lies the Hebrew Bible, the book that Jews call Tanak (or Tanakh) and Christians call the Old Testament. Preexilic Israel produced the raw materials out of which most of the Bible was constructed, but it was Second Temple Judaism that created the Bible, venerated the very parchment on which it was written, and devoted enormous energies to its interpretation."[10] It was the move to the scribe, to erudition, that enabled both Jews and Judaism to survive. The scribes took these ancient texts and made them enduringly relevant to their particular eras. This is still the genius of Judaism today. The study of Torah from that day to this has kept Jews and Judaism alive. When the Second Temple was destroyed and the priest as well as the king disappeared, the Torah and the rabbis remained. These scholars and sages were able to re-form Judaism once again around study and prayer because they had done it before—they are still doing it.

The History of the Second Temple Era

The history of the Second Temple is the history of the rise and fall of great empires. Babylon gave way to the Persians: Cyrus took control of Babylonian territories including that of Israel in 539 BCE. Under Darius I (522–486 BCE) the kingdom expanded: "When Darius died Persia was at the height

9. Shaye J. D. Cohen, *From the Maccabees to the Mishnah*, 3rd ed. (Louisville: Westminster John Knox, 2014), 11.

10. Cohen, *From the Maccabees*, 11.

of its territorial expansion and material wealth. Its borders ranged from the Indus and Jaxartes (Syr Darya) rivers in the east to Egypt and the Aegean in the west, and from the Persian Gulf in the south to the Caspian and Black seas in the north."[11] Under Cyrus Jews were permitted to return to the land of Israel, and under Darius the Second Temple was built. Jews flourished in Babylon during the Persian Empire, establishing a community that would remain perhaps the most significant center of learning and piety for more than a millennium. The impact of Persian culture and religious thought on Judaism is greatly debated.[12] But there can be no doubt regarding the profound influence of the empire that would follow.

In 334 BCE the young Macedonian ruler Alexander routed the Persian army. By 331 BCE he had taken Syria, Palestine, and Egypt from the Persians. But he was far from finished. He finished off the Persian Empire and marched his army all the way to India, where he was forced to end his conquests. In the years to come, Greek philosophy and religion, Greek architecture and city planning, Greek culture and art would come to dominate the ancient world. Even the rise of Rome did not blunt the impact of what came to be called Hellenism. The Greek language was the language of commerce, learning, and politics throughout the Middle East, Europe, and North Africa. The towering influence of the philosophers of Greece's classical age continues to this day. There is no doubt that the struggle with Hellenism, with the influence of the Greeks, was one of the most formative factors in Second Temple Judaism. Some Jews resisted this influence mightily. Some eagerly assimilated to the glittering new culture. Some sought to integrate Greek learning with Judaism and remain faithful Jews. But all were impacted by Hellenism.

Following Alexander's death his kingdom was divided among his most important generals. In Syria and the east the general was Seleucus and his kingdom called the Seleucid. In Egypt the general was Ptolemy and his kingdom the Ptolemaic. Both generals claimed the ancient land of Israel and their successors fought over possession of this vital link between east and west as well as north and south. The Seleucid dynasty had gained control of the land of Israel by the second century BCE. The Seleucid king Antiochus IV Epiphanes, for reasons that are obscure to this day, "desecrated the temple by erecting in the sacred precincts a cult object or an altar of a foreign god"

11. Robert E. Stone II, "Persia," in *Eerdmans Dictionary of the Bible*, ed. David Noel Freedman (Grand Rapids: Eerdmans, 2000), 1031–34.

12. See Lester L. Grabbe, *Judaism from Cyrus to Hadrian*, vol. 1, *The Persian and Greek Periods* (Minneapolis: Fortress, 1992), 101–2.

and "tried to compel the Jews to abandon their traditional religious practices (circumcision, Sabbath, abstention from pork, etc.). The goal of the king and his supporters was to remove the features of Judaism that made it different from the other religions of the world."[13] The result was the Maccabean revolt, which eventually drove out the Seleucid forces, purified and restored the temple (an event celebrated in the Jewish holiday Hanukkah), and established the Jewish "Hasmonean" dynasty of kings. This dynasty lasted for a century before internal squabbling brought in the Romans. The Hellenistic influence remained powerful throughout the long centuries of Roman occupation, whether directed from Rome itself or, later, from Constantinople.

The Influence of Hellenism on Second Temple Judaism

It was once fashionable to argue that there was a significant difference between the Judaism of the "Hellenistic Jews" of the Diaspora and the "normative Judaism" of the land of Israel. Most scholars, both Jewish and Christian, would not make that argument today. As Cohen states, "All the Jews of antiquity were Hellenized to some degree. All shared in the material culture of the larger world and were exposed to the Greek language."[14] The Maccabean revolt originated in the attempt of a Greek ruler to undermine the Jewish law and compromise the worship of the temple. And yet, as Lester Grabbe writes,

> No doubt the Maccabean revolt included reactions against certain elements of Hellenization that were the most overt elements of the Seleucid oppression, a common factor in anticolonial revolts. Many elements of Greek culture were already a part of the Jewish world, however, and were probably not even recognized as Greek in origin. More important is the fact that Hasmonean rule brought no change to the status of Hellenistic culture in Judea. Therefore, the claim often made that the Maccabean revolt was a revolt against Hellenization is misleading.[15]

The Hasmonean kings were simultaneously, at least in their own eyes, thoroughly faithful Jews and recognizably Hellenistic rulers. How would

13. Cohen, *From the Maccabees*, 22.

14. Cohen, *From the Maccabees*, 33.

15. Grabbe, *Persian and Greek Periods*, 308; see pp. 147–70 for greater detail.

individual Jews and groups of Jews negotiate the tensions and pressures of one of the most powerful cultures the world had ever known? How would they remain faithful when they were relatively powerless and impacted by that culture whether they wanted to be or not?

Elite Individuals and Formative Groups of the First Century CE

Since the destruction of the First Temple, the Jews had suffered exile and restoration, rule by powerful empires from Persia, Greece, and Rome, and a century of deeply ambiguous rule by Jewish kings. They had been scattered throughout the Middle Eastern and Mediterranean worlds. By the first century CE it must have seemed to many that the glorious promises of the prophets were more remote than ever. Throughout the centuries of exile and domination by gentile powers Jews were forced to ask hard questions. Why are we being punished so severely? Has God abandoned us? When will the promised redemption finally arrive? What does it mean to live as a Jew in Babylon, in Alexandria, in Rome? How much can a Jew "fit in" and remain faithful to God's covenant with his people? What does it really mean to live in obedience to God's Torah? Is there really still any point to doing so? The range of options included apostasy and assimilation at one extreme and sectarian withdrawal at the other. Examples of both extremes are not hard to find in Second Temple Judaism and its literature.

Ironically, the surviving Jewish literature of the most critical first century CE could not be considered representative of what would become normative Judaism in the wake of the destruction of the Second Temple. The philosophical works of Philo of Alexandria and the historical and apologetic works of Josephus illustrate one option. They represent the efforts of highly educated elite Jews to integrate their Judaism with the dominant Hellenistic and Roman modes of thought. The other major surviving Jewish works of the first century are the Gospels and letters of the New Testament. They represent a totally different way of mediating Jewish life and thought to a largely gentile audience. However hostile the Gospels are to figures like the "scribes and Pharisees," they provide a picture of Jewish life in both Judea and the Diaspora not otherwise available in first-century literature.

The other important source of information about first-century CE Judaism is the Mishnah. Produced around 200 CE, it includes some sayings and stories about rabbis of the first centuries BCE and CE. While traditional Jews accept the veracity of these stories and sayings, many modern Jewish scholars are more skeptical.[16] Unlike Philo, Josephus, and the New Testament, the Mishnah was not written with an eye to the gentile world. It was written for an exclusively Jewish audience and focused on how Jews were to *live* and reflects a refusal to compromise with the dominant culture. The Mishnah and its development will be the subject of a subsequent chapter.

Elite Individuals: Fitting in but Remaining Faithful

Philo was from a wealthy, distinguished Alexandrian Jewish family. He was a man of immense erudition, learned in both Torah and the philosophical traditions of Greece: "He . . . seized the opportunity to fuse Judaism systematically with the thought of the Hellenistic world in a corpus that today occupies some twenty-five hundred printed pages. This contribution would be passed on by the church fathers and virtually ignored by the Jewish people, only to be rediscovered by them during the Italian Renaissance."[17]

Philo, like other Jews, was very attentive to the text of the Torah. He was an exegete. But like other sophisticated Jews at the time, Philo was troubled by the image of God and the actions of his Jewish forebears depicted in the Torah:

> Philo finds it impossible to believe that Moses spent forty days and nights with God only to return with a book filled with unedifying stories about the domestic troubles of one ancient clan; obviously the stories of Genesis about the patriarchs must be trying to reveal something significant. For Philo, the stories, when properly decoded, are about the ascent of the soul from the world of matter to the world of the archetypes and the Monad. The episodes in the lives of the patriarchs are way stations in the journey of the soul.[18]

This way of reading is called *allegory.* The literal level remains significant but there is a deeper meaning that transcends the occasional crudities on the surface. Philo's approach was very congenial to sophisticated Hellenists and accounts for his popularity with the church fathers who used the same methods to read the Gospels.

16. See Cohen, *From the Maccabees*, 155–58.
17. Schiffman, *From Text*, 94–95.
18. Cohen, *From the Maccabees*, 204.

But this does not mean that Philo rejected his Jewish way of life. That there were deeper meanings attached to the stories and laws of Torah did not mean that the commands should be rejected. In fact, "he criticized fellow Jews who thought that the underlying meaning of Jewish rituals negated the necessity of their observance. Philo argued that they were essential markers of community identity."[19] For Philo, circumcision, Sabbath observance, festivals and holidays, and dietary regulations were all critical to maintaining a Jewish identity. In this he was unlike his nephew Tiberius Julius Alexander who, according to Josephus, "did not maintain his ancestral traditions."[20] Tiberius became a high-ranking Roman official and was at the side of the future emperor Titus when Jerusalem was destroyed—as was Titus Flavius Josephus.

Josephus provides another model. He was a younger contemporary of Philo born in Jerusalem to a prominent family. He was a born survivor. A general during the first Jewish revolt, he managed to ingratiate himself to the emperor Vespasian and returned with him to Rome where he wrote critically important works of history and apologetics.[21] Our knowledge of Jewish history of the Greek, Hasmonean, and Roman periods would be greatly impoverished without Josephus's massive output. Like Philo, Josephus's work was also "lost to the Jewish people," finding greater popularity among Christians.[22] The value of the historical work of Josephus is universally acknowledged, but Josephus himself has been scorned as a traitor and a toady for the Romans.

> He was more devious than a turncoat—and more consistent. Without some measure of slyness, how could he have told as much of the truth as he did? Faced with an alien, often contemptuous audience, he was under the patronage of men whose indulgence could never be taken for granted. . . . From the moment he devised a way not to share the fate of the other defenders of Jotapata [during the Jewish revolt] Joseph was alone. Isolated from other Jews, he was sentenced to life in the solitary confinement of his own memories and reactions.[23]

19. Gregory E. Sterling, "Philo," in Collins and Harlow, *Eerdmans Dictionary of Early Judaism*, 1063–70.

20. Gregory E. Sterling, "Tiberius Julius Alexander," in Collins and Harlow, *Eerdmans Dictionary of Early Judaism*, 1309–10.

21. Steven Mason, "Josephus," in Collins and Harlow, *Eerdmans Dictionary of Early Judaism*, 828–32.

22. Schiffman, *From Text*, 171.

23. Frederic Raphael, *A Jew among the Romans* (New York: Anchor Books, 2013), 126.

And yet Josephus too considered himself a good Jew, a defender of the Jews, their history, and traditions. Although Josephus and Philo wrote to defend and preserve the Jewish people and Jewish way of life; although elite Jews over the coming centuries would face similar struggles to fit in and remain faithful, neither Philo nor Josephus would provide a viable model for Jewish faithfulness—until, perhaps, the modern era. But two of their contemporaries did provide a way forward that has endured to this day. They were Hillel and Shammai.

Elite Individuals: The Rabbinic Roots

Hillel and Shammai and the "schools" they founded were the roots of a rabbinic tradition that flourished in the decades following the destruction of the Second Temple. The fruits of this tradition were the Mishnah, the Talmud, and the rich exegetical embroidery of midrash. The soil that nourished this tradition was the scribal tradition traceable to Ezra and the oral tradition stretching back, for traditional Jews, to Moses. As the Mishnah puts it, "Moses received the Law from Sinai and committed it to Joshua and Joshua to the elders, and the elders to the Prophets; and the Prophets committed it to the men of the Great Synagogue. They said three things: Be deliberate in judgement, raise up many disciples, and make a fence around the Law."[24]

According to tradition, Hillel arrived in Israel from Babylon sometime during the second half of the first century BCE. He was known for his learning, his piety, and his patience. The stories and legal rulings credited to Hillel show him to be passionately committed to Torah and the oral tradition. At the same time he was creative and flexible in his interpretation. His "legal decisions portray a leader of strong authority who was capable of providing creative legal solutions to redress situations of potential social inequity. Hillel's leadership and legal authority, as well as his respect for the people as significant partners in the legal process," are well attested.[25]

Hillel wanted to make it possible for ordinary people to follow the Torah and live as faithful Jews. This was a complex challenge for a people living under foreign domination, with scant social or political power. Modern Judaism traces its lineage to Hillel and his famous offspring: Gamaliel I and II and Judah the Patriarch.

24. *m. Avot* 1:1.

25. Paul Mandel, "Hillel," in Collins and Harlow, *Eerdmans Dictionary of Early Judaism*, 742–43.

Shammai, his contemporary, was known for "his irascibility and intransigence as opposed to the patience and flexibility of Hillel."[26] Whether or not this tradition is accurate, two schools or streams of traditional interpretation traced their origins to the conflicts between these great masters and their pupils. These arguments and contentions play out in the pages of the Mishnah. The Mishnah and Jewish tradition in general do not consider such contention an evil. They consider it a necessity. To this day students of Torah sit in pairs and passionately argue out their interpretations of Torah. Rabbinical literature makes no attempt to eliminate the conflicting decisions of the rabbinic masters but goes out of its way to preserve them. "Any controversy that is for God's sake shall in the end be of lasting worth, but any that is not for God's sake shall not in the end be of lasting worth. Which controversy was for God's sake? Such was the controversy of Hillel and Shammai. And which is not for God's sake? Such was the controversy of Korah and his company."[27]

Hillel and Shammai were certainly not alone in their attempts to assure the enduring relevance of the Torah to the Jewish people. There were several groups and movements seeking to answer the questions of identity and purpose that haunted faithful Jews in the fateful decades of the late first century BCE and the early decades of the first century CE. They were often in direct conflict with each other. Their impact would be felt in the years leading up to and following the Jewish War of 66–73 CE.

Groups: Seeking Faithfulness to Torah

The book of Ezra tells us that "Ezra came up from Babylon, a scribe expert in the Teaching of Moses" (Ezra 7:6). He had dedicated himself to the study of the Torah "so as to observe it, and to teach laws and rules to Israel" (7:10). The arrival of Ezra began a religious revival of sorts in the land of Israel. Cohen argues that Ezra the scribe, although of priestly lineage himself, set himself in opposition to the restored priesthood of the Second Temple. "In effect, Ezra 'published' the Torah by making it accessible to the masses. This was a direct threat to the political hegemony of the priesthood. . . . By giving the masses free access to the Torah, Ezra was curbing the power of

26. Paul Mandel, "Shammai," in Collins and Harlow, *Eerdmans Dictionary of Early Judaism*, 1224–25.

27. *m. Avot* 5:17.

the priestly magistrates. In his work he was aided by the Levites, a group that was at odds with the priesthood throughout the Second Temple period."[28]

Ezra was arguing that God's Torah was not only the purview of the priests, but of ordinary people, intellectuals as well as peasants. This had perhaps become clear to Ezra and others in the Babylonian exile. Unless the Torah became the possession of *all* Jews, regardless of their proximity to the land and the temple, Jewish life itself would be at risk.

Thus were laid down the lines of tension and conflict that shaped not only the Second Temple period, but the development of Judaism itself. The conflict centered not only on the temple and its management, but on whose halakah ordinary Jews should follow. Overshadowing all this was the large question of how both ordinary Jews and elite Jews should relate to the dominant imperial power as they sought to follow God's will. And, they wondered, when will God finally act to liberate his people? Could God's people do anything to hurry this eventuality along? Out of these conflicts and questions were born a number of important groups: "the Scribes and the Pharisees," "the priests and the Sadducees," and "the Essenes and the Zealots."

Scribes and Pharisees

Few people were literate in the ancient world. Scribes were necessary not only for recording business transactions and keeping the tax rolls up to date but also for helping ordinary people write letters and preserve important bits of family business.[29] But scribes were also the scholars, the academics of the ancient world. They were the teachers who passed on the traditions of the community. According to Ben Sira, a text written in the second century BCE, a scribe

> devotes himself to the study of the law of the Most High! He seeks out the wisdom of all the ancients, and is concerned with prophecies; he preserves the sayings of the famous and penetrates the subtleties of parables; he seeks out the hidden meanings of proverbs and is at home in the obscurities of parables. He serves among the great and appears before rulers; he travels

28. Cohen, *From the Maccabees*, 137.

29. D. Andrew Teeter, "Scribes and Scribalism," in Collins and Harlow, *Eerdmans Dictionary of Early Judaism*, 1201–4.

> to foreign lands and learns what is good and evil in the human lot. He sets his heart to rise early to seek the Lord who made him, and to petition the Most High; he opens his mouth in prayer and asks pardon for his sins.[30]

For Ben Sira, the scribe is a model of both intellect and piety. He is a student not only of the laws of God but also of the ways of the wider world. He is a teacher as well as a learner, communicating his wisdom to all who will listen.

In the Second Temple era the Jewish scribes were "Torah scholars" and reflected the text orientation that had been growing since the days of Ezra. It is likely that different groups within the larger Jewish community had their own scribes, experts in their own traditions and interpretations. In the New Testament the "scribes" are associated not just with the Pharisees but with the Sadducees and the "high priests." It seems that the Pharisees, the Sadducees, the high priestly elite, and other groups within and beyond the land of Israel all had their own scribes, their own scholars. It also seems likely that each group's "scribes" promoted their own "halakah" with the halakah of the Pharisees differing from that of the Sadducees, the priestly elite, and that of the Essenes and Qumran sectarians. Although all sought to ground their teachings in Torah, they followed differing traditions of reading and applying the text to the lives of the academic and spiritual elites as well as ordinary Jews.

The most prominent group of Jews in the Second Temple period is perhaps the Pharisees. While the Pharisees are often depicted as opponents of Jesus in the Gospels, both Jesus and the early Christians were closer to the Pharisees than any other first-century CE group. Although Jesus is critical of the Pharisees, he takes their side on the question of the resurrection (see Mark 12:18–27) and tells one he is "not far from the kingdom of God" (Mark 12:34). Paul declares that he was a Pharisee in Philippians 3:5 and in Acts 23:6 we are told that he created an uproar in the Sanhedrin when he shouted, "My brothers, I am a Pharisee, descended from Pharisees. I stand on trial because of the hope of the resurrection of the dead." Luke comments, "The Sadducees say there is no resurrection, and that there are neither angels nor spirits, but Pharisees believe all these things" (Acts 23:7)—as did the early Christians. In fact, according to Luke some of the earliest followers of Jesus came from the Pharisees (Acts 15:5).

The Pharisees are also the most important forebears of post–70 CE Judaism. As one rabbi friend proudly told me, "I am a Pharisee." Their origins

30. Sir 38:34b–39:5, trans. Charlesworth.

are obscure, but like other Jewish groups they were seeking to enable Jews in difficult circumstances to live faithfully to God's Torah. This required a good deal of intellectual effort since Jews lived in radically different times from that of the Patriarchs and Moses or the kings and the prophets. In these new situations they sought the sanctification "of the whole nation (not just the priests)." Every Jew "stands under the command to be holy (Exod 19:6). The way to holiness is a life according to Torah."[31] The halakah of the Pharisees was developed "so that it could be practiced by as many people as possible during their daily routine."[32] This concern is clearly represented in the Mishnah. The Pharisees' halakah was rooted in the "traditions of the elders" or the "Oral Torah" that formed the basis of the Mishnah (see Mark 7:1–23).

While the conflicts in the Gospels between Jesus and the Pharisees are fierce, it is important to remember that readers of the Gospels are listening in on an inter-Jewish conflict. We often argue most insistently with those to whom we are closest. The halakah of Jesus was obviously different from that of the Pharisees. But Jesus, and the movement he began, had and has many similarities to the Pharisees. Perhaps contemporary Jesus followers cannot proudly say with my rabbi friend, "We are Pharisees!" But Christians have to acknowledge there is still a good deal of the spiritual DNA of the Pharisees within our community. And this is not a bad thing.

Priests and Sadducees

The locus of the work of the Pharisees was evidently in the synagogue, an institution of obscure beginnings and varied function. By the first century there were synagogues throughout the Jewish world. They were community centers, schools, and places of prayer. Not surprisingly, the earliest synagogues are found in the Diaspora.[33] There they were called "prayer-houses." Synagogues were apparently for the most part lay-led rather than led by "clergy," whether priests or rabbis, though both groups likely participated in their ongoing life. Both priests and rabbis, for example, were likely involved in the teaching of youth. The institutional center of the priests and Sadducees, however, was the temple in Jerusalem. When it was

31. Roland Deines, "Pharisees," in Collins and Harlow, *Eerdmans Dictionary of Early Judaism*, 1061–63.

32. Deines, "Pharisees."

33. Cohen, *From the Maccabees*, 111.

destroyed, they were, for the most part, destroyed along with it. Jewish religious life, of course, was not destroyed. "The concomitant development of the synagogue as an institution, along with the gradual ascendancy of prayer over sacrifice as a means of worship, prepared Judaism for the new situation brought about by the destruction of the Temple. By the time the Temple was taken away, its replacement had already been created. From that time on the daily prayers would serve in place of sacrifice, and the synagogue, the 'Temple in miniature,' would replace the central sanctuary in Jerusalem."[34]

While the temple stood, it continued to exercise a great deal of influence upon Jews, even those who would never see it. Not only did Jews from the Diaspora send tithes to support the temple, many of them made the arduous journey to celebrate one of the great feasts in its courts. Acts 2 tells us that on the Day of Pentecost "there were staying in Jerusalem God-fearing Jews from every nation under heaven . . . Parthians, Medes and Elamites; residents of Mesopotamia, Judea and Cappadocia, Pontus and Asia, Phrygia and Pamphylia, Egypt and the parts of Libya near Cyrene; visitors from Rome (both Jews and converts to Judaism); Cretans and Arabs" (Acts 2:4, 9–11a). The temple was the domain of the priesthood, especially the high priest and his allies among the Sadducees. The high priest had for generations operated as a kind of de facto head of state for the Jews, wielding significant power on behalf of Israel's imperial rulers of the day.[35]

The high priests and their families became Jewish aristocracy. They were wealthy and powerful and, according to many Jews, corrupt. The Essenes were especially critical of the priesthood and the ritual practices of the Second Temple: "They complained that . . . the temple was polluted, the temple priests were illegitimate, the temple cult was not conducted in accordance with the correct calendar, or the correct purity laws."[36] There was also tension between the high priests and other elite priests in Jerusalem and the "simple priests" who lived in the countryside and came in "courses" to carry out priestly duties in Jerusalem. According to Cohen, "The social turmoil that preceded the outbreak of the war in 66 CE shows that the tension between the simple priests and the high priests was as great as that between the lay masses and the high priests. All priests were entitled to receive tithes

34. Schiffman, *From Text*, 166.

35. James C. VanderKam, "High Priests," in Collins and Harlow, *Eerdmans Dictionary of Early Judaism*, 1179–81.

36. Cohen, *From the Maccabees*, 160.

and officiate in the temple, but only the high priests enjoyed the full measure of power that such a position could bestow."[37] The war was not simply a revolt against the Romans; in the end, especially in Jerusalem proper, it was a vicious civil war.

The Sadducees were apparently an elite group within an elite group. They were part of the priestly aristocracy, but there were also high priests who were not Sadducees.[38] All the information we have about them comes from sources hostile to them (e.g., the New Testament and rabbinic literature). They left no written record of their beliefs. According to Josephus they were few in number and, unlike the Pharisees, had no following among the people. Both the New Testament and the rabbis say the Sadducees denied the resurrection of the dead. Josephus says they "denied fate," that is, they were not predestinarian or deterministic. They evidently had their own halakah and approach to purity. It is likely they had their own "oral tradition" that was different in some respects from that of the Pharisees. Conflicts over purity and other matters between the Sadducees and Pharisees are found in the Mishnah.[39] Their "party" did not survive the Jewish War and they are remembered for the most part only as the opponents of both the Pharisees and, perhaps ironically, Jesus of Nazareth.

Essenes and Zealots

The Essenes and the Qumran community, like the Pharisees and the Sadducees, had their own halakah and vision of how the Jerusalem temple and its ritual should be managed. Unlike the Pharisees, they were, in Shaye Cohen's words, "sectarian."[40] Two documents describe the vision of the Essenes: the Damascus Document, discovered in a Cairo synagogue in 1896, and the Rule of the Community, found in the famous Qumran caves.[41] "The *Rule of the Community* envisions a society of celibate men living in isolation from

37. Cohen, *From the Maccabees*, 106.

38. Gunter Stemberger, "Sadducees," in Collins and Harlow, *Eerdmans Dictionary of Early Judaism*, 1179–81.

39. See Cohen, *From the Maccabees*, 154, for an example.

40. Cohen, *From the Maccabees*, 123–71.

41. See Charlotte Hempel, "Damascus Document," and Sarianna Metso, "Rule of the Community (1QS + Fragments)," in Collins and Harlow, *Eerdmans Dictionary of Early Judaism*, 510–12 and 1169–71, respectively.

their fellow Jews, while the *Damascus Covenant* envisions a community of men, women, and children, living among Jews (and gentiles!) who are not members of the group."[42]

The Essenes and Qumran sectarians thought the temple and its priesthood corrupt, their ritual practices flawed, and their calendar mistaken. This meant they thought the community of Israel celebrated their festivals and holidays at the wrong times and in the wrong way. The Essenes looked forward to a day when all this would be corrected and a just and holy priesthood restored. There was an apocalyptic element to the Qumran community as the so-called War Scroll illustrates.[43] Both the Qumran community and the Essenes disappeared in the wake of the Jewish War.

The final group that warrants attention is the "Zealots." These were revolutionaries and assassins virulently opposed to the Roman occupation. "The basic tenet of this group, which was founded by Judas the Galilean (or the Gaulanite) and Zadok the Pharisee was 'No king but God.' The slogan seems anarchic in character since it justifies the rejection of all political institutions, but in practice Judas and his followers attacked only Romans and those Jews who supported or cooperated with the Romans. This group first appeared in 6 CE, when it rebelled against the Romans; the rebellion was crushed (Acts 5:37)."[44]

There is a direct line from the agitation of these early violent revolutionaries to the rebellion against Rome in 66 CE. It culminated in the destruction of the temple, the slaughter of many thousands of Jews, and the destruction of most of the important institutions and groups. The Pharisees were left to pick up the pieces and reconstitute Jewish life in the wake of this unparalleled disaster. I will pick up their story after examining two first-century Jews whose impact extended far beyond the confines of the land of Israel and Judaism itself: Jesus of Nazareth and Paul of Tarsus. The focus of these two chapters will be upon what Jews themselves have said about these two figures over the centuries. For the last 150 years or so, Jewish scholars have begun to reclaim, especially, Jesus the Jew. Paul has had a harder road, but even this controversial figure is now being recognized as a Jew by his fellow Jews.

42. Cohen, *From the Maccabees*, 151.

43. For English translations of "The Community Rule," the "Damascus Document," and the "War Scroll," see Florentino García Martínez, *The Dead Sea Scrolls Translated*, trans. Wilfrid G. E. Watson (Grand Rapids: Eerdmans, 1996).

44. Cohen, *From the Maccabees*, 163.

QUESTIONS FOR DISCUSSION

1. How did the Babylonian exile and its aftermath shape Judaism?
2. What was the influence of Hellenism on both the Jews of the Diaspora and the Jews of the land of Israel?
3. Who were the most important groups in Second Temple Judaism and how did they differ from one another?

FURTHER READING

Cohen, Shaye J. D. *From the Maccabees to the Mishnah.* 3rd ed. Louisville: Westminster John Knox, 2014.

Collins, John J., and Daniel C. Harlow, eds. *The Eerdmans Dictionary of Early Judaism.* Grand Rapids: Eerdmans, 2010.

Schiffman, Lawrence. *From Text to Tradition: A History of Second Temple and Rabbinic Judaism.* Hoboken, NJ: Ktav, 1991.

Segal, Alan. "The Second Temple Period." Pages 34–57 in *The Cambridge Guide to Jewish History, Religion, and Culture*, edited by Judith R. Baskin and Kenneth Seeskin. Cambridge: Cambridge University Press, 2010.

CHAPTER 9

Jesus the Jew

After John was put in prison, Jesus went into Galilee, proclaiming the good news of God. "The time has come," he said. "The kingdom of God has come near. Repent and believe the good news."

—Mark 1:14–15

But when the set time had fully come, God sent his Son, born of a woman, born under the law, to redeem those under the law, that we might receive the adoption to sonship.

—Galatians 4:4–5

He [Jesus] was a Jew, a Pharisean Jew with Galilean coloring—a man who shared the hopes of his time and who believed that these hopes were fulfilled in him. He did not utter a new thought, nor did he break down the barriers of nationality. . . . He did not abolish any part of Judaism; he was a Pharisee who walked in the way of Hillel, did not set the decisive worth on every single external form, yet proclaimed "that not the least tittle should be taken from the Law; the Pharisees sit in Moses' seat, and when they speak, you should observe and obey."

—Abraham Geiger

From my youth onward I have found in Jesus my great brother.

—Martin Buber

Jesus was a Jew and a Jew he remained till his last breath. His one idea was to implant within his nation the idea of the coming of the Messiah and, by repentance and good works, hasten the "end."

—Joseph Klausner

After two thousand years of ignorance, the time has come for the church and synagogue, Jews and Christians, to understand our intertwined histories, to see Jesus as a Jew who made sense to other Jews in a Jewish context, to learn how our two traditions came to a parting of the ways, to recognize how misunderstandings of Jesus and Judaism continue even today to foster negative stereotypes and feed hate and to explore how the gains in interfaith relations made over the past several decades can be nurtured and expanded.

—Amy-Jill Levine

In Ephesians 2, Paul argues that Jews and gentiles, once estranged from one another, "have been brought near by the blood of Christ" (Eph 2:13). He continues: "For he himself is our peace, who has made the two one and has destroyed the barrier, the dividing wall of hostility, by setting aside in his flesh the law with its commands and regulations. His purpose was to create in himself one new humanity out of the two, thus making peace, and in one body to reconcile both of them to God through the cross, by which he put to death their hostility" (Eph 2:14–16). The terrible irony of this passage is that, of course, the very things the apostle thought would unify and liberate the Jews and gentiles became the source of bitter division, tragic alienation, and even violence and death. Jesus and his cross, rather than becoming the way to eliminate the barrier wall, became themselves an even higher and more formidable barrier. The importance of the Jewishness of Jesus was, because of this mutual animosity and ignorance, obscured if not lost entirely for many centuries. Since the middle of the nineteenth century, Jewish scholars have been among the most important proponents of the recovery of Jesus the Jew, sometimes forcing Christian scholars to reconsider their own sacred texts and traditions.

Premodern Jewish Conceptions of Jesus

Before the modern era there is relatively little in extant Jewish literature that refers to Jesus of Nazareth.[1] Passages that scholars think might refer to Jesus are often obscure, uncertain, and late. Some of the clearest references in the early era are found in the Babylonian Talmud. These eastern rabbis, being under Persian rule, were not threatened by the oppressive western Christian authorities and could write more frankly: "The majority of anti-Christian texts in this latter period (third to sixth centuries CE) are in the Babylonian Talmud. Here, too, these texts are an exceptionally small part of that vast compendium. The Babylonian Talmud recounts stories about the trial and crucifixion of Jesus (b.Sanh. 43a), Jesus' repudiation by his disciples (ibid.), Jesus' punishment in hell (b.Git. 57a), and the dishonesty of Christian judges (b.Shabb. 116a–b; parodying Mt. 5:14–17)."[2]

1. See Burton L. Visotzky, "Jesus in Rabbinic Thought," and Martin Lockshin, "Jesus in Medieval Jewish Tradition," in *The Jewish Annotated New Testament*, ed. Amy-Jill Levine and Marc Zvi Brettler (Oxford: Oxford University Press, 2011), 580–82.

2. Visotzky, "Jesus," in Levine and Brettler, *Jewish Annotated New Testament*, 580.

In the early medieval world critiques of Jesus came, perhaps not surprisingly, from Jews in the Islamic world. Claims of Jesus's divinity were disputed in a ninth-century work called "Polemic of Nestor the Priest." But perhaps the most famous or infamous work was *Toledot Jeshu*. Its origins are obscure, but it argued that Jesus was a sorcerer who pronounced the divine name to work his sorcery.[3] Such works have little or no value in reconstructing the "historical Jesus," but rather understandably expressed Jewish frustration at their mistreatment and marginalization under Christian powers.

For many if not most Jews, Jesus was a heretic who had abandoned his people. Given the nature of the Jews' relationship with the church and the constant attacks on them by western Christian authorities, it was hard to think otherwise. Christian claims for Jesus's divinity and the doctrine of the Trinity appeared to Jews to indicate that Christians had two or three gods in spite of their claims to be monotheists. If Jesus was the founder of Christianity, obviously he was the one who led the Christians away from the one true God into idolatry—a most heinous sin. Before the modern era there appeared to be little to commend Jesus of Nazareth to a faithful Jew.

The Question of the "Historical Jesus"

With the rise of rationalism and historical criticism, the histories and sacred scriptures of both Judaism and Christianity found themselves under increased scholarly scrutiny. Jesus himself was not exempt from such historical reappraisals. Albert Schweitzer famously called this mostly nineteenth-century phenomenon "the quest of the historical Jesus."[4] Schweitzer began the modern quest with the work of one Herman Samuel Reimarus (1694–1768), the son of a clergyman who had himself studied theology and would become part of the philosophical faculty at Wittenberg.[5] His *Apology or Defense of the Rational Worshippers of God* was only published in 1778, some ten years after his death. Most controversial was the section "On the Intention of Jesus and His Disciples." According to Reimarus, "Jesus was a pious Jew, dedicated to calling Israel to repentance in order to establish the kingdom of God on earth.

3. Lockshin, "Jesus," in Levine and Brettler, *Jewish Annotated New Testament*, 581.

4. Albert Schweitzer, *The Quest of the Historical Jesus*, trans. W. Montgomery, Susan Cupitt, and John Bowden (Minneapolis: Fortress, 2001).

5. Herman Samuel Reimarus, *Reimarus: Fragments*, ed. Charles H. Talbert, trans. Ralph S. Fraser (Philadelphia: Fortress, 1970), 2–4.

He did not intend to introduce novel teaching or found a new religion. As time went on Jesus made the fatal mistake of embracing political messianism. His miscalculated popular support, and his belief in divine intervention was misplaced. He died disillusioned with the God who had forsaken him (Mk. 15:34)."[6] Reimarus's work anticipated similar assessments of Jesus that would come from both Christian and Jewish authors in the coming centuries.

Especially important in the decades following the publication of Reimarus's groundbreaking publication were the seminal works of major German writers and theologians: H. E. G. Paulus, Friedrich Schleiermacher, and, especially, David Friedrich Strauss and his famous *The Life of Jesus Critically Examined.*[7] In general, these works rejected the miraculous, cast doubt on Jesus's resurrection, and denied or reshaped the nature of Jesus's divine consciousness. Strauss famously used the category of "myth" to explain the Gospels. Such works produced a cottage industry of responses from furious orthodox critics and enthusiastic supporters. Their impact is felt to this day.

While these debates were raging in the Christian world, significant changes were impacting the European Jewish world. Throughout Europe, Jews were to greater or lesser extents being "emancipated."[8] Jews were attending university and entering the professions in greater numbers than previously permitted. Large and ornate synagogues were being built in the great capitals of Europe, and urbane, sophisticated Jews were seeking to enter the European mainstream. Jewish historians and theologians were beginning to ask the same historical and theological questions of their texts and histories as Christians in Germany and elsewhere were of theirs. This led to a Jewish "quest of the historical Jesus." A key figure in this Jewish quest was Abraham Geiger.

Abraham Geiger's Jewish Jesus

Jewish emancipation was a two-edged sword. It made it possible for brilliant individuals like Geiger to get a first-rate classical education along with a traditional Jewish education, as he did, in Bible and Talmud.[9] Emancipation

6. Colin Brown, "Quest of the Historical Jesus," in *Dictionary of Jesus and the Gospels*, ed. Joel B. Green, Jeannine K. Brown, and Nicholas Perrin, 2nd ed. (Downers Grove, IL: InterVarsity, 2013), 718–56.

7. Brown, "Quest," 721–29.

8. Karesh and Hurvitz, "Emancipation," *Encyclopedia of Judaism*, 136–37.

9. On Geiger, see Susannah Heschel, *Abraham Geiger and the Jewish Jesus* (Chicago: University of Chicago Press, 1998), 23–49.

also meant that many Jews were leaving the practice of Judaism behind to fit in more with the cultures of Europe. From his synagogue in Breslau, Geiger began to lead a liberalization of Judaism that he thought would enable these sophisticated Jews to continue living as Jews and be successful in the gentile world. Geiger, considered the father of Reform Judaism, "wanted to eliminate from Judaism any ritual that separated Jew from non-Jew. He was mainly concerned with upholding Jewish ethical laws; any ritual that did not support the ethical laws was not needed, and served only to separate the Jew from the modern non-Jew. . . . Under Geiger's leadership Reform Jews rejected observance of Jewish dietary laws . . . wearing a *kippah* (head covering), and putting on *tefillin* (phylacteries)."[10]

But Geiger was also concerned to address the gentile world. His study of early Christianity and the life of Jesus suggested to him that Christian anti-Semitism was rooted in gross misunderstandings and misrepresentations of Judaism and even Christianity's key figure, Jesus of Nazareth. Geiger was particularly irritated with Christian depictions of the Pharisees. For Geiger the Pharisees represented not a crimped legalism but the source of the great humanist Jewish tradition: "If Judaism represents the essence of religion, the Pharisees must be the Jews par excellence. Geiger describes them as 'the kernel of the people.' They exemplify the highest level of religiosity. 'Their struggle was [for] the equality of all classes, their struggle was a struggle that in all times, where there is competence, repeats itself, a struggle against priesthood and hierarchy, against privilege of single classes, a struggle precisely for that which does not seek higher worth only in the external, but in the inner, religious character.'"[11]

Geiger's great hero was the towering first-century Rabbi Hillel. He saw Jesus himself as a Pharisee and a follower of Hillel, although he considered Hillel his superior. Jesus was an ordinary Pharisee, he argued, whose memory was corrupted under the influence first of "fantastical, uneducated Galilean Jews" and further corrupted by Hellenistic paganism.

> He was a Jew, a Pharisean Jew with Galilean coloring—a man who shared the hopes of his time and who believed that these hopes were fulfilled in him. He did not utter a new thought, nor did he break down the barriers

10. Karesh and Hurvitz, "Geiger, Abraham," *Encyclopedia of Judaism*, 168–69.

11. Heschel, *Abraham Geiger*, 148. Hereafter, page references to this work are given in parentheses in the text.

> of nationality. . . . He did not abolish any part of Judaism: he was a Pharisee who walked in the way of Hillel, did not set the decisive worth on every single external form, yet proclaimed "that not the least tittle should be taken from the Law; the Pharisees sit in Moses' seat, and what they speak, you should observe and obey." It is true that, if the accounts are faithful, when someone met him, he allowed himself to be carried away to trifling depreciatory expressions concerning one object or another, when he was opposed; but he never faltered in his original convictions. (149)

For Geiger there was nothing original or unique about Jesus. Like many before and since, he considered the true innovator in Christianity to be Paul of Tarsus. His was the corrupting influence that reshaped the Jesus movement into something that would appeal to a pagan, gentile audience. Geiger argued that it was the weakness and corruptness of the Greco-Roman world that made it ripe for conversion to early Christianity. "A man who was at the same time a god, was the center; but the manner of his appearance, the teaching connected with the belief in him, had impressed upon that new religion a character that had, until then, never appeared. It must have made a deep impression, acted as a caustic, and gave new excitement to the enervated souls. Thus, the doctrine of Christianity, in its third phase . . . penetrated into the heathen world . . . it was then Christianity completely severed from Judaism" (152). Geiger thus set a pattern of "rescuing" the Jewish Jesus from early Christian corruptions and reclaiming him for Judaism as a true heir of the irenic Pharisee Hillel.

According to Susannah Heschel, Geiger wrote to produce "a radically altered depiction of Judaism during the Second Temple and Mishnaic periods" (187). In this he was only partially successful. Christian scholars in Germany were receptive to his ideas regarding the Sadducees, Karaites, and Samaritans. But his prized goal of renovating the reputation of the Pharisees was a failure: "Geiger's contention regarding the nature of Pharisaism and the usefulness of Rabbinic texts as historical sources were rejected out of hand [and] his argument that Jesus was a Pharisee aroused hostility and claims that Geiger was expressing thereby a form of Jewish contempt for Christianity" (187).[12] It would take a century for most Christian scholars and theologians to begin to take Geiger's arguments about the Pharisees and Jesus seriously.

12. Heschel's entire chapter 7 bears close reading.

Joseph Klausner's Jesus of Nazareth

Jewish scholars continued to write about Jesus of Nazareth in the wake of Geiger's pioneering work.[13] For the English-speaking world, the liberal British Jew C. G. Montefiore was particularly important.[14] But by far the most important and famous early twentieth-century book on Jesus by a Jew was *Jesus of Nazareth* by Jacob Klausner.[15] Klausner is a complex and fascinating character. He was born in 1874 in present-day Lithuania, then a part of Imperial Russia.[16] He was a brilliant student, eventually securing a degree from Heidelberg. He was a passionate advocate of the recovery of Hebrew as a modern language and an ardent Zionist. He was particularly drawn to the study of the Second Temple period. Following World War I, he immigrated to Palestine and settled in Jerusalem. He taught for decades at Hebrew University, though he was disappointed not to be assigned to teach Jewish history.

His work on Jesus was an outgrowth of his interest in the Second Temple period. It created a stir among both Christians and Jews with praise and blame from both quarters. In *We Jews and Jesus*, Samuel Sandmel calls Klausner's work a "bad book," suggesting "his approach to the Gospels exhibits a unique capacity to have reviewed much of the Gospel scholarship and to have remained immune from reflecting on it; Klausner was the amateur Talmudist and amateur psychologist applying dilettantism rather whimsically to Gospel passages."[17] Klausner makes elaborate claims to historical objectivity and for his "scientific" approach.[18] David Sandmel, son of Samuel Sandmel, argues in his 2002 dissertation on Klausner that in reality Klausner's approach was anything but scientific and objective. "Severing Jesus from subsequent Christianity while simultaneously claiming him as an authentic Jew has strong polemical overtones. Christianity is reduced to a misguided faith based not on the real Jewish Jesus but on

13. Donald A. Hagner, *The Jewish Reclamation of Jesus* (Eugene, OR: Wipf and Stock, 1997), 60–71.

14. Samuel Sandmel, *We Jews and Jesus* (Woodstock, VT: Jewish Lights Publishing, 2006), 88–91.

15. Jacob Klausner, *Jesus of Nazareth: His Life, Times, and Teachings* (New York: Macmillan, 1926).

16. Samuel Werses, Meir Menden, and David Flusser, "Klausner, Joseph Gedaliah," *Encyclopedia of Judaism*, 215–17.

17. S. Sandmel, *We Jews and Jesus*, 92–93.

18. Klausner, *Jesus of Nazareth*, 10.

a fiction created by a diaspora Jew [Paul] and eventually accepted by millions of pagans."[19]

Klausner, according to David Sandmel, wanted to have his cake and eat it too. "Part of him wants to claim Jesus, while another part wants to find a flaw in Jesus that is irreconcilable with true Judaism."[20] Klausner's work is full of tensions and contradictions: "Jesus was both humble and tolerant, but on the other hand possessed a belief in his mission that verged on self-veneration. In his teaching he was a Pharisaic rabbi, but concerned with *haggada* rather than *halacha*; however, he invested himself with authority and unlike the Pharisees depended little on Scripture."[21] Although Klausner insisted on the Jewishness of Jesus and the unique influence of Palestine, he argued that there were serious points of disagreement between Jesus and Judaism. Although a Pharisee, his critique of the legal tradition of the Pharisees, particularly the "ceremonial law," opened the door for later abuses by the early Christians.[22]

Klausner also, in effect, critiqued the narrow focus of Jesus's ministry. His teaching was not sufficient to form a culture, to undergird a national project. His ethics were unrealistic: "ethical precepts like these can only appeal to priests and recluses . . . whose only interest is religion; while the rest of mankind all pursue a manner of life that is wholly secular or pagan."[23] Jacob Neusner echoes this latter critique in his *A Rabbi Talks with Jesus.*[24] According to David Sandmel, Klausner is conflicted. He appears to want "to expose Jesus as nothing more than an eccentric, misdirected, first-century Jew and to enshrine him as another of Judaism's gifts to humanity."[25]

Although Klausner's *Jesus of Nazareth* cannot claim the stature of David Strauss's *The Life of Jesus Critically Examined*, it produced a similar if smaller stir. It was praised and denounced by Christians and Jews alike. Some Jews thought him too friendly to Jesus and Christianity. Some Christians denounced his denial of Jesus's divinity. Careful reviewers critiqued Klausner's methodological inconsistencies, his Zionist lenses, and his at times odd

19. David Fox Sandmel, "Into the Fray: Joseph Klausner's Approach to Judaism and Christianity in the Greco-Roman World" (PhD diss., University of Pennsylvania, 2002), 77.

20. D. Sandmel, "Into the Fray," 77.

21. S. Sandmel, *We Jews and Jesus*, 91.

22. D. Sandmel, "Into the Fray," 183.

23. D. Sandmel, "Into the Fray," 190.

24. See Jacob Neusner, *A Rabbi Talks with Jesus* (Montreal: McGill-Queen's University Press, 2000).

25. D. Sandmel, "Into the Fray," 197.

psychologizing.[26] Whatever the flaws of Klausner's work, Donald Hagner rightly considers it one of the "outstanding representations of the Jewish perspective on Jesus."[27] According to David Sandmel,

> Before the publication of *Jesus of Nazareth*, few Christian scholars paid attention to Jewish scholarship or ancient Jewish literature bearing on the time of Jesus. . . . German scholarship, in particular, had constructed a Jesus in contrast to the Judaism of his day. Klausner was neither the first to offer a different perspective, nor did he single-handedly change the course of scholarship. However, the time of the publication of *Jesus of Nazareth* combined with the unique appeal of the author and the accessibility of the volume added support to the movement . . . toward a more balanced and inclusive approach to [Second Temple Judaism] that has become the standard in scholarship today.[28]

Although a flawed book, it is still worth reading today. For Klausner, even though the seeds of the later Christian break with Judaism are found within the thoroughly Jewish Jesus,

> In his ethical code there is a sublimity, distinctiveness and originality in form unparalleled in any other Hebrew ethical code; neither is there any parallel to the remarkable art of his parables. The shrewdness and sharpness of his proverbs and his forceful epigrams serve, in an exceptional degree, to make ideas a popular possession. If ever the day should come and this ethical code be stripped of its wrappings of miracles and mysticism, the Book of the Ethics of Jesus will be one of the choicest treasures of the literature of Israel for all time.[29]

Samuel Sandmel's We Jews and Jesus

Samuel Sandmel's *We Jews and Jesus* was published forty years after Klausner's book came out in English translation. A new edition of this justly famous work was published in 2006. It included a preface by Sandmel's son,

26. D. Sandmel, "Into the Fray," 204–7.
27. Hagner, *Reclamation*, 28.
28. D. Sandmel, "Into the Fray," 207.
29. Klausner, *Jesus of Nazareth*, 414.

Rabbi David Sandmel, setting the context of his father's work as a rabbi, scholar, and proponent of interfaith dialogue.[30] Samuel Sandmel was perhaps the first American Jew to do a doctoral degree on the New Testament. During his distinguished career he taught at Vanderbilt University, Hebrew Union College, and the University of Chicago. In addition to his book on Jesus he wrote *A Jewish Understanding of the New Testament, We Jews and You Christians*, and *The Genius of Paul*.[31]

Sandmel wrote during an era of radically changing relationships between Jews and Christians, especially in the United States. The postwar era with the horror of the Holocaust and the reestablishment of the State of Israel was bringing Jews and Christians into conversation as never before. Christian scholars were also beginning to ask questions about historic perceptions of Jews and Judaism and even beginning to reconsider how they had read and understood the Jewishness of both Jesus and Paul. Jews and Christians were also beginning to read one another's texts and scholarship more seriously and carefully. Sandmel's education as a New Testament scholar had been rooted in the more skeptical Protestant scholarship of the early and mid-twentieth century. Donald Hagner, who admired and respected Sandmel, argued that he was "the most pessimistic of Jewish scholars" on the question of a truly historical reconstruction of Jesus and was "by no coincidence . . . the Jewish scholar most influenced by radical Protestant Gospel criticism."[32]

For Sandmel, and most critical scholars of that era, it was impossible to disentangle the views of the early church, the prejudices of the Evangelists, and the actual words and deeds of Jesus: "The Gospels are not telling about the man that scholarship seeks, but about the human career of a divine being. To search the Gospels for the man seems to me to involve a distortion of what is in the Gospels. New Testament scholarship has not succeeded in isolating the man Jesus, Jesus the Jew."[33]

This does not mean that Sandmel despairs of saying anything about Jesus. He sees in Jesus "a Jewish loyalty at variance with the views of both Christians and Jewish partisans who through opposing motives that cancel

30. D. Sandmel, "Preface to the New Edition," in S. Sandmel, *We Jews and Jesus*, vii–xiii.

31. S. Sandmel, *A Jewish Understanding of the New Testament* (Cincinnati: Hebrew Union College Press, 1956); *We Jews and You Christians: An Inquiry into Attitudes* (Philadelphia: Lippincott, 1967); *The Genius of Paul* (Philadelphia: Fortress, 1979).

32. Hagner, *Reclamation*, 75.

33. S. Sandmel, *We Jews and Jesus*, 108. Hereafter, page references to this work are given in parentheses in the text.

each other out, detach him from Judaism" (109). Jesus, in other words, was a loyal Jew, but it is likely his loyalty would not fit the schemes of either his Christian or Jewish interpreters. Sandmel argues that Jesus "believed that the end of the world was coming soon" and that he himself was "the Messiah, and that those scholars who deny this are incorrect" (109). He sees "no originality in the teaching of Jesus." Nevertheless, "there is more in the teachings of Jesus that I admire than I do not" (43). Jesus was "a teacher, a Jewish loyalist, a leader of men, with a personality unquestionably striking enough to be a leader." He was, Sandmel concludes,

> a martyr to his Jewish patriotism. So many Jews became martyrs at the hands of later Christians that his martyrdom seems to us perhaps too unexceptionable for special notice. We Jews have so suffered, because Christians in ages past made us suffer, that it is difficult for us to acknowledge that Jesus suffered unusually. I believe that he did. There is to my mind both in the Epistles of Paul and in the Gospels the recurrent note that the career of Jesus was one of triumph; I can certainly acknowledge that martyrdom partakes of the overtone of triumph. Yet the dominant note to me of his career is overwhelmingly one of pathos, of sympathy, that a man, with the normal frailties of men, aspired and labored and worked, and yet experienced defeat. (110)

Hagner, though disagreeing with Sandmel's assessment of Jesus, argues that, however pessimistic he is about the historical reliability of the Gospels, Sandmel "is fairer to the documents themselves" than many of his fellow Jewish (and, for that matter, Christian) scholars.[34] In the decades since the publication of Sandmel's works on Jesus and Paul, scholarship has moved on. Some of the distinctions he used to explain the peculiarities he sees in both Jesus and Paul (e.g. the differences between "Palestinian" and "Diaspora" Jews) have been challenged. An enormous amount of work has been done on Second Temple Judaism that would no doubt cause Sandmel to reassess some of his conclusions and perhaps some of his skepticism. But one important point remains: both Jews and Christians continue to distort both the Gospels and historical criticism to find a Jesus congenial to their preestablished convictions. In the process they fail to hear the voice of Jesus *as the Gospels present him.* This failure Jacob Neusner set out to address in his striking book *A Rabbi Talks with Jesus.*

34. Hagner, *Reclamation,* 269.

Jacob Neusner's A Rabbi Talks with Jesus

Jacob Neusner was a prodigious and controversial scholar whom some credit (or blame) for bringing Judaism into the wider world of religious studies.[35] He wrote or edited some 900 volumes and "translated, analyzed, and explained virtually the entire rabbinic canon," making "Judaism and its study available to scholars and laypeople of every background and persuasion."[36] Like Sandmel he was interested in interfaith dialogue and produced works addressing both Christians and Muslims. In *A Rabbi Talks with Jesus*, Neusner approaches both the Gospels and Jesus uniquely. He is certainly not unaware of the historical challenges of a straightforward reading of the Gospels, but he takes the Gospel of Matthew's account of Jesus and his teaching seriously. He imagines himself as an ordinary Galilean Jew following Jesus around as he teaches and heals. He is both attracted to and perplexed by this charismatic figure. He interviews both Jesus and his disciples. In the end he parts ways with Jesus with some sadness and disappointment.

In 2007 Pope Benedict XVI published *Jesus of Nazareth.*[37] In the course of his discussion of the Sermon on the Mount the Pope makes a startling assertion about Neusner's book: "more than other interpretations known to me, this respectful and frank dispute between a believing Jew and Jesus, the son of Abraham, has opened my eyes to the greatness of Jesus's words and to the choice that the Gospel places before us."[38] High praise indeed for a Jewish reader of the Christian Gospels. The Pope cites Neusner extensively throughout his volume and agrees that Neusner has rightly discerned why a believing Jew would reject Jesus's message both then and now.[39] What was it about Matthew's Jesus that Jacob Neusner found so troubling?

Neusner's problem with Jesus is not so much that his Torah teaching is different from that of other Jews or even that he is critical of certain Pharisees. It is not, in other words, that Jesus is the wrong sort of Jew. Neusner's problem is first with *the claims Jesus makes for himself*, and second *that Jesus does not address Israel, "eternal Israel," as a whole.* To take the second charge first, Neusner argues that

35. W. Scott Green, "Neusner, Jacob," *Encyclopedia of Judaism*, 15:124–25.

36. Scott Green, "Neusner, Jacob."

37. Joseph Ratzinger, Pope Benedict XVI, *Jesus of Nazareth* (New York: Doubleday, 2007).

38. Ratzinger, *Jesus*, 69.

39. Ratzinger, *Jesus*, 103–27.

> Jesus addresses not eternal Israel, but a group of disciples. His focus time and again, defines a limited vision. But eternal Israel comes forth from Sinai, not a collection of families, but something more: a collectivity that adds up to much more than the sum of the parts, much more than families, but rather, a people, a nation a society: "a kingdom of priests and a holy people." As the teaching unfolds, I begin to wonder whether there is not a missed mark here—not a sin, but not a target squarely hit either. Jesus on the mountain addresses not "all Israel," this one and that one, individuals and families.[40]

This critique is similar to that of Klausner, who did not find in Jesus a way to found a *nation*, to sustain a *people.* Jesus does not help the Jewish *people* know how to live as a people, offering his message to heroic individuals rather than the people as a whole. Later Neusner concludes,

> Jesus and his disciples went their way, off the stage of Israel's enduring life, and I would have thought then, as I think now, that Israel was right to let them take their leave. For theirs—at least in the spectacle of Matthew's picture—was a message for individuals, but the Torah spoke to us all. Leave home, follow me; give it all up, follow me; take up your (personal) cross, follow me—but then what of home, what of family and community and the social order that the Torah had commanded Israel bring into being? (157)

These are apt questions. In the next chapter when we address Jewish views of Paul these questions will emerge again. In one sense this was *the* question Paul was addressing. The question of whether gentiles should be circumcised and keep the Law of Moses was not simply a question of what practices gentiles should observe. It was a question of whether and how a *particular* tradition could become *universal.* Were gentiles to be integrated into what Neusner calls "eternal Israel" or were both "eternal Israel" and gentile Jesus followers now part of a new, universal community? If so, how is one to understand the covenant with Abraham and, especially, the Sinai covenant made with Israel? If Neusner is correct and Jesus was suggesting through his teachings that his movement was to go beyond "eternal Israel," the questions and struggles of the early church found in Paul make perfect sense.

But how was it that Jesus's teachings created such a movement? If he

40. Neusner, *A Rabbi,* 45. Hereafter, page references to this work are given in parentheses in the text.

was simply, as many Jewish and Christian scholars have asserted, an orthodox Jewish teacher, how did Christianity emerge? Many have, of course, suggested that it was Paul who was the hero (or villain) of the piece. He was the real "founder" of Christianity. Neusner would suggest that it was Jesus himself who paved the way for the moves that Paul and others would make. Paul is correct to locate a "new age" not simply in Jesus's teaching, death, and resurrection but in Jesus's self-understanding. For well over a century both Jewish and Christian scholars have tried to make a distinction between the "Jesus of the Gospels" and the "Christ of faith." Neusner begs to differ:

> I find myself unable to recognize that abyss between the man, Jesus, and the Christ of faith. Jesus makes sense . . . only in the setting of the Christ of faith. When we compare what he says on the commandment to honor parents with what other sages have to say, indeed, when we find our way to an appropriate comparison—one in which each side of the equation really does correspond to the other—we see in the Jesus of history precisely the Christ of faith that, for twenty centuries Christians have found as much in Matthew's Jesus as in Paul's Christ. (69)

To Neusner's Galilean peasant on the road with Jesus it seems that Jesus sees himself as Moses: "Sir, how can you speak on your own say-so, and not out of the teachings of the Torah given by God to Moses at Sinai? It looks as though you see yourself as Moses, or more than Moses?" (48). Not only this, but this perplexed Galilean will later ask one of Jesus's disciples, "'And is your master God?' For, I now realize, only God can demand of me what Jesus is asking" (68). So, for Neusner, it is not simply that Jesus imagined himself to be messiah or was waiting, along with the rest of Israel, for the kingdom of God. He was claiming to be God's singular spokesperson, a second Moses, and, more than that, he would be the agent of a new community made up of individuals; a community that would leave "eternal Israel" behind. He would not simply reinterpret Torah, he would *replace* Torah (94). For Neusner, Paul and the later Christians came by their "Christology" and communal struggles honestly. They were very much rooted in the life and teaching of Jesus himself (69).

Assessing the "Jewish Jesus"

From the very beginning of their investigations of Jesus of Nazareth, Jewish scholars have understandably defended and corrected misapprehensions of

Judaism past and present. They have defended the Pharisees against perceived slanders by Christian scholars. They have explained the character and function of Jewish literature and Jewish practices. They have sought to set Jesus in the clear historical context of Second Temple Judaism. They have had, in other words, an *apologetic* purpose. And in this they frequently called upon Jesus as an ally: Jesus was a lover of Torah; exclusively sent to the "lost sheep of the house of Israel"; was looking forward to the redemption of Israel and reasoned and argued like any other first-century rabbi. For many, Jesus's teachings and actions were neither unusual nor original. There was nothing special or even particularly profound in his teaching. He was exceeded, in fact, by such revered figures as his contemporary, Hillel. So how is his influence explained?

For many Jews and, for that matter, Christians, the villain (or hero) of the piece was the apostle Paul. He took the simple teachings of Jesus intended for the restoration of Israel and the proclamation of the coming kingdom of God and turned the Jesus movement into a Hellenistic mystery religion. Either Paul was a Diaspora Jew who had not been sufficiently exposed to the "purer" Judaism of Palestine or he was deeply compromised by Hellenism and paganism, or overly eager to make gentile converts. As a result, he imposed upon Jesus a divine consciousness he lacked and a messianic role he never claimed. The Gospel writers are also seen as problematic—again, this is true of both Jewish and Christian scholars. They told the story of Jesus through the later lenses of myth and ecclesial theology, making it difficult if not impossible to disentangle the "real Jesus" from the church's "Christ."

Both Samuel Sandmel and Jacob Neusner argued that these attempts at disentangling were not only largely fruitless but unfair to the Gospel writers. In pursuing what was essentially a literary archeological dig, both Jewish and Christian scholars frequently failed to grapple adequately with the Jesus the various Gospels actually depict. The "historical Jesus" that results from these studies is often an ersatz Jesus. And however strongly critical scholars warn against creating a Jesus in one's own image or a Jesus who fits one's own political or religious vision, nearly all of them end up with a Jesus congenial to their purposes. Neusner further insisted that he found it difficult if not impossible to separate the "historical Jesus" from the "church's Christ." In fact, what made Jesus unique and enabled his disciples to found an enduring movement were the claims Jesus made for himself and not an identity later imposed upon him. Jesus claimed to take the place of Torah, to be a new Moses, and even to speak for God himself. *It was the person of Jesus himself* that made his teaching and vision to endure. Neusner found himself unable to follow Jesus. He thought it right that Israel rejected him. But he recognized that this was no ordinary rabbinic teacher. The Jesus of "critical" scholars both Jewish and Christian is, in comparison to the Jesus of the Gospels, hardly compelling. It is to Neusner's credit that he recognizes this and gives Matthew's Jesus a fair hearing.

It is clear that Jewish work on Jesus and early Christianity will continue. Jewish scholarship has forced Christians to take more seriously the actual historical and religious setting of Jesus's life and ministry. Perhaps to their own surprise Jewish scholars have found in Jesus a "brother" they can understand and appreciate, if not follow. To many Jews, Jesus makes sense. The apostle Paul is another matter. But in the next chapter we will examine how even Judaism's old enemy is now being reconsidered. This, for many Jews, is a much harder reappraisal. Paul seems the ultimate antagonist who despised Torah and relegated Israel to the dustbin of history. Rehabilitating him is a tall order. But even with Paul, seeing him with Jewish eyes has cast new light on his life and letters.[41]

QUESTIONS FOR DISCUSSION

1. How did Jews come to "reclaim" Jesus as one of their own?
2. What are the differences between the Jesus of Klausner, Sandmel, and Neusner?
3. What is problematic for both Sandmel and Neusner with the Jesus of critical scholarship?

41. In addition to the books considered in this chapter, I would recommend the following Jewish works on Jesus: Amy-Jill Levine, *The Misunderstood Jew* (New York: HarperCollins, 2006); Amy-Jill Levine, Dale C. Allison, and John Dominic Crossan, eds., *The Historical Jesus in Context* (Princeton: Princeton University Press, 2006); Amy-Jill Levine, *Short Stories by Jesus: The Enigmatic Parables of a Controversial Rabbi* (New York: HarperOne, 2015); David Flusser with R. Steven Notley, *The Sage from Galilee* (Grand Rapids: Eerdmans, 2007); Paul Fredricksen, *From Jesus to Christ*, 2nd ed. (New Haven: Yale University Press, 2000); Geza Vermes, *Jesus the Jew* (Philadelphia: Fortress, 1981). Vermes has authored a number of additional books on Jesus's life and teaching.

FURTHER READING

Heschel, Susannah. *Abraham Geiger and the Jewish Jesus.* Chicago: University of Chicago Press, 1998.

Klausner, Joseph. *Jesus of Nazareth: His Life, Times, and Teaching.* Translated by Herbert Danby. New York: The Macmillan Company, 1926.

Levine, Amy-Jill. *The Misunderstood Jew: The Church and the Scandal of the Jewish Jesus.* New York: HarperCollins, 2006.

Neusner, Jacob. *A Rabbi Talks with Jesus.* Rev. ed. Montreal: McGill-Queen's University Press, 2000.

Sandmel, Samuel. *We Jews and Jesus: Exploring Theological Differences for Mutual Understanding.* Preface by David Sandmel. Woodstock, VT: Jewish Lights, 2006.

CHAPTER 10

Paul the Jew

If others think they have reasons to put confidence in the flesh, I have more: circumcised on the eighth day, of the people of Israel, of the tribe of Benjamin, a Hebrew of Hebrews; in regard to the law, a Pharisee; as for zeal, persecuting the church; as for righteousness based on the law, faultless.

—Philippians 3:5–6

It . . . becomes incomprehensible why Paul fought against the law with all the determination of his faith, as if it were a life and death struggle for his religious existence.

—Leo Baeck

Although Paul called himself a Pharisee, one cannot say that he was clearly identified with Palestinian Judaism before his conversion.

—Samuel Sandmel

Jesus, yes! Paul, never!

—Richard Rubenstein

Paul is unambiguously Jewish—ethnically, culturally, morally and theologically.

—Pamela Eisenbaum

Paul was evidently proud of his Jewish identity. Writing to the Philippians, he provides an impressive Jewish resume. But he follows up this list by insisting that all of this was nothing, indeed "garbage" in comparison to "knowing Christ Jesus my Lord" (Phil 3:7–11). This would not exactly endear him to his Jewish readers. Throughout history Paul has frustrated and enraged Jews. His attitude to the law has historically perplexed them. Of course, it is fair to say that he has perplexed many of his Christian interpreters as well. But it was more than the law. To many Jews it seemed that he had rejected Judaism entirely and assigned it to the dustbin of history. In fact, "the historical Jewish attitude to Paul has been presented as portraying him as the 'ultimate enemy of Judaism . . . [and] supreme apostate,' 'its greatest heretic,' 'the quintessential convert . . . [and] a villain,' 'the arch self-hating Jew,' and the one 'single-handedly responsible for two thousand years of Christian brutality toward Jews.'"[1] Making a case for Paul as a faithful Jew would seem, to say the least, an uphill battle. But remarkably a number of contemporary Jewish and Christian scholars are doing exactly that.[2]

Paul has always had his critics. They dogged his steps in his own day and lurk behind the more polemical parts of his letters. Paul was not gentle with them: "As for those agitators, I wish they would go all the way and emasculate themselves!" (Gal 5:12). He seemed to relish the conflict. And even his friends found Paul at times perplexing: "Paul's . . . letters contain some things that are hard to understand, which ignorant and unstable people distort, as they do the other Scriptures" (2 Pet 3:16). In spite of the difficulty of his teachings, Paul became for Christians *the* apostle. His letters would make up a significant portion of the New Testament, and for what was to

1. Daniel R. Langton, *The Apostle Paul in the Jewish Imagination* (New York: Cambridge University Press, 2010), 23–24.

2. For ongoing reassessments of Paul as a Jew, in addition to the works cited in this chapter, see Michael Bird, *An Anomalous Jew: Paul among Jews, Greeks, and Romans* (Grand Rapids: Eerdmans, 2016); Mark D. Nanos and Magnus Zetterholm, eds., *Paul within Judaism: Restoring the First-Century Context to the Apostle* (Minneapolis: Fortress, 2015); Reimund Bieringer and Didier Pollefeyt, eds., *Paul and Judaism: Crosscurrents in Pauline Exegesis and the Study of Jewish-Christian Relations* (London: T&T Clark, 2012); Gabriele Boccaccini and Carolos Segovia, eds., *Paul the Jew: Rereading the Apostle Paul as a Figure of Second Temple Judaism* (Minneapolis: Fortress, 2016).

This chapter is a revised version of my essay, "(Re)reading Paul: Jewish Reappraisals of the Apostle to the Gentiles," in *Doing Theology for the Church: Essays in Honor of Klyne Snodgrass*, ed. Rebekah A. Eklund and John E. Phelan Jr. (Eugene, OR: Wipf and Stock, 2014), 79–93.

become Christianity, his vision, however misunderstood, would become normative. The church's greatest thinkers from Augustine in its formative years, to Luther and Calvin during the Reformation, to Karl Barth in the modern era, laid their theological superstructures on a Pauline (or at least a supposed Pauline) foundation.

The amount of scholarly work done on Paul in the last two hundred years alone has been staggering. And yet, the apostle remains as elusive and perplexing as ever. Paul has been both vilified and adored—even by Christians. He is seen as a misogynist and a liberator, as patriarchal and egalitarian, as Christianity's first great theologian and as the betrayer of the simple message of Jesus. And Paul continues as a, or perhaps *the*, battleground for Jews and Christians. For Jews Paul has not been the *apostle*, but the *problem.* While since the nineteenth century, at least, Jewish scholars have been able to reappropriate Jesus as a Jew, Paul is another matter. For many, if not most Jews, it has been, as Richard Rubenstein puts it, "Jesus, yes! Paul, never!"

The Jews' problem with Paul is not simply that his approach to the Jewish law is unacceptable and that his understanding of Jesus's nature perplexing but, according to Jonathan Sacks, the former Chief Rabbi of the United Synagogue in the United Kingdom, he was "the architect of a Christian theology which deemed that the covenant between God and his people was now broken. . . . Pauline theology demonstrates to the full how remote from and catastrophic to Judaism is the doctrine of a second choice, a new election. No doctrine has cost more Jewish lives."[3] Christian theologian George Lindbeck would, to a certain extent, agree, insisting that "the understanding of the church as the replacement of Israel is the major ecclesiological source of Christian anti-Judaism."[4] Many contemporary scholars would *not* agree that Paul is the architect of the "replacement theory" or "supersessionism."[5] To read Paul in this way is, for many, to misread him and ultimately misuse him.

In spite of all this, over the last few decades some Jewish thinkers have been taking another look at Paul. In this they have been aided by Christian scholars' willingness to reappraise their own views of Judaism in general and first-century Judaism in particular. Christian reappraisals of Judaism

3. Cited in Daniel R. Langton, "Paul in Jewish Thought," in Levine and Brettler, *Jewish Annotated New Testament*, 586.

4. George Lindbeck, "What of the Future? A Christian Response," in *Christianity in Jewish Terms*, ed. Tikva Frymer-Kensky et al. (Boulder, CO: Westview Press, 2000), 358.

5. Lindbeck, "What of the Future?," 358–59.

have led in turn to a reappraisal of Paul's thought by Jews and Christians alike. Paul's Jewishness and his commitment to the Jewish people are being reconsidered. Daniel Langton, however, offers this sobering assessment: "In contrast to the figure of Jesus, who has, in the main, been reclaimed as a good Jew of one sort or another, Paul remains an object of hostility and suspicion. While there have been a number of scholarly exceptions to this rule, one should not expect him whose likening the Law to 'sin' and 'death' still echo down the centuries to enjoy a more general Jewish reclamation any time soon."[6] Nevertheless, in what follows I will consider six books written by Jewish scholars and published in the last sixty years that reclaim Paul the Jew to one extent or another.

Paul in the Nineteenth and Early Twentieth Centuries

The nineteenth century in Europe brought with it the development of sophisticated forms of anti-Semitism. This was not the anti-Semitism of superstitious peasants, but the intellectualized loathing of Jews by both Christian and anti-Christian thinkers. In some cases it is what has been called "anti-Christian anti-Semitism." The Jews were blamed not only for being Jews, but also for giving the world Christianity and particularly the Roman Catholic Church. This strain of anti-Semitic thought was also frequently anti-Paul. Hans Joachim Schoeps cites two examples of this, one Christian, one definitely not Christian. Friedrich Nietzsche despised Paul. For him Paul was the "eternal Jew *par excellence.*" According to Nietzsche, Paul "shattered essential and original Christianity." He was "a genius in hatred, in the vision of hate, in the ruthless logic of hate. What has not this nefarious evangelist sacrificed to his hatred. He sacrificed first and foremost the Savior, he crucified him on his cross." Paul, "that morbid crank," is responsible for the "falsifications of true Christianity."[7]

For Paul de Lagarde, renowned German orientalist, biblical scholar, and anti-Semite, Paul was responsible for the "transformation and falsification of original Christianity." De Lagarde shows himself an heir of Marcion when he writes: "Paul brought into the church for us the Old Testament, under the influence of which the gospel, as far as was possible, perished. Paul favored

6. Langton, "Paul in Jewish Thought," 587.

7. H. J. Schoeps, *Paul: The Theology of the Apostle in Light of Jewish Religious History*, trans. Harold Knight (Philadelphia: Westminster, 1959), 276.

us with the Pharisaic mode of interpreting scripture, which proves everything from everything, and has ready resources for discovering in the text the meaning that has to be discovered, then boasting that it follows only the word of scripture. Paul brought home to us the Jewish theory of sacrifice and all that depends on it; the whole Jewish understanding of history was foisted on us by him."[8] From this it is a short road to the Aryan Jesus and truncated Bible of the National Socialists.[9]

Such analyses led to the search for alternative origins for Paul's thought outside of Judaism. Surely Paul, Protestantism's great hero, did not bring about the destruction of the gospel. Surely Paul did not foist on the early church the perverse and peculiar ways of the Jews. Nineteenth- and early twentieth-century liberalism sought to disconnect Paul from both the Jews and Christian orthodoxy. For the so-called history of religions school, Paul's theological sources were not Jewish at all, but Hellenistic. Many Jewish thinkers found this analysis congenial. Paul's strange deviations from "normative" Judaism could be explained by his being a heterodox Hellenistic Jew. According to Langton, "As German Christian scholarship emphasized Paul's role in injecting pagan elements into the religion of Jesus, it comes as no surprise that the prominent American Reform rabbi, Kaufman Kohler . . . found Gnostic influences and Hellenistic religions to account for many of Paul's teachings."[10]

Martin Buber

Perhaps the most important early-twentieth-century figure to attach Paul to Hellenism was Martin Buber. In his book *Two Types of Faith,* Buber "argued that Judaism and Christianity represented two entirely different forms of religion, even if they were historically intertwined."[11] Hellenistic Judaism, Buber argued, distorted Judaism by associating the God of Israel with the notion of "fate." "For Paul (and other Hellenistic Jewish writers), the fusion of Hellenistic fate with the Jewish belief in God created an enormous chasm between human beings and God, and, thereby, a need for reconciliation."[12]

8. Schoeps, *Paul,* 277.

9. See Susannah Heschel, *The Aryan Jesus: Christian Theologians and the Bible in Nazi Germany* (Princeton: Princeton University Press, 2010).

10. Langton, "Paul in Jewish Thought," 586.

11. Pamela Eisenbaum, *Paul Was Not a Christian: The Original Message of a Misunderstood Apostle* (New York: HarperCollins, 2009), 57.

12. Eisenbaum, *Paul Was Not,* 57.

Although Paul's theology was rooted in a form of Judaism, it was a distorted form.[13] Buber was not the only scholar to follow this path.

Leo Baeck

For Leo Baeck, the religion of Paul was a form of "Romanticism." He wrote, "Christianity accepted the inheritance of ancient—Greek and oriental—romanticism. At an early date, the traditional national religion of the Hellenic lands had been joined by a victorious intruder, probably from the north: another religion, phantastic and sentimental—the Dionysian or Orphic cult. . . . It had all the traits of romanticism: the exuberance of emotion, the enthusiastic flight from reality, the longing for experience."[14] Paul combined this Hellenistic romanticism with the power of Judaism to create a merger of "Orient and Occident" (62). In Paul's thought "Judaism and paganism were now reconciled and brought together in romanticism, in the world of mystery, of myth, and of sacrament" (64).

According to Baeck, faith, for Paul, is

> so completely everything that down here nothing can be done for it; . . . all "willing or running" is nonsensical and useless. The salvation that comes through faith is in no sense earned, but wholly received; it comes only to those for whom it was destined from the beginning. God effects it, as Luther later explained the words of Paul, "in us and without us." Man is no more than the mere object of God's activity, of grace or of damnation; he does not recognize God, God merely recognizes him; he *becomes* a child of redemption or of destruction, "forced into disobedience" or raised up to salvation. (65–66)

He concludes, "The conception of the finished man which appears here—truly the child of romanticism for which truth is only a living experience, became one of the most effective ideas of the entire Pauline doctrine" (67).

Jewish scholar and seminary professor Pamela Eisenbaum argues that there is a flaw in Baeck's analysis: "Baeck's understanding of Paul's theology

13. An excerpt from Buber's *Two Types of Faith* is found in *Jewish Perspectives on Christianity*, ed. Fritz A. Rothschild (New York: Crossroad, 1990).

14. Leo Baeck, "Romantic Religion," in Rothschild, *Jewish Perspectives*, 60–61. Hereafter, page references to this work are given in parentheses in the text.

is entirely mediated by Luther. Of course, his description of this form of religion reveals his negative assessment. When Baeck says that the person is 'the object of virtue and of sin,' he means that this Romantic form of religion, 'Pauline religion,' is one in which people are not understood as ethical beings, because they are not subjects who act, but rather are objects who are acted upon, either by God's grace or by sin, and thus they are not accountable for their actions."[15] There could be nothing more at variance with traditional Judaism than this. But is it true to Paul's thought? Eisenbaum does not think so. Eisenbaum argues that Baeck and Buber's views of Paul were distorted because "they took for granted the typical German Protestant understanding of Paul. . . . For Luther and the German Protestants who followed in his interpretive path, Paul's theology represents the pinnacle of human religiosity; for Buber and Baeck, it is the nadir. Buber and Baeck used Paul as a lens to critique Christianity, just as their Christian contemporaries used him to critique Judaism."[16]

The apparent ethical indifference, the vision of a passive human acted on by either fate or God without reference to their own actions, was anathema to Jews such as Buber, Baeck, and, another critic of Paul, Joseph Klausner. The last concludes his book *Jesus and Paul* with these words: "It is permissible to say—of course with certain reservations—that it was not Jesus who created (or more correctly, founded) Christianity, but Paul. Jesus is the source and root of Christianity, its religious ideal, and he became all unconsciously its lawgiving prophet." But, he continues, it was Paul who "made Christianity a religious system different from both Judaism and paganism, a system mediating between Judaism and paganism but with an inclination toward paganism."[17]

Paul at Mid-Century

In the middle of the twentieth century, things began to change. It may seem that the so-called new perspective on Paul sprang newly formed from the minds of Krister Stendahl and E. P. Sanders. But this overlooks the significant work of scholars such as Johannes Munck of Denmark and W. D. Davies of Wales, who carried out much of his teaching and scholarship in the United

15. Eisenbaum, *Paul Was Not*, 56–57.

16. Eisenbaum, *Paul Was Not*, 58.

17. Joseph Klausner, *From Jesus to Paul* (New York: Macmillan, 1943), 581–82.

States.[18] Stendahl, in his foreword to Munck's *Christ and Israel*, says, "It was reading this book more than twelve years ago which for the first time opened my eyes to Paul and his mission."[19] Munck laid the groundwork for Stendahl's programmatic essays in *Paul among Jews and Gentiles* and for the substantial rethinking of Paul's understanding of the Jewish people reflected in the "new perspective."[20] Both scholars took Paul's Jewish and even rabbinical background seriously. At the same time, Jewish scholars were also beginning a reappraisal of Paul, in part in reaction to the work of Stendahl and Davies.

H. J. Schoeps

H. J. Schoeps's *Paul: The Theology of the Apostle in Light of Jewish Religious History* came out at the same time as Munck's *Paul and the Salvation of Mankind*. Schoeps was a German Jew who taught at Erlangen University. For Schoeps, "The theology of the apostle Paul arose from overwhelmingly Jewish religious ideas. In the age of tense Messianic expectation, Saul the Pharisee, following the religious convictions which came to him as a result of his Damascus experience and believing that the Messianic event had occurred, corrected traditional eschatology and refashioned it by means of the apocalyptic teaching about two aeons."[21]

Paul's messianic expectations were all understandable within the Judaism of his day. On the other hand, Schoeps argued that Paul's Christology came from a combination of Jewish and pagan ideas, and that "by his doctrine of Christ's divinity Paul oversteps the bounds of Judaism, which has never known the idea of a divine Messiah, and has never attributed soteriological functions to the Messiah" (259).

Paul also misconstrued the law by separating the Torah from the covenant. "The law as a whole, resting on the covenant relationship, had ceased to be a living and personal possession for Paul the Diaspora Pharisee and Septuagint Jew." This led Paul to the question, "senseless for a Jew, whether the

18. See Johannes Munck, *Christ and Israel*, trans. Ingeborg Nixon (Minneapolis: Fortress, 1967) and *Paul and the Salvation of Mankind*, trans. Frank Clarke (Richmond, VA: John Knox, 1959); W. D. Davies, *Paul and Rabbinic Judaism* (London: SPCK, 1958) and *Jewish and Pauline Studies* (London: SPCK, 1984).

19. Munck, *Christ and Israel*, vii.

20. Krister Stendahl, *Paul among Jews and Gentiles* (Philadelphia: Fortress, 1976).

21. Schoeps, *Paul*, 259. Hereafter, page references to this work are given in parentheses in the text.

law as a whole was 'fulfillable'" (260). For Schoeps, then, however important Paul's Jewish origins, his Diaspora Judaism and identification of Jesus as messiah led him to misconstrue the law and God's covenant with Israel. Schoeps further argued that Paul "fixed the relationship of the new people of God to the old by maintaining that the election had been transferred to God's new Israel, the Messianic church formed of Jews and Gentiles" (261). So, for Schoeps, however Jewish Paul was, however rooted his expectations were in the messianic expectations among the Jews of his day, he fundamentally misrepresented the Jewish position on the law and the covenant, and believed that God had thrust the "old people" of God aside for the new.

Samuel Sandmel

A second important voice was that of Samuel Sandmel, who published *The Genius of Paul* in 1958. As noted in the previous chapter, Sandmel was an American Jew with an unusual academic pilgrimage. According to his son David Fox Sandmel, Dean Harvie Branscomb III of Duke encouraged Samuel Sandmel to pursue a degree in New Testament.[22] Sandmel subsequently taught at Vanderbilt University and Hebrew Union College—Jewish Institute of Religion where he served as professor of Bible and Hellenistic Literature (it being unlikely that Hebrew Union College would have a professor of New Testament). Shortly before his untimely death in 1979, he moved to the University of Chicago as the Helen A. Regenstein Professor of Religion. He was a major interpreter of Christianity for the Jewish world and made a significant contribution to Jewish-Christian dialogue. He was, perhaps not surprisingly, a close friend of Krister Stendahl, who called him "a gift of God to both Jews and Christians."[23]

Samuel Sandmel insists that "Paul in his own mind has not deviated from Judaism; it is these opaque Jews who do not share his conviction who have deviated and gone astray."[24] Nevertheless, Sandmel wonders, "what was there about Paul or his environment which questioned the continued validity, indeed the eternity of the Law of Moses?" (37). Sandmel, like Schoeps,

22. See David Sandmel's biographical essay on his father in S. Sandmel, *We Jews and Jesus*, vii–xiii. The original publication date of *We Jews and Jesus* was 1965.

23. S. Sandmel, *We Jews and Jesus*, ix.

24. S. Sandmel, *The Genius of Paul*, 37. Hereafter, page references to this work are given in parentheses in the text.

thinks it is Paul's origin in Diaspora Judaism that accounts for his misunderstanding and abandonment of the law. Diaspora Judaism, remote from the temple, steeped in pagan surroundings, faced challenges unthinkable in remote Jerusalem. In fact, "the living Judaism of Paul and his contemporaries was scarcely identified with the Biblical religion" (46). Paul (and Philo, for that matter) reduced the Law, Torah, to "laws." But, "to Palestinian Jews, and their spiritual descendants, the word *Torah* never had so restricted a connotation; they equated *Torah* with our word 'revelation.' While they would have conceded that the Torah was a revelation which *included* 'law,' they would properly have denied that revelation and 'law' were interchangeable" (47).

Sandmel is not impressed with W. D. Davies's attempts to locate Paul's thought in Palestinian Judaism. "Davies' book is an admirable book, indeed, a great one—and one with which I disagree almost one hundred per cent" (223). He sees little connection between Paul and what would become rabbinic Judaism. For Sandmel, as for Schoeps, Paul, the Diaspora, Hellenized Jew, fundamentally misunderstands his own tradition and therefore offers a distorted view of the function of Torah within Judaism.

Schoeps and Sandmel represent a generation of Jewish scholars who were more willing to acknowledge Paul's essential Jewishness. Both clearly located Paul's thought within the Judaism of his day, even if that Judaism, Diaspora Judaism, deviated from "normative Judaism" in significant ways. In this way they can account for Paul's essential Jewishness as well as for the ways Paul misunderstands and misrepresents the Torah and the covenant. Subsequent scholarship, however, has questioned the once ironclad distinction between Hellenistic and Palestinian Judaism. According to John J. Collins, due to the extensive Hellenization within Palestine, "the old distinction between 'Palestinian' Judaism and 'Hellenistic' (= Diaspora) Judaism has been eroded to a great degree in modern scholarship."[25] He continues, "Diaspora Judaism, no less than its counterpart in the land of Israel, had its frame of reference in the Torah."[26] Paul's apparent deviations from Judaism cannot be explained with reference to his origins in the Diaspora. Furthermore, in subsequent years both Jewish and Christian scholars began to wonder if Paul's apparent misreading of the Law and the covenant had more to do with Protestantism than Hellenism.

25. John J. Collins, "Early Judaism in Modern Scholarship," in Collins and Harlow, *Eerdmans Dictionary of Early Judaism*, 16–17.

26. Collins, "Early Judaism," 16–17.

New Perspective for Jews and Christians

The story has by now been told many times. A sea change in the way Paul is read began with a slim book of essays by Krister Stendahl. He argued that Paul had been misunderstood for generations because he had been read through the experience of Luther and "the introspective consciousness of the west."[27] Paul did not agonize over his inability to keep the law; in fact, he had a rather "robust conscience"—or, as my former teacher A. C. Sundberg used to put it, a "robust ego" (81). Furthermore, his so-called conversion was more of a "call" than a conversion. Paul was not a Jew who "converted" to another religion or *started* a new religion. He was a Jew who, like the prophets of old, experienced the call of God (7–23). Protestants, Stendahl insisted, have read Paul the Jew not in his own terms, but in the terms of Martin Luther's internal struggles with late medieval Catholic piety (83–86).

Stendahl's book was based on lectures he did in the 1960s, although the book itself was not released until 1976. A year later, E. P. Sanders published *Paul and Palestinian Judaism: A Comparison of Patterns of Religion.* The book changed the conversation on Paul forever. He argued that Christians have misread Judaism as a religion of legalists determined to pursue salvation via "works righteousness." On the contrary, "God chose the Jews as his elect people and gave them the Torah to live by as their covenant obligation. God rewards obedience and punishes transgression. The Torah includes provisions for forgiveness and atonement. Those who maintain their covenant membership through obedience to Torah will be saved by God's grace." Jews, in other words, did not believe that their works made them righteous before God in the sense that Christians had claimed. It was the mercy of God's election of and his covenant with Israel that assured Israel of salvation.[28] Sanders thus called the entire framework of Protestant Pauline interpretation into question.

Sanders's book, along with his subsequent works, produced a cottage industry for Sanders fans and Sanders critics. As Pamela Eisenbaum puts it, "Sanders's book is one of those rare works whose influence on subsequent scholarship is difficult to overstate."[29] Christian scholars like James Dunn and

27. Stendahl, *Paul among Jews and Gentiles*, 78–95. Hereafter, page references to this work are given in parentheses in the text.

28. Mark A. Chancey, "Sanders, Ed Parish," in Collins and Harlow, *Eerdmans Dictionary of Early Judaism*, 1191–92; E. P. Sanders, *Paul and Palestinian Judaism* (Philadelphia: Fortress, 1977).

29. Eisenbaum, *Paul Was Not*, 64.

N. T. Wright, taking their cue in part from Sanders, reassessed every part of Paul's thought in light of Sanders's reassessment of Judaism. And Jewish scholars have done the same. Scholars such as Alan Segal, Daniel Boyarin, Mark Nanos, and Pamela Eisenbaum have been able to come to Paul from a fresh Jewish perspective, assured of a more favorable hearing from both Jews and Christians than they may have had before Stendahl and Sanders.

Alan Segal

Alan Segal was for many years a professor of Jewish studies at Barnard College. He is best known for his book *Paul the Convert*, published in 1990.[30] Segal points out that Paul "is one of only two Pharisees to have left us any personal writing" and the "only first century Jew to have left confessional reports of mystical experiences (2 Cor 12:1–10)." In fact, Paul "should be treated as a major source in the study of first century Judaism."[31] A bit later he says that in light of this "it is a pity that few Jewish writers have attempted to understand Paul. Because of the polemical context that forms the basis of Paul's letters, Christianity has been sadly bereft of all but the most daring of Jewish scholars' observations of Paul."[32] Thankfully, since Segal published his volume in 1990, this has begun to change.

Segal focuses on Paul's mystical/apocalyptic experience, arguing for a link in Judaism between mystical experience and apocalyptic speculation. Paul, for Segal, represents this important stream of Judaism. He even suggests that Paul's Christology is not alien to the Judaism of his day: "the identification of Jesus with the manlike appearance of God is both the central characteristic of Christianity and understandable within the context of Jewish mysticism and apocalypticism."[33] Segal not only sees continuity with contemporary Jewish apocalyptic mysticism, he sees a profound connection with what would become rabbinic Judaism. He explores Romans 11, a text that will become increasingly important in Jewish assessments of Paul. He notes the strange ambiguity in Romans 9–11. On the one hand, "Paul implies that only those who accept Christ will be saved," but he never actually says

30. Alan F. Segal, *Paul the Convert* (New Haven: Yale University Press, 1990).

31. Segal, *Paul the Convert*, xi.

32. Segal, *Paul the Convert*, xv.

33. Segal, *Paul the Convert*, 44. See also Daniel Boyarin, *The Jewish Gospels* (New York: The New Press, 2012); and Peter Schafer, *The Jewish Jesus* (Princeton: Princeton University Press, 2012).

so. "He surprisingly asserts the rabbinic notion that all Israel will be saved (11:26)." He continues, "rather than merely abandon the unbelieving members of the Jewish community, Paul asserts that God's promises to them are still intact: 'For the gifts and call of God are irrevocable' (11:29)."[34]

Paul's angry words in Galatians about agitators who are attempting to impose the law on his gentile converts are changed to words of alarm in Romans when he begins to see what could happen to the Jews in a majority gentile community (see Rom 14). Christians who read Paul's words in defense of a threatened minority in a situation of a now comfortable majority misuse those words and undermine Paul's purpose. For Segal, then, Paul's "conversion," his Christology, and even his understanding of the covenant are firmly rooted in the varieties of first-century Judaism, including the stream that lead to rabbinic Judaism.

Daniel Boyarin

Daniel Boyarin, in his 1994 volume *A Radical Jew*, echoes Segal's concern that Paul has been neglected as a source for exploring first-century Pharisaic Judaism.[35] He would also like "to reclaim Paul as an important Jewish thinker. On my reading of the Pauline corpus, Paul lived and died convinced he was a Jew living out Judaism. He represents, then, one option which Judaism could take in the first century" (2). Nevertheless, Paul represents a serious challenge to Boyarin as a Jew. Paul's vision was a universal one that included both Jews and gentiles. "While Paul's impulses toward the founding of a non-differentiated, non-hierarchical humanity were laudable in my opinion, many of its effects in terms of actual lives were not. In terms of ethnicity, his system required that all human cultural specificities—first and foremost, that of the Jews—be eradicated, whether or not the people in question were willing." The outcome of this would be inevitably the "merging of all people into the dominant culture" (8).

All of this places Boyarin in an almost intolerable tension: "the claims of difference and the desire for universality are both—contradictorily—necessary; both are equally problematic." The necessity of tolerance, solidarity,

34. Segal, *Paul the Convert*, 280.

35. Daniel Boyarin, *A Radical Jew: Paul and the Politics of Identity* (Berkeley: University of California Press, 1994), 2. Hereafter, page references to this work are given in parentheses in the text.

and equality in a world characterized by difference cannot be underestimated. But "just as surely the insistence on the value of ethnic—even genealogical—identity that the Rabbis put forth cannot be ignored or dismissed because of the reactionary uses to which it can and has been put" (10). Boyarin wants to reclaim Paul as an "internal critic of Jewish culture" and not as the founder of a new religion. To view him as a founder of a new religion is to "marginalize" him, when his critique is needed for both Judaism and Christianity (12).

Boyarin appreciates the rereading of Paul "undertaken in the wake of the treatises of Krister Stendahl, W. D. Davies, and his student E. P. Sanders. . . . Perhaps, not surprisingly, this book is part of the movement to thoroughly discredit the Reformation interpretation of Paul and particularly the description of Judaism on which it is based." Boyarin argues that this reading is not only unsupportable in scholarly terms, but an "ethical scandal as well, and one that does Christianity no credit." Paul does offer a critique of Judaism, he says, but not "the slanderous libel that Luther accused him of" (11). It should be said that later Jewish scholarship on Paul would not be so sure that Paul was the sort of critic of Jewish particularity Boyarin imagined him to be. Both Eisenbaum and Nanos are convinced that Paul was perfectly happy for Jews to remain Jews in all their particularity in spite of Paul's insistence that Jews and gentiles are now "one in Messiah."

Mark Nanos

One of the most interesting contemporary Jewish interpreters of Paul is Mark D. Nanos, who teaches at the University of Kansas. His book *The Mystery of Romans*, published in 1996, was the winner of the National Jewish Book Award for Jewish-Christian Relations.[36] Nanos denies that Paul rejected the continuing election of Israel or sought to undermine Jewish adherence to Torah. "This study," Nanos writes, "finds the Paul behind the text of Romans to be a practicing Jew—'a good Jew'—albeit a Jew shaped by his conviction in Jesus as Israel's Christ, who did not break with the essential truths of the Judaism(s) of his day, who was committed to the restoration of his people as his first and foremost responsibility in the tradition of Israel's

36. Mark D. Nanos, *The Mystery of Romans* (Minneapolis: Fortress, 1996). See also Mark D. Nanos, *The Irony of Galatians* (Minneapolis: Fortress, 2002), and Mark D. Nanos, ed., *The Galatians Debate* (Peabody, MA: Hendrickson, 2002).

Deuteronomic prophets."[37] We are a long way here from Baeck, Buber, and Klausner, or, for that matter Schoeps and Sandmel.

For Nanos, the problem that Paul is facing in Romans is very different from the one he is addressing in Galatians. In the latter text the threat is from Jews who want to make sure Paul's gentile converts are properly integrated into Israel through circumcision and Torah keeping. In Romans, Paul is concerned with a majority gentile community of Jesus followers who are marginalizing the Jews in their community. Nanos insists that the Jews Paul is concerned with in Romans are not Jewish followers of Jesus, but Jews proper. He imagines that the gentile and Jewish followers of Jesus are still part of the synagogues of Rome. Overly liberated gentiles not only create offense but undermine Paul's mission "to the Jew first."[38]

The most succinct account of Nanos's understanding of Paul is found in the *Jewish Annotated New Testament.*[39] He argues that Paul continued to be a Torah-practicing Jew. He did not think that Jews who did not yet follow Jesus as messiah were "outsiders to God's family." Jewish privileges were intact as far as Paul was concerned (see Rom 9:4–5). Nanos thinks that Paul expected that all Jewish Christ followers would remain faithful to their Jewish covenant identity by the observance of Torah.[40] He even argues that both Paul and Jewish synagogue officials understood him to be under the authority of the synagogue since Paul was subjected to the discipline of the synagogue (see 2 Cor 11:24). Nanos makes the idiosyncratic suggestion that the "powers that be" in Romans 13 are not the imperial governing authorities, but the Roman synagogue authorities.[41] In short, as Jewish New Testament scholar Amy-Jill Levine once said to me, "Mark Nanos's Paul is so Jewish my daughter could date him."

Pamela Eisenbaum

Pamela Eisenbaum's book *Paul Was Not a Christian* has already been cited several times in this article. Eisenbaum teaches New Testament at Iliff School of Theology in Denver. Like Boyarin, Eisenbaum sees Paul address-

37. Nanos, *Mystery of Romans*, 9.

38. Nanos, *Mystery of Romans*, 12–16.

39. Nanos, "Paul and Judaism," in Levine and Brettler, *Jewish Annotated New Testament*, 551–54. See also his commentary on Romans in the same volume.

40. Nanos, "Paul and Judaism," 552.

41. Nanos, *Mystery of Romans*, 289–336.

ing issues critical to her self-understanding as a Jew: "I have come to regard Paul as a Jew who wrestled with an issue with which many American Jews wrestle: how to reconcile living as a Jew with living in and among the rest of the non-Jewish world."[42] Also, like Boyarin, she is wary of Paul's solution but understands the power of critique. Like Nanos she believes "Paul was a Jew before and after his experience of Christ." She agrees with Stendahl that Paul was "called rather than converted" (3). She insists "Paul's belief in Jesus would not have branded him a heretic—a pain in the neck perhaps, but not a heretic" (8).

On the two major issues of Torah and covenant she argues first that Paul's audience was made up of gentiles, so everything he says about the law applied to *them*, unless specified otherwise. As many have noted, Paul's morality, even as it applied to his gentile converts, was thoroughly Jewish and rooted in the Torah. Although there were certain aspects of Torah observance that Paul thought unnecessary for his gentile converts, "Paul never speaks against Jews' observance of Torah—never" (224). Furthermore, the law is not meant to condemn humanity; it serves a positive pedagogical function. She argues that Paul is not as cynical about human capacity to obey God and do good as Luther, Calvin, and their followers would be. From this it follows that "the doing of good works is not the opposite of faith" (233). Finally, "Gentiles do not need to be circumcised to be in accord with Torah. But they *are* obligated to be in accord with Torah." Nanos and Eisenbaum, unlike many Jewish readers of Paul before them, see Paul not as an opponent and critic of the law, but as an upholder of the law, for both Jews and gentiles in their separate ways.

To the question "Does God have two plans of salvation, one for Jews and another for gentiles?" Eisenbaum seems to say both yes and no. There is only one God who shows mercy on all. The right question is not "How will I be saved? Rather it is [Paul's] answer to the question, how will the world be redeemed and how do I faithfully participate in the redemption?" (252). Paul does not, she argues, "collapse Jew and Gentile into one generic mass of humanity. All will be kin; none will be strangers but the Gentile will not become Jew, and the Jew will not become Gentile." She concludes, "I think everyone can agree that Paul's message was about grace. Why is it necessary to put limits on this grace? Let's let Paul's message of grace stand as it is" (255).

42. Eisenbaum, *Paul Was Not*, 3. Hereafter, page references to this work are given in parentheses in the text.

Assessing the Jewish Paul

How has Pauline scholarship in general and the Christian world in particular benefited from a Jewish reappraisal of Paul? Alan Segal, as noted above, thought it a pity that so few Jewish writers had attempted to understand Paul. This reluctance to study the one many thought their great enemy left Christianity "sadly bereft of all but the most daring of Jewish scholars' observations of Paul." The more favorable views of Jews and Judaism emerging in the wake of concerted interfaith dialogue following the horrors of World War II, along with the reappraisal of Paul's relationship to Judaism by Stendahl, Sanders, and company, have made it possible for many more Jewish scholars to study and comment on Paul and the rest of the New Testament. The distinguished list of contributors to the *Jewish Annotated New Testament* bears eloquent witness to this new openness. Scholars such as Shaye J. D. Cohen, Adam Gregerman, Susannah Heschel, Amy-Jill Levine, and David Fox Sandmel are making significant contributions to the understanding of the New Testament. For this Christian scholars can only give thanks. Reading Paul and, for that matter, any part of the New Testament "with Jewish eyes" can provide fresh insight into that profoundly Jewish text.[43] The Jewish context of Paul's life and thought is no less important than that of Jesus.

Pamela Eisenbaum alludes to a second benefit of the Jewish reading of Paul. Eisenbaum viewed Paul through her American Jewish experience—an experience that includes teaching at a Christian institution. As a Diaspora Jew and then a Jew following Jesus as messiah, Paul faced a similar struggle and question as Eisenbaum. How does one live as a Jew in a culture that does not support one's way of being? Paul's attempts to carve out a space for Jews and gentiles to worship and work together in the shadow of a frequently hostile Roman imperial system offered Eisenbaum a model for reflection and emulation. As Eisenbaum profited from considering Paul's struggle to remain faithful to his vision and his God, Christians in an increasingly secular and hostile environment can benefit from the long experience of marginalization suffered by the Jews. Christianity has throughout history struggled to maintain itself as a minority culture. The Jewish experience of faithfulness in the most hostile of circumstances offers Christians hope. For Christians, reading Paul from the

43. See Levine and Brettler, *Jewish Annotated New Testament.*

margins could be a salutary experience. This might mean reading Paul less as a theologian and more as a pastor struggling to hold his churches together and enable them to bear witness and show love in increasingly hostile situations.

Third, the recent Jewish interpreters of Paul have also shown that both Christians and Jews share additional common struggles and questions. As Boyarin notes, both traditions struggle with the tension between universalism and particularity and the risk of being absorbed by the majority culture. Both constantly ask what it means in individual circumstances to be obedient to God. Both wonder what it might mean for the world to be redeemed and what their respective communities might do to collaborate with God in that redemption. Both wonder how God can honor the covenant promises made to Israel while including the gentiles in the conversation.

Finally, both groups can now acknowledge that the New Testament actually belongs to both communities. For Jews, the New Testament bears witness to the nature of Judaism in the first century. It contains books written by Jews and for Jews facing situations not unfamiliar to contemporary Jews. In light of this, Christians must recognize that they are "reading someone else's mail" and could use a partner to add the other half of the conversation. Jews are still justly wary of Paul and his Christian readers. But courageous and competent Jewish readers of Paul are helping both Jews and Christians to see the Apostle to the Gentiles in a different and more positive light. Perhaps both communities can profit from reading Paul together, learning from his passion and wisdom in an increasingly hostile political and religious setting.

QUESTIONS FOR DISCUSSION

1. Why is Paul more difficult for Jews to reclaim than Jesus?
2. What is the "new perspective" on Paul and why is it important and controversial?
3. Both Boyarin and Eisenbaum speak with appreciation and concern of Paul's universal vision. From a Jewish standpoint, what is problematic about it?

FURTHER READING

Boyarin, Daniel. *A Radical Jew: Paul and the Politics of Identity*. Berkeley: University of California Press, 1994.

Eisenbaum, Pamela. *Paul Was Not a Christian: The Original Message of a Misunderstood Apostle*. New York: HarperCollins, 2009.

Sandmel, Samuel. *The Genius of Paul: A Study in History*. Philadelphia: Fortress, 1979.

Segal, Alan F. *Paul the Convert: The Apostolate and Apostasy of Saul the Pharisee*. New Haven: Yale University Press, 1990.

CHAPTER 11

The Rabbis

When the temple was destroyed, Abraham came before God, weeping, plucking out his beard, tearing out the hair of his head, striking his face, rending his garments and with ashes on his head; then he went to the temple and mourned and cried.

—*Lamentations Rabbah*, Introduction, 24

It would have been better if the earth had not produced Adam, or else, when it had produced him, had restrained him from sinning. For what good is it to all that they live in sorrow now and expect punishment after death? O Adam, what have you done? For though it was you who sinned, the fall was not yours alone, but ours also who are your descendants. For what good is it to us, if an eternal age has been promised to us, but we have miserably failed.

—4 Ezra 7:116–18

All Israel will have a share in the world to come. The biblical proof is Isa. LX, 21, "They shall all be righteous." The following have no share in the world to come. He who says the Resurrection of the dead is not indicated in the Law . . . , he who says the Law is not from heaven . . . , and the Epicureans.

—*b. Sanhedrin* 10:1, 2, 96b, and 105a

[Vespasian asked] "Are you Johanan b. Zakkai? What shall I give you?" He replied, "All I ask of you is that I may go to Jabneh [Yavneh], and teach my disciples there, and fix a place of prayer there, and carry out all the commandments." He answered, "Go, and all that pleases you to do there, do."

—Avot of Rabbi Nathan 4:11b–12a

Shaye J. D. Cohen has argued that before the destruction of the Second Temple in 70 CE, Judaism was "sectarian."[1] During the Greek and Roman periods, and especially in connection with the rule of the Hasmoneans, internal conflicts had festered. Separatist groups, frustrated with the direction of their leaders in Jerusalem, had clashed with kings and priests. Some had fled to the wilderness to await the final intervention of God on their behalf. Others had stayed in Jerusalem and fought it out. In the Diaspora some Jews clung faithfully to their sacred texts and traditions, some assimilated, and some, like Philo of Alexandria, attempted a synthesis of Greek philosophy and Jewish Torah. Other Jews, in Palestine and the Diaspora, were impatient with the quietism and waiting. They hoped by their activism, even violence, to prod God into action. By the first century CE these various groups had coalesced into the well-known Pharisees, Sadducees, Essenes, and Zealots. Surely there were others now lost to history.

When the Jewish rebellion against Rome broke out in 66 CE, Jews found themselves in conflict with not only the Roman legions but also their fellow Jews. While the Romans were building siege works to reduce the walls of Jerusalem to rubble, Jewish factions were engaging in a nasty civil war within the city. The great prize was the Temple Mount.

> The militant revolutionaries, who had weapons and experience in using them . . . staged a violent coup d'état in the Winter of 67/68, seizing the Temple Mount, appointing a high priest, and killing the high priests, Ananus son of Ananus, Jesus son of Gamala and other leaders of the first government. . . . Once in control, the militants began systematically eliminating opponents, but the two main rebel leaders . . . soon quarreled. . . . The city was divided into three areas, and in the factional battles many Jews were killed, and the city's food reserves were destroyed. Thus, the city and its swollen population were severely weakened when Titus began the siege during Passover, 70 C.E.[2]

The lessons of this horrendous rebellion and its brutal aftermath were not lost on the Jews who picked up the pieces in its wake. Both rebellion and sectarianism threatened the very existence of the Jewish people. New forms

1. Shaye J. D. Cohen, "The Significance of Yavneh: Pharisees, Rabbis and the End of Jewish Sectarianism," *HUCA* 55 (1984): 17–53.

2. Jonathan J. Price, "Revolt, First Jewish," in Collins and Harlow, *Eerdmans Dictionary of Early Judaism*, 1146–49.

of individual, communal, and institutional life needed to focus on ways to live within the commands of Israel's God while dominated by the gentiles.

These lessons did not sink in immediately. Some sixty years after the first rebellion, another attempt to throw off Roman authority also failed, with even more devastating results. But beginning with Rabbi Yohannan Ben Zakkai and his followers in the seaside community of Yavneh, a new direction was mapped out. Cohen argues that the new approach would entail

> the creation of a society which tolerates disputes without producing sects. For the first time Jews "agreed to disagree." The major literary movement created by the Yavneans and their successors testifies to this innovation. No previous Jewish work looks like the Mishnah because no previous Jewish work, neither biblical nor post-biblical, neither Hebrew nor Greek, neither Palestinian nor diasporan, attributes conflicting legal and exegetical opinions to named individuals who, in spite of their differences, belong to the same fraternity. The dominant ethic here is not exclusivity but elasticity.[3]

According to Cohen, the destruction of the temple taught Jewish leaders that sectarianism was dangerous and destructive. If the Jews could not learn to "agree to disagree," they might not survive. But the destruction of the temple also eliminated the very thing that engendered a great deal of the conflict: the temple itself.

Much of the sectarian conflict of the Second Temple era was over how the temple was to be managed. Who should be in charge? Who should be high priest? What ritual practices should be followed? What purification rites should be practiced? Which calendar should be followed? The Essenes and the Qumran sectarians had definite ideas about all of these things. When God intervened on their behalf, their sect would rule in a purified temple with a purified priesthood. The Sadducees, the dominant temple aristocracy, surely thought their priests and rituals were to be preferred. Even the Pharisees existed in part because of their insistence on particular ritual and purity practices associated with the temple.[4] As noted above, the first thing the revolutionaries did when they seized the Temple Mount was kill the old high priests and appoint a new one. The temple was at the heart of it all.

3. Cohen, "Significance of Yavneh," 29.

4. See Roland Deines, "Pharisees," in Collins and Harlow, *Eerdmans Dictionary of Early Judaism*, 1061–63.

But now the temple was gone. A new way needed to emerge to be faithful to God's covenant or Israel would not survive. "The new goal," Cohen writes, "was not the triumph over other sects but the elimination of the need for sectarianism itself. As one tannaitic midrash remarks, . . . 'Do not make separate factions . . . but make one faction together.'"[5] Israel became a community of *dispute* rather than a community of factions. The rabbis would not always agree. They would argue fiercely with one another. But rather than driving out their opponents, the rabbis would include them, argue with them, and even learn from them. This was the genius of the movement that began in Yavneh and continues to this day.

The Rabbinic Tradition

Yohanan Ben Zakkai, Yavneh, and the Tannaim

It didn't happen overnight. Although their ranks were depleted by war, famine, and despair, neither the Sadducees, Essenes, Zealots, nor, certainly, the Pharisees disappeared entirely. The Bar Kokhba rebellion alone makes it clear that many Jews were still hoping to drive out the Romans and reestablish their own state. Apocalyptists, such as the Ezra of *4 Ezra* in the second century CE, were still receiving direct revelations from God regarding the fate of Israel.[6] The later rabbis would denounce both rebellions and direct revelations from God as dangerous threats to the integrity and survival of the Jewish people. They were both the result of and continuing source of sectarianism. As time went on, the emerging Jesus movement within Judaism became itself a sect that intended to replace, if not destroy, Judaism and the Jewish people. While this threat was not likely apparent to Yohanan Ben Zakkai and his disciples, it certainly became clear as the decades passed. And it was clear to those sages that the Jewish people needed a new source of unity and cohesion.

According to tradition, Yohanan Ben Zakkai was a leading Pharisee in the decades before the destruction of the temple in 70 CE.[7] He is credited

5. Cohen, "Significance of Yavneh," 29.

6. *4 Ezra* is a Jewish work set in the Babylonian exile but actually written in Hebrew or Aramaic at the end of the first century CE about the same time as the book of Revelation. See Karina Martin Hogan, "Ezra, Fourth Book of," in Collins and Harlow, *Eerdmans Dictionary of Early Judaism*, 623–26.

7. Ra'anan Boustran, "Yohanan Ben Zakkai," in Collins and Harlow, *Eerdmans Dictionary of Early Judaism*, 1355–56.

with enabling the survival of Judaism in the wake of the temple's destruction and the end of the sacrificial system that had so dominated Jewish faith and practice. According to a famous story in the *Avot de Rabbi Nathan*, Yohanan Ben Zakkai's escape from war-torn Jerusalem was dramatic.[8] As the story goes, Rabbi Yohanan pleaded with the defenders of Jerusalem to surrender to the Romans, save the city and the temple, and many thousands of lives. But they refused. General, soon to be Emperor, Vespasian, had heard that Yohanan was "a friend of the emperor." His mission a failure, Rabbi Yohanan had his disciples put him in a coffin and smuggle him out of the city:

> The gatekeeper said, "What is this?" They said, "A corpse is in it, and, as you know, a corpse must not be left in the city overnight," so they said, "If it be a corpse, carry it forth." So they carried him forth and brought him to Vespasian. He said, "Are you R. Johanan b. Zakkai? What shall I give you?" He replied, "All I ask of you is that I may go to Jabneh [Yavneh], and teach my disciples there, and fix a place of prayer there, and carry out all the commandments." He answered, "Go, and all that it pleases you to do there, do."[9]

Robert M. Seltzer tells the traditional story of Rabbi Yohanan's accomplishments at Yavneh: "In the town of Yavneh, near the Judean seacoast, a rabbinic blueprint for Jewish survival was articulated. . . . Although rabbinic Judaism took as its central task the development of the legal component of Torah, it was also the fulfilment of an essential implication of classical prophecy: that the religious life does not depend on a functioning sacrificial cult but on ethical and penitent action in the mundane world."[10] According to Seltzer, at Yavneh the term *rabbi* came into common usage, the teachings of the schools of Hillel and Shammai were collected, the canonization of Scripture was completed, a more precise form of the daily prayers was developed, and some of the observations associated with the temple and Jewish festivals were transferred to the synagogue and Sanhedrin.[11] Additionally, an ordination procedure for

8. On the story in *Avot of Rabbi Nathan* or "The Fathers according to Rabbi Nathan," see Jacob Neusner, *Invitation to Midrash* (New York: Harper & Row, 1989), 225–33.

9. *Avot Rab. N.* 4:11b–12a in Montefiore and Loewe, *Rabbinic Anthology*, 266.

10. Seltzer, *Jewish People*, 245–46.

11. Seltzer, *Jewish People*, 247.

rabbis was introduced and the Sanhedrin "assumed supreme legislative and regulatory functions, such as the right to control the date of the New Year and leap months."[12]

Many of these things were undoubtedly accomplished by the emerging rabbinic community at Yavneh. But some contemporary scholars contend that this picture of a proactive, authoritative rabbinical assembly is a bit too neat. Although the work was begun at Yavneh, some of it took many decades to complete and perhaps some of it (e.g., canonization) had already been substantially accomplished. Shaye Cohen writes, "All that is known of Yavneh is based on the *disjecta membra* of the Mishnah and later works, all of which were redacted at least a century after the events."[13] Elsewhere he suggests, "Most of this reconstruction has unraveled in recent years." But this does not diminish the significance of Yavneh, Rabbi Yohanan, or the work they did there, whether or not it included everything on Seltzer's list: "the significance of Yavneh lies in the fact that the rabbinic sages after the destruction of the Temple began the process that would, almost a century later, produce the Mishnah. That book became the basis of a new and distinct kind of Judaism, a Judaism that would endure one way or another from that day to this. . . . This is an accomplishment."[14]

These early sages were called "the Tannaim." According to Rabbi Adin Steinsaltz, "the name *tanna* means one who studies, repeating and handing down what he has learned from his teachers."[15] The tannaim were the great collectors and organizers of the oral tradition. The period of the tannaim began in the last years of Hillel and Shammai and ended with the editing and publication of the Mishnah. The rabbis of Yavneh and those who followed them began the process of shedding sectarianism and taking up a new means of community formation. It would be the oral tradition represented finally in the Mishnah that replaced the temple at the center of Jewish life. In collecting and organizing this material the tannaim were not afraid to let even the dissident voices be heard. In the generations following, this new approach would be vital as the Jewish people faced yet another crisis that threatened their very survival. In the midst of this conflict one of the Jewish people's most important teachers and martyrs emerged: Rabbi Akiva.

12. Seltzer, *Jewish People*, 247.

13. Cohen, "Significance of Yavneh," 29.

14. Shaye J. D. Cohen, "Yavneh," in Collins and Harlow, *Eerdmans Dictionary of Early Judaism*, 1355.

15. Adin Steinsaltz, *The Essential Talmud*, trans. Chaya Galai (New York: Basic Books, 2006), 49.

From the Bar Kokhba Rebellion to the Amoraim

The Babylonian Talmud records a story of a heavenly journey and experience of time travel by Moses:

> When Moses ascended on high [to receive the Torah] he found the Holy One, blessed be He, sitting and tying knots on the letters. [Moses] said to Him, "Lord of the Universe, what are those for?" He replied, "After many generations a man will be born called Aqiva ben Joseph; he will infer stacks of laws from each of these marks." [Moses] said to Him: "Lord of the Universe, show him to me." He said, "Move back!" [Moses] went and sat in the eighth row [of Aqiva's school], but could not make sense of what they were talking about and grew faint. When [the disciples] reached a certain point [in the discussion], they asked [Aqiva], "Master, on what do you base this?" He replied, "It is Torah [received by] Moses at Sinai." Moses was reassured.[16]

This story not only illustrates the greatness of Akiva, so great that even Moses grows faint at his teaching, but it demonstrates the process of the rabbis—the inference of "stacks of laws" from both the Written and Oral Torah. It also makes clear that the rabbis thought the Written and Oral Torah and the "stacks of laws" they inferred went back to Moses himself.

According to tradition, Akiva came late to the study of Torah. He was a simple man in his 40s when he fell in love with the daughter of a wealthy man. His father-in-law immediately disowned his daughter. She, however, insisted that Akiva leave to study Torah.[17] In spite of his age and his ignorance, he became the most celebrated scholar of his time. His efforts to collect and organize what he had learned became the basis for the work of Rabbi Judah the Prince on the Mishnah. According to a later tradition Rabbi Judah said of Rabbi Akiva, "To what may Rabbi Akiva be compared? To a worker who goes out with his basket. He finds wheat and puts it in to his basket, barley and puts it in, spelt and puts it in, beans and he puts them in, lentils and he puts them in. When he arrives home he separates out the wheat, barley, spelt, beans and lentils. This is what Rabbi Akiva did. He arranged the Torah rings by rings."[18] Akiva

16. *b. Menah.* 29b in Solomon, *The Talmud*, 591.

17. For what follows see Benyamin Lau, *From Yavneh to the Bar Kokhba Revolt*, vol. 2, *The Sages: Character, Content and Creativity*, trans. Ilana Kurshan (Jerusalem: Maggid Books, 2011), 191–208.

18. *Avot Rab. N.* 18 in Lau, *From Yavneh*, 202.

was continuing the work of Yohanan Ben Zakkai and the sages of Yavneh. But in one sense he was very unlike Rabbi Yohanan. According to tradition, when rebellion against Rome came, he supported it.

The beginning of the second century CE saw Jewish riots and rebellions in Alexandria, Cyprus, and Cyrenaica between 115 and 117. But a more serious revolt broke out in the land of Israel. It was led by one Simeon Bar Kosiba, who was given the name Bar Kokhba, "Son of a Star." Hailed as messiah by many, Simeon managed to defy Rome and establish a Jewish state. According to the Palestinian Talmud, Akiva hailed Bar Kokhba as messiah and was brutally martyred by the Romans. Some modern scholars dispute these assertions, but Akiva nonetheless became a model for faithfulness to Torah in the face of death.[19] After a brutal invasion by the Roman legions of the emperor Hadrian, Bar Kokhba's rebellion was crushed. Judah in particular was ravaged. Tens of thousands of Jews were killed, and many more tens of thousands were sold into slavery.

The emperor Hadrian's defeat of Bar Kokhba had a devastating effect on the Jews of the land of Israel. They were forbidden to reside in Jerusalem, which became a pagan city. For a time they were forbidden to circumcise their sons or teach Torah. Hadrian was known as a second Antiochus Epiphanes. The center of rabbinic life moved north to Galilee. Hadrian's successor, Antoninus Pius, rescinded his harsh decrees and allowed a measure of Jewish self-government: "Under Rabban Simeon ben Gamaliel II (first half of the second century C.E.) and later under Rabbi Judah the Prince (latter half of the second and beginning of the third century C.E.), the editor of the Mishnah, the patriarchate and other institutions of the Jewish community reached their height. Taxes poured into the patriarchal coffers even from the Diaspora, where the emissaries of the rabbis of Palestine attempted to foster the spread of tannaitic Judaism."[20]

Rabbi Judah the Prince (or Judah ha-Nasi) is a towering figure in rabbinic Judaism. He was the son of Rabbi Simeon ben Gamaliel II and "'Rabbi' par excellence in rabbinic literature. . . . [He] was a quasimonarchical personage, a scholar of great stature, and a pivotal figure in the history of rabbinic law."[21] His major accomplishment was the refining and redacting of the oral teachings earlier collected by Rabbi Akiva and others. This was

19. Azzan Yadin, "Akiba (Aqiva)," in Collins and Harlow, *Eerdmans Dictionary of Early Judaism*, 315–16.

20. Schiffman, *From Text*, 174.

21. Seltzer, *Jewish People*, 250–51.

published at the beginning of the third century CE in what we now know as the Mishnah (repetition or teaching). "The Mishnah contains primarily material of a legal character; anonymous rulings, rulings ascribed to named sages, and debates between sages. The Mishnah also contains anecdotes, maxims, exhortations, scriptural exegesis, and descriptions of the rituals of the Jerusalem temple."[22]

The Mishnah is a kind of curriculum. It provides more than legal decisions in particular cases; it teaches a method of reasoning, a manner of disputation. It also indicates how Jews are to read Tanakh, what Christians call the Old Testament. From the time of the Mishnah on, Jews will read their sacred books through the rabbinic lenses provided in the Mishnah and subsequent rabbinic literature. This is true even though Tanakh is seldom quoted in the Mishnah. Nevertheless, one must have a firm grasp of Tanakh to make sense out of the Mishnah. "Bible and *Mishnah* constitute together the matrix of subsequent rabbinic Judaism."[23]

The Mishnah is divided into six "orders." These are themselves divided into "tractates." There are sixty-three tractates in all. The result is a substantial volume—nearly eight hundred pages in Danby's English translation.[24]

> The six orders are: *Zera'im* ("Seeds"), on the disposition of the agricultural products of the land of Israel; *Mo'ed* ("Feasts" or "Appointed Times"), on Sabbath, festivals, and pilgrimage to the Temple; *Nashim* (Women), on marriage, divorce, and family law; *Neziqin* ("Damages"), on civil and criminal law, and judicial procedure; *Qodashim* ("Holy Things"), on Temple sacrifices and rituals; and *Toharot* ("Purities"), on the maintenance of ritual purity and the removal of ritual impurity.[25]

There is a timeless quality to the Mishnah. It is characterized by a "seeming obliviousness to its time and place."[26] The Mishnah discusses, for example, in great detail matters pertaining to a temple and priesthood that no longer exist. This timelessness served the rabbinic and wider Jewish community well in the centuries to come. It gave permission for subsequent rabbinic sages to study the Mishnah not simply with reference to Israel of the sixth

22. Cohen, *From the Maccabees*, 212.

23. Seltzer, *Jewish People*, 251.

24. See Danby, *Mishnah.*

25. Cohen, "Mishnah," in Collins and Harlow, *Eerdmans Dictionary of Early Judaism*, 960–61.

26. Cohen, "Mishnah."

century BCE or Roman Palestine of the second century CE, but with reference to their own times and settings. It provided, as noted before, a curriculum, a method of disputation, and a model for decision-making that would shape, and continues to shape, Judaism. "In sum, the Mishnah represents not just a new literary form in the history of Judaism, but also a new way of thinking and ultimately a new religiosity."[27] But the rabbinic conversation did not cease with the publication of the Mishnah.

The Talmud

The Rise of Babylon and the Creation of the Talmud

Jews were removed from Judah to Babylon before the First Temple, Solomon's Temple, was destroyed. The young King Jehoiachin had surrendered to the besieging Babylonians and been carried to Babylon along with some of his officials, fighting men, skilled workers, and artisans (2 Kgs 24:8–14). According to 2 Kings 25, Jehoiachin's uncle Zedekiah became king and ruled for some nine years before foolishly rebelling against Nebuchadnezzar. After a brutal two-year siege, the Babylonians broke through the walls. The temple was burned to the ground along with every other important building in Jerusalem. Another large group was taken away into exile. Only "the poorest people of the land" were left behind "to work the vineyards and fields" (2 Kgs 25:12). These devastating events continue to reverberate through canonical and extra-canonical literature of both Jews and Christians to this day.

The prophet Jeremiah, in a letter to the exiles, speaking on behalf of God, told the exiles, "build houses and live in them, plant gardens and eat their fruit. Take wives and beget sons and daughters; and take wives for your sons, and give your daughters to husbands, that they may bear sons and daughters. Multiply there, do not decrease. And seek the welfare of the city to which I have exiled you and pray to the LORD in its behalf; for in its prosperity you shall prosper" (Jer 29:5–7).

And prosper they did. Although we know very little about the religious, social, and commercial lives of the Jews who lived under the Babylonians and then the Persians, by the time of the death of Rabbi Judah the Prince a thriving community existed. "By the second century CE at the latest, the Persian king had recognized as official head of the Jews an exilarch, . . . who

27. Cohen, "Mishnah."

claimed descent from the kings of Judah taken in captivity by Nebuchadnezzar. The exilarch collected taxes from Jews, appointed judges and supervised the court system and represented the people in the Persian royal court."[28]

There was clearly a lively and continuous communication between the Jews of Persia and those of the land of Israel. During the second century CE scholars moved freely between the two communities. "Some Palestinian scholars temporarily settled in Babylonia during the Bar Kokhba war and Hadrianic persecutions, and afterward, Babylonian Jews came to study in the academies of the Galilee."[29] The communities shared their traditions and legal rulings with each other. The publication of the Mishnah gave new impetus to the serious study of these rulings and traditions. It provided a common curriculum for scholarly discussion, comment, and interpretation and created a new class of sages: "the codification of the Mishnah and the death of R. Judah marked the beginning of a new era, the period of the *amoraim* (from the verb *amar*, to speak or interpret), interpreters of the Mishnah."[30] While the collection of the oral tradition continued, with the Amoraim a process began that would lead to the publication of the Palestinian and Babylonian Talmuds.

Sometime after the publication of the Mishnah a second, even more substantial volume was published: the Tosefta ("supplement" or "collection"). It is organized in the same manner as the Mishnah. The relationship between the Mishnah and Tosefta is complex: "the Tosefta often repeats the Mishnah's words verbatim without explication; contains material not found in our Mishnah; presents Mishnaic material in different form (sometimes using different language to make the same point as the Mishnah). . . . There is a growing consensus . . . that some Toseftan material is earlier than the Mishnah."[31]

According to Rabbi Adin Steinsaltz, the school of Rabbi Nehemiah, a student of Rabbi Akiva, was responsible for the Tosefta.[32] Additionally, there were the so-called *baraitot*, "any rabbinic teaching or ruling from the generation of the *tannaim* (between the years 10 and 220 CE) that was not included in the Mishnah."[33] These were part of the oral tradition and only appeared

28. Seltzer, *Jewish People*, 256–57.

29. Seltzer, *Jewish People*, 257.

30. Steinsaltz, *Essential Talmud*, 63.

31. Shaye J. D. Cohen, "Tosefta," in Collins and Harlow, *Eerdmans Dictionary of Early Judaism*, 1317–18.

32. Steinsaltz, *Talmud*, 63.

33. Karesh and Hurvitz, "Baraita (pl. baraitot)," *Encyclopedia of Judaism*, 44.

later within the Tosefta or Talmud. While the Mishnah remained the primary text, all of this material became grist for the mills of the Amoraim. "After the Mishnaic period, the sages regarded themselves as *amoraim* Mishnah. Their task was to explain and expound the text to the people, rather than to create independent *halakha*."[34]

The Christianization of the Roman Empire also had a dramatic impact on the Jews within the empire and the Jews of Palestine in particular. During the fourth century CE, Christian rulers began to limit communication between the Jews of Galilee and Babylonia. The patriarchate and the Sanhedrin began to lose influence beyond Galilee. Things only got worse in the fifth century CE. "When the Patriarch Gamaliel IV died in the 420s, the Roman government refused to approve a successor. In the early fifth century Jews were excluded from government posts."[35] Although Jews survived in Palestine and sages continued to teach disciples and collect materials, the center of Jewish life moved to Babylonia.

Rabbi Abba Ben Ibo, "one of the outstanding Palestinian scholars, ordained by R. Judah himself," returned to his native Babylonia and "settled in the small town of Sura." There he "established an academy" that would attract "thousands of disciples."[36] Rabbi Abba came to be called simply "Rav," and "the authority of the Sura center over most of Jewish Babylonia was recognized and the Sura academy survived in various forms for 700 years."[37] Other great academies were founded and for generations the engagement with and explication of the Mishnah flourished. Some of the towering figures of rabbinic literature left their mark in Babylonia: "their intellectual output was so great in quantity and so profound in quality that the scholars of the next generation [the fifth generation of Amoraim]—R. Papa, R. Nahman Bar Isaac, and R. Huna Ben Rav Joshua—engaged, to a large extent, in elaborating the theories of those sages and deriving conclusions from them. It was later recognized that the age of Abbaye and Rava [the fourth generation of Amoraim] constituted a turning point in Torah scholarship."[38] The stage was set for the collection and redaction of what would become the Babylonian Talmud.

34. Steinsaltz, *Essential Talmud*, 64.
35. Seltzer, *Jewish People*, 254–55.
36. Steinsaltz, *Essential Talmud*, 65.
37. Steinsaltz, *Essential Talmud*, 66.
38. Steinsaltz, *Essential Talmud*, 68.

The Production of the Talmud

We know little about the actual editors of the Talmud. They were called the Stammaim, the "anonymous ones." According to the tenth/eleventh-century CE *Epistle of Sherria Gaon*, the work of these initial editors was completed by "a group of rabbis in the sixth century CE called the Savoraim [expositors] [who] added the final flourishes to the Talmud, clarifying ambiguous statements, and inserting some teachings of their own."[39] Both the Babylonian and the earlier but much less polished Palestinian Talmud are made up of two main sections: the Mishnah and the Gemara (variously interpreted as "completion" or "teaching tradition"). The Gemara functions as a commentary and expansion of the Mishnah and follows its order. For traditional Jews "God's word . . . consist[s] of two complementary components, the 'written law' represented by the Hebrew Bible and the 'oral law' represented by the Talmud and other rabbinic works."[40] For a Jew, to study any of it is to study Torah.

Neither the Palestinian nor Babylonian Talmud comments on the entire Mishnah. Of the sixty-three tractates, the Palestinian Talmud comments on thirty-nine and the Babylonian comments on thirty-seven. The Babylonian Talmud is much longer—some two-and-a-half million words to the Palestinian's 750,000.[41] Given the interactions between the Palestinian and Babylonian rabbis, the two documents have much in common, although the more comprehensive and polished Babylonian Talmud has proved to be the most authoritative. "Most of the Gemara is in dialogue form: a chain of questions and answers, objections and rejoinders, refutations and counterrefutations. Each phrase of the Mishnah is carefully interpreted by the amoraim; apparent discrepancies are resolved and redundancies explained. Conflicting opinions of tannaim are contrasted and reconciled, often by defining the specific circumstances to which each opinion explicitly refers."[42]

The legal discussions are illustrated by stories, folktales, and parables. According to Seltzer, as much as one-third of the Babylonian Talmud consists of such material (or haggadah).[43] According to Rabbi Adin Steinsaltz, there was never an official end to the writing and editing of the Talmud,

39. Beth A. Berkowitz, "Babylonian Talmud," in Collins and Harlow, *Eerdmans Dictionary of Early Judaism*, 413–15.

40. Berkowitz, "Babylonian Talmud."

41. Seltzer, *Jewish People*, 265.

42. Seltzer, *Jewish People*, 265–66.

43. Seltzer, *Jewish People*, 267.

"hence the significant saying: 'The Talmud was never completed.' There was never a time when intellectual activity founded on the Talmud came to a standstill, and it continued to take on new forms for many generations to come."[44]

Today's Talmud

Such a vast literature was difficult and expensive to copy and preserve before the advent of printing. Tragically, over the centuries during times of Christian oppression many precious copies of the Talmud were consigned to the flames. Other copies were censored by Christians to remove what was considered anti-Christian. According to Rabbi Steinsaltz, the Talmud text used today "is mainly that of Rashi (Rabbi Shlomo ben Yitzhak, 1040–1105). He himself studied and compared a great number of manuscripts of the Talmud, and many of his emendations were later included within the text itself."[45] Rashi also produced a commentary on the Talmud that is today printed on the inside column of the page beside the text of the Talmud itself. On the outside column is a running commentary called the "tosafot." These comments were produced by Rashi's grandsons, great-grandsons, and students from his academy. They often disagree with Rashi or go into greater depth on particular topics.[46] The commentary of Rashi and the tosafists surround a section of the Mishnah and the Gemara addressing it. A page of Talmud is complicated visually as well as intellectually.

Studying the Talmud Today

Jews have been studying the Talmud, arguing about its contents, and seeking to apply its rulings for the last fifteen hundred years. The range of study today is great—from sages in the great rabbinical academies of Israel, to Orthodox boys in a *beit midrash* in Brooklyn, to boys and girls in a suburban Reform synagogue in Atlanta preparing for their Bar or Bat Mitzvah, to now both men and women preparing for the rabbinate in Jewish yeshivas and seminaries in Jerusalem, New York, and Cincinnati. And, of course, ordinary Jews

44. Steinsaltz, *Essential Talmud*, 70.
45. Steinsaltz, *Essential Talmud*, 116.
46. Karesh and Hurvitz, "Tosafot," *Encyclopedia of Judaism*, 523–24.

are involved in "Torah study" with their rabbis or other experts in some form or other in virtually every synagogue in the world.

Wherever the Talmud is taught, Jacob Neusner insists that there is a preferred way to study it: "You do not 'read' the Talmud, you 'learn' it, preferably with a *haver*, or a fellow student, and always with a rabbi. . . . In the traditional *yeshivah*, the Talmud is not 'learned' in a monotone. The Talmud is the music for a choir of voices; it is sung, and the music conveys the thrust and parry, the give and take of argument, which is what is truly Talmudic about the Talmud."[47]

The Talmud, however filled with abstract reasoning and detailed arguments over what may often appear to be minor matters, is a document of faith. You don't learn the Talmud as an academic or intellectual exercise, though it clearly is that. The sages, Neusner insists, were not merely learned men, they were saints invested in "a most serious and substantive effort to locate in trivialities the fundamental principles of the revealed will of God to guide and to sanctify the most specific and concrete actions in the workaday world."[48]

The study of the Talmud is detailed and particular. One learns the text page by page, line by line, step by step. A close study of the Talmud requires "abstract, rational criticism of each tradition in sequence and of the answers hazarded to the several questions."[49] How did the various sages come up with their rulings? What were their reasons? Are they logically well founded? Do they rationally cohere with other rulings within the larger tradition? That the reasoning is abstract and rational does not mean that the Talmud remains in the realm of the abstract. Far from it. The goal of all this reasoned engagement is, according to Rabbi Steinsaltz, to provide a "model" that can be used for a variety of very concrete and practical contemporary decisions.[50] The point of the learning is, after all, to determine how a Jew might fulfill God's will *today*. When the Talmud is read as a religious text and not merely as an exercise in antiquarian interest, reason is in service of love and obedience.

Philological and literary criticism have long been critical to the study of the Talmud and other canonical Jewish texts.[51] The editors of the Talmud

47. Jacob Neusner, *Invitation to the Talmud*, 2nd ed. (San Francisco: HarperCollins, 1984), xv.

48. Neusner, *Invitation*, xvi–xvii.

49. Neusner, *Invitation*, 267.

50. Steinsaltz, *Essential Talmud*, 263.

51. Neusner, *Invitation*, 267.

as well as the later commentators struggled with the meanings of words in the Mishnah as well as Tanakh. What did the ancients mean to say? This required, and continues to require, a close reading of the text in comparison with other ancient texts to tease out meanings of words, sentences, and paragraphs. The medieval commentators were obsessed with such matters. For them individual words and their meanings were key. Some of the words and phrases of the Mishnah were baffling to them. The later readers of the Talmud would, of course, face the same challenges with its words. Religious texts often reshape the meaning and significance of words or use them in technical ways understood by their first hearers or readers but opaque to later readers. Additionally, the Talmud is a literary genre in itself—a unique literary form. Genres "work" in a certain way. A student needs to understand how a genre "works"; to learn the unwritten "rules" of the genre before the modes of communication and argument make sense.[52] This is absolutely critical with the Talmud.

As Rabbi Steinsaltz pointed out, the key concern of the Talmud and other Jewish literatures is how people live their lives: what could be called "practical criticism," the pursuit of "what people actually do in order to carry out their religious obligations."[53] This, after all, was the point of the whole enterprise. How was a Jew to live in accordance with God's commands in any time or place? The Talmud lays claim on the Jew who studies it. A true "learner" is a disciple who follows their rabbi as their rabbi follows Moses, who the rabbis claimed studied Torah with God. And wherever Jews have lived and struggled to be faithful to God's Torah, whether in North Africa, the Rhineland, or the United States, "the Talmud [has been] the central pillar of Jewish culture. This culture is many faceted, but each of its numerous aspects is connected in some way with the Talmud. . . . It is impossible to approach biblical exegesis or Jewish or esoteric philosophy without knowledge of the Talmud."[54]

Finally, Jacob Neusner and many modern Jewish scholars have also argued for the application of the canons of modern historical criticism to the Mishnah and the Talmud.[55] Many modern scholars have raised the question of the trustworthiness of many of the narratives concerning and say-

52. See Steinsaltz, *Essential Talmud*, 262–67.
53. Neusner, *Invitation*, 267.
54. Steinsaltz, *Essential Talmud*, 296.
55. Neusner, *Invitation*, 267.

ings ascribed to the ancient rabbis. Modern scholars have used the same historical-critical tools to investigate the Christian Gospels. Scholars have long questioned whether Jesus (and for that matter Peter and Paul) did and said everything the New Testament claims. Neusner and many modern Jewish scholars are equally skeptical that the Talmud is completely historically reliable. While traditional Jews and Christians continue to be troubled by some of the conclusions of critical scholars, it is impossible today, whether studying the Talmud or the New Testament, to ignore the claims of historical scholarship. The contemporary desire to find out "what actually happened" cannot be evaded, even if it is virtually impossible to do so. And even the most skeptical scholar can shine new light on the history and meaning of the text for religious readers of such texts.

Transitions

The end of the seventh century CE marks a time of significant transition for the Jews and the Eastern Roman/Byzantine and Persian worlds. A new religious force would arise in Arabia under the Prophet Muhammad and over the next centuries sweep nearly all before it. The Byzantine emperors in Constantinople would struggle to survive in the face of relentless Arab raids and invasions. The empire would eventually lose Palestine, Egypt, and North Africa to the powerful Arab armies and to Islam. The Jewish Diaspora would continue to grow and move into Europe. Eventually there would be two poles of Jewish spiritual and intellectual life: one in Spain and North Africa and another in Europe. During the medieval era Judaism was blessed with men of such intellectual and spiritual genius that their impact is felt to this day. There were exegetes, philosophers, mystics, and poets with a messiah or two thrown in. To their story we now turn.

QUESTIONS FOR DISCUSSION

1. How did the rabbis re-form Judaism after the disasters of the late first and early second centuries CE?
2. Who was Rabbi Judah the Prince and what did he accomplish?
3. What is the Mishnah and how does it function as a sacred text in Judaism?

FURTHER READING

Neusner, Jacob. *Invitation to the Talmud: A Teaching Book.* Rev. and expanded ed. New York: HarperCollins, 1984.

Seltzer, Robert M. *Jewish People, Jewish Thought: The Jewish Experience in History.* New York: Macmillan, 1980.

Steinsaltz, Adin. *The Essential Talmud.* Translated by Chaya Galai with a new preface by the author and two new chapters. New York: Basic Books, 2006.

Urbach, Ephraim E. *The Sages: The World and Wisdom of the Rabbis of the Talmud.* Translated by Israel Abrahams. Cambridge, MA: Harvard University Press, 1987.

CHAPTER 12

The Age of Genius

My heart is in the East
And I am at the edge of the West.
How can I possibly taste what I eat?
How could it please me?
I'd gladly leave behind me
all the pleasures of Spain
if only I might see
the dust and ruins of your Shrine.

—Judah Halevi

When I determined to make a town out of the village of Speyer, I Rudiger, surnamed Huozmann, Bishop of Speyer, thought that the glory of Speyer would be augmented a thousand-fold if I were to bring Jews.

—Bishop Rudiger of Speyer

Having broken the locks and knocked [down] the doors, they seized and killed seven hundred who vainly sought to defend themselves against forces far superior to their own; the women were also massacred, and the young children, whatever their sex, were put to the sword.

—Albert of Aix, describing the massacre
at the Mainz Jewish community

Maimonides yearns for the Messianic era "not so that Israel may rule the world and subjugate other nations or that it may be called to high honors by other nations or that it may give itself over to excessive pleasure and immoderate joy; but so that it may be free of any constraint and devote itself undisturbed to studying the doctrine of God and knowledge and partake of everlasting bliss."

—Abraham Joshua Heschel

It is now acknowledged by modern scholars that the rather dismissive term "The Middle Ages" does not do justice to the intellectual, economic, political, and spiritual accomplishments of the years 500 to 1500 CE. These were not simply "the Dark Ages" of abject poverty, crippling ignorance, and brutal violence—although there was poverty, ignorance, and violence aplenty. For the Jews these years represented times of intellectual, spiritual, and economic flourishing as well as times of marginalization, persecution, and nerve-wracking insecurity. Jews lived their lives in the east under Muslim rule and in the west under Christian rule by sufferance of rulers who alternatively found them useful and a nuisance. Throughout the millennium, Jews were forced to flee persecutions and forced conversions perpetrated by both Christian and Muslim fanatics. At the end of the era, in 1492, the Jews of Spain suffered expulsion from Spain, where once learning and culture had flourished under both Muslim and Christian rulers.

As the finishing touches were being put on the Talmud by the sages of Babylon, the vast majority of Jews were living in the east. The Babylonian academies would dominate the religious lives of Jews for hundreds of years. With the arrival of Islam most of these Jews found themselves under Muslim rule, although many still lived within the orbit of Byzantium. "Jews formed only a tiny portion of the population of Latin Christendom, and they constituted only a miniscule portion of world Jewry."[1] But as the Latin west began to develop politically and economically, this began to change. "Arguably the most important development of the second half of the Middle Ages (roughly the eleventh through the fifteenth centuries) was a pronounced shift in the center of gravity in Jewish population, power, and creativity. During this period, Jews began the process of becoming a predominantly European people, centered in the Latin Christian areas of the Western World."[2]

During these centuries, rabbinic/Talmudic Judaism solidified its hold on Jews throughout the world in spite of threats from the external challenges of Islam and Christianity and the internal challenge of the Karaites (about which more later). Sages continued to refine, organize, and comment on the Talmud. Prayer books and religious poetry enriched the worship lives of Jews from Spain to Babylonia. Towering figures such as Saadia Gaon, Judah Halevy, Moses Maimonides, and many others sought to defend Judaism rationally in the light of emerging or reemerging philosophical traditions,

1. Robert Chazan, "Jewish Life in Western Christendom," in Baskin and Seeskin, *The Cambridge Guide*, 113.

2. Chazan, "Jewish Life," 113–14.

especially Aristotelianism. Biblical commentators like Rabbi Solomon ben Isaac (Rashi) insisted on the importance of the "plain meaning" of the text. His commentaries on the Bible and the Talmud are central to Jewish study and reflection to this day.[3] Jewish mystics sought a deeper experience of the one God through esoteric knowledge and spiritual experiences. And throughout the millennium Jews continued to hope for the messianic redemption, especially during times of persecution. It is perhaps not too much to say that these centuries, more than any other, set the terms for the conversations that continue to engage Jews today.

Political Changes: The Arrival of Islam and the Conflicts between East and West

Muhammad is said to have had his first revelation at the age of 40 and continued to have them throughout his life. These are collected in the Qur'an, the holy book of Islam. Muhammad's radical monotheism appealed to Arab tribesmen and Islam grew with astonishing speed. In the seventh century CE, Muslim armies marched against the powerful Persian and Byzantine empires and crushed them. "By 644 Syrian Palestine, Egypt, Iraq and Persia had been occupied by Muslim troops. The eastern frontier of the Byzantine empire had been pushed back to Asia Minor; the Persian state had been destroyed. By the 660s the Umayyad dynasty of caliphs . . . had consolidated their control of the Muslim empire from their capital at Damascus. Muslim armies continued to campaign at the extremities of the realm."[4]

It seemed that the whole world would be swept by the forces of Islam. Their advance into Europe through the Iberian Peninsula was halted by the Frankish leader Charles Martel in 732. In the east the Byzantine emperors suffered defeats at times of Muslim unity and were able to push back against the Caliphs in times of Muslim disunity and civil war.

Islam saw itself as an heir and fulfillment of both Judaism and Christianity: "Islam recognized figures like Moses, David, Solomon, and Jesus as true prophets; Muhammad, however was to be the 'seal of prophecy,' the

3. On Rashi see John Efron, Steven Weitzman, and Matthias Lehmann, *The Jews: A History*, 2nd ed. (Boston: Pearson, 2014), 187–89.

4. Seltzer, *Jewish People*, 329.

last prophet whose task it was to reestablish the true, pure divine revelation that, according to Islamic theology, had been corrupted by Jews and Christians."[5] Muhammad was evidently frustrated when the Jews did not accept this new revelation. In one passage from the Qur'an, Muhammad warns, "You will find that the most implacable of men in their enmity to the faithful are the Jews and the pagans, and that the nearest in affection to them [the Muslims] are those who say, 'We are Christians.' That is because there are priests and monks among them; and because they are free from pride" (Sura 5:82).[6]

Jews and Christians were generally tolerated within the Muslim realms, but their lives were significantly circumscribed. According to the "Pact of Omar," Jews and Christians could not "make converts, build new churches or synagogues, or make a public display of their rituals (church bells, processions); they were not to live in houses higher than those of Muslims, carry weapons, or ride horses (only donkeys). They were supposed to wear distinctive clothing."[7] They also had to pay poll taxes and land taxes and were not permitted to exercise any political authority over Muslims. According to Seltzer, these restrictions were not always enforced, but there was always the danger that a fanatical new leader could make life difficult for Jews and Christians under his jurisdiction.[8]

The impact on Jewish livelihoods under Islam and, eventually, under Christianity was enormous. Jews were forced off the land. While the Mishnah and the Talmud are significantly concerned with agricultural matters, within a few centuries "Jews became almost completely urban. Confiscatory land taxes made it almost impossible for [Jews] to remain farmers and peasants."[9] In both the east and the west, Jews moved (or were moved) off the land into the city. They became merchants and tradespeople, scholars and money-lenders. Outside of medicine, very few of the "professions" were open to them, and with only rare exceptions they never possessed significant political power. However, there were places and times when Jewish life flourished under Muslim rule: in Babylon, in Spain, and in Egypt, especially.

5. Efron et al., *The Jews*, 151.
6. Cited in Efron et al., *The Jews*, 153.
7. Seltzer, *Jewish People*, 331.
8. Seltzer, *Jewish People*, 331.
9. Seltzer, *Jewish People*, 331.

The Exilarch and Gaon under Islam

The Umayyads fell to the rival Abbasid dynasty in 750 CE. The capital of the new empire was moved from Damascus in Syria to the new city of Baghdad in Babylonia. This realignment of power was critical for Babylonian Jews and especially the leaders, or Gaonim, of the rabbinic academies. "The heads of the Babylonian Jewish leadership . . . now found themselves right in the political center of the Islamic empire. By the ninth century, the two yeshivot of Sura and Pumpedita had relocated to Babylon where their respective leaders competed for power and influence with the nominal head of the Babylonian Jewish community, the so-called 'exilarch' . . . who claimed to be a descendent of the biblical Davidic dynasty and represented the community to the caliphal authorities."[10] The Gaonim would eventually win the battle for influence within the community of Baghdad and with the wider Jewish community. But the battle for power would be a bitter one and is perhaps best illustrated in the life and work of the most famous of the Gaons, Saadiah ben Joseph, or simply Saadiah (or Saadyah) Gaon (882–942).

Saadiah is known for far more than his leadership of the Babylonian community. He is one of the most important Jewish thinkers in history. His scholarly output was prodigious and varied. "Saadiah was a prolific author who made pioneering contributions to such fields as Hebrew philology, Jewish liturgy, and halakhah; he polemicized against the Karaites (and his rabbinic enemies); he translated most of the Bible into Arabic and commented on many of its books; and produced the first major Jewish theological treatise: *The Book of Beliefs and Opinions.*"[11] His intention in the latter volume was to refute the religious claims of Christians, Muslims, and Zoroastrians. "He argued that there are four sources of knowledge: sense experience, intuition of self-evident truths, logical inference, and reliable tradition. The fourth category, derived from the first three, is the mainstay of civilization; it was given by God to man [*sic*] to provide guidance and protection against uncertainty since the vast majority of humanity is incapable of engaging in philosophical speculation."[12]

For Saadiah, then, reason and revelation were compatible. Through the use of reason alone he thought one could establish the truths of the Oral and Written Torah. For those who could not arrive at truth through the rigors of

10. Efron et al., *The Jews*, 155.
11. Seltzer, *Jewish People*, 377.
12. Cohn-Sherbok, *Judaism*, 176.

philosophy, God's revelation of Torah sufficed. But in the end, "there could be no contradiction between reason and faith, between philosophical thinking and the revealed truth of Torah."[13] The question of the respective roles of reason and revelation in religious life would trouble Muslim, Jewish, and Christian thinkers for years to come.

Babylon was a place of many religions, sects, and traditions. Muslims, Jews, Christians, Zoroastrians, and pagans interacted more or less freely (rather too freely for some more traditional Muslims). But Saadiah and his fellow rabbis had more than Christians and Muslims to contend with. A group of Jews who rejected rabbinic Judaism had risen to prominence in Palestine, Iraq, and Persia. They had established an academy in Jerusalem and would eventually establish synagogues throughout the Middle East. Called Karaites ("readers"), they were a sort of "back to the Bible" group. They rejected the rabbinic texts in favor of a strict reading of the Torah. There is no need for the Oral Torah or the extended disputes of the Talmud, they argued, since God has revealed all that was necessary in the Written Torah. They were much more rigorous in their practices, rejecting what they saw as weak compromises by the rabbinic tradition. "The main characteristics of Karaism in the first centuries of its history are asceticism, yearning for an end to exile, rejection of rabbinic authority, individualistic biblical interpretation, and growing interest in rationalistic criticism of rabbinic Judaism and rationalistic defense of the Jewish faith."[14]

Saadiah Gaon composed a treatise attacking their founder Anan ben David, whose guiding principle was, "search thoroughly the Scripture and do not rely on my opinion."[15] Saadiah shows himself not above character assassination, accusing Anan of "persistent unruliness and irreverence." His purpose, according to Saadiah, was not to pursue truth but "cause a schism because he was frightened of the government of the time." Anan became a rival exilarch (145).

Ironically, at perhaps the height of its power, the Jewish community of Babylon shared in the fate of a disintegrating Muslim empire. By the end of the tenth century CE the Islamic world was divided into separate states and spheres of influence. "The rabbinic academies of Babylon began to lose their hold on the Jewish scholarly world" (151). Local centers of learning began to

13. Efron et al., *The Jews*, 156.

14. Seltzer, *Jewish People*, 341.

15. Cohn-Sherbok, *Judaism*, 142. Hereafter, page references to this work are given in parentheses in the text.

replace the great academies of Baghdad and the east. Old centers reasserted themselves—in Palestine especially—and new centers arose in Egypt and elsewhere in North Africa. But "it was in Spain that the Jewish community attained its greatest level of achievement" (151). In medieval Spain Muslims, Christians, and Jews joined in conversation and conflict in what has been called, rightly or wrongly, a "golden age." The influence of the Spanish Jewish sages, poets, and mystics would be enormous in the centuries to come. These were times of great learning, profound spirituality, and cultural brilliance—and ultimately, of bitter conflict and terrible tragedy.

Jews under Christian Rule: Spain, France, and the Rhineland

We know from the New Testament that there were significant Jewish communities in Europe during the first century of the common era. Acts tells us that Paul found Jews in Macedonia: in Philippi, Thessalonica, Beroea, and Corinth (Acts 16–18). In each of these cities he visited Jewish places of prayer and proclaimed his message of Messiah Jesus. Paul also wrote letters to at least three of those communities. Jews had also long been on the Italian Peninsula. Acts alludes to the edict of the emperor Claudius driving the Jews out of Rome (Acts 18:2). They would soon return. Paul's most important letter, Romans, was written to the capital city at least in part to address conflicts between the gentile and Jewish followers of Jesus within the community. At the end of that letter he expresses a desire to visit the church in Rome and from there go on a mission to Spain. This suggests that Paul expected to find Jews there as well.

There were also already Jews in what is now southern France. But during the latter half of the "Middle Ages" Jews began to move into northern and central Europe in significant numbers. Political and economic developments made these areas increasingly attractive to Jews. Early in the period, as illustrated by Bishop Rudiger, cited in an epigraph to this chapter, Christian communities saw the clear advantages of having entrepreneurial Jews in their midst. Jewish merchants had contacts throughout the known world and Jewish crafts and trades were very useful in an expanding economy. Unfortunately, this openness would not last. According to Robert Chazan,

> During the eleventh and early twelfth centuries, ecclesiastical law, church teachings, and popular opinion were relatively unformed and flexible. By the middle decades of the twelfth century, however, the church and the

> populace at large had begun to articulate more clearly and more forcefully their positions. In the case of the church, the demands for wide-ranging limitations on the expanding Jewish community became more vocal; in the case of the populace at large, perceptions of Jews as hostile and threatening emerged and spread rapidly and widely.[16]

Jewish learning developed alongside Jewish commerce and trade. Jews in the Rhineland, Mainz, and Worms and in northern France in Troyes and Sen developed centers of learning and scholarship to rival Babylonia. They produced

> such leading scholars as the legal expert Rabbanu Gershom of Mainz (960–1028) and the greatest commentator of the medieval period, Solomon ben Isaac of Troyes (known as Rashi: 1040–1105). In subsequent generations the study of the Talmud reached great heights: in Germany and northern France scholars known as *tosafists* . . . utilized new methods of Talmudic interpretation. In addition Ashkenazic Jews of this period composed religious poetry modelled on the liturgical compositions (*piyyutim*) of fifth- and sixth-century Israel.[17]

Tragically, it was some of these very communities that suffered from crusading knights and local mobs in the wake of Pope Urban's call for a crusade to free the Holy Land from Muslim control. In 1096 crusading knights marched through the Rhineland, leaving thousands of Jews dead and many thousands of others forcibly baptized.[18] Whole communities were destroyed, among them the significant communities of Mainz and Worms.

According to Efron et al., these communities made surprisingly quick comebacks with the support of sympathetic Christian rulers. But these traumas had a lasting impact on the European Jewish communities. "What matters perhaps even more than the events of 1096 was the way they were remembered in subsequent generations" (191). In the following decades and centuries when European Jews were under pressure to convert or otherwise threatened with extinction, they would recall these stories of courage and suffering. The Crusade narratives engraved "the image and ideal of

16. Chazan, "Jewish Life," 116–17.

17. Cohn-Sherbok, *Judaism*, 155.

18. Efron et al., *The Jews*, 190–93. Hereafter, page references to this work are given in parentheses in the text.

martyrdom—*kiddush ha-shem,* or 'sanctification of [God's] Name' into the collective memory of Ashkenazi Jewry" (192). And they would need these memories far too frequently in the coming centuries.

In this same period Judaism was flourishing in another part of Europe: Spain. Muslims ruled most of what is now Spain and Portugal during the eighth century. Almost immediately Christian kingdoms began the process of attempting to wrest territory back from the Muslim conquerors. This process, called the *Reconquista,* lasted many centuries and was not complete until 1492. During those long centuries Christian and Muslim rulers alternatively fought one another and allied with one another against threatening neighbors of whatever faith. Jews were often caught in the middle of these conflicts. Sometimes they would flee Christian rule and at other times Muslim rule. Under the Umayyad caliphate of Cordoba, however, both Islamic and Jewish culture flourished. Abd ar-Rahman III, who ruled from 912 to 961, was a man of learning and culture: "Cordoba at the time was a vast and sophisticated city of 100,000 or more inhabitants and home to great libraries—the caliph's collection was said to hold 400,000 volumes—, a magnificent mosque and a huge royal palace constructed on the outskirts of the city at Madinat az-Zahra. Just as al-Andalus appeared like a land of unequaled riches and beauty in the medieval Muslim imagination, Jewish observers too praised the land for its natural beauty and also as a center of trade and culture" (161).

Famously, a series of Jewish officials actually exercised political power and influence during this "golden age." Hasdai ibn Shaprut rose to power through his skill as a physician (a pattern other Jews would emulate in years to come). He was a trusted diplomat for the Umayyads, entering "negotiations with Byzantine Emperors" and "establishing relations with various Christian rulers in Europe" (162). Jewish scholars and poets were supported by men like Hasdai ibn Shaprut. As Muslim Spain began to disintegrate into smaller principalities, Jews continued to exercise unusual influence. Samuel Ibn Negrela of Granada was not only an important Jewish courtier but also "knowledgeable about mathematics and philosophy, wrote in Hebrew and Arabic, and served as vizier of Granada for thirty years."[19] The arrival of Christian pressure from the north and successive waves of fanatical Muslims from the south would bring this era to a crushing end. "On December 20, 1066, Joseph ha-Nagid [Samuel's son] was assassinated in a popular uprising. His body was crucified upon the city's main gate. The Jewish quarter of

19. Cohn-Sherbok, *Judaism,* 152.

Granada was attacked by a rampaging mob that slaughtered its inhabitants and razed it to the ground."[20]

Judah Halevi and the Longing for Zion

Judah Halevi (or Halevy), a brilliant scholar and poet, was born in Toledo, in Christian Spain in 1075. As a teenager he made his way to Granada. The Jewish community there had against all odds recovered from the catastrophe of 1066. It was a time of literary flowering and intellectual genius. But it was not to last. Halevi would reflect with frustrated longing on his experience of Granada for the rest of his life. When the Muslim rulers of Granada called on Berber warriors of Morocco to help in the battle against Christians, "the warriors were ascetic, militant, hostile to laxness and luxury, and all of that—needless to say—was bad for the Jews."[21] After a time in Muslim-controlled Lucena he once again was forced to flee another wave of fanatical Muslims to Seville. Eventually he settled in Christian Castile where he lived for some twenty years but "it seems never to have been a place where he felt secure or especially happy."[22]

> All this perilous shuttling between rival sets of persecutors had changed Halevi. He was now middle aged and, perhaps understandably given to raining curses on the persecutors of the Jews, Christian and Muslim alike. A dawning, bitter conviction that the Jews could expect no refuge, no succor, no understanding from anyone except their God and their religion, was drawing him away from the possibility of a genuine coexistence with either Muslims or Christians and towards an intense communion with his Judaism.[23]

This drew him as he grew older toward Jerusalem, in spite of the fact that Christians ruled there and had slaughtered the Jewish community when they seized the city in 1099. He left for the Holy Land in 1140. For a time he remained in Egypt, where he had many admirers in both Alexandria and

20. Norman A. Stillman, "The Jewish Experience in the Muslim World," in Baskin and Seeskin, *The Cambridge Guide*, 105.

21. Schama, *The Story of the Jews*, vol. 1, *Finding the Words*, 280.

22. Schama, *Finding the Words*, 281.

23. Schama, *Finding the Words*, 282.

Cairo. It is not clear that he ever made it to Jerusalem. Although legend has it that he was killed in Jerusalem, it appears he died in Egypt.[24]

Halevi is certainly remembered for his poetry. But perhaps his greatest work grew out of his love for Judaism and the Jewish people. His book *The Book of Argument and Proof in Defense of the Despised Faith*, more popularly known as the *Book of the Khazar*, is an apologetic for Judaism and defense of its people. It is presented as a dialogue between the king of the Khazar people and a Jewish sage. At the end of this dialogue, the king is converted to Judaism. Although philosophically savvy, Halevi leans into Judaism's revelation in opposition to reason and philosophy.

> Except for a few remarks about Christianity and the Karaites, the main position that Halevy opposed in the *Kuzari* was Aristotelian philosophy, which he considered the greatest internal danger to Jewish faith in his day. Halevy's argument stems from the conviction that biblical revelation—not philosophy—provides the proper guidance to life in communion with God. To be sure, reason is useful for religion inasmuch as it indicates that an understanding of the world leads to the idea of a single divine cause. (389)

In the end, for Halevi, neither reason, Aristotelianism, nor any other human philosophy is sufficient for a good life in communion with God. Such a life is rather based upon Torah.

Halevi was not entirely dismissive of philosophy. Although he recognizes the limits of reason and of Aristotelianism in particular, there is, according to Seltzer, a "paradox" in Halevi's thought. "Although critical of philosophy, he offers in rebuttal a theory that explains the distinctiveness of Israel and of biblical prophecy in naturalistic, even biological terms. Similar to Neoplatonism, Halevi's theology is based on the idea of an emanation that pours out from God to elicit the special potential of each lower lever of reality, under suitable conditions" (391–92).

Nevertheless, human reason alone cannot find its way to an appropriate personal and social ethic. Here Halevi opposes earlier Jewish philosophers like Saadiah Gaon. "Halevy's conception of the significance of biblical law is almost the obverse of Saadiah's. Whereas Saadiah had defended its rationality, Halevy emphasized those features that are not explicable" (392). Human intellect cannot find its way to God's will and purposes. Human reason,

24. Seltzer, *Jewish People*, 382. Hereafter, page references to this work are given in parentheses in the text.

"science," and philosophy all have their place, but in the end revelation and prophecy are supreme. These arguments about reason and revelation and the roles of philosophy and "science" would only intensify in the wake of the work of perhaps the greatest of all of the medieval Jewish sages, Moses Maimonides.

Maimonides: A Genius and His Critics

In his magisterial account of Maimonides's life and thought, Moshe Halbertal argues that he "attempted to bring about two far-reaching and profound transformations in the Jewish world." He intended, first of all, to rationalize the study of Jewish law (halakah) by addressing the complexities of the Talmud, changing it from "a fragmented and complex system to one that was transparent and unambiguous."[25] This was the purpose of his great *Mishnah Torah*, in which all "the halakhic give and take, the disagreements, and the minority opinions" were omitted. The rulings that remained were straightforward, clear, and rationally presented.

His second mission was to bring about "a substantive shift in Jewish religious consciousness." He would do ferocious battle with "anthropomorphism" and the idolatry, not just of the figural representation of the divine, but of the *mental* image of God. This required him to struggle especially with the biblical text, offering "a systematic reinterpretation of Jewish religious language and of religious language in general" (2). In this he was attacking the religious imaginations of ordinary people and challenging cherished notions of the divine. Maimonides also sought to change the Jewish religious consciousness by substituting natural causality for miracle: "God's wisdom, as revealed in nature, was seen to be the highest expression of His revelation." This change "required Maimonides to reinterpret some of Judaism's basic concepts, such as providence, creation, prophecy, and revelation. All of them seemingly based on a revelation of divine will and a fracturing of the normal causal order" (2). All of these changes were perhaps rooted in the most critical change Maimonides sought: understanding "philosophy and science as the medium for attaining the heights of religious experience—love and awe of God" (2).

Maimonides (also known as Rambam) thus set the terms for the following centuries of theological and halakhic conversations among the most

25. Moshe Halbertal, *Maimonides: Life and Thought* (Princeton: Princeton University Press, 2014), 1. Hereafter, page references to this work are given in parentheses in the text.

important Jewish sages of the medieval and early modern periods. There were Maimonidean enthusiasts, Maimonidean critics, and some who sought to go even further than the great man himself. Halbertal concludes, "To be sure, historically speaking, he did not succeed in bringing about the change in religions consciousness he hoped for. Nevertheless, once Judaism had passed through the refining blaze of Maimonidean interpretation, it acquired a different and distinctive voice that offered a genuine alternative to the then conventional understanding. This distinctive Maimonidean voice shook the rafters in its day and posed a lasting challenge to all later Jewish thought" (3).

The impact of his work extended beyond Judaism. The great medieval Christian theologian Thomas Aquinas acknowledged a debt to Maimonides. Maimonides's greatest works, *Mishnah Torah* and *Guide for the Perplexed*, continue to influence Jewish life and thought to this day.

In some ways Maimonides's life paralleled that of his great predecessor Judah Halevi. Born in 1135, just a few years before Halevi's death, he and his family were also forced to flee the fanatical Almohads, wandering through Spain and North Africa looking for a place to practice their faith and learn in peace. For five years they lived in Fez, in present-day Morocco. In 1160 they fled to Egypt where, excepting a brief stay in the Holy Land, Maimonides lived out his life.[26] Also, like Halevi, he became a physician, gaining such a reputation that he became one of the court physicians of the Muslim ruler of Egypt.[27] Maimonides was drawn, as were many of his philosophically oriented peers, to the newly reemerging works of the ancient Greek philosopher Aristotle. He joined Muslim and Christian thinkers in the attempt to reconcile the thinking of their respective religious communities with the greatest of the Greeks. "In everything he wrote, Maimonides strove to demonstrate that philosophy and religion point to the same truth. . . . [N]othing in Judaism could contradict reason."[28] In some ways Maimonides resembled his great philosophical predecessor Philo. However speculative his thought, he remained faithful to Jewish law and an advocate for a life faithful to halakah. His learning never drew him away from a life in Torah.

In the following centuries, Jewish philosophers either opposed Maimonides, supported and furthered his work, or found some middle ground between appreciation and condemnation. "Though Maimonides was admired as a halakhic authority, some Jewish scholars were troubled by his

26. Seltzer, *Jewish People*, 393.
27. Seltzer, *Jewish People*, 393.
28. Seltzer, *Jewish People*, 395.

views. In particular they were dismayed that he appeared not to believe in resurrection; that he viewed prophecy, providence, and immortality as dependent on intellectual attainment; that he regarded the doctrine of divine incorporeality as a fundamental of Jewish faith; and that he felt the knowledge of God should be based on Aristotelian principles."[29]

The antagonism between the fans and critics of Maimonides changed only when "Dominican inquisitors in France burned copies of Maimonides' writings."[30] Although the initial fierce opposition was muted, Maimonides continued to be studied with both appreciation and skepticism in the centuries to come. Perhaps the greatest of Maimonides's later critics was Hasdai Crescas (ca. 1340–1414), who offered "an alternative account of the basic principles of Jewish faith in opposition to Maimonides' thirteen principles." Crescas was also critical of Maimonides's Aristotelianism, offering an alternative that is in certain ways, according to some scholars, strikingly modern.[31]

The Pietists, the Mystics, and the Kabbalah

Alongside the ongoing developments in philosophical, biblical, and halakhic studies was the flourishing of Jewish mysticism. We return to the Jews of Spain, this time in Christian Spain. Moses ben Nahman or Nahmanides (1194–1270) was born in Girona in Catalonia but late in his life moved to the Holy Land. He was a prolific writer. "He left his imprint in several areas, in particular through his commentary on the Bible and his writings on the Talmud. He was responsible more than anyone for introducing the kind of Talmud study to the Sephardic world that had been developed by the tosafists of northern France, and he created a new synthesis of the Talmudic scholarship of Spain, northern France, and Provence."[32]

He was also a respectful but sharp critic of Maimonides's approach to Jewish law in *Mishnah Torah.* Nahmanides, perhaps most importantly, left his imprint on Jewish mysticism. In his commentary on the Bible he was "the first to integrate the teaching of Kabbalah" (the Jewish mystical tradi-

29. Cohn-Sherbok, *Judaism*, 185.

30. Cohn-Sherbok, *Judaism*, 185.

31. Cohn-Sherbok, *Judaism*, 188; see also Seltzer, *Jewish People*, 413–18; Efron et al., *The Jews*, 202–4.

32. Efron et al., *The Jews*, 199.

tion) into the study of the biblical text. "He often cites the interpretation of a verse 'by way of the plain meaning of the Scriptures' followed by another interpretation that he introduces with the words, 'by the way of Truth,' that is, its interpretation is in the spirit of Kabbalah."[33]

Although Jewish mysticism was ancient, the arrival of new forms of mysticism during the twelfth and thirteenth centuries perhaps represented "a response to the challenge of philosophy."[34] The doctrines of the mystics were, not surprisingly, often secret and esoteric. Certain texts were particularly important to the mystics. Ezekiel with its description of the divine chariot (*Merkavah*) was a favorite text. "It was the aim of the mystic to be a '*Merkavah* Rider' so that he would be able to penetrate the heavenly mysteries."[35] Their experiences are described in the so-called *hekhalot* ("palaces") literature, dating from the seventh through the eleventh centuries. "In order to make their heavenly ascent, these mystics followed strict ascetic disciplines, including fasting, ablutions and the invocation of God's name. After reaching a state of ecstasy, the mystic was able to enter the seven heavenly halls and attain a vision of the divine chariot" (194).

These mystical texts were studied by Ashkenazic Jews, especially in the Rhineland. These "pietists" were drawn to the mystery of God—the divine glory (*kavod*). "The aim of German mysticism was to attain a vision of God through a cultivation of a life of pietism (*hasiduth*)—which embraced devotion, saintliness and contemplation" (202). It is perhaps not surprising that this form of mysticism developed in the Rhineland during the twelfth and thirteenth centuries. Their prayers and practices "provided a means of consolation and escape from the miseries of the Rhineland communities" during this era of oppression and violence (202).

Another form of Kabbalah was developing in southern France. This form was based on Neoplatonism, a tradition that had an enormous impact upon both Jewish and Christian mysticism. The various forms and developments of Kabbalistic mysticism of this era are vastly complicated. This is especially represented in the text of the *Zohar* composed by Moses ben Shem Tov de Leon (1250–1305) in Spain. "Written in Aramaic, the text is largely a *midrash* in which Torah is given a mystical or ethical interpretation" (206). According to these various systems,

33. Efron et al., *The Jews*, 200.

34. Efron et al., *The Jews*, 200.

35. Cohn-Sherbok, *Judaism*, 194. Hereafter, page references to this work are given in parentheses in the text.

> God in Himself lies beyond any speculative comprehension. To express the unknowable aspect of the Divine, early kabbalists of Provence and Spain referred to the Divine infinite as *Ayn Sof*—the absolute perfection in which there is no distinction or plurality. The *Ayn Sof* does not reveal itself. It is beyond all thoughts and at times is identified with the Aristotelian First Cause. In Kabbalistic teaching, creation is bound up with the manifestation of the hidden God and His outward movement. According to the *Zohar*, the *sefirot* emanate out of the hidden depths of the Godhead-like flame. (206)

The *sefirot* are divine qualities that flow from the *Ayn Sof* without compromising its unity and simplicity. All existence is, in fact, an emanation from the Deity. "He is revealed in all things because he is immanent in them" (207).

These mystics were not simply contemplating the Godhead in supreme indifference to the fate of the world. Quite the contrary. "For the mystics deeds of *tikkun* (cosmic repair) sustain the world, activate nature to praise. . . . Such repair is accomplished by keeping the commandments which were conceived as vessels for establishing contact with the Godhead and for ensuring divine mercy" (207). The mystics, like the philosophers, were not content to contemplate the emanations of the divine. They too were committed to a life in Torah, not in spite of their mysticism, but because of it. There were differences between the mystics and the philosophers. "Whereas Jewish philosophers had necessarily pointed to common features between their and other monotheistic faiths, the Kabbalists emphasized the vast difference between the role of the Jewish people in the spiritual destiny of the universe and that of other religious communities. Thus the Kabbalah justified the agonies suffered by Jews who remained committed to their faith and reaffirmed the unique destiny of Israel among the nations."[36]

The Jewish people would need these resources to survive in the coming centuries. Resurgent Christian kingdoms in Spain and France would make life miserable for the Jews during the early modern period. And the Protestant Reformation would bring enormous changes to Europe. It would break the hold of the Roman Catholic Church over much of Europe. The outcome would be massive social change, bitter theological and political conflicts, and, most disastrously, war. Very often Jews would be caught in the middle of these conflicts and suffer bitterly. But with the arrival of the "Enlighten-

36. Seltzer, *Jewish People*, 450. See his entire lengthy and valuable discussion of Jewish mysticism, 419–50.

ment," Jews as well as Christians began to ask questions about their received traditions and how they would fit in this emerging "modern world."

QUESTIONS FOR DISCUSSION

1. How was Babylon important in the development of Judaism?
2. How did the church help and make difficult the lives of the growing Jewish communities in Europe?
3. Who was Maimonides and why is he important to this day?

FURTHER READING

Chazan, Robert. "Jewish Life in Western Christendom." Pages 113–39 in *The Cambridge Guide to Jewish History, Religion, and Culture.* Edited by Judith R. Baskin and Kenneth Seeskin. Cambridge: Cambridge University Press, 2010.

Cohn-Sherbok, Dan. "The Philosophy of Maimonides." Pages 180–84 in *Judaism: History, Belief and Practice.* London: Routledge, 2003.

Halbertal, Moshe. *Maimonides: Life and Thought.* Translated by Joel Linsider. Princeton: Princeton University Press, 2014.

Stillman, Norman. "The Jewish Experience in the Muslim World." Pages 85–112 in *The Cambridge Guide to Jewish History, Religion, and Culture.* Edited by Judith R. Baskin and Kenneth Seeskin. Cambridge: Cambridge University Press, 2010.

CHAPTER 13

Jews in Early Modernity

No historian . . . can recover the horror, dismay, fear and pathetic agony of the Jews who heard the implacable death sentence now imposed on communities which had indeed seemed their "Jerusalem in Spain," where the language, turned into Ladino, had flowered; where rabbis had studied and written; where songs liturgical and songs loving had been composed, chanted and sung.

—Simon Schama

It was in its Renaissance that western Europe achieved what the Middle Ages had at most dreamed of: a world free of Jews.

—David Nirenberg

One might think that the humanist Renaissance, with its sense of new possibilities and criticism of old stereotypes, would have acted as a counterweight to the Iberian declaration of war on Judaism. The reality was that Jews benefited from the Renaissance even less than women.

—Diarmaid MacCulloch

Know, O adored Christ, and make no mistake, that aside from the Devil, you have no enemy more venomous, more desperate, more bitter, than a true Jew who truly seeks to be a Jew. Now whoever wishes to accept venomous serpents, desperate enemies of the Lord, and to honor them, to let himself be robbed, pillaged, corrupted, and cursed by them, need only turn to the Jews.

—Martin Luther, *Against the Jews and Their Lies*

The Besht used to say: No child is born except as the result of joy and pleasure. In the same way, if a man wants his prayers to be heard, he must offer them up with joy and pleasure.

—Baal Shem Tov

Throughout the centuries, to be a Jew has been to be in exile. Jews were scattered by the Assyrians in the eighth century BCE, the Babylonians in the sixth century BCE, the Romans in the first and second centuries CE, and Christian and Muslim rulers in the following centuries. On some occasions, as in Edward I's England and Ferdinand and Isabella's Spain, they were driven out. On too many occasions to mention, they fled for their lives. Although there were always Jews in the land of Israel, the vast majority could only look longingly to that land from an always insecure exile.

Expulsion from Spain

The expulsion of the Jews from Spain and its various territories is one of the hinges of Jewish history. According to Diarmaid MacCulloch, this expulsion was "the greatest single disaster for the Jewish people since the Roman Empire's destruction of Jerusalem back in 70 CE."[1] Simon Schama vividly describes how Spanish Jews, after much denial, bargaining, and desperation, were finally forced to flee their homes: "Panic set in along with sickening despair. Frantic attempts were initiated to sell everything that was not to be confiscated: houses, shops, bodegas, gardens, cherry orchards, vineyards, olive groves. . . . They were lucky to get . . . 10 percent of the value; and then there was the question of finding some sort of means to take it with them over the borders to Navarre and Portugal or over the sea to wherever would receive them."[2]

Their community leaders pled and attempted bribery, but Ferdinand and Isabella, bolstered by the inquisitor Torquemada, remained implacable. It was too much for some. About 40,000 decided to convert, among them "the chief rabbi himself, Abraham Seneor, [who] was baptized along with his son Melamed (the teacher) Meir . . . in the presence of the king and queen who stood as the octogenarian's godparents."[3] Thus ended the great Andalusian Jewish culture that had produced the poetic fire of Judah Halevi, the intellectual ice of Moses Maimonides, and the mystical wonder of the *Zohar*.

1. Diarmaid MacCulloch, *The Reformation: A History* (New York: Penguin, 2003), 688.
2. Schama, *Finding the Words*, 411.
3. Schama, *Finding the Words*, 411.

Seeking New Lands

As desperate as this moment was, for those Jews trudging to Spanish harbors or the borders of what they hoped would be friendlier lands, they carried with them their holy books, their songs of lament and hope, and, especially, their national story. According to contemporary witnesses, as the Jews left, their women and girls sang and played tambourines on the road. Schama comments,

> The Sephardim left Spain with their beautiful music filling their ears. But why, in particular, did the rabbis call on the women to sing? Because, of course, this was an exodus, one that must have been ordained by God as a new departure as He had when they had been delivered from Egyptian bondage. . . . [I]t was Moses' sister Miriam who sang and danced after the Israelites had passed safely through the Red Sea and the waters had closed over the hosts of Pharaoh. . . . God would [again] provide miracles and lead them from servitude to the Promised Land.[4]

And there would be new lands and new opportunities: in the east, in Asia Minor, North Africa, and Palestine, the Ottoman Turks would welcome the Jews. And in Eastern Europe, in Lithuania and Poland, a great, learned, and pious Jewish community would rise and flourish. It would remain the heartland of European Jewry (and in many ways world Jewry) until the Nazis murdered nearly the entire community. A few thousand Jews remain today in a land where millions once served their God in faithfulness to his Torah and in hope of his redemption. But as had happened so many times in the past and would happen again in the years to come, in the wake of the horror and disaster of the expulsion new life would break out and the Jewish people would flourish in new and unfamiliar places.

Jews in the Ottoman Empire

It was said that the Ottoman sultan Bayezid II (1447–1512) invited the expelled Spanish Jews to settle in his realm. The Turks had recently succeeded in conquering and dismantling the Byzantine Empire; Constantinople had finally fallen in 1453. Syria and Palestine had also succumbed to their armies. The

4. Schama, *Finding the Words*, 413.

ancient Byzantine capital now "was converted into the capital of an Islamic empire, that, at its peak stretched from Algeria in the west to Iraq in the east, from Hungary in southwestern Europe to Yemen at the southern tip of the Arabian Peninsula."[5] Before the Spanish Jews were expelled, Jews from Western Europe had been attracted to the empire. Rabbi Isaac Zarfati recommended his fellow Jews in Germany immigrate to Turkey: "I proclaim to you that Turkey is a land wherein nothing is lacking and where, if you will, all shall be well with you. The way to the Holy Land lies open to you through Turkey. . . . Here every man may dwell at peace under his own vine and fig tree."[6] Jews and Christians still had to live with the restrictions of being *dhimmis*, but they were at least able to practice their respective faiths in relative peace.

One of the Jews who made her way to Constantinople was scion of a prominent Marrano family of Portugal. Dona Garcia (1510–69) began her life as Beatriz de Luna, part of an old and very wealthy and prominent family. Ostensibly good Christians, her family, along with many others in Spain and Portugal, kept their Judaism alive within their homes. The tale of Beatriz and her sister Brianda is worthy of a novel. As thrillingly told by Simon Schama, it is a story of secret marriages and narrow escapes, imprisonments and threatened executions, greedy kings and grand deceptions.[7] The patriarch of the family, Diogo Mendes, had made a fortune in the spice trade. Dying, he entrusted his fortune not to his wife, Brianda, but to his sister-in-law, Beatriz. The Christian rulers of Portugal, Italy, and the Holy Roman Empire were loath to see the Mendes money leave their lands. Charles V was particularly concerned that it not fall into the hands of his enemies, the Turks. But through guile, deception, and an occasional well-placed bribe, the sisters and their wealth arrived in Constantinople in 1553.

The family did not bring their money to Constantinople simply to live in ease and worship in relative freedom:

> The women and the men of the family had endured the terrors of prison, the endless comings and goings in boats and closed carriages, the encounters with armed and brutal men all for this: to keep guard over the Mendes-Benveniste money which, whether self-interest or altruism, they had come to think of as a Shield of Israel. . . . [T]he sisters . . . shared an understanding

5. Efron et al., *The Jews*, 217.

6. Efron et al., *The Jews*, 217.

7. See Simon Schama, *The Story of the Jews*, vol. 2, *Belonging, 1492–1900* (New York: HarperCollins, 2017), 29–65.

> that God had preserved their good fortune for something other than patrician self-indulgence, that it was the capital of *tzedakah*, righteous care.[8]

Dona Gracia, as she was now called, was deeply concerned for the survival of the Jewish people. She became renowned for her generosity and acts of charity: for building schools and synagogues and for helping poor Jews who had fled to the Ottomans. She has come down to us as "one of the greatest of living blessings: she is Miriam, Deborah, Esther and Judith; no mere paragon of the domestic hearth but the epitome of the strong Jewish woman: courageous, resourceful and wise."[9] For many Jews she was "the Messiah in skirts." She remains to this day the model of the strong, shrewd Jewish woman in service of her people.

Jews settled elsewhere in the Ottoman Empire. Especially famous was the city of Safed in Palestine. Scholars from Spain fled to the city in such numbers that it was said, "Let us be grateful to the kings of Spain for having expelled our sages and judges, so that they came here and re-established the Torah to all its pristine glory."[10] Mystics and scholars came to Safed especially to study Kabbalah. Among them were luminaries like Joseph Karo (1488–1574), a mystic and halakhist, Isaac Luria (1534–1572), who developed an approach to Kabbalah that endures to this day, and Moses Cordovero (1522–1570), whose commentary on the *Zohar* laid the groundwork for many Kabbalists, including Luria. Jews also made their way to Morocco and established a vibrant community that survived for centuries: "Fez alone is said to have received 20,000 in the decades after 1492. . . . The Sephardi rabbinic elite (the 'sages of Castile') came to dominate the religious life of Moroccan Jewry."[11] The influence of these scattered Sephardi revitalized Jewish life in Asia Minor, North Africa, and the land of Israel. But the Ottoman Empire was not the only refuge for the Jews.

Poland and Lithuania

Throughout the fifteenth and sixteenth centuries, the situation of Jews in Western Europe became increasingly precarious. We have seen that Jews were expelled (or forced to convert) in Spain, in Portugal, in certain regions

8. Schama, *Belonging*, 59.
9. Schama, *Belonging*, 65.
10. Efron et al., *The Jews*, 221.
11. Efron et al., *The Jews*, 223.

of France, and, increasingly, in the territories of the Holy Roman Empire. Jews had already been driven out of England centuries before during the reign of Edward (1239–1307). From the late thirteenth century on, however, the various rulers of the territory of Poland/Lithuania offered the Jews access to land for new communities and opportunities to serve as agents for the state and regional noblemen. "By the beginning of the fifteenth century the Polish Jewish community numbered 10–15,000 Jews, and in the next century the population grew to more than 150,000. In the sixteenth and seventeenth centuries, the Polish nobility, who owned large tracts of land in the Ukraine, employed Jews on their estates: there they collected taxes, fees, tolls, and produce from the serfs."[12]

With the aid and support of these noblemen the Jews established towns and villages made up entirely (or nearly so) of Jews. They developed their own form of local self-government. "Each local community (*kehillah*) engaged a Board of Trustees that collected taxes for the government and provided educational and other necessary facilities of Jewish life. In the larger cities, the *kehillot* were supervised by paid officials including rabbis who were usually employed for three-year periods to serve as authorities in matters of Jewish law as well as heads of Talmudic academies."[13]

Poland would become a great center of Jewish scholarship and would remain so until well into the twentieth century. Polish sages developed their own unique approach to Talmudic scholarship. According to Seltzer, "In the yeshivah, Talmudic disputation became almost an end in itself; the method of *pilpul* (literally, 'pepper') or *billuk* (subtle differentiation and reconciliation of rabbinical opinions)" became so dominant that some Polish Talmudists complained it was "losing a firm connection to reality."[14]

At the heart of the Polish Jewish enterprise was the education of their young men in the intricacies of the Talmudic and rabbinic texts. The account of an eighteenth-century chronicler cited in Seltzer describes "the Ashkenazic educational ideal":

> Each community maintained young men and provided for them a weekly allowance of money that they might study with the head of the academy. And for each young man they also maintained two boys to study under

12. Cohn-Sherbok, *Judaism*, 226.

13. Cohn-Sherbok, *Judaism*, 226.

14. Seltzer, *Jewish People*, 478. Hereafter, page references to this work are given in parentheses in the text.

> his guidance, so that he would orally discuss Gemara, the commentaries of Rashi, and the Tosafot, which he had learned, and thus would gain experience in the subtlety of Talmudic argumentation. . . . If the community consisted of fifty householders, it supported not less than thirty young men and boys. (477–78)

Polish Jews even formed a regional government of sorts. Representatives "from several Ashkenazic communities" would meet "to resolve conflicts between them, deal with special crises, and head off threats posed by notorious anti-Jewish agitators." A national body called "The Council of the Four Lands" would meet twice a year to assign the tax burden, select advisors to the Polish court, and issue ordinances "in matters of education, public morals, and qualifications for the rabbinate" (479).

Tragically, the Jews of Poland would suffer from a vicious program called "the Chmielnicki Massacres" in 1648. This was a peasants' revolt against the Polish nobility that targeted Jews because of their association with the nobility in tax collection and estate management. Thousands of Jews were slaughtered in what was both a religious and political conflict. Years of war and violence followed with the Jewish community caught between the armies of Sweden, Poland, and Russia. "The catastrophe of 1648 ranks with the First Crusade, the Black Death, and the Spanish attacks of 1391 in Jewish history for its devastation. Despite the magnitude of the disaster, however, the Council of the Four Lands undertook measures to save as many Jews as possible, and many communities were re-established afterwards, even in the Polish Ukraine. But the economic prosperity and security that made the high degree of Polish rabbinic culture possible remained shattered for decades" (482).

The Polish Jewish community and Talmudic scholarship would endure and grow to be "the Jewish heartland." The rabbinic academy in Vilna in Lithuania would become world renowned. It would be known for its rigorous intellectualism and commitment to the close reading of the Talmud. Perhaps its most powerful and influential figure, Rabbi Elijah ben Solomon Zalman, the Vilna Gaon, would find himself at the end of the era in conflict with the emerging, pietistic Hasidic movement—a conflict that echoes to this very day.

The Impact of Martin Luther and the Reformation

The confluence of the "new learning" of the European humanists and the perceived corruption of the late medieval Roman Catholic Church produced what would come to be called the Protestant Reformation. It undid a millennium of substantial religious and cultural unity in Western Europe. Erasmus's Greek New Testament introduced scholars to the original text of the Gospels and Epistles. Martin Luther's German translation made it possible for even German peasants to hear the Bible in their own language. William Tyndale's English translation, though deemed "heretical" and suppressed in England, was mass-produced and smuggled into the country regardless of the protests of Henry VIII and his bishops. As many have noted, the printing press became the true engine of reform. Vernacular Bibles, sophisticated theological treatises, and scurrilous tracts poured off the presses of, especially, the low countries. The genie was well and truly out of the bottle.

Although the call for reform was an old one, Martin Luther's belligerence and intransigence became the catalyst for something more than reform: a revolution. Within a few decades the boundaries of the various states of Western Europe were not merely "national," but religious. Protestant princes favored Protestant religion. Catholic princes preserved the old religion. Henry VIII's England attempted to straddle the fence in his quest for an heir. For Europe a century of off-and-on conflict threatened the economic stability, political identity, and very lives of Europe's citizens. At the beginning of the seventeenth century, the Thirty Years' War brought devastation, famine, disease, and death.

But what of Europe's Jews during these cataclysmic years? By the beginning of the Reformation, Jews had already been driven out of many parts of Europe. For those Jews on the outskirts of Europe the Reformation had little impact. Robert Seltzer suggests that in the long run Jews would benefit from the Reformation. When toleration was eventually extended to dissident Christians it would be extended to Jews as well. Some Reformed communities would be more receptive to Jews than others. Dutch Calvinists and English Puritans were drawn to the imagery and thought of the Old Testament/Tanakh. Calvinists would find more value in "the Law" than many Protestants. Such Protestants would learn Hebrew to read not only the Bible in the original language, but, somewhat controversially, to read Jewish books. But for Jews who remained in Western Europe, especially in the German lands, there was certainly no improvement: "In the short run . . . the rise and spread of Protestantism in the sixteenth and the first half of the seventeenth centuries did not bring about an improvement in the status of the Jews in Germany (although fewer Jews were slaughtered while Christians were killing each other)" (501). In the very long run, Martin Luther's attitude toward the Jews would be utterly disastrous for the Jews of Europe in the middle of the twentieth century.

Luther was not alone in his virulent anti-Semitism. The humanist hero Desiderius Erasmus (1466–1536) was a notable Jew-hater. When a colleague remarked favorably on the study of Jewish literature, Erasmus retorted, "I see [the Jews] as a nation full of the most tedious fabrications who spread a kind of fog over everything. Talmud, Cabala, Tetragrammaton, Gates of Light—words, words, words. I would rather have Christ mixed up with Scotus than with that rubbish of theirs."[15] Erasmus's excuse for not taking up repeated invitations to come to Spain was that it was "full of Jews."[16] The efforts of Ferdinand and Isabella to drive the Jews out of Spain must have pleased him no end. Luther, however, proved to be a special case.

It has been popular to argue that Luther did not begin as an anti-Semite. His early work *That Jesus Christ Was Born a Jew* (1523) was a remarkably tolerant piece that argued that Christians "have dealt with the Jews as if they were dogs rather than human beings; they have done little else than deride them and seize their property."[17] Later, the argument goes, when he realized the Jews were not going to convert, he became unhinged and penned his infamous *Against the Jews and Their Lies* (1542). His recent biographer Lyndal Roper argues that this is simply not the case. "Anti-Semitism was not just a product of his later years, but in fact appears time and again."[18] In his exegetical work, his pamphleteering, and his casual conversation, one reads demeaning, dismissive, and crude words about the Jews. He complained about there being too many Jews in Frankfurt. He suggested in a letter that it was vain to baptize Jews "because they are rascals." He refused to intervene with the Elector of Saxony to enable the free movement of Jews in that region. His extreme supersessionism is perhaps his greatest and most tragic theological legacy. Time and time again he made the Jews the villains of their own holy texts. He intended to expel Jews from the Tanakh as they were expelled from Spain.[19]

But it was *Against the Jews and Their Lies* that had the longest and most tragic impact. This was, as Roper puts it, Luther off the leash. He is at his most cruel, his most biting, his most crude in this scurrilous tract. Luther de-

15. MacCulloch, *The Reformation*, 689.

16. MacCulloch, *The Reformation*, 681.

17. Lyndal Roper, *Martin Luther: Renegade and Prophet* (New York: Random House, 2016), 378.

18. Roper, *Martin Luther*, 379.

19. Roper, *Martin Luther*, 379–81.

clares that their synagogues should be set on fire and utterly destroyed. Their homes should likewise be broken down and destroyed, "for they perpetuate the same things there that they do in their synagogues." He continues:

> They should be deprived of their prayerbooks and *Talmuds* in which such idolatry, lies, cursing and blasphemy are taught. . . . [T]heir rabbis must be forbidden under threat of death to teach any more. . . . [P]assport and travelling privileges should be absolutely forbidden to the Jews. . . . [T]hey ought to be stopped from usury. . . . [L]et the young and strong Jews and Jewesses be given the flail, the axe, the hoe, the spade, the distaff, and spindle, and let them earn their bread by the sweat of their noses.[20]

He concludes that the German nobility ought to "be free of this insufferable devilish burden—the Jews." MacCulloch justifiably calls Luther's tract "a blueprint for the Nazis' *Kristallnacht* of 1938."[21] His writings against the Jews were (and are) perennially popular with anti-Semites. Rabbi and historian Reinhold Lewin (1888–1942/3) wrote in 1911, "whoever writes against the Jews, and for whatever reason, feels justified in referring triumphantly to Luther."[22] David Nirenberg remarks that Lewin's words "applied just as well to the National Socialists at whose hands, decades later, he probably perished."[23] Nazi biblical scholars and theologians through such organizations as the "Institute for the Study and Eradication of Jewish Influences on German Religious Life" eagerly produced new editions of Luther's anti-Jewish works.

At the end of his life Luther was still in bitter combat with the Jews. Nirenberg describes a winter journey to his birthplace of Eisleben:

> A number of Jewish refugees from other expulsions had recently been granted asylum there, a grant he hoped to reverse. As he rode through the town, he wrote to his wife on the first of February, it seemed to him that the presence of the Jews and their guilt raised a bitter wind against him, one that sought to freeze his brain, leaving him weakened and ill. He would do all he could, he told her, to see that they were driven out. To this end he preached some hard-edged sermons to the faithful: "If they will not con-

20. Cited in Cohn-Sherbok, *Judaism*, 231–32.

21. MacCulloch, *The Reformation*, 690.

22. David Nirenberg, *Anti-Judaism: The Western Tradition* (New York: W. W. Norton, 2013), 266.

23. Nirenberg, *Anti-Judaism*, 266–67.

vert, we should neither tolerate nor endure them among us." Luther's chill worsened, and these turned out to be the final sermons of his life.[24]

There were few exceptions to the Protestant intolerance and hatred of the Jews. Among European theologians the Lutheran Andreas Osiander, for one, "stood out strongly against such sentiments." He deplored Luther's attitude and wrote "a devastating attack on the 'blood-libel' myth about Jewish slaughter of Christian children."[25] He was perhaps the exception that proved the rule. But there was one region of Protestant Europe that welcomed Jews: the United Provinces of the "Low Countries" and especially the city of Amsterdam. Both the city and the Jews flourished because of their presence there.

The Jews of Amsterdam

At the end of the sixteenth century, Portuguese *conversos*, often skilled in trade, made their ways to congenial port cities, Hamburg, Livorno, and, especially, Amsterdam. William of Orange had led a revolt against the Spanish Hapsburgs that resulted in the formation of the independent United Provinces in 1581. The result was a Protestant trading state that quickly became "the foremost center of world trade in the seventeenth century."[26] The Protestant rulers of the United Provinces, like medieval Catholic princes before them, saw the advantage of tolerating Jews in their new republic. Portuguese Jews had long played a significant role in international commerce. Their presence in this new, wide open society (at least by sixteenth-century standards) would only enhance the wealth and power of the fledgling state. "The Amsterdam Jews were not only engaged prominently in the Dutch Atlantic trade and the importation of colonial goods, but also in related crafts—for example operating sugar refineries, tobacco workshops, workshops cutting and polishing diamonds and chocolate-making facilities. They were also successful as brokers in the Amsterdam stock exchange."[27]

Efron, Weitzman, and Lehmann argue that the Amsterdam Sephardim are considered "the first modern Jews." They had to reinvent a tradition

24. Nirenberg, *Anti-Judaism*, 266.
25. MacCulloch, *The Reformation*, 690.
26. Efron et al., *The Jews*, 247–48.
27. Efron et al., *The Jews*, 249.

that they had significantly lost. Some of them had been born to families who had spent generations as Roman Catholics. "The former *conversos* who emigrated to Amsterdam in the seventeenth century had to learn Judaism from scratch."[28] They would be called "new Jews."

In Amsterdam and elsewhere in the United Provinces, Jewish literature was produced and an educational system was developed to reintroduce these Jews to their ancient tradition. They had to learn the basics: Hebrew prayers, the content of the Torah and the Prophets, and, critically, halakah. At the same time the Portuguese and Spanish Jews continued to use the languages of their homeland and read with enthusiasm the poetry and literature of the "'Golden Age' . . . of Spanish literature, reading the works of Gongora and Quevedo, staging Spanish plays in the Amsterdam theater, and establishing literary academies modeled on the Spanish literary circles of the time."[29] These were "hyphenated Jews"—Jews at home in more than one culture.

In Amsterdam and other Dutch cities one may perhaps experience the first stirrings of "Jewish enlightenment" and nascent modernism. It was in Holland that the unfortunate Uriel Acosta (1590–1640) "argued that Torah was probably not of divine origin since it contained many features contrary to natural law."[30] He was excommunicated more than once in more than one city and committed suicide in Amsterdam in 1640. The greatest Jewish enlightenment thinker was Baruch (or Benedict) Spinoza (1632–77). Like Acosta, he denied the divine origin of the Torah and developed "a metaphysical system based on a pantheistic conception of nature."[31] His work *Tractatus Theologico-Politicus* had a major impact on the development of modern philosophy. He too was excommunicated by the Jewish community. Since he never returned to Judaism or converted to Christianity, some consider him the first "secular Jew." In the coming centuries he would find many companions, both former Jews and former Christians.

Mysticism, Messianism, and *Mitnagdim*

Jewish mysticism (or Kabbalah) has a long and varied history in Judaism. Ezekiel's visions of the chariot and throne of God had, over the centuries,

28. Efron et al., *The Jews*, 249.
29. Efron et al., *The Jews*, 250.
30. Cohn-Sherbok, *Judaism*, 253.
31. Cohn-Sherbok, *Judaism*, 253.

provided the most mature scholars access to profound, and, at times, dangerous mystical experiences. The Talmud tells us that four great sages "entered the Garden": Ben Azzai, Ben Zoma, Elisha Ben Abuya, and Akiva. Ben Azzai died; Ben Zoma went mad; Elisha Ben Abuya became a heretic; Akiva "emerged in peace."[32] The medieval rabbis would insist that only married men over 40 should engage in the study of Kabbalah. It was a practice for the intellectual and spiritual elite. In the early modern period this study would be democratized. The most famous mystical text of Judaism is the *Zohar*, ascribed to Shimon Ben Yochai of second-century Palestine. Modern scholars consider it the work of Moses De Leon, a Jewish mystic of thirteenth-century Castile.[33] The greater part of the *Zohar* is mystical interpretations of the weekly Torah portions. It was to have an enormous impact on Jews throughout the world—an impact that endures to this day.

Kabbalah is complex, varied, and often perplexing. At the heart of the system as it came to reside in the *Zohar* and other mystical texts is the notion of God as *Ayn Sof*, "the infinite":

> God's essence is unknowable to men, but [the mystics] combined this with a system of positive attributes drawn from earlier Jewish writings and from their own mystical intuitions. According to Kabbalah, the "root of roots" in God is the Ayn Sof, the infinite, limitless, impersonal First Cause, which cannot be grasped by human thought. . . . Out of the hidden depths, latent powers and lights of the Ayn Sof break forth—the sefirot. The sefirot are revealed divinity, in their unity constituting the personal God of religion to which prayer and meditation are directed.[34]

The sefirot "are degrees or stages issuing forth from the absolute mystery of the Ayn Sof; they are not intermediary forces between God and the material world as in Neo-Platonism."[35] The names of the ten sefirot are Divine Will (or "Supreme Crown"), Wisdom, Understanding, Greatness, Power, Beauty, Endurance, Majesty, Foundation (or "Righteous One"), Kingdom (or "Divine Presence"). "The meaning of each sefirah in relation to the whole is the subject of inexhaustible and loving kabbalistic meditation."[36]

32. *b. Hag.* 2:14b in *The Talmud: A Selection*, trans. Solomon.
33. Karesh and Hurvitz, "Zohar," *Encyclopedia of Judaism*, 573–74.
34. Seltzer, *Jewish People*, 430.
35. Seltzer, *Jewish People*, 430.
36. Seltzer, *Jewish People*, 431.

By the sixteenth century Kabbalah was no longer the province of elite scholars. The printing press enabled the *Zohar* to be available as never before. And a new system of Kabbalah was developed in Safed by Moses Cordevero and Isaac Luria:

> The system promulgated by Isaac Luria and his disciples offered a startling creation myth that accounted for the presence of evil in the world as a result of a breakdown in the divine system. Using the teachings of the *Zohar* as a base for exegesis, Lurianic Kabbalah also offered a reinterpretation of ritual. . . . [Luria] taught that Jewish ritual performance not only played a role in maintaining the cosmic order but also was fundamental to the redemption of the world. With each properly performed ritual, a repair (*tikkun*) was made to the fallen world order, and a piece of the Godhead was restored.[37]

The result was the production of new rituals and new customs that both scholars and ordinary Jews could participate in. The rituals were thought by many to pave the way for the messianic redemption. Perhaps only the scholarly and mystical elite could experience the raptures of the divine throne room. But ordinary Jews by their obedience to the commandments and their engagement in ritual practices could involve themselves in the repair of the world and pave the way for messiah. This contributed to the rise of one of the most important and startling messianic pretenders in early modern Judaism.

Shabbatai Zevi

In the late seventeenth century, Jews were suffering the results of the challenges and dislocations described earlier in this chapter. The expulsions from Spain and Portugal had seen Jews seek refuge wherever they could find it—especially in the Ottoman Empire. The Protestant Reformation had destabilized Western Europe and seen Jews driven from Germany into Poland. The Thirty Years' War that further disrupted Europe had been followed by the Chmielnicki Massacres. The Ottoman Turks were in firm control of a vast and increasingly aggressive empire. It would seem a good time for the messiah to come. A Jew from Smyrna named Shabbatai Zevi (or Zvi) became a student of Lurianic Kabbalah, participating in Kabbalistic groups

37. Adam Shear, "Jews and Judaism in Early Modern Europe," in Baskin and Seeskin, *The Cambridge Guide*, 157, 159.

in Cairo and Gaza. In Gaza, Abraham-Nathan Ashkenazi (Nathan of Gaza) proclaimed Zevi the messiah in 1665. "Nathan sent letters to Jews in the diaspora asking them to repent and recognize Shabbatai Zevi as their redeemer. Shabbatai, he announced, would take the Sultan's crown, bring back the lost tribes, and inaugurate the period of messianic redemption."[38] The effect on world Jewry was electric.

In her seventeenth-century memoir, Glickl of Hameln describes what happened when the news of Shabbatai Zevi reached Hamburg. "Our joy, when the letters arrived [bringing news about Shabbatai Zvi] is not to be told. . . . The Sephardic youth came dressed in their best finery and decked in broad green silk ribbons, the gear of Shabbatai Zvi. 'With timbrels and with dance' . . . they one and all trooped to the synagogue. . . . Many sold their houses and lands and all their possessions, for any day they hoped to be redeemed."[39]

But it was not to be. Shabbatai Zevi was arrested and imprisoned by the Ottoman authorities in 1666. This did not diminish the excitement or the expectations of many Jews. The Ottoman authorities soon wearied of the movement. Zevi was brought before the Sultan and given the choice of converting to Islam or death: he chose to convert. His conversion ended Shabbatainism as a mass movement. "Many individuals, including some leading rabbis . . . continued to believe in his messianic mission, interpreting the apostasy as part of the process leading to redemption."[40] Even Zevi's death in 1676 did not end his movement. "Nathan of Gaza declared that Shabbatai had ascended to the supernal world" and a number of small groups continued to believe in his messianic message.[41] In the eighteenth century, Joseph Frank (1726–91) would declare himself the reincarnation of Zevi.[42]

Scholars and Pietists: The Hasidim and Their Opponents

Alongside developments in Jewish mysticism were important developments in Jewish law. Joseph Karo (or Caro) set himself the task of developing a new code of Jewish law. Entitled *Schulhan Arukh* ("the set table"),

38. Cohn-Sherbok, *Judaism*, 220.
39. Cited in Efron et al., *The Jews*, 257.
40. Efron et al., *The Jews*, 258.
41. Cohn Sherbok, *Judaism*, 221.
42. Cohn-Sherbok, *Judaism*, 221.

it was a digest of all the binding rulings of the halakah. "This collection, which appeared in 1564, became the authoritative code of law in the Jewish world."[43] It is in use to this day. In the 1570s an Ashkenazi rabbi named Moses Isserles "changed Ashkenazi Jewry profoundly. . . . [H]e published in Cracow a new edition of Karo's *Shuhlan Arukh* with his own comments, in which he clarified the Ashkenazi practice where it differed from Karo's opinion."[44] Although originally controversial with some rabbis, Karo's work with Isserles's comments created "a sense of Ashkenazi identity" over a wide geographic area, including "Poland-Lithuania, the Hapsburg lands of Bohemia and Moravia, and the Jewish communities of Germany."[45] Perhaps the most important of these communities was that in Poland-Lithuania, where great learning and great piety would clash at the beginning of the modern era.

The Jerusalem of Lithuania

While the rest of Polish Jewry struggled to recover from the disasters of the Chmielnicki Massacres, Lithuania flourished: "Owing to its proximity to Prussia and trade connections with the West and with Russia, the Jews of Vilna and several other Lithuanian towns maintained a certain prosperity in the eighteenth century. Vilna became an important focus of Jewish intellectual life from the mid-eighteenth century until the twentieth century. (Vilna came to be called the Jerusalem of Lithuania—a lively center not only of traditional rabbinic scholarship, but of the nineteenth-century Jewish Enlightenment and Jewish social radicalism as well.)"[46]

A key figure in the eighteenth century was Rabbi Elijah ben Solomon Zalman, known as the Vilna Gaon. He espoused a "rigorous intellectuality" rejecting "elaborate argumentation . . . and espoused an exact, meticulous, interpretation of the common-sense meaning of the text."[47] He was even willing to criticize "the scholars of the rabbinic age when he felt they had not interpreted adequately the foundations of rabbinic law in the Mishnah."[48] The Vilna Gaon had many disciples, produced many books, and was in his

43. Cohn-Sherbok, *Judaism*, 212.
44. Efron et al., *The Jews*, 241.
45. Efron et al., *The Jews*, 241.
46. Seltzer, *Jewish People*, 483–84.
47. Seltzer, *Jewish People*, 485.
48. Seltzer, *Jewish People*, 485.

lifetime considered a saint. But he would find himself contending with a Jewish revival movement that would alarm him and other intellectuals of Vilna, the Hasidim.

Israel ben Eliezer, the Baal Shem Tov (Master of the Good Name), was very different from the Vilna Gaon. He was "a kabbalist, a faith healer, a writer of amulets designed to ward off illness, and an exorcist."[49] The aftermath of the Chmielnicki Massacres resulted in many Polish Jews becoming obsessed with their sins, the extreme evil of the world, and the need for penance and extreme asceticism—all with the intention of hastening the arrival of the messiah. A Polish Jew named Solomon Maimon, looking back on his youth, remembered these times of misery and fear. He describes how a scholar named Simon of Lubtsch, distressed by the weight of his sins, starved himself to death. In spite of this Maimon says many looked on him as a saint. He continues, "Jossel of Klezk proposed nothing less than to hasten the advent of the Messiah. To this end he performed strict penance, fasted, rolled himself in the snow, undertook nightwatches and similar severities. By all sorts of such operations he believed that he was able to accomplish the overthrow of the legion of evil spirits, who kept guard on the Messiah, and placed obstacles to his coming."[50]

The group around Baal Shem Tov (Besht) took a different tack. They rejected the extreme penances and obsessive guilt and "denounced melancholy as a state of mind that created a barrier between man and God."[51] Their worship and prayer practices were perhaps their most distinctive contribution to Jewish life. They focused not on the absence of God, but on God's omnipresence: "There is no place where God is not." "A main characteristic of Hasidism was complete trust in God's goodness and providence—a faith that is realized in total cleaving (*devekut*) of the soul to God in worship." The worship was characterized by "joy, humility, gratitude and spontaneity."[52] They sought to remove any barriers and distractions between the individual and God. The practices of the Hasidim became very popular with the common Jews of Poland. The stories of the wit and wisdom of those early Hasidim still delight contemporary hearers.[53]

49. Efron et al., *The Jews*, 289.

50. Seltzer, *Jewish People*, 490.

51. Seltzer, *Jewish People*, 490.

52. Seltzer, *Jewish People*, 491.

53. See Martin Buber, *Tales of the Hasidim*, trans. Ocla Marx (New York: Schocken, 1948), and Buber, *The Legend of the Baal-Shem*, trans. Maurice Friedman (New York: Harper & Brothers, 1955).

The learned elites of Lithuania were not pleased with the Hasidim. Critics of their practices came to be called the *mitnagdim* (opponents). Early on the rabbinic authorities objected that uneducated Jews were being introduced to the esoteric practices of Kabbalah. They were also concerned about matters of halakah. They were worried about untrained ritual slaughterers, lack of attention to Torah study, their establishment of specifically Hasidic places of worship and study, and their lack of decorum in worship.[54] They were also concerned that the Hasidic holy man, the *tzaddik,* was robbing the elite rabbis of their traditional authority. The opponents "insisted on the stark separation of the material and the spiritual worlds and emphasized that Torah study was the only legitimate way to approach God. Similarly, they considered the idea that God was present in the world of the mundane and material to be an affront."[55]

The Vilna Gaon became the most important voice of the *mitnagdim.* He considered Hasidism to be a heresy and attempted, unsuccessfully, to stamp it out. In spite of the efforts of the learned of the *mitnagdim,* the writs of excommunication, and denunciations, Hasidism survived. "The religious revival that was Hassidism continued to blossom; within about three generations of its founding, Hasidism had captured the hearts and minds of nearly two-thirds of eastern European Jewry."[56] The Hasids and their opponents would make their peace only when they faced a greater enemy than each other—the *Haskalah* or Jewish enlightenment.

As the modern world emerged, the three streams of early modern Judaism converged: the rigorous intellectualism of the rabbinic academies represented by the learned of Poland-Lithuania and especially the Vilna Gaon; the mystical intensity of the sages of Safed represented by Lurianic Kabbalah; and the joyous piety of the Hasidim represented by the Baal Shem Tov. Together these formed a European and, indeed, international Jewish culture that for centuries would produce great scholars, pious "rebbes," and ordinary Jews deeply formed by the Torah and practices of these varied streams. This culture would in the centuries to come face the fires of secularism and the bitter outcome of more than a millennium of European anti-Semitism. The world made by those scattered Sephardi, the mystics of the Kabbalah, and the pious and learned communities of Poland and Lithuania is to this day part of the spiritual and intellectual DNA of contemporary Jews.

54. Efron et al., *The Jews,* 294.
55. Efron et al., *The Jews,* 295.
56. Efron et al., *The Jews,* 295.

QUESTIONS FOR DISCUSSION

1. What was the impact of the expulsion of Jews from Spain?
2. How did Jews fare in the Ottoman Empire?
3. What was Martin Luther's view of the Jews and how did the Reformation impact them?

FURTHER READING

Buber, Martin. *The Legend of the Baal-Shem.* Translated by Maurice Friedman. London: Horowitz, 1956.

Cohn-Sherbok, Dan. "The Rise of the Hasidic Movement." Pages 233–40 in *Judaism: History, Belief and Practice.* London: Routledge, 2003.

Nirenberg, David. *Anti-Judaism: The Western Tradition.* New York: W. W. Norton, 2013.

Scholem, Gershom. *Major Trends in Jewish Mysticism.* With a new foreword by Robert Alter. New York: Schocken Books, 1995.

Shear, Adam. "Jews and Judaism in Early Modern Europe." Pages 140–68 in *The Cambridge Guide to Jewish History, Religion, and Culture.* Edited by Judith R. Baskin and Kenneth Seeskin. Cambridge: Cambridge University Press, 2010.

CHAPTER 14

Emancipation, Reform, and Danger

Reward and punish no doctrine, tempt and bribe no one to adopt any religious opinion! Let everyone be permitted to speak as he thinks, to invoke God after his own manner or that of his fathers, and to seek eternal salvation where he thinks he may find it, as long as he does not disturb the public felicity and acts honestly toward the civil laws, toward you and his fellow citizen.

—Moses Mendelssohn

It was not the "Orthodox" Jews who introduced the word "orthodoxy" into the Jewish discussion. It was the modern "progressive" Jews who first applied this name to "old," "backward" Jews as a derogatory term. . . . "Orthodox" Judaism does not know any varieties of Judaism. It conceives Judaism as one and indivisible.

—Samson Raphael Hirsch

Today we accept as binding only the moral laws and maintain only such ceremonies as elevate and sanctify our lives, but reject all such as are not adapted to the views and habits of modern civilization.

—The Pittsburg Platform of American Reform Judaism, 1885

Jews were portrayed as a people shaped by their desert origins and their dispersed condition into a calculating, nomadic, and parasitic tribe that could thrive only by attaching itself to larger and more rooted peoples and, in the process, both exploiting and weakening them.

—Peter Hays

As long as he is a Jew, his Jewishness must be stronger in him than his humanity, and keep him apart from non-Jews. He declares by this segregation that this, his Jewishness, is his true, highest nature, which has to have precedence over his humanity.

—Bruno Bauer, German Protestant theologian

The great German philosopher Immanuel Kant was scheduled to lecture at the University of Konigsberg in 1777. A small, hunchbacked Jewish man made his way into the lecture hall, much to the displeasure of the assembled students. A student recalled, "As to be expected there began sneering and jeering that eventually turned into clicking, whistling and stamping."[1] The mere presence of a Jew at a Christian university in Germany was enough to set off a near riot. The crowd settled down as Kant began his lecture. "At the conclusion of the lecture," the student reports,

> the Jew pushed himself forward with an intensity, which starkly contrasted with his previous composure, through the crowd to reach the Professor. The students hardly noticed him, when suddenly there again resounded a scornful laughter, which immediately gave way to wonder as Kant, after briefly looking at the stranger pensively and exchanging with him a few words, heartily shook his hand and then embraced him. Like a brushfire there went through the crowd, Moses Mendelssohn. "It is the Jewish philosopher from Berlin." Deferentially the students made way as the two sages left the lecture hall hand in hand.[2]

Freedom and Faithfulness in the Enlightenment

The eighteenth century was a time of "enlightenment" throughout Europe. The new learning was challenging old thinking about nearly everything. Modern science and philosophy (often the same thing) were asking uncomfortable questions about God and the world. Human reason was now touted as the only secure route to truth and understanding of the world. Both Jews and Christians were confronted with the question of how this emerging science and modern philosophy fit with their long-accepted assumptions about the nature of God and the world. Moses Mendelssohn was one of the most important voices in this conversation in the latter half of the eighteenth century. He became famous in Germany in 1763 when his *Treatise on Metaphysical Evidence* came in first place in an essay contest put on by the Berlin Royal Academy. Immanuel Kant's essay came in second.[3] For many Germans, this was a different sort of Jew.

1. Efron et al., *The Jews*, 300.
2. Efron et al., *The Jews*, 301.
3. Martin Goodman, *A History of Judaism* (Princeton: Princeton University Press, 2018), 457.

Moses Mendelssohn

Mendelssohn insisted that a Jew could accept the emerging truth of the Enlightenment, live as a loyal citizen of the German state, and remain faithful to the religion of his or her forebears. He argued that Jews need not convert to Christianity to flourish in modern Europe. In his great book *Jerusalem, or, On Religious Power and Judaism*, he advised his fellow Jews to adapt themselves to their respective states. They should follow the secular laws of the country in question but should also "hold fast to the religion of your fathers." He recognized this could be a burden, especially for professional Jews who spent a good deal of their time interacting with non-Jews. The food laws, the intricacies of the calendar, and the required times for prayer would make them stand out. But Mendelssohn was convinced that it was possible to live a modern, enlightened life in Germany and remain faithful to Torah.[4] The Jews Mendelssohn addressed were urban Jews, for the most part; Jews who had made their way in the great cities of Europe. They longed to be part of their communities, accepted as equals in the universities and professions. They hoped to be *emancipated*, to receive the same civil and political rights as other citizens of their respective cities and states. But how would they do this and remain Jews?

This was the great question faced by the increasingly educated, sophisticated, and successful Jewish community of Western Europe. Would "emancipation" require Jews to become un-Jewish, or at least less Jewish? Could a Jew be faithful to the revelation of God to Moses and accept the findings of science and the assertions of the philosophers? Christians, of course, were asking similar questions. Mendelssohn, among others, thought this was indeed possible. A Jew not only *could* but *must* remain faithful to the religion of Israel in spite of the difficulties it created in normal urban life. In the coming century, some Jews would disagree. They began to recommend significant changes in Jewish law and practice—going beyond anything suggested or perhaps imagined by Mendelssohn. Many would set aside the food laws and distinctive practices of prayer and worship, and the calendar. The result would be a Judaism divided for the first time into the "denominations" explored in the first half of this book.[5] They did not intend to destroy Judaism—quite the contrary. They intended to make a place for Jews and Judaism within Christian European society. This would prove more difficult than they could imagine.

4. Goodman, *A History*, 458.
5. See above, pp. 17–19.

Mendelssohn's family is a case study in the challenge "enlightened" Jews faced in retaining their Jewish faith. Conversion to Christianity was viewed by many elite Jews as a means for social and political advancement. Mendelssohn's son Abraham consequently raised his children as Lutherans and would later, with his wife, also convert.[6] Early nineteenth-century German Romanticism would make things even more difficult for Jews. The rational and legal nature of Judaism was singularly unappealing to the emerging German Romantics who "grounded faith on feeling and subjective experience."[7] Two of Mendelssohn's daughters, Dorothea and Henriette, would, under the influence of Romanticism, also convert to Christianity.[8] Only his son Alexander remained a Jew to the end of his life. None of his grandchildren (including the famous composer Felix Mendelssohn) were practicing Jews. This was, in fact *is*, the dilemma for modern Judaism: How does a Jew remain faithful to the Torah, to the God of Israel, live in the modern world, and flourish as a citizen of a modern state? Does "emancipation" necessarily mean assimilation?

The Paths to Emancipation

The countries of Europe pursued varied paths to the emancipation, or at least partial emancipation, of their Jews. They also experienced different forms of resistance and pushback to the full inclusion of Jews as citizens. Dan Cohn-Sherbok argues that "in many respects the medieval period extended into the eighteenth century for the Jewish community."[9] Jews in many locations were subject to centuries-old restrictions, taxations, and humiliations. The Enlightenment began to raise serious questions about the justice of this treatment. In the German states, Wilhelm Christian Dohm, a Prussian politician and writer, famously argued for the emancipation of the Jews in his work *Concerning the Amelioration of the Civil Status of the Jews* in 1781. In the same year, the Holy Roman Emperor Joseph II "abolished the Jewish badge as well as taxes imposed on Jewish travelers," eventually issued an edict of toleration for Jews in Vienna, and abolished other restrictive regulations.[10]

6. Efron et al., *The Jews*, 263.
7. Seltzer, *Jewish People*, 583.
8. Efron et al., *The Jews*, 263.
9. Cohn-Sherbok, *Judaism*, 291.
10. Cohn-Sherbok, *Judaism*, 291.

In fairness, these changes were perhaps intended more for the good of the states involved than for the good of the Jews.

Substantial changes in the status of Europe's Jews came only with war and revolution. The French Revolution produced the landmark "Declaration of the Rights of Man and the Citizen" that insisted "all men are born, and remain, free and equal in right" and that "no person shall be molested because of his opinions, even such as are religious, provided that the manifestation of those opinions does not disturb the public order established by law." Some French officials wondered if this included France's Jews, especially the Ashkenazi Jews of the Alsace who had immigrated from the east. They were viewed as "other." In the end, Jews who could take the "civic oath" were to be recognized as citizens. In principle, "Judaism was to be treated exactly like Christianity by the state."[11]

When Napoleon seized power, he convened an "Assembly of Jewish Notables" to determine whether Judaism was compatible with full citizenship in the new French state. Napoleon was satisfied with their answers and the potential loyalty of French Jews. He would go on to establish a "Great Sanhedrin." He was hoping to determine, in consultation with these Jewish leaders, which of the laws of Judaism could be safely set aside for the good of the state. He wanted citizens who could contribute to France without the complications of peculiar religious restrictions. An army that required different foods, different times of worship, and different clothing would not be as cost-effective or unified as one with the same food, same times of worship, and same clothing. Civic unity demanded some essential conformity.[12] He would establish "consistories" throughout the country to "regulate Jewish life for the benefit of the state."[13]

The influence of French policies would be felt outside of France. Wherever the French army conquered, both before and during the time of Napoleon, Jews were liberated. In Holland, northern Italy, and the Rhineland, Jewish civic equality was affirmed. With the conquests of Napoleon in central Europe many Jews would receive a measure of emancipation for the first time. When the French established the client kingdom of Westphalia, the Jews were given equality with other citizens. The city of Frankfurt gave Jews equal rights in 1811, as did Prussia. Jews received full citizenship and civil rights throughout the realms con-

11. Seltzer, *Jewish People*, 522–23.
12. Goodman, *A History*, 442.
13. Goodman, *A History*, 442.

quered by the French.[14] When Napoleon invaded Poland and Russia, Jews initially greeted him as "an enemy of Polish backwardness and Russian autocracy." But they would turn against him when he failed to bring liberation to the Jews of Eastern Europe. Like most Europeans they would eventually come to see Napoleon "as a tyrant to be crushed, a symbol of a failed revolution."[15]

The defeat of Napoleon brought pushback against Jewish emancipation. The various German states and cities rescinded the recently received citizenships and civil rights of Jews. In response to the French conquests, the Germans had become increasingly xenophobic and nationalistic. Any freedoms granted by the French were immediately suspect. Jewish emancipation was set back for a generation. It was not until 1869 that the Northern German Federation liberated its Jews and only in 1871, with the unification of Germany under the Hohenzollerns, that Germany's Jews were finally granted citizenship and civil rights.[16] The revolutionary movements of 1848 in Europe forced monarchs in several European states to grant additional rights to their citizenry, including the Jews. Freedom of religion was assured in Austria in 1848 and eventually in Hungary as well. Jewish equality was recognized in most Italian states and when Italy was united, emancipation of the Jews of Italy was complete.[17]

Restrictions in Eastern Europe

Eighteenth-century Russia was an autocracy. It seemed impervious to western-style liberalizations and would never countenance emancipation of its peasants, let alone its Jews. When it annexed the Polish-Lithuanian Commonwealth it acquired nearly one million Jews.

The empress Catherine the Great restricted Jewish settlement by edict. An enormous region called "the Pale of Settlement" was established. It included Lithuania, White Russia, western Ukraine, and Poland. Jews were not permitted to live in Russia proper with the exception of a handful of elite merchants.[18] While Jews were being granted citizenship and religious

14. Seltzer, *Jewish People*, 524–25.

15. Efron et al., *The Jews*, 274–75.

16. Cohn-Sherbok, *Judaism*, 242–43.

17. Seltzer, *Jewish People*, 531–32.

18. Marsha L. Rozenblit, "European Jewry: 1800–1933," in Baskin and Seeskin, *The Cambridge Guide*, 184.

freedom in Western Europe, the Russian Tsars pursued hostile policies. Nicholas I (1825–55) sought to convert Jews to Christianity. He undertook an extremely cruel conscription policy. The state drafted Jewish boys as young as twelve into the army, separated them from their families, and pressured them to convert.[19] Some would never see their families again. Nicholas also sought to assimilate Jews through "crown schools" that provided a "secular, modern" education for Jewish children. He also undermined the traditional Jewish communal authorities and structures.[20] Things did not greatly improve for Jews during the reign of Nicholas's successor, Alexander II. More wealthy and elite Jews were permitted to live outside of the Pale of Settlement. But with Alexander's assassination things would become much worse for Russia's Jews.[21]

The Jewish Enlightenment: Reform and Resistance

Moses Mendelssohn's life and work were examples of the Jewish enlightenment or *Haskalah* (from the Hebrew *sekhl*, "intellect"). Mendelssohn and his enlightened peers "encouraged Jews to study European languages, philosophy, and science. They discouraged the use of Yiddish, a Jewish language with both German and Hebrew elements, as a barrier to integration."[22] The leaders of the Jewish enlightenment were called *maskilim* and were drawn for the most part from the wealthy and educationally elite segments of European Jewish society. Germany became a center of *Haskalah*. The "Jewish Free School" was opened in Berlin in 1778, offering courses in German, French, math, mechanics, geography, history, and the sciences. Germany, over the next few generations, would produce a cadre of "scientifically trained, skeptically inclined" Jews. In the nineteenth century these Jews would offer intellectual and spiritual leadership to the whole of Jewish and, for that matter, Christian Europe.[23]

The *maskilim* produced a wealth of publications spreading the message of enlightenment. In 1806 the journal *Sulamith* was launched with the purpose of "the promotion of culture and humanism among the Jewish nation."

19. Rozenblit, "European Jewry," 185.
20. Rozenblit, "European Jewry," 187.
21. Cohn-Sherbok, *Judaism*, 249.
22. Karesh and Hurvitz, "Haskalah," *Encyclopedia of Judaism*, 199–200.
23. Efron et al., *The Jews*, 302.

It became clear that the goal of the Jewish enlightenment was "harmonizing Judaism with European culture."[24] Mendelssohn had insisted that Jews could be enlightened, sophisticated citizens of Europe and faithful to the laws and traditions of their forebears—fully practicing Jews. His successors were not satisfied with this. Men like David Friedlander were not content to live comfortably within German culture. They sought political equality as well as social acceptance. For this to happen, Friedlander and other prominent Jews imagined that Jewish religious life and practice needed to be reformed. Friedlander wanted Hebrew to be abandoned, along with study of the Talmud, Kabbalistic references in prayers, and references to the restoration of Jerusalem. He wanted services of greater dignity and order—more like those in Germany's Protestant churches—to be held on Sunday rather than on the Sabbath.[25]

One of the most important early reformers was a wealthy layman named Israel Jacobson. Jacobson was deeply invested in both Judaism and the principles of the Enlightenment.[26] During the time of Napoleon's reign in Westphalia, he opened the first Reform temple in the town of Seesen in central Germany. After Napoleon's defeat, the old order was restored, and he moved to Berlin and opened a private synagogue in his home. Jewish traditionalists succeeded in getting it closed down. Finally, in 1818, Eduard Kley, who had participated in the Reform group in Berlin, became the head of a new Jewish school in Hamburg. He opened a Reform synagogue in Hamburg that was faithful to the views of Friedlander and Jacobson. The sermons and prayers were in German. Choral singing was accompanied by an organ, as it would be in the local Lutheran Church.[27] A new prayer book eliminated parts of the traditional service, including the prayers for return to the land of Israel and the messianic age. Not surprisingly, the more traditional rabbis of Hamburg were outraged.

Perhaps the most important response to these developments in Germany was penned by a brilliant young scholar named Samson Raphael Hirsch (1808–88). In 1836 he published *Nineteen Letters on Judaism.* The format of the book was a series of essays written by a rabbi to a young friend considering abandoning his Judaism. The purpose of life, Hirsch argued, was not to acquire wealth and power, to be happy and self-satisfied—but to obey God's will. This was as true for gentiles as it was for Jews. If the people

24. Efron et al., *The Jews*, 303.
25. Efron et al., *The Jews*, 303.
26. Seltzer, *Jewish People*, 580.
27. Seltzer, *Jewish People*, 581.

of Israel left off obeying the laws of God given at Sinai, they were not only abandoning God's Torah but abdicating their role to demonstrate to the entire world what a life of obedience and faithfulness entailed. The prophetic call to love, justice, and peace for the entirety of humanity could be lost.[28] By abandoning some of the practices of their forebears, Reform Judaism was abdicating this role of modeling a life of obedience to God.

Hirsch was no obscurantist. He had studied classical languages, history, and philosophy at the University of Bonn. He has been credited (or blamed) for the origin of a Jewish Neo-Orthodoxy. His brand of orthodoxy embraced rather than rejected modernity. He fully believed that one could "combine a commitment to the Torah with active participation in the life of the state and society."[29] Other Orthodox critics of the reform were not so sure. Rabbi Moses Sofer (1762–1839) was one of the most important opponents of reform. He was the rabbi of Pressburg in Hungary, an important center of traditional Judaism. He wrote,

> May your mind not turn to evil and never engage in corruptible partnerships with those fond of innovations. . . . Do not touch the books of Rabbi Moses [Mendelssohn] from Dessau, and your foot will never slip. . . . The daughters may read German books but only those in our own way [Yiddish], according to the interpretation of our teachers. . . . Be warned not to change your Jewish names, speech and clothing—God forbid. . . . Never say, "Times have changed."[30]

Rabbi Sofer's concerns reflect those of the devotees of traditional cultures and religions to this day. How much contact with the "outside world" is advisable or even permissible? What will eventually compromise your commitment to your faith and tradition? As time went on it became clear to both the "Reform" and the "Orthodox" camps that reform came about via "Jewish contact with non-Jewish society, exposure to general education, and one's social status and class." This would divide Jews socially, intellectually, economically, and spiritually. In many parts of Jewish Europe there were two groups of Jews: "one poorer and traditional the other wealthier and religiously progressive."[31] As this split within Judaism grew wider, some

28. Cohn-Sherbok, *Judaism*, 260.
29. Efron et al., *The Jews*, 320.
30. Cited in Efron et al., *The Jews*, 317.
31. Efron et al., *The Jews*, 317.

would come to believe the only answer to the threat of assimilation was total isolation from a corrupt culture.

Today's Heredim (the fearful of God) represent those Jews (sometimes called ultra-Orthodox) who make every effort to keep themselves separate from the decadence of modern society, including the apostasy, as they see it, of other groups of Jews. They live in separate enclaves in Israel and throughout the Diaspora. By segregating themselves, they hope to minimize, if not eliminate, contact with the outside world, especially popular culture. Their children are educated in separate schools. The educational focus is upon living a life in obedience to Torah.[32] Some communities cautiously send their young people to university to receive training deemed necessary for the community: medicine, teaching, computers, and the like. Their educations are carefully monitored. Hirsch would perhaps wonder how such a life in isolation contributes to the mission of modeling a life of obedience to the wider world; Sofer would perhaps argue that is exactly the point of such a life.

Europe's Jews over the course of the late eighteenth and nineteenth centuries offered various routes of surviving as Jews in an increasingly complex and "enlightened" world. Some Jews found non-conformity too difficult and converted to Christianity, assuming this was their pass into acceptance in society. Others, like Mendelssohn and Hirsch, sought an accommodation with European society. They insisted that Jews could be enlightened, educated, and accommodated without being assimilated. The advocates of Reform went further. They insisted that, to survive, Judaism needed to make larger changes than Mendelssohn and Hirsch had imagined. Unless Judaism was updated to fit the needs of modern Jews, they would lose many Jews to secularism—especially younger Jews. A final group rejected all of these options. They would remain faithful to the practices of their forebears regardless of how the world around them had changed. To this day, Jews continue to struggle with the implications and varieties of these options—as do Christians. The question of what it means to be a believer in a secular and sometimes hostile world continues to trouble many.

The Scientific Study of Judaism

While Jacobson, Friedlander, and their colleagues were rethinking Jewish practice and worship, Jewish scholars were reconsidering Jewish history. Eu-

32. Goodman, *A History*, 499.

ropean scholars, especially in Germany, began to apply the same historical-critical tools they had used to study the history of Egypt, Greece, and Rome to the origin stories of Judaism and Christianity. Hermann Samuel Reimarus, for example, attacked the historical basis of the Christian origin story in his *Apology or Defense of the Rational Worshippers of God.* It was published after Reimarus's death by Gottfried Ephraim Lessing, a close friend of Moses Mendelssohn. Reimarus argued that Jesus was a simple, pious Jew who had no thought of beginning a separate religion. He wanted to see the kingdom of God established on earth. That was the sole focus of his teaching. His mistake was embracing a political form of messianism and believing he had more support among the masses than he actually did. He was arrested and executed by the Romans and died in despair and disappointment, believing God had abandoned him.[33] The response to the publication of Reimarus's work was predictable. One critic refuted his work line by line. But thus began what Albert Schweitzer would call "the Quest of the Historical Jesus."[34] In the nineteenth century, Jews would find their own history and origin stories similarly challenged.

The "scientific study of Judaism" could actually be traced to a certain extent to Baruch Spinoza and Uriel Acosta in the seventeenth century. Both raised questions about Jewish history and practice on the basis of their enlightenment rationalism. Spinoza denied that God had revealed the Torah to Israel and insisted that the various laws of Israel "were the articles of the constitution of a now-defunct state."[35] But serious historical work on the history of the Jews began in the nineteenth century with Leopold Zunz (1794–1886), Isaac Marcus Jost (1793–1860), and, especially, Heinrich Graetz (1817–91). All three sought to apply modern historical-critical approaches to Jewish literature and history. Zunz aimed "to obtain command over the entire corpus of medieval Jewish literature and historically situate each work."[36] Jost published a nine-volume *History of the Israelites from the Maccabean Period to Our Own Day*. It was at least in part an apologetic work whose "principal thrust was to demonstrate the loyalty Jews had displayed to their host societies throughout history."[37]

33. Brown, "Quest of the Historical Jesus," 725.

34. Albert Schweitzer, *The Quest of the Historical Jesus*, trans. W. Montgomery, Susan Cupitt, and John Bowden (Minneapolis: Fortress, 2001; orig. published 1906).

35. Efron et al., *The Jews*, 298. On the "Positive-Historical School" of Judaism, see Karesh and Hurvitz, "Positive Historical School," *Encyclopedia of Judaism*, 490–91.

36. Efron et al., *The Jews*, 315.

37. Efron et al., *The Jews*, 316.

Graetz produced his eleven-volume *History of the Jews* between 1853 and 1876. His work was unique. It was written with great passion and verve. It has been called "suffering and scholarship history" because of its laser focus on the grim history of Jewish suffering.[38] For Graetz, the Jews were not simply members of a religious community, but constituted a "spiritual nationhood," "a living folk . . . acting out, under providential guidance, their role as a 'messianic people.'"[39]

Perhaps the era's most important scholar/rabbi was Abraham Geiger. He was trained as a rabbi and educated at the universities of Heidelberg and Bonn. While serving as a rabbi of Reform communities in Wiesbaden and Breslau he produced an array of articles and books reframing Jewish history, practice, and theology. Geiger argued that religion "was rooted in the human recognition of finitude and the quest for the infinite." Judaism, he believed, was a faith "founded on the trust in the one who guides the universe and in the task imposed upon Jews to practice justice and mercy."[40] For Geiger, Judaism had gone through a series of developmental stages. The final stage, the age of critical study, meant that "legalism was transcended through historical research." Although the halakah was no longer binding, "this does not imply Judaism is cut off from the past." The laws were to be appreciated as stages in the development of Judaism rather than "the core of the Jewish faith."[41] Geiger was convinced that his brand of Reform Judaism was superior not only to that of the "Orthodox" and "Neo-Orthodox" but also to Christianity. He thought Judaism as he conceived it could become a unifying force in a divided world.[42]

Robert Seltzer helpfully summarizes the intellectual and spiritual questions faced by the eighteenth- and nineteenth-century reformers and their critics. First, to what extent did Judaism need modernization? The Orthodox would say, not at all. The Neo-Orthodox of Hirsch would insist that traditional Jewish practice could and must be maintained even as Jews study in and live in the modern world. The more radical reformers would shed the practices of traditional Judaism entirely while clinging to what they considered the "kernel" of the Jewish faith. Second, to what extent was Judaism a "revealed religion"? The Orthodox and Neo-Orthodox insisted Torah "was a timeless, immutable, changeless pattern for the ideal human life." The re-

38. Efron et al., *The Jews*, 316.
39. Seltzer, *Jewish People*, 612.
40. Cohn-Sherbok, *Judaism*, 269.
41. See Seltzer, *Jewish People*, 596–97.
42. Seltzer, *Jewish People*, 596.

formers and the critical historians argued that to one extent or another the revelation was a "historical process" rather than a singular event. Finally, for the Orthodox, the Jewish state would one day be established in the messianic age through divine intervention. For Neo-Orthodox and Reform Jews, Judaism was a religious confession, not a nation. Jews could for this reason fully participate as citizens in their respective states. Seltzer suggests that they all had one thing in common: the feeling that "a rejuvenation of the Jewish religion was about to take place. The people of Israel had a unique mission in history, pointing to the messianic age. . . . Jewish thinkers were optimistic about the future—the future of Judaism and the future of humanity."[43] Ironically and tragically in light of this optimism, the greatest threats to the survival of Jews and Judaism lay ahead of them with the rise of modern anti-Semitism and in the coming bloodshed and tragedy of the twentieth century.

The Rise of Modern Anti-Semitism

European rulers who promoted emancipation for the Jews often did so with the expectation that Jews, by participating in the intellectual, political, and spiritual life of their respective countries, would become less Jewish. Eventually, it was thought, they would intermarry with gentiles, convert to Christianity, and become indistinguishable from other French or German citizens. Emancipation was intended, in part, to *eradicate* Judaism. This is why many reformers were looking for ways to modernize Judaism. They thought it would enable young Jews to remain Jews instead of succumbing to the temptations of conversion. A modernized Judaism was perhaps deemed better than no Judaism. They were right to be concerned. Attempts to persuade the Jews over the centuries to convert via argument and violence had largely failed. Jews who had been forcibly converted to Christianity (or Islam) frequently reverted to their ancestral faith as soon as they were able to do so. But secularism proved itself an even more formidable foe. It had the capacity to erode Jewish identity entirely.

Some late nineteenth-century thinkers argued that it didn't matter that a Jew converted; it made no difference that a Jew intermarried, lived, ate, dressed, and enjoyed the same entertainments and opinions as his or her fellow countrymen. For them, the problem with Jews was not their odd religion, strange customs, and sharp practices, but their *biology*. German jour-

43. Seltzer, *Jewish People*, 617–18.

nalist Wilhelm Marr coined the term "anti-Semitism" in the 1870s. Marr's anti-Semitism was not based on Jewish religion but on biological descent. Jews were a threat to the purity of "native Teutonic stock." According to Marr, Jews dominated culture, commerce, and politics. The German people and culture faced a struggle for survival with this alien, corrupting force.[44] Much earlier, in 1843, theologian Bruno Bauer (cited in the superscription) had written an essay entitled "The Jewish Question." There he argued that the "Jewishness" of a Jew took "precedence over his humanity." This is actually an old complaint. The Jews' sense of being a "chosen people" with a unique role to remain obedient to God's Torah had annoyed many over the centuries. The Roman writers Tacitus and Juvenal complained that Jews were misanthropic. The church father Origen suggested that the Jews had "formed a conspiracy against the human race." It is not hard to find such complaints throughout history in pagan, Christian, and Muslim sources.[45] This racial, essentialist anti-Semitism would prove the deadliest form of anti-Semitism to date. It would also be the most persistent. It endures in both religious and secular society to this day.

The late nineteenth century saw a dramatic rise in such biological anti-Semitism. An anti-Semitic congress was held in Germany in 1882. Explicitly anti-Semitic political parties and politicians arose and gained prominence in France, Germany, and Austria.[46] But perhaps the most dramatic event of the late nineteenth century occurred in France: the trial and conviction of the Jewish soldier Captain Alfred Dreyfus for passing military secrets to the Germans. The incident divided the country. "For the antisemites, the affair was proof of Jewish treachery. For the defenders of the French Revolution and the Third Republic, Dreyfus was an innocent victim of a terrible Conservative conspiracy."[47] The great impressionist painters Renoir, Degas, and Cézanne were convinced of Dreyfus's guilt. Degas was virulently anti-Semitic and "given to violent tirades against them." Pissarro, Monet, and Signac, on the other hand, were "firmly in Dreyfus' camp."[48] The left-wing supporters of the Revolution were eventually proven correct. It was a "vast right-wing conspiracy," and Dreyfus was eventually vindicated. But the whole incident shook European Jews. One young man, Theodor Herzl,

44. Cohn-Sherbok, *Judaism*, 273. See also Nirenberg, *Anti-Judaism*, 423–59.
45. Efron et al., *The Jews*, 329–30.
46. Cohn-Sherbok, *Judaism*, 274.
47. Efron et al., *The Jews*, 339.
48. Efron et al., *The Jews*, 339.

became convinced that Jews would never be accepted in Europe, no matter how much they integrated. For Herzl, the only solution was a Jewish homeland. I will take up his story in the next chapter.

While the Jews of Western Europe were being troubled by rising anti-Semitism and the Dreyfus Affair, Russian, Polish, and Lithuanian Jews were experiencing "pogroms." The term comes from the Russian word meaning "to wreak havoc." "It was used to describe an organized attack or massacre, often with government support, against any non-Russian ethnic group." The term eventually came to be especially associated "with the anti-Jewish pogroms of Russia of the period 1881 to 1921."[49] Pogroms began in earnest with the assassination of Alexander II in 1881. The Jews of the Ukraine suffered successive waves of attacks; Jews were expelled from Moscow. As late as 1911, a Jew named Mendel Beilis was accused in Kiev of ritual murder, but fortunately exonerated.[50]

During this era one of history's most notorious anti-Semitic texts was produced: *The Protocols of the Elders of Zion.* It was composed by the Russian secret police in Paris between 1896 and 1898. It was supposedly the minutes of a meeting of Jewish leaders to plot world domination. Jews are deemed responsible in the *Protocols* for many of the ills of modern society most feared by conservative autocratic societies: liberalism, parliamentary democracy, capitalism, Marxism, and anarchism.[51] This farrago has remained immensely popular. It has been used to prove that the Jews are behind the abuses of capitalism and communism, responsible for World Wars I and II and the Russian revolution, and just about every financial crisis that has occurred. Even today you will hear complaints about "Jewish bankers" and Jewish domination of the media and entertainment industry. Automaker Henry Ford published the *Protocols* in the United States. The Nazis cited it to justify their anti-Semitic program. Not only is it still popular among groups like the Ku Klux Klan and the Aryan Nation in the United States, but it is extremely popular in the Arab world, where it is used in speeches and proclamations against Israel and Zionism by Arab leaders as if it was a true and accurate depiction of Jewish intentions.[52] Scores of anti-Semitic books and pamphlets would pour off the presses of Europe in the late nineteenth

49. Karesh and Hurvitz, "Pogrom," *Encyclopedia of Judaism*, 395–96.

50. Cohn-Sherbok, *Judaism*, 274.

51. Efron et al., *The Jews*, 344.

52. Karesh and Hurvitz, "*Protocols of the Elders of Zion*," *Encyclopedia of Judaism*, 407–8.

and early twentieth centuries. They would shape the worldview of many, including a young Austrian named Adolf Hitler.

The Education of Adolf Hitler

If Judaism is merely a religion, like Christianity or Islam, a Jew who converts is no longer a Jew. If a Jew is a member of a nation and decides to become "naturalized" as a citizen of France, Germany, or the United States, then, once again, she or he is no longer a Jew. But if a Jew is a member of a "race" with particular invariable characteristics and perspectives, it no longer matters whether a Jew becomes a Christian or a citizen of France, he or she is still a Jew.

The early integrationists had argued that converting Jews to Christianity and forming them as citizens of the great European nations would destroy the unfortunate characteristics of their "Jewishness." The racial anti-Semites thought otherwise. It did not matter how long a Jew or a Jewish family had been Christian or citizens, they were always and forever Jews. As Jews they were a danger to the body politic and needed to be marginalized or driven out. For anti-Semites, Christian civilization was in a great battle for its soul with the Jews.

When Adolf Hitler moved to the Austrian capital Vienna from his hometown of Linz, he came to what recent biographer Volker Ullrich calls "a major stomping ground for anti-Semites" and "a fertile ground for crass racist theories."[53] Not only would Hitler learn in Vienna of the corrupting influence of the Jews on the German people, but he would revel in the inherent superiority of the Aryan race. "Without doubt, part of the poisoned legacy of Hitler's Vienna years was that in the course of his autodidactic studies, he was introduced to the broad repertoire of anti-Semitic clichés and prejudices popular among local nationalists and racists."[54] Hitler was for the most part self-taught and during those years read voraciously. But like most self-taught people, his reading was deep rather than broad. The books, papers, and journals he read reinforced what he had already come to believe.

Ullrich argues that "a central motif running through almost all Hitler's speeches was his declaration of war on the Jews. From the beginning, he treated this topic in the most radical of terms." In August of 1920 he gave a

53. Volker Ullrich, *Hitler: Ascent 1889–1939* (New York: Alfred A. Knopf, 2016), 43–44.
54. Ullrich, *Hitler*, 102.

speech entitled "Why Are We Anti-Semitic?" The speech demonstrates the effect of Hitler's reading of articles and books like "Judaism in Music," by Richard Wagner, *Handbook on the Jewish Question*, by Theodore Fritsch, *The Law of the Nomad and Today's Jewish Domination*, and perhaps most important, *Foundations of the Nineteenth Century*, by Houston Steward Chamberlain. "The speech was a murky mixture of pseudo-scientific and vulgar anti-Semitic clichés." Jews were called "parasites on the bodies of other peoples," driven by "Mammonism and materialism." They were said to be "incapable of any productive work and cultural achievement." The National Socialists, he declared, intended to "combat this destructive force by 'awakening and inciting the instinctual antipathy of our people for Jewry.'" His final "ultimate unchangeable goal [was] 'the removal of Jews from our people.'"[55] This would lead inexorably to the "final solution" of the Jewish problem.

Conclusion

On the brink of the twentieth century Jews had reasons to be optimistic and reasons to be concerned. The accomplishments of Jewish writers, scholars, artists, and intellectuals had been dazzling. In most European states, in England, and in the United States, Jews had arrived at an unprecedented level of civic engagement and acceptance. On the other hand, most Jews in the east were still poor and under threat from an autocratic and frequently anti-Semitic regime in Russia. The pogroms sent shockwaves through the populace, causing one of the largest Jewish migrations in history with hundreds of thousands migrating to Western Europe, and especially, the United States. In the coming century the centers of Jewish population would alter dramatically. The growing racial anti-Semitism was not simply a recasting of an ancient antipathy. It was something new and infinitely more dangerous. It targeted Jews not simply as devotees of a passé religion or as an alien nation, but as an inherently corrupting race. This would lead in the twentieth century to a horror impossible to imagine.

Jews responded to these challenges and opportunities in a variety of ways in the decades to come. But perhaps the most significant movement began at the end of the nineteenth century and was spurred by the decades of war and bloodshed that lay ahead: Zionism. In the following chapter we will look at the rise of the Zionist movement, its leading figures and controversies

55. Ullrich, *Hitler*, 102–3.

and its outcome in the foundation of the State of Israel. We will also consider the contributions of Christians to the success of Zionism—especially Christians in the United States. The twentieth century would prove to be a period of hope, despair, and hope renewed for the Jewish people. They would confront murderous antipathy and survive. Today, in the twenty-first century, there are Jews who worry that that survival is still in doubt. The murderous antipathy remains, as do the dangers of assimilation and destruction.

QUESTIONS FOR DISCUSSION

1. What did the "emancipation" of the Jews entail? What were the advantages and disadvantages of emancipation?
2. Who was Moses Mendelssohn and what was the Jewish "enlightenment"?
3. What was the "Orthodox" response to the "enlightenment"?

FURTHER READING

Cohn-Sherbok, Dan. "The Emergence of Jewish Thought in the Enlightenment." Pages 254–58 in *Judaism: History, Belief and Practice.* London: Routledge, 2003.

———. "The Status of Jews in Europe." Pages 241–46 in *Judaism: History, Belief and Practice.* London: Routledge, 2003.

Hertzberg, Authur, and Aron Hirt-Manheimer. *Jews: The Essence and Character of a People.* New York: HarperCollins, 1998.

Rosenblit, Marsha L. "European Jewry: 1800–1933." Pages 169–207 in *The Cambridge Guide to Jewish History, Religion, and Culture.* Edited by Judith R. Baskin and Kenneth Seeskin. Cambridge: Cambridge University Press, 2010.

CHAPTER 15

From the Rise of Zionism to the State of Israel

At Basel I founded the Jewish state. If I said this out loud today I would be answered by universal laughter. Perhaps in five years, and certainly in fifty, everyone will know it.

—Theodor Herzl

For the living the Jew is a dead man; for the natives, an alien and a vagrant; for property holders, a beggar; for the poor, an exploiter and millionaire; for patriots, a man without a country; for all citizens, a hated rival.

—Leon Pinsker

Why not give Palestine back to [the Jews] again? According to God's distribution of nations, it is their home—an inalienable possession from which they were expelled by force. . . . Why shall not the powers which under the treaty of Berlin in 1878 gave Bulgaria back to the Bulgarians and Servia to the Servians not give Palestine back to the Jews?

—William Blackstone

Two important phenomena, of the same nature but opposed, which have still not drawn anyone's attention, are emerging at this moment in Asiatic Turkey. They are the reawakening of the Arab nation and the latent effort of the Jews to reconstitute on a very large scale the ancient kingdom of Israel. Both these movements are destined to fight each other continually until one of them wins. The fate of the entire world will depend on the final result between these two peoples representing two contrary principles.

—Negib Azoury

The Russian pogroms and the Dreyfus Affair filled Jews throughout Eastern and Western Europe with dread. As a result, the always latent longing for Zion, for a Jewish state, came to the surface in the late nineteenth century and produced a variety of forms of Zionism. Perhaps the most important form was the *political Zionism* of Theodor Herzl and the World Zionist Organization. Herzl was a journalist and was sent by his Viennese newspaper to cover the Dreyfus trial. He witnessed Dreyfus's humiliation as he was stripped of his rank and drummed out of the French army. Outside of the gates, a howling mob shouted curses on the Jews. Herzl was shaken. Although he was a sophisticated, secular intellectual, he had a powerful attachment to the Jewish people. He became convinced that however much Jews adapted themselves to their host countries, however they contributed to their flourishing, however often they came to their defense in war, they would always be suspect and even hated. He would insist in works like "The Jewish State" that the only way the Jews could survive would be with a state of their own—ideally in Palestine. With this goal in mind he founded the World Zionist Organization in Basel in 1897.[1]

Ahad Ha-Am (Asher Ginsberg) advocated for *cultural Zionism*. Although not necessarily opposed to a Jewish state in Palestine, he sought a spiritual and cultural renewal, including the return of Hebrew as the spoken language of the Jewish people. He was skeptical of the political ambitions of the secular Zionists. Although he attended the conference in Basel, he would say he felt like a mourner at a wedding feast. The answer to Europe's "Jewish problem," he would argue, was not a homeland in Palestine. Even if a Jewish state was established Jews would continue to live in the Diaspora and face the ongoing struggles of assimilation and difference. And the establishment of a state in Palestine would be fraught with difficulty, not the least of which was the population of Arab residents already there. In "The Jewish State and the Jewish Problem," he argued that having a Jewish state would be a good thing. But without a cultural and spiritual renewal the state would not accomplish its goals of the unification of the Jewish people. A merely political solution alone was ultimately no solution at all.[2]

Labor Zionism was committed to establishing a socialist state in Palestine, seeing its establishment as part of the ongoing, international class struggle.

1. See Theodore Herzl, "The Jewish State," in *The Zionist Idea*, ed. Arthur Hertzberg (New York: Atheneum, 1972), 262–69.

2. See Ahad Ha-Am (Asher Zvi Ginsberg), "The Jewish State and the Jewish Problem," in Hertzberg, *Zionist Idea*, 262–69.

The Socialists were concerned to return Jews to the land—quite literally, to agriculture. They foresaw the development of a strong Jewish "proletariat" alongside its intellectuals and professionals. They advocated, among other things, the establishment of cooperative settlements in the land where labor and social benefits would be shared within the community. Men like Nahmen Syrkin argued that socialism was the *only* way to form a Jewish state. "It is inconceivable," he wrote, "that people will agree to the creation of an autonomous state based on social inequality."[3] Although many Labor Zionists were secular, they were not Marxists (although there were Marxist Zionists). They saw the Jewish state as a place for all Jews—religious Jews included. The ideals of Zionist socialism were enshrined in the Israeli Labor Party that dominated the political life of Israel for decades.[4] When the State of Israel was established, the Labor Party, in good socialist fashion, insisted that the government was responsible for health care, education, and social services for all its citizens.[5]

Although many Orthodox Jews were hostile to the efforts to build a Jewish state in Palestine, there were also *religious Zionists*. The Mizrachi movement "combined strict adherence to tradition and nominal acceptance of Zionism." While many rabbis feared that a secular state would lead younger Jews away from the commandments, members of Mizrachi argued that the establishment of the state could lead Jews to fulfill the commandment to return to the land.[6] It saw its role as "spreading Zionism among religious Jews and Judaism among secular Zionists."[7] Over the following decades many forms of religious Zionism would develop. All saw the establishment of the State of Israel as both a challenge and an opportunity. Assimilated Jews could be brought back to Torah and religious Jews could find their place in a country that would support their values and enable their religious lives. The conflict between the secular and religious visions of Israel is an enduring one.

Early Immigration

Beginning in the late nineteenth century, successive waves of Jewish immigration into Palestine increased the Jewish population substantially. In 1882

3. Nahem Syrkin, "The Jewish Problem and the Socialist-Jewish State," in Hertzberg, *Zionist Idea*, 349.

4. Karesh and Hurvitz, "Labor Party," *Encyclopedia of Judaism*, 283–84.

5. Karesh and Hurvitz, "Labor Party," *Encyclopedia of Judaism*, 283–84.

6. Karesh and Hurvitz, "Mizrachi Movement," *Encyclopedia of Judaism*, 334–35.

7. Karesh and Hurvitz, "Mizrachi Movement," *Encyclopedia of Judaism*, 334–35.

the Jewish population of Palestine (then part of the Ottoman Empire) was some 24,000, about 10 percent of the population.[8] Immigration from Russia and elsewhere in Eastern Europe brought the Jewish population to 85,000, and to 90,000 by the outbreak of World War I. These "were not old men who came to study, pray, and die, but young men and women who came to work, build and live."[9] They included men such as David Ben-Gurion, the future Prime Minister of Israel. They would organize trade unions, launch newspapers, establish collective farms, and seek to inculcate a renewed Jewish culture and language in their communities.[10] Many of these early immigrants were rigorously secular and sometimes scornful of religious Jews.

They would begin to alarm the Arab population of Palestine. The Arabs of the Middle East had been incorporated into the Ottoman Empire when the Ottoman Turks secured their conquest of the Muslim world. From a small state in Asia Minor the Ottomans gradually "absorbed other Turkish principalities and extended their rule in southeastern Europe and the Middle East. By the mid-fifteenth century they had conquered large areas of the Balkans and Greece."[11] They would go on to put an end to the Byzantine Empire, take Syria, Palestine, and Egypt, and Iraq. Eventually they would control Arabia, North Africa, and many of the islands of the Eastern Mediterranean. By the late nineteenth century, their power was on the wane. Arabs as well as Jews were beginning to entertain national aspirations. Some were secretly considering how to throw off the Ottoman yoke. The so-called Great Powers would take advantage of this growing Arab frustration during and after World War I.

The initial Arab concerns over Jewish immigration were practical. When the Jews set up farming communities, they often purchased the land from absentee landowners. The upshot was that Palestinian peasants who had farmed the same small patch of land for generations were dispossessed. Lands once open to the whole community for grazing sheep were now closed off and taken for agricultural development. As early as 1891, a "group of Arab notables in Jerusalem" sent a note to the Grand Vizier in Istanbul complaining about the immigration of Russian Jews and seeking his support in stopping both Jewish immigration and land purchases.[12] Such bans were

8. Bernard Lewis, *Semites and Anti-Semites* (New York: W. W. Norton, 1986), 165.
9. Lewis, *Semites and Anti-Semites*, 165.
10. Cohn-Sherbok, *Judaism*, 280.
11. Seltzer, *Jewish People*, 455–56.
12. Lewis, *Semites and Anti-Semites*, 170.

largely unsuccessful and yet "remained the basic Arab demands" until the end of British rule in 1948.[13] The officials in Istanbul, while certainly concerned with Jewish immigration, were much more concerned with what was going on in the wider Arab world. Zionism and the idea of a Jewish state seemed laughable. Arab nationalism, on the other hand, was a real threat.

By 1914 Jews had purchased some 130,000 acres of land. In twenty-six agricultural communities, 90,000 of those acres were under cultivation.[14] The new arrivals used the latest farming techniques and, in some cases, saw yields the Palestinian peasants could only dream of. According to one report, during the 1912–13 growing season Jewish planters were getting 638 boxes of oranges per acre compared to the 350 boxes typical for the Arab growers.[15] Arab officials and editorialists complained that the local growers could not stand up to the competition. If the officials in Istanbul were not yet convinced the Jews were a threat to Arab survival in Palestine, those on the ground in Jerusalem and Haifa were increasingly alarmed. The ultimate question, a question that endures to this day, was, Who now had a right to the land? A young Arab nationalist, Khalil al-Sakakini, would write in his diary on February 23, 1914, "if this country is the cradle of the Jews' spirituality and the birthplace of their history, then the Arabs have another inalienable right [to Palestine] which is that they propagated their language and culture in it. [The Jews'] right had died with the passage of time; our right is alive and unshakable."[16]

When World War I shattered the Ottoman Empire it gave hope to national aspirations of both the Jews and the Arabs. The deceptions and postwar bungling of the Great Powers, particularly Britain and France, ensured this bitter rivalry would turn into a conflict with international implications.

William Blackstone and the Origins of Christian Zionism

Jews were not the only ones interested in the reestablishment of the State of Israel. Throughout the nineteenth century many American Christians became deeply interested in Bible prophecy and obsessed with the return of Christ. Most famously, the followers of William Miller had predicted the re-

13. Lewis, *Semites and Anti-Semites*, 170.
14. Jonathan Schneer, *The Balfour Declaration* (New York: Random House, 2010), 11.
15. Schneer, *The Balfour Declaration*, 13.
16. Schneer, *The Balfour Declaration*, 13–14.

turn between March 1843 and March 1844. When March 1844 passed without the Parousia, a new date was set: October 22, 1844. When this failed, many were understandably disillusioned. Others clung to their expectation that Christ's return was imminent and founded the first Adventist Churches.[17] At roughly the same time in England, a former Church of Ireland priest, John Nelson Darby, was making an intensive study of the prophetic material of the Bible. The approach he developed—Dispensationalism—would have an even greater impact on American Christianity.

Darby would come to believe that God worked with his people in different ways during different "dispensations" or periods of time. For Darby there were two principal stories in the Bible—not one. There was Israel's story and the promises made to the Jewish people. There was the church's story and the promises made to those who follow Israel's rejected messiah, Jesus Christ. Darby and his followers would argue that the promises to Israel, in spite of the Jews' rejection of Jesus, had not been abrogated—only delayed. Israel's rejection of Jesus led to a hiatus, the "times of the Gentiles" (Luke 21:24), the era of the church. At the end of this era Jesus would return—but in a secret "rapture" to remove the church from the coming "tribulation." Following the tribulation, Christ would return once more, this time to defeat his enemies and establish his "millennial reign."[18] This reign would be "a Jewish kingdom, complete with a restored Jerusalem temple, daily animal sacrifices, and a powerful King Jesus reigning from Jerusalem and extending Jewish hegemony over the rest of the world."[19] In the course of this all people, Jews included, would either turn to the messiah or be destroyed.

When Dispensationalism arrived in the United States, it found a ready hearing. In prophecy conferences clergy and Bible scholars would pore over the visions of Daniel and Revelation to discern "the signs of the times." One thing was clear: for the prophecies to be fulfilled, the Jews would have to reestablish a state in their ancient homeland. One man in particular would take up the cause of the Jews' restoration to their homeland. William Blackstone was a layman—he had attended neither college nor seminary. But he was an avid Bible student and consumer of Christian literature. Blackstone was a wealthy Chicago real estate developer and friend of evangelist Dwight L.

17. "William Miller," in *The Westminster Dictionary of Church History*, ed. Jerold C. Brauer (Philadelphia: Westminster, 1972), 553.

18. See Timothy P. Weber, *On the Road to Armageddon* (Grand Rapids: Baker, 2004), 20–26, for a brief overview.

19. Weber, *On the Road*, 25.

Moody and Horatio Spafford (who would later establish the American Colony in Jerusalem). Convinced that the end was very near, he sought to prepare the masses for what was surely coming by writing a small book that would have enormous influence: *Jesus Is Coming*. It was the *Late Great Planet Earth* of its day. It would go through many printings and editions, growing from a slim 96 pages in 1878 to 256 pages in 1906.[20] By his death in 1935, more than a million copies of the book had been printed, and the book had been translated into forty-eight languages.[21] Along with C. I. Scofield's reference edition of the Bible, it reshaped how millions of Americans read their Bibles and understood their world.

Many dispensationalists were passive, willing to merely observe God's plan unfold. The urgent task for the Christian was not to turn the world away from the coming violence and chaos—that was impossible. The church was a lifeboat in the storm, and the most that could be done was to rescue others from that storm by pulling them into the lifeboat. Blackstone was different. No less convinced of the dreadful chaos that was coming, he was eager to help the process along by working for a Jewish homeland in Palestine. He organized and chaired the first meeting between Christians and Jews in Chicago in 1890. Many, if not most, of the Jews at the conference were unimpressed with his advocacy for a Jewish homeland. Rabbi Emil Hirsch said, "We modern Jews do not wish to be restored to Palestine. We have given up hope in the coming of a political, personal Messiah . . . . We will not go back . . . to form again a nationality of our own."[22]

Other Jews proved more receptive to Blackstone's vision. Jewish leaders such as businessman Nathan Strauss, Rabbi Stephen Wise, Supreme Court Justice Felix Frankfurter, and, especially, Justice Louis Brandeis became friends and supporters. Brandeis reportedly called Blackstone "the true 'father of Zionism' since his work 'antedates' that of Theodore Herzl."[23]

20. Weber, *On the Road*, 103.

21. Matthew Avery Sutton, *American Apocalypse: A History of Modern Evangelicalism* (Cambridge, MA: Belknap Press of Harvard University Press, 2014), 9.

22. Weber, *On the Road*, 103.

23. Sutton, *American Apocalypse*, 72. "The Blackstone-Brandeis relationship became even more bizarre in 1917. Blackstone oversaw a trust for world evangelism established by evangelical millionaire oilman Milton Stewart. Blackstone wanted to ensure that the money was used effectively. He asked Brandeis to help him draw up legal documents to transfer the trust to Brandeis to use for the Zionist cause in the event of the rapture. Apparently Brandeis agreed to help. The justice maintained a safe deposit box with Blackstone's legal papers, copies of his premillennial tracts, and sealed documents that Blackstone instructed

As early as 1891, citing the suffering of Russian Jews, Blackstone argued that just as Bulgaria had recently been returned to the Bulgarians, and Serbia to the Serbians, so Palestine should be returned to the Jews. He sought the signatures and support of prominent politicians and businessmen for this project and forwarded the petition to President Benjamin Harrison. All this occurred a year before the first "Love of Zion" societies were formed in the United States and five years before Herzl's "The Jewish State" was published.[24] In the decades that followed, Blackstone continued his efforts on behalf of the Jewish homeland, attracting millions of ordinary American Christians to his cause with his writing and insistent advocacy. He was joined in this by a growing trans-denominational movement and scores of popular magazines, journals, and newsletters given to discerning "the signs of the times."

World War I came as no surprise to the prophetic prognosticators. Southern Baptist leader Victor Masters spoke for many when he insisted that "never before did the world face a situation which seemed so completely to fulfill this prophecy as it does today."[25] Blackstone worked tirelessly to use the opportunity the war provided to encourage the US government to support a Jewish homeland. He wrote to Secretary of State William Jennings Bryan, "'May it be' . . . that the United States will serve as 'the instrument which God has prepared' to establish a Jewish state in Israel."[26] As the war progressed, the British moves toward Palestine excited the expectations of the dispensationalists. Many were convinced that the collapse of the Ottoman Empire was imminent. As early as 1916 the *Weekly Evangel* had declared, "As God is working with the nations, He will drive the Turk out of Palestine and cause his ancient people to take possession of it."[27]

In November 1917 the British captured the city of Jerusalem, and shortly thereafter the "Balfour Declaration" was published: "His Majesty's Government view with favour the establishment in Palestine of a national home for the Jewish people, and will use their best endeavours to facilitate the achievement of this object, it being clearly understood that nothing shall be done which may prejudice the civil and religious rights of existing non-

Brandeis to open only in the event of the rapture. These documents would further instruct Brandeis on how to find salvation in a world ruled by the Antichrist."

24. Weber, *On the Road*, 103–4.

25. Sutton, *American Apocalypse*, 50.

26. Sutton, *American Apocalypse*, 50.

27. Weber, *On the Road*, 109.

Jewish communities in Palestine or the rights and political status enjoyed by Jews in any other country."[28]

Some dispensationalists were overwhelmed. A. B. Simpson, in Chicago for a conference, "had to retreat to his hotel room, where he wept for joy." After composing himself, he addressed the crowd at the Moody Tabernacle with "a stirring address on the fulfillment of prophecy in Palestine."[29] Although the British were in fact still in control of the land, the dispensationalists had no doubt that this was only a temporary expediency and that sooner or later a Jewish state would be established. W. Fuller Gooch confidently declared, "We are . . . likely to see in the near future a Jewish State in Palestine. It may be in a month or two, it may be in a year or two, but the intention is to restore the land to the people and the people to the land."[30] It would, in fact, take another thirty years, an additional world war, and an unbearable tragedy for the Jewish people.

From Balfour to World War II

World War I utterly changed the world. The great prewar empires were either destroyed or badly mauled. The German Empire, the Austro-Hungarian Empire, the Ottoman Empire, and the Russian Empire were no more. New states would be carved out of the remnants of the fallen empires, setting the stage for future conflicts. The Bolshevik Revolution in Russia would create a new political and military threat for Europe and the east. Even the victorious British were seriously damaged by the war. Their empire would also begin to melt away. The European states were devastated economically and had barely begun to recover when hit with a devastating worldwide economic depression in the 1930s. A whole generation of young men had been decimated. France lost 1,150,000, either dead or missing, on the battlefield; Great Britain nearly 750,000; Russia a staggering 1,700,000. Millions more were permanently disabled by battlefield injuries.

The Versailles Treaty sought revenge upon and reparations from Germany. It created resentment not only in Germany but also in the Middle East, where the British and French appeared to renege on promises made to the Arabs. The British Mandate in Palestine became a particular sore point. In

28. Karesh and Hurvitz, "Balfour Declaration," *Encyclopedia of Judaism*, 43–44.

29. Weber, *On the Road*, 110.

30. Weber, *On the Road*, 111.

the interwar years it was popular to say that democracy had failed. The new powers in the world were ruled by strongmen who brought discipline and pride to humiliated populations. They were invariably nationalistic and increasingly racist. Heinrich von Treitschke had enunciated the German creed before the war: the individual existed to serve the state, not vice versa; war was a positive good; any treaty that limited that state should be ignored; the state should be racially homogenous.[31] This nationalist creed was replicated in varied ways in Italian Fascism, German National Socialism, and even Russian Communism. The great democracies faced their own challenges from nationalists of both the Fascist and Communist varieties.

The war was especially disastrous for Europe's Jews. The anti-Semitism of the late nineteenth century was only exacerbated, in spite of the fact that Jews had fought bravely for their various countries. Some 500,000 Jews fought for the Russian Empire; some 70,000 were killed in action. German Jews were particularly patriotic and enlisted in huge numbers. Ominously, as the war went badly for Germany, anti-Semites complained that Jews were shirking. This inspired the government to do a "Jew Count" to determine if Jews were enlisting in sufficient numbers or dodging military service. When the report determined that in fact the Jews had enlisted in disproportionately large numbers, the report was quietly shelved.[32] After the war, throughout Germany, Jews were blamed for its outcome. Jewish capitalists would be blamed for the world financial collapse and the suffering of the working classes. Jews would be blamed for the rise of Communism in Russia and "modernism."[33] Jews became the most convenient scapegoat in both Europe and the United States for the world's ills.

Despite the continuing miseries of Jews, especially in Eastern Europe, the interwar years saw a great flowering of Jewish culture and intellectual achievement. According to philosopher Martin Buber, even in Germany there was "a renaissance of Jewish culture." Along with Franz Rosenzweig (1886–1929), an assimilated Jew who had reclaimed his Judaism, Buber established a school for Jewish adults.[34] It intended the "'reappropriation' of Jewish knowledge through the teaching of classical Jewish texts and traditions."[35] German Jews also produced two substantial Jewish encyclope-

31. Schneer, *The Balfour Declaration*, 141.
32. Efron et al., *The Jews*, 370.
33. Nirenberg, *Anti-Judaism*, 423–59.
34. Efron et al., *The Jews*, 382.
35. Efron et al., *The Jews*, 383.

dias—one of which had to be abandoned with the rise of the Nazis.[36] Jewish writers found fame in Germany and beyond, and Yiddish theater was extremely popular. Yiddish literature and theater would also flourish in Poland, in spite of the suffering of its Jews. The most famous of the Jewish writers from Poland were Isaac Bashevis Singer and his brother Israel Joshua Singer. Isaac would be awarded the Nobel Prize for Literature in 1978. Throughout Western Europe, Jewish intellectuals and scholars would make enormous contributions to science and literature in spite of restrictions and prejudices.

In spite of Arab resistance, the Jewish population continued to grow in British Mandate Palestine in the wake of the war. By 1929 there were 160,000 Jews and some 110 agricultural settlements. Over the next decade, the numbers rose to 500,000 and 253. Urban Jewish population also grew: Tel Aviv to 150,000, Jerusalem 90,000, and Haifa 60,000.[37] Both the Arabs and the English sought to put limits on Jewish immigration into Palestine—not entirely successfully. Tensions increased between the Arabs and Jews, resulting in outbreaks of violence, most notably in August of 1929 and during the "Arab Revolt" of 1936–39.[38] As a result the Jews formed a defense force, the Haganah, which eventually formed the core of the Israeli army. Eventually some Jews would bring the fight to the occupying British forces as well as the Arabs. In light of the ongoing conflict, the British set up the Peel Commission to make recommendations for the partition of Palestine into Jewish and Arab states. The Zionists "grudgingly" accepted it while the Arabs flatly rejected it. The stage was set for the post–World War II conflict over the creation of the State of Israel.

The Nazis and the Shoah

The racial anti-Semitism of the late nineteenth century, the scapegoating of Jews in the wake of World War I, and the bitter resentments of German nationalists produced a most bitter fruit. Adolf Hitler rode these resentments to power in Germany and plunged the world once again into a brutal and destructive war that would again remake not only Europe but the entire world. In prosecuting his war, he sought to destroy world Jewry as the ultimate solution to Europe's "Jewish problem." "Was there any form of filth

36. Efron et al., *The Jews*, 383.
37. Cohn-Sherbok, *Judaism*, 290.
38. Efron et al., *The Jews*, 400.

or profligacy," he wrote, "particularly in cultural life, without at least one Jew involved in it? If you cut even cautiously into such an abscess you found like a maggot in a rotting body, often dazzled by the sudden light—a *kike.*"[39] Jews and other "inferior" races were like infections endangering the pure Aryan race. These corrupting inferiors needed to be destroyed or reduced to slavery on behalf of their "superiors."

The Nazis began by making life in Germany nearly impossible for its Jewish residents. Increasingly restrictive laws made it difficult for Jews to make a living. Jews were driven out of the professions, in spite of the large proportion of Jews who were physicians and lawyers. They lost their jobs at German universities and research institutes. Jewish radicals were imprisoned along with others who dared resist the regime. When Germany moved against Poland and then Russia, the fanatical SS sent *Einsatzgruppen* ("action groups") to round up and murder Jews. The largest of these "actions" was the murder of 34,000 Jews at Babi Yar outside of Kiev in 1941. As many as one-and-a-half to two million Jews were murdered by being shot or gassed by the *Einsatzgruppen* in occupied Russia in 1941–42.[40] Many more Jews were murdered in death camps. They were shot, gassed, and worked to death. Gruesome experiments were perpetrated upon them. Ninety percent of Poland's vast Jewish community was killed. The same percentages apply to the Baltic States, Germany, and Austria. Over 70 percent of the Jews of Bohemia, Slovakia, Greece, and the Netherlands were murdered. Half of the Jews of White Russia, the Ukraine, Yugoslavia, Romania, and Norway perished.[41] The names Auschwitz, Majdanek, Treblinka, Belzec, Chelmno, and Sobibor live in infamy.

From the Shoah to the State of Israel

In December 1942, Rabbi Stephen Wise wrote to *The Christian Century* to alert the readers of the leading Protestant publication to the murder of Jews in Poland. He offered precise figures based on information collected by a number of Jewish organizations. The editors took exception to Wise's report. Surely he was exaggerating—especially when he suggested the bodies were being processed into soap and fertilizer. To them this all sounded like

39. Cited in Cohn-Sherbok, *Judaism*, 299.
40. Seltzer, *Jewish People*, 668.
41. Cohn-Sherbok, *Judaism*, 306.

the "cadaver factory" stories of World War I. Wise was furious. "It would appear," he wrote, "you are more interested in seeking to prove that figures I gave out . . . are inaccurate in respect to Jewish mass massacres . . . than you are in making clear to American Christians how unspeakable has been the conduct of Hitlerism against the Jewish people."[42] The editors of *The Christian Century* were not alone in their skepticism concerning the extent of the horror Hitler was perpetrating on the Jews. It was only as the camps began to be liberated by western armies that the full horror began to set in.

As the pictures and newsreels began to appear in American newspapers and theaters, even the skeptics struggled to deny their awful reality. An editorial in *The Signs of the Times* in May 1945 was entitled simply, "So It Was True!" It described the American liberation of Bergen-Belsen. The traumatized soldiers found in one village the partially burned bodies of more than a thousand prisoners who had been crowded into a barn and set afire. At Belsen itself they found bodies heaped up for the burial their torturers were unable to accomplish before they fled. Thousands more, the editorial reported, were "still alive, but walking skeletons."[43] The soul-searching began almost immediately. Could America and American Christians have done more to rescue the Jews of Europe? Did our government and our own prejudices blind us to the realities on the ground—realities reported by credible sources? And, perhaps most seriously, to what extent did Christianity itself contribute to the murder of those millions of innocents?

After the war, hundreds of thousands of Jewish survivors found themselves in "displaced persons" camps managed by the allies. Perhaps it is not surprising that in spite of their suffering few countries were willing to take in refugees. From 1945 to 1948 the *Brichah* (Flight) organization smuggled, very much against the will of the British, some 100,000 of these Jews into Palestine.[44] Throughout the war, Jewish paramilitary organizations, principally the Irgun led by future prime minister Menachem Begin and *Lehi* (an acronym for "Warriors for the Freedom of Israel") led by another future prime minister, Yitzhak Shamir, led the resistance to British rule. By 1947, weakened by the war, the British had had it. They turned Palestine over to the newly formed United Nations. The United Nations revived the old partition plan rejected by the Arabs in 1939. On November 29, 1947, the

42. Robert W. Ross, *So It Was True: The American Protestant Press and the Nazi Persecution of the Jews* (Minneapolis: University of Minnesota Press, 1980), 174.

43. Ross, *So It Was True*, 233.

44. Efron et al., *The Jews*, 444.

United Nations voted 33-13 for the creation of separate Arab and Jewish states, with Jerusalem under an international trusteeship. Civil war began immediately.[45]

On May 14, 1948, after the British departure, David Ben-Gurion read out the "Scroll of Independence," declaring the creation of the State of Israel—the war for independence was launched. The armies of Egypt, Transjordan, Lebanon, Syria, and Iraq attacked the fledgling state. By the war's completion in January of 1949, Israel had established itself in some 8,000 square miles of Palestine (as opposed to the 6,200 under the partition agreement). Egypt controlled the Gaza Strip; Jordan controlled the West Bank of the Jordan river and east Jerusalem. Israel signed truce agreements with the various Arab governments and was admitted to the United Nations on May 11, 1949. During the war, some 650,000 Arab inhabitants of Palestine either fled or were driven out of territory that would become part of the State of Israel. A refugee problem that exists to this day was created for both Israel and the Arab states.[46]

So far as the Arab states were concerned, the truce was merely temporary. President Gamal Abdul Nasser of Egypt worked to create pan-Arab agreements to eventually eliminate the State of Israel and, of course, Israel's Jews. In 1956 he closed the Suez Canal to Israel and made agreements with Saudi Arabia, Yemen, Jordan, and Syria. With logistical help from Britain and France, Israel launched a preemptive strike on Egypt. It was a crushing and embarrassing defeat for Nasser and his forces. Israel's survival seemed assured. But an even greater victory was coming.[47] In 1967 the armies of Egypt, Syria, and Jordan once again decided to attempt to destroy Israel. On May 15, 1967, Nasser moved 100,000 troops to the Sinai and ordered the United Nations forces there to leave—which they meekly did. Once again, on June 5 Israel launched a preemptive strike, destroying the Egyptian air force on the ground. Two days later the Israelis captured the Old City of Jerusalem from the Jordanians and occupied the rest of the West Bank on the following day.[48] Israel went on to capture the Golan Heights in the north and the Sinai Peninsula in the south. It was all over in six days.

45. Seltzer, *Jewish People*, 674.

46. Cohn-Sherbok, *Judaism*, 314.

47. For a comprehensive history of the wars and the earliest days of the State of Israel see Martin Gilbert, *Israel: A History*, rev. and updated ed. (New York: Harper Perennial, 2008).

48. For a moving account of the Six Day War, the outcomes, and the lives of some of the men who fought in it, see Yossi Klein Halevi, *Like Dreamers: The Story of the Israeli Paratroopers Who Reunited Jerusalem and Divided a Nation* (New York: Harper, 2013).

The response of the world's Jews was immense relief and great pride. During that nervous week they had come to fear a second Shoah. Rabbi Jonathan Sacks was a philosophy major at Cambridge when the ominous news of Egypt's buildup to war was reported. Like many others, he feared another tragedy was about to occur. But then, in sophisticated Cambridge, something remarkable began to happen. Students and professors, some of whom had never particularly identified as Jews, crowded into the synagogue to pray. "Everyone wanted to help in some way," Sacks writes, "to express their solidarity, their identification with Israel's fate."[49] Sacks would later discover that the same thing was occurring around the world. Jews in the United States, in Russia, and throughout Europe were united first in fear and then in celebration of Israel's survival. But not only Jews. The capture of the Old City and especially the Temple Mount would excite the dispensationalists. L. Nelson Bell said that the capture of the Old City "gives a student of the Bible a thrill and a renewed faith in the accuracy and validity of the Bible." John Walvoord of Dallas Theological Seminary was even more expansive. This was "one of the most remarkable fulfillments of biblical prophecy since the destruction of Jerusalem in A.D. 70."[50]

It would seem in 1967 that Israel, after a mere twenty years of existence, was at last secure. But the seeds of future wars and stresses were sown in victory. Immediate questions were raised by Israel's conquests: How much of the land now occupied should be kept? What was to be done with the Arab refugee population and the Arabs now living under occupation? Should Israeli Jews be permitted to live and build communities in the occupied territories? On what basis? These questions continue to dominate conversations in Israel and in Arab and western capitals to this day. Israel would go to war over and over again in the following decades. It would find itself locked in an increasingly unpopular, violent, and dangerous occupation of Arab lands and facing a growing terrorist conflict with the Palestine Liberation Organization and other state and non-state parties that would result in the deaths of thousands of Jews and Arabs. It would see its status in the world erode. It would go from being seen as a group of out-gunned but courageous freedom fighters, carving out living space for an oppressed people, to a brutal colonial power oppressing another people. The problem of two peoples with legitimate claims to the same small space seems, to this day, intractable.[51]

49. Jonathan Sacks, *A Letter*, 28.

50. Weber, *On the Road*, 184.

51. See Yossi Klein Halevi, *Letters to My Palestinian Neighbor* (New York: HarperCollins, 2018).

The Christian response to Jews, Judaism, and the State of Israel continues to be complicated. Many Christians, Catholic, mainline Protestant, and evangelical, celebrated the creation of the State of Israel. Over the next couple of decades, in their different ways, the various Christian denominations began to confront their anti-Semitism. They began to ask questions, not only about their relationships with and opinions of individual Jews, but about how Christian theology had contributed to the mistreatment of Jews throughout the life of the church. Groups of Jews and Christians began to meet seriously for the first time, seeking understanding and pursuing reconciliation. The Roman Catholic Church took a critical step during Vatican II with its statement *Nostra Aetate*. In the first decades of the twenty-first century, in spite of all that occurred in the twentieth, anti-Semitism is once again on the rise. Christians are once more in conflict with Jews, often, but not always, over the actions of Israel. Conversations that once were hopeful are increasingly hostile and hopeless. What now is to be done?

QUESTIONS FOR DISCUSSION

1. What was the Dreyfus Affair and how did it impact the rise of Zionism?
2. Who was William Blackstone and what was/is "Christian Zionism"?
3. Why were/are some Jews so opposed to the reestablishment of a Jewish state in the land of Palestine?

FURTHER READING

Confino, Alon. *A World without Jews: The Nazi Imagination from Persecution to Genocide*. New Haven: Yale University Press, 2014.

Hertzberg, Arthur, ed. *The Zionist Idea: A Historical Analysis and Reader*. New York: Atheneum, 1972.

Heschel, Susannah. *The Aryan Jesus: Christian Theologians and the Bible in Nazi Germany*. Princeton: Princeton University Press, 2008.

Ross, Robert W. *So It Was True: The American Protestant Press and the Nazi Persecution of the Jews*. Minneapolis: University of Minnesota Press, 1980.

Schneer, Jonathan. *The Balfour Declaration: The Origins of the Arab-Israeli Conflict*. New York: Random House, 2010.

CHAPTER 16

Dialogue and Hope

Let us offer, then, as a working principle the following: No statement, theological or otherwise, should be made that would not be credible in the presence of burning children.

—Irving Greenberg

The record of most theologians and churchmen in England and America as well as the Third Reich was confused and weak where not outright wicked.

—Franklin Littell

Born in suffering, Christianity became a source and pretext of suffering to others.

—Elie Wiesel

First they came for the communists—
but I was not a communist—
so I did nothing.
Then they came for the social democrats—
but I was not a social democrat—
so I did nothing.
Then they came for the trade unionists,
but I was not a trade unionist.
And then they came for the Jews,
but I was not a Jew—
so did little.
Then when they came for me,
there was no one left who could stand up for me.

—Martin Niemoller

On April 27, 2019, the last day of the Passover celebration, a clean-cut, white American teenager named John Earnest burst into a Poway, California, synagogue with a semiautomatic weapon and opened fire.[1] Lori Gilbert-Kaye was killed and three others, including Rabbi Yisroel Goldstein, were injured. When his rifle jammed, Earnest fled the scene, but he was soon apprehended by the San Diego police. In a manifesto accompanying the shooting, he recited standard white supremacist charges against Jews and Judaism, including the "meticulously planned genocide of the European race." But more striking was Earnest's citation of the New Testament and Christian theology to justify his actions. Earnest was a member of the Orthodox Presbyterian Church, a small conservative denomination that split from the mainline Presbyterian Church. He was a regular attender, and his father was an elder. Both his local congregation and the leadership of the Orthodox Presbyterian Church were horrified and condemned the attack, declaring that such anti-Semitism was antithetical to their doctrine and self-understanding.

Some seventy-five years after the death camps were liberated, after the worst fears of the Jewish world were realized, Christian communities are once again being forced to reckon with the horrific outcomes of toxic readings of their sacred texts. Earnest's pastor, reading his manifesto, acknowledged that "we can't pretend as though we didn't have some responsibility for him—he was radicalized into white nationalism from within the very midst of our church."[2] Although many of Earnest's white nationalist views came from sources far from the Christian mainstream, his anti-Jewish views were deeply rooted in the ancient Christian "teaching of contempt" and readings of the Christian Bible that blame Jews for the death of Jesus (deicide), for refusing to respond to the gospel, and for persecuting the early Christians. This guilt is held as not only the guilt of some Jews in the past, but of all Jews for all time. Seventy-five years after the Shoah, the same toxic brew that produced the Shoah—nationalism, racial hatred, and the Christian teaching of contempt—were present in Earnest's manifesto and led him to religiously motivated murder.

Since the Shoah, Christian leaders from all parts of the Christian world, Roman Catholic, mainline Protestant, Orthodox, and evangelical, have de-

1. Julie Zauzmer, "The Alleged Synagogue Shooter Was a Churchgoer Who Talked Christian Theology, Raising Tough Questions for Evangelical Pastors," *The Washington Post*, May 1, 2019.

2. Zauzmer, "The Alleged Synagogue Shooter."

nounced anti-Semitism and sought to address, to one extent or another, the "teaching of contempt." Jews and Christians have been in serious dialogue for many decades now. Leaders from the various communities have sought to get to know each other and, in many cases, have come to respect and love each other. And yet anti-Semitic hate speech, violence, and murder are increasingly common in the United States and around the world. Some of the outrage is directed toward the State of Israel and its treatment of the Palestinians. But the line between political critiques and anti-Semitic attacks is sometimes a very thin one. Unwittingly, many scholars, pastors, and laypersons, people of good will, perpetuate anti-Jewish tropes in their preaching, teaching, interpretation of the Bible, and political advocacy. Often this is done in ignorance, but the outcome of such casual, often invisible anti-Judaism can be tragic.

Before, During, and After the Shoah

In his book *So it Was True: The American Protestant Press and the Nazi Persecution of the Jews* historian Robert W. Ross examined fifty-two Protestant periodicals from the years 1933–45.[3] These periodicals were, in Ross's terms, liberal, mainline Protestant, evangelical-conservative, and fundamentalist. They included denominational periodicals, non- or interdenominational periodicals, and specialized periodicals (e.g., magazines concerned with Jewish evangelization). Included were such flagship magazines as *The Christian Century, The Christian Herald, The Moody Bible Institute Monthly,* and *The Gospel Herald,* among others. Ross makes it clear that throughout the period leading up to the war and during the war itself Christian readers who were paying attention to their own religious press had no excuse for their ignorance of the murder of Europe's Jews. Ironically, it was the agencies and periodicals dedicated to the evangelization of the Jews that were most explicit and, it turns out, most accurate. Not only did these periodicals publish frantic accounts of the ongoing slaughter, but they also took out alarming and explicit ads in other Christian magazines to alert the wider Christian world.

According to Ross, an alert Christian reader would have known that firing squads were part of the "radical solution" to the "Jewish problem" in conquered territories as early as the fall of 1941. And in 1942 multiple

3. Ross, *So It Was True*, xiv. Hereafter, page references to this work are given in parentheses in the text.

magazines reported that the Jews were being rounded up and slaughtered. One source described it as a story of "persecution, murder, mass slaughters, tortures of prisoners, brutal treatment of women" (277). And yet, after the war many of the editors and readers of these very magazines seemed shocked at the scale of the tragedy. There had been warnings throughout the war that these "atrocity stories" sounded very much like the charges against the Germans in World War I—charges that had proven to be false. Jewish leaders and others who raised the alarm were considered untrustworthy rumor mongers. Even before the war it appeared that many thought the Jews were either overly sensitive or even deserved what they got. Consider the words of G. F. Hedstrand in a letter to *The Christian Century*:

> The Jews are not persecuted in Germany because of their religion, but because of their political and economic activity. They are communist many of them and "persecuted" the nationalists before they came to power. . . . They are children—reminding one of the colored race—in their mental makeup. They must be spoken to with authority, or they will not believe you. That is just what the nationalists are doing. They are not persecuting the Jews—they are talking to them in the only language they know. (26–27)

This was not the only letter or editorial that used such reasoning to suggest the Jews were not deserving of sympathy.

In the wake of the war it became immediately clear that the Third Reich's murder of the Jews was neither rumor nor propaganda. The grisly photos and films from the camps, the reports that filtered back home to the United States from ordinary soldiers, military chaplains, aid workers, and reporters made it clear that this time the atrocity stories were all too true. As the scale of the disaster became clear, the shock and horror only increased. Some Christian leaders were quick to raise the most obvious and most painful question: How could this have happened in the heart of Christian Europe, in the homeland of the Protestant Reformation? But not far behind was the question of why so many American and European Christians were either willfully ignorant of or indifferent to the fate of Europe's Jews until it was far too late to address their plight. Ross cites an editorial in the *Federal Council Bulletin* that acknowledged, "The Jews were victims; Christians, those who proved to be 'callously indifferent,' including American Protestant Churches, must bear the weight of 'a standing reproach'" (263).

The problem, of course, is that Christians were not merely indifferent and uninformed. Throughout Europe, baptized Christians aided and abetted or enthusiastically joined in the slaughter. Adolf Hitler died a Roman Catholic. Hermann Goering died a Lutheran. Neither man was excommunicated by their respective churches. Franklin Littell, a Methodist pastor who spent ten years in postwar Germany acting as an advisor to the Allied High Command was deeply affected by what he experienced. In his searing book *The Crucifixion of the Jews*, he accuses the postwar churches in both Europe and the United States of failing to grasp the enormity of the theological challenges of the Holocaust. He is scornful of the leaders and theologians who attempted to evade the church's responsibility by arguing that the Nazis were actually pagan or by citing the handful of Christian martyrs and resisters.[4]

Karl Barth, Dietrich Bonhoeffer, and Martin Niemoller spoke out against the Nazis and anti-Semitism. And yet their records reveal anti-Jewish stances and equivocal support for Germany's Jews until it was once again too late. In his earliest preaching, Bonhoeffer cited the deicide myth. Barth admitted to Eberhard Bethge, Bonhoeffer's biographer, that he had himself failed to make the suffering of the Jews a central issue. He also said that, had he attempted to put a strong statement supporting the Jews in the Barmen Declaration, the Confessing Church would not have accepted it.[5] And Martin Niemoller, who spent years in a concentration camp for his resistance to Hitler, in a sermon given in 1937 spoke of the "sinister history" of the Jews and alluded to "the 'Eternal Jew' . . . a restless wanderer who has no home and cannot find peace." I am sure he thought his conclusion was gracious: "[nevertheless], we have no license empowering us to supplement God's curse with our hatred."[6] No wonder he later acknowledged that, so far as the Jews were concerned, he "did little." In 1968 he would write that "the Jewish question" was actually "the key question of the Church Struggle. But if we seek the resistance which was raised in the Protestant Church in this matter, we come to a miserable result."[7]

In spite of the Shoah, many Christians appeared to go on theologizing after World War II as if nothing had happened, as if the questions raised against their theology of the Jews were unimportant or had already been addressed. Reformed theologian Loraine Boettner could write in 1958 that after the death of Christ "the old Mosaic order died never to be revived . . .

4. Franklin H. Littell, *The Crucifixion of the Jews* (Macon, GA: Mercer University Press, 1986), 47–55.

5. Littell, *Crucifixion*, 46–47.

6. Stephen R. Haynes, *Reluctant Witnesses: Jews and the Christian Imagination* (Louisville: Westminster John Knox, 1995), 85.

7. Littell, *Crucifixion*, 46.

Judaism is a thing of the past." He acknowledges that "it may seem harsh to say that 'God is through with the Jew.' . . . But the fact of the matter is that He is through with them as a national group."[8] It seems not to have occurred to Boettner that it was this very notion that had caused the Jews so much grief throughout their history and had made it easier for the Christian world to countenance their destruction. Littell also notes an astounding postwar article in a "liberal Methodist journal" that complained of the Jews' refusal to assimilate properly into American society. The writer suggested that Jews had always been a problem. Even in Egypt, Babylon, and Rome they had been "conspirators, saboteurs, and subversives." Littell scathingly suggests that this writer apparently believed it was wrong for the Jews to resist the slavery, oppression, and idolatry of these empires as God had commanded them.[9] Such thoughtless postwar anti-Jewish sentiments would be repeated many times.

Jewish Responses

Not surprisingly, Jews were scathing regarding Christian participation in and response to the Holocaust. Rabbi Eliezer Berkovits would see no hope for Christianity: "The final result of that [Christian] age is bankruptcy. The moral bankruptcy of Christian civilization and the spiritual bankruptcy of Christian religion. After nineteen centuries of Christianity, the extermination of six million Jews, among them one and a half million children, carried out in cold blood in the very heart of Christian Europe, encouraged by the criminal silence of virtually all of Christendom, including that of an infallible Holy Father in Rome was the natural outcome of that bankruptcy."[10] Berkovits wanted nothing to do with Christians and was scornful of Jews who sought dialogue.

Jews such as Jules Isaac thought differently. Isaac, the author of the influential *Teaching of Contempt: Christian Roots of Anti-Semitism*, would famously meet with Pope John XXIII to begin a new conversation between Roman Catholics and Jews. The outcome of their friendship would be the famous Vatican II statement *Nostra Aetate*, which redefined the relationship

8. Littell, *Crucifixion*, 32–33.

9. Littell, *Crucifixion*, 39.

10. Eliezer Berkovits, "Judaism in the Post-Christian Era," in *Disputation and Dialogue: Readings in the Jewish Christian Encounter*, ed. F. E. Talmage (New York: Ktav, 1975), 287–88.

between the two communities.[11] It affirmed God's enduring covenant with Israel, it denied that Jews through all of time should be held guilty for the death of Jesus, it urged preachers and teachers to avoid anti-Jewish statements, and it called for dialogue. Subsequent popes have strengthened the position of the Catholic Church—especially Pope John Paul II, who condemned anti-Semitism as "a sin against God and humanity."[12]

Many Jews, Berkovits among them, thought it was all too little, too late. Others recognized that a Jewish future still would require addressing Christian attitudes toward Jews and Judaism. Even after the war, Jewish lives were at stake.

The Holocaust Theologians

In June of 1974 a remarkable meeting was held in the Cathedral of St. John the Divine in New York City: the International Symposium on the Holocaust. The speakers were a who's who of the emerging conversation about the implications, theological and otherwise, of the Shoah. Many of those present would come to be known as "Holocaust theologians." The Christians involved were among the first to struggle with both the history of Christian anti-Judaism and the agonizing theological questions raised by the murder of six million Jews in Christian Europe. The Jewish voices included that of survivor Elie Wiesel, whose writing was shining a harsh light on the human depravity that produced and sustained those murders. In the decades to come, many of these scholars and thinkers would produce significant theological, ethical, political, social, and even spiritual reflections on the Shoah.[13]

Roman Catholic scholar Rosemary Radford Ruether presented an unremitting critique of the church's treatment of the Jews.[14] In her historical review of the relationship, she demonstrated the increasing hostility of Christian writers, theologians, and officials over the first three centuries of the church's existence. When the church acquired the coercive power of

11. Gilbert S. Rosenthal, "Introduction," in *A Jubilee for All Time: The Copernican Revolution in Jewish-Christian Relations*, ed. Gilbert S. Rosenthal (Eugene, OR: Pickwick, 2014), xv.

12. Rosenthal, *A Jubilee*, xvii.

13. Eva Fleischner, ed., *Auschwitz: Beginning of a New Era?* (New York: Ktav, 1974), 465–68.

14. Rosemary Radford Ruether, "Anti-Semitism and Christian Theology," in Fleischner, *Auschwitz*, 79–92.

the Roman Empire, the church's treatment of the Jews only became worse. Her depiction of the western church's treatment of the Jews over the centuries is unbearably grim. But Ruether did more than recite history. She suggested that Christianity faced an agonizing theological challenge. "Anti-Judaism," she argued, "developed theologically in Christianity as the left hand of Christology." If Jesus is the Jewish messiah and heir of the Jewish messianic hopes, then the Jews are obviously wrong to expect those hopes to be otherwise fulfilled. And if they are wrong, they must be opposed and, if possible, silenced.[15] Anti-Judaism, Ruether argued, grew out of the church's understanding of the accomplishments of Jesus of Nazareth.

For Ruether, then, anti-Judaism is baked into the claim that Jesus is messiah. Even belief in Jesus's resurrection is deemed anti-Jewish, because if Jesus had been vindicated by God, it was at the expense of the Jews. Critics charged that Ruether and other (but not all) Christian "Holocaust theologians" seemed to think that the only way to deal with Christian anti-Judaism was essentially to cease being Christian in any meaningful sense. Any attempt to remove Jesus as messiah and resurrected Lord from the New Testament would seem a task worthy only of a new Marcion. Did fellowship, cooperation, mutual learning, and friendship between Jews and Christians require that either or both give up what was central to their religious self-understanding? In response to the Shoah, were Christians really required to give up on their Christianity or change it into something unrecognizably Christian?

The response to Ruether was given by Jewish historian Yosef Hayim Yerushalmi. He found himself in the awkward position of suggesting that Ruether had rather overstated her case. He comments, "Throughout her summary of Christian theological anti-Semitism I could not help but ask: if this was the teaching why did they not destroy the Jews?"[16] Backed by the power of the Roman Empire and then the various Christian states of Europe, the church certainly had power to do so. It had shown itself ruthless with heresy, seeking to completely stamp out heretical groups. And yet, from the days of Augustine on, leaders of the church, while denigrating and oppressing the Jews, insisted that they not be destroyed. He argues that while life for the Jews was often miserable, they were never without rights and protections. Why was this so?

15. Ruether, "Anti-Semitism," 79–80.

16. Yosef Hayim Yerushalmi, "Response to Rosemary Radford Ruether," in Fleischner, *Auschwitz*, 98.

Yerushalmi suggests that the presence of the Hebrew Scriptures in the Christian canon preserved a continuity between the two communities. Christians believed in the God who made a covenant with Israel at Sinai and even expected that the Jews would in the end turn to Jesus as messiah. "One shudders to contemplate," he wrote, "what might have been the fate of the Jews had Marcion been victorious."[17] Fair enough, but "at least we were not exterminated" hardly vindicates the church. And Yerushalmi is certainly not making a defense of the bitter history of Jewish-Christian relations. As a historian, he suggests that he could add to the litany of misery recounted by Ruether. Rather, he is pointing a way forward that really does not require Jews to cease being Jews or Christians to cease being Christians. He makes four points that I paraphrase here:

1. If healthy relationships require Christians to cease being Christians and Jews to cease being Jews, we are in a bad way.
2. Christians should not spend their entire time in relationship with Jews in constant expressions of "mea culpa." To acknowledge what was done to the Jews in the name of the crucified messiah is perfectly appropriate, but, he comments, "I do not want to encounter Christians as confessor and penitent."
3. Christian theology is an internal Christian affair and a question for Christians to discuss. "I want to know," he continues, "why Rosemary Ruether is my friend, and one of the . . . righteous among the Gentiles."
4. He concludes, "I hope that the condition of our dialogue is not our mutual secularization. . . . You do not have to repudiate everything in the Christian past concerning the Jews. Much of the record is dark. There were also patches of light. . . . Be it known to you, however, that not by your ancestors, but by your actions, will you be judged. For my people, now as in the past, is in grave peril of its life. And it simply cannot wait until you have completed a new *Summa Theologica*."[18]

There is a great deal of wisdom here, but at one point I would disagree with Professor Yerushalmi. It is certainly true that Christian theology is an internal Christian affair, and that Christian friendship with and commitment to the survival of the Jewish people are more important than the reformation of our theology. At the same time, the incidents in Poway and Pitts-

17. Yerushalmi, "Response," 101.
18. Yerushalmi, "Response," 107.

burgh and the ongoing threats to the survival of the Jews of Israel make it clear that our Christian theology *does* and *should* matter to Jews. Over and over we have seen anti-Jewish theology used to justify Jewish deaths. And since, as Yerushalmi suggests, Christian theology is an internal Christian affair, *Christians* must address these perversions of their sacred texts and traditions and repudiate anti-Jewish preaching, teaching, and writing. Professor Yerushalmi is correct—Jewish lives are at stake. And some of those lives are at stake because of anti-Jewish ideas that are sometimes invisible to Christians.

Anti-Jewish Understandings

In the following section I will consider four dangerous Christian anti-Jewish readings that are actually distortions of our own sacred texts and traditions. They are:

1. that the Jews are under a "curse" and even "Satanic";
2. that the Jews were responsible for the death of Jesus (deicide);
3. that God is "through with the Jews";
4. that the Pharisees were all hypocrites and legalists, as are all the Jews.

To this day you will find each of these points stated in popular books, in study Bibles, and by popular preachers and teachers. In many cases the "Jews" referred to by these books and speakers are clearly abstractions, mythical figures, and not real Jews. But in the end, real Jews may and in fact have borne the brunt of such dangerous and misguided teaching. But these readings are required by neither our sacred texts nor Christian theology.

"Satanic" Jews

In his book *Evangelical Interpretations After Auschwitz*, Robert W. Bleakney cites egregious examples of such anti-Jewish readings from the evangelical world.[19] Two historically problematic verses come from the Johannine literature. In John 8:44, in a conflict with Jewish leaders Jesus says, "You

19. Robert W. Bleakney, *Evangelical Interpretation After Auschwitz* (Atlanta: Hebraic Heritage Press, 2019).

belong to your father, the devil, and you want to carry out your father's desires." Similarly, Revelation 2:9 and 3:9 refer to people who say they are Jews but are not, and are instead a "synagogue of Satan." Both of these texts have historically been read in anti-Jewish ways. Bleakney cites editions of the New International Version Study Bible that, commenting on John 8:44, suggest "the Jew's relationship to Satan was now stated explicitly. . . . Being oriented toward Satan, they were bent on murder (v. 37) and would eventually succeed (v. 28)." The MacArthur Study Bible states, "Since the Jews exhibited the patterns of Satan in their hostility toward Jesus and their failure to believe in Him as Messiah, their paternity was the exact opposite of their claims, i.e., they belonged to Satan." Similar interpretations are found in the Dake Annotated Reference Bible and the English Standard Version Study Bible.[20] Perhaps most shockingly, commenting on Revelation 2:9 and 3:9, the MacArthur Study Bible concludes, "With the rejection of the Messiah Judaism becomes as much a tool of Satan as emperor worship."[21]

These are clearly difficult verses, but they should not be read in an explicitly anti-Jewish manner. Many scholars have noted that John's reference to "the Jews" need not be interpreted to refer to all Jews for all time. In fact, it seems clear that while sometimes John appears to use the term "the Jews" to refer to the Jews of his day as a people, at other times he seems to be referring to a specific group within Judaism—perhaps especially the Jewish leadership in Jerusalem, a group depicted as Jesus's opponents in Judaea. In these contexts some would even translate the word as "Judaeans" rather than "Jews." This is supported by John 9:22, where the parents of the man born blind are said to be fearful of "the Jews." Since the parents and their son are Jews, it seems clear that a particular Jewish group is intended—perhaps "the Jewish leaders" would be a better translation. Today's New International Version translates it in this way; the Common English Bible has "the Jewish authorities" as does the Revised English Version. In any event, that Jesus engaged in conflict with Jewish leaders in the first century and accused them of resisting his efforts clearly does not suggest that all Jews for all time are somehow "Satanic" or cursed. In fact, Jesus told the woman at the well that "salvation is from the Jews" (John 4:22).[22] And Paul, of course, insisted in Romans 11 that the Jews are still "loved" by God (Rom 11:28–29).

20. Bleakney, *Evangelical Interpretation*, 194–95.

21. Bleakney, *Evangelical Interpretation*, 195.

22. For a Jewish discussion see Adele Reinhartz, "The Gospel according to John," in Levine and Brettler, *Jewish Annotated New Testament*, 155–56.

The "synagogue of Satan" in Revelation 2:9 and 3:9 is generally taken to refer to Jewish groups in the Asia Minor towns of Ephesus and Philadelphia, who were making things difficult for their Christian communities. Perhaps they were alerting the imperial authorities to the presence of dissenting bodies within their midst. This could lead in those Christian communities to persecution and even death. But there are problems with this view. Curiously, John writes, "They say they are Jews, but are not." What could this mean? Are these gentile converts to Judaism who are "outing" their fellow gentiles? Or is John referring to the kind of gentile Jesus followers that troubled Paul—gentiles who insisted that to follow Jesus one must follow the Jewish law in its entirety. Or, as David Frankfurter suggests in his commentary in the *Jewish Annotated New Testament*, it could be just the opposite. The "synagogue of Satan" could refer to Christian groups that took the apostle Paul too seriously. They were not, as John would expect, following the necessary purity codes, and they were compromising with the empire by participating in what he considered idolatrous.[23] Whatever the case, it seems clear that John is referring to something very specific and that this text should not be used to condemn the Jews or the "synagogue" for all time and should certainly not be used to declare that Judaism was as bad as emperor worship.

"His Blood Be Upon Us and Our Children"

In Matthew's account of the crucifixion, Jesus is brought before the "chief priests and the elders," who persuade the "crowd" to call for Jesus's death. When Pilate tries to get Jesus released, they cry out for Jesus to be crucified. Pilate, who alone has the power to condemn Jesus, accedes to their demands. Then he washes his hands before the crowd and declares, "I am innocent of this man's blood." The people respond, "His blood be upon us and our children" (Matt 27:20–26). Bleakney notes that modern popular study Bibles still interpret this verse (27:25) to refer to the enduring guilt of "the Jews" for the death of Jesus. The MacArthur Study Bible comments, "The Jews accepted the blame for the execution of Jesus and did not hold the Romans responsible." The Dake Annotated Reference Bible states, "The Jews quickly assumed full responsibility for His death. We accept the punishment due for such a crime; let it be upon us and our children. They were

23. David Frankfurter, "The Revelation to John," in Levine and Brettler, *Jewish Annotated New Testament*, 469.

visited with the same kind of punishment and worse." It goes on to say that "the Jews" were the "persecutors of the church everywhere."[24] Those Jews who cried out for Jesus's blood, in other words, cursed all Jews for all time to suffer misery and alienation.

In his commentary on Matthew, Frederick Dale Bruner notes the bitter fruit of such Christian interpretations of this verse. In the fourth century, the church father Jerome wrote, "This imprecation rests at the present time . . . upon the Jews, the Lord's blood is not removed from them." Some fourteen centuries later, the German scholar Bengel commented, "This record against the Jews explains their present exile."[25] Bruner goes on to argue that it is hard to imagine that Matthew would think this "curse" would rest upon all Jews throughout all time.[26] But it is undeniable that this verse was used over the centuries to demonize and brutalize the Jewish people. Rivers of Jewish blood flowed because of such readings. But why should the verse be read in such a deadly manner? The great Jewish New Testament scholar Samuel Sandmel puts it well:

> Perhaps we [Jews] might be willing to say to ourselves that it is not impossible that some Jews, even leading Jews, recommended the death of Jesus to Pilate. . . . [I]f we admit—not confess!—that some Jews were involved, then why blame us all, both then and now? And since Jesus was a Jew, is it not more reasonable to say that *people* killed Jesus, than to put the statement as though Jesus were not a Jew, but his opponents were? Is it not equally unfair to say *the* Americans killed Lincoln and Kennedy?[27]

It is clearly as idiotic to blame all Jews over all time for the death of Jesus as it would be to blame all Italians over all time for his death because Pilate was a Roman official. It is time to abolish this reading of the guilt of "the Jews" for the death of Jesus.

24. Bleakney, *Evangelical Interpretation*, 205, 220.

25. Frederick Dale Bruner, *Matthew: A Commentary*, vol. 2, *The Churchbook*, 2nd ed. (Grand Rapids: Eerdmans, 2004), 723.

26. Bruner, *Matthew*, 2:724.

27. S. Sandmel, *We Jews and Jesus*, 141.

God Is "through with the Jews"

The "replacement theory" or "supersessionism" suggests that Israel is passé. With the death and resurrection of Jesus a new order has arrived and the old one has been abolished. There are passages which seem to suggest this upon first reading. Consider Jesus's parable of the "wicked tenant farmers." In Mark 11, Jesus finds himself in conflict with "the chief priests, the teachers of the law, and the elders." He addresses a familiar parable to them in Mark 12:1–12. The group of tenant farmers not only fail in their task of delivering the required portion but beat up the servants sent by the owner and eventually kill his son in a bid to seize the vineyard for themselves. Jesus declares that the vineyard will be taken from them and given to others. The chief priests, teachers of the law, and elders realize Jesus has "spoken the parable against them" but are afraid to arrest him on the spot (Mark 12:12). Subsequent interpreters have taken this to be a reference to the "church" taking over the vineyard from "Israel," but no such interpretation is required. What Jesus appears to be saying here is that the vineyard (a common symbol for Israel) will soon have a new group of stewards—not that Israel itself would be utterly rejected. Clearly, so far as the New Testament is concerned, with the death and resurrection of Jesus something new has been unleashed in the world. And clearly a move has been made beyond ethnic Israel with the inclusion of the gentiles. But this just as clearly does *not* mean that the Jews have been rejected or Israel replaced.

In the latter part of the letter to the Romans, Paul agonizes over the fate of his people. He has been shocked that so few of them have responded to the message of Messiah Jesus and ponders several explanations. Perhaps only a chosen remnant will be saved (Rom 9). They appear to have rejected the message where the gentiles have accepted it (Rom 10). But what does this mean? Paul wonders if God rejected his people. Were they replaced, superseded, damned? Paul's answer is clear: "By no means! . . . God did not reject his people, whom he foreknew" (Rom 11:1–2). While there is a remnant that has responded, even those who have rejected or not heard are not finally rejected. Paul argues that Israel's rejection of his message made room for gentile acceptance and that they are fully capable of being "regrafted" into the "old olive tree." Paul will go on to make two stunning affirmations: "Israel has experienced a hardening in part until the full number of the gentiles has come in, and then all Israel will be saved" (11:25–26, my translation).[28]

28. The Greek word *outos*, which I have translated "then," has been variously trans-

However things have changed with the death and resurrection of Messiah Jesus, "God's gifts and his call are irrevocable" (11:29). The Jews have not been rejected by God. The promises to them have not been revoked. Jews and Christians will certainly disagree about how the final salvation of Israel will occur. But that God's covenant with Israel endures is absolutely clear.

The Pharisees Were All Legalists and Hypocrites

It is grating for many Jews to hear Christians use the word "Pharisee" to refer to people who are hypocritical, harsh, or legalistic. Sometimes you will even hear preachers suggest that the Pharisees were purveyors of a "sterile legalism" that was lifeless and hopeless. I trust that I have communicated sufficiently that the tradition of the Pharisees was far from "sterile" and "lifeless." It was the efforts of the Pharisees in the wake of the destruction of Jerusalem and its temple that enabled the Jewish people to survive. It was the teaching of the Pharisees and their successors, the rabbis, that was lovingly collected into the Mishnah and elaborated in the Talmud. When I first met my rabbi friend, he announced to me, "I am a Pharisee." It is clear, of course, that Jesus engaged in conflict with the Pharisees—almost from the beginning of his ministry. In the early chapters of Mark, Jesus engages in debate with the Pharisees over when it was appropriate to fast and whether it was appropriate to "pick grain" or heal on the Sabbath. He engages in biblical interpretation in order to prove his point—as any Jewish rabbi would. At the same time, it is certainly true that at times Jesus can be rather hard on the Pharisees—or at least some of them (see Matt 23).

However harsh his critiques, it is nevertheless clear that Jesus was closer to the Pharisees than to any other early group in first-century Palestine. Like the Pharisees, and unlike the Sadducees, Jesus believed in the resurrection of the dead (see Mark 12:18–27). Jesus would charge the Sadducees with knowing neither the Scriptures nor the power of God. Following his response to the Sadducees, a "teacher of the Law"—who Matthew notes is a Pharisee—"noticing that Jesus had given them a good answer," asked a question about the greatest commandment. He is pleased with Jesus's answer and tells him so. Jesus replies, "You are not far from the

---

lated. The TNIV has "in this way"; the NRSV has "and so"; the CEB has "in this way"; the REB translates "once that has happened."

kingdom of God" (Mark 12:34). Even in Matthew 23, where Jesus harshly berates the Pharisees, he acknowledges that "the teachers of the law and the Pharisees sit in Moses's seat. So you must be careful to do everything they tell you." This is a rather striking statement if Jesus thought the Pharisees were utterly bankrupt in life and thought. We know from the book of Acts that many of the earliest Jesus followers were Pharisees (see Acts 15:5). And Paul himself, when standing before the Sanhedrin, shrewdly read the room and saw that there were both Sadducees and Pharisees trying him. "My brothers," he cried, "I am a Pharisee, descended from Pharisees. I stand on trial because of the hope of the resurrection of the dead" (Acts 23:6). Not surprisingly, the Sanhedrin descended into chaos and Paul had to be rescued. The Pharisees, Acts tells us, "argued vigorously. 'We find nothing wrong with this man'" (23:9).

Family feuds are almost always the worst. The closer you are, the more bitter the conflict. It is important for Christians to recognize that when they are listening to the New Testament, they are often overhearing an inter-Jewish squabble. Jesus argued with the Pharisees not because he was so distant from them, but because he was so close. Paul proudly acknowledged both his Jewish and Pharisaic heritage even as he, too, engaged in conflict with certain members of the Jewish community. We make a serious mistake when we approach these conflicts as "Christians" over against "Jews." Neither Jesus nor Paul saw their conflicts with the leaders of Israel in this way. Perhaps the Pharisees were critiqued so strongly, not because they were so far from the kingdom of God, but because they were so close. It is no fairer to say all Pharisees were hypocrites than to say all churchgoers are hypocrites—a charge you often hear. In Romans 14 it seems that the sandal is on the other foot: apparently gentile Jesus followers are criticizing Jewish Jesus followers for their "legalism," and Paul is having none of it. When it comes to what one should eat or what calendar one should follow, Paul insists that the Jews and gentiles of the Roman church should respect one another rather than viewing one another with contempt. "Who are you," he asks, "to judge someone else's servant?" (Rom 14:4). The Jew who lives a halakhically faithful life does so for the Lord. The gentile who is not required to do so also lives for the Lord. "Accept one another," he concludes, "just as Christ accepted you. . . . For I tell you that Christ has become a servant of the Jews on behalf of God's truth, so that the promises made to the patriarchs might be confirmed and, moreover, that the Gentiles might glorify God" (15:7–9).

The Jews are not under a curse, are not responsible for the death of Jesus, are not passé, and are not heirs of an arid legalism. Jews and Christians clearly differ in how they view the identity and accomplishments of Jesus of Nazareth; they clearly differ in how faith in the God of Abraham is to be lived out; they clearly differ in how that God is to be worshiped. As this book has demonstrated, whatever the commonalities, the differences are great. But this does not require Christians to demonize or denounce or slander either the Jews of Jesus's day or the Jews of our own.

A Way Forward?

In July of 1947, a group of Christians and Jews met in the Swiss town of Seelisberg to consider the scourge of anti-Semitism and the responsibility of Christianity for its flowering in the past and its prevention in the future.[29] "An Address to the Churches" was published as a result of the conference. It noted that, in spite of the murder of millions of Jews, "antisemitism has lost none of its force but threatens to extend to other regions, to poison the minds of Christians and to involve humanity more and more in a grave guilt with disastrous consequences."[30] There follow "Ten Points" to shape future conversations between Jews and Christians and to frame Christian teaching and preaching. The first four points deal with commonalities: the one God of both Judaism and Christianity; the Jewishness of Jesus and his love for his own people; the Jewishness of the disciples and early Christian martyrs; the fundamental commandment of both Judaism and Christianity to love God and neighbor. The next six warnings deal with contemporary relationships:

1. Avoid distorting or misrepresenting biblical or postbiblical Judaism with the object of extolling Christianity.
2. Avoid using the word "Jews" in the exclusive sense of the enemies of Jesus, and the words "the enemies of Jesus" to designate the whole Jewish people.

29. James K. Aitken, "Seelisberg Conference," in *A Dictionary of Jewish-Christian Relations*, ed. Edward Kessler and Neil Wenborn (Cambridge: Cambridge University Press, 2005), 399.

30. "An Address to the Churches (The Ten Points of Seelisberg)," Council of Centers on Jewish-Christian Relations, http://ccjr.us/dialogika-resources/documents-and-statements/ecumenical-christian/seelisberg.

3. Avoid presenting the Passion in such a way as to bring the odium of the killing of Jesus upon all Jews or upon Jews alone. . . .
4. Avoid referring to the scriptural curses, or the cry of a raging mob: "His blood be upon us and our children," without remembering that this cry should not count against the infinitely more weighty words of our Lord: "Father, forgive them for they know not what they do."
5. Avoid promoting the superstitious notion that the Jewish people are reprobate, accursed, reserved for a destiny of suffering.
6. Avoid speaking of the Jews as if the first members of the church had not been Jews.[31]

That each of these errors needs to be addressed more than seventy years after this conference suggests Christians have not yet entirely learned the bitter lessons of the Shoah or sufficiently addressed their own anti-Semitism.

In spite of this, the words of Professor Yerushalmi should be recalled: "I do not want to encounter Christians as confessor and penitent."[32] The bitter failures of Christianity should and must be acknowledged, but shame-faced guilt is not the basis for a relationship. And, as is abundantly clear, Jewish lives are still at stake. In light of all this, how should Christians and Jews meet and engage one another? In a famous and moving essay entitled "No Religion Is an Island," Abraham Joshua Heschel suggests a way forward. We meet first "as human beings who have much in common: a heart, a face, a voice, the presence of a soul, fears, hope, the ability to trust, a capacity for compassion and understanding, the kinship of being human."[33] For Christians and Jews, the human being is not simply a representative of the species *Homo sapiens* but one who bears the image of God. To be in the presence of a human being is to be in the presence of God.[34] If we disagree about matters of faith, "does the image of God I face disappear? Does God cease to stand before me? Do the differences in commitment destroy the kinship of being human? Does the fact that we differ in our conceptions of God cancel what we have in common: the image of God?"[35] The answer to each of these questions is clearly No.

31. "An Address to the Churches."

32. Yerushalmi, "Response," 106.

33. Abraham Joshua Heschel, "No Religion Is an Island," in Abraham Joshua Heschel, *Moral Grandeur and Spiritual Audacity*, ed. Susannah Heschel (New York: Farrar, Straus, and Giroux, 1996), 238.

34. Heschel, "No Religion," 238.

35. Heschel, "No Religion," 239.

Perhaps most important for Heschel is that, whatever our differences, we meet as people of faith, as *believers* in the One God of Abraham, Isaac, and Jacob. Heschel calls this "the dimension of faith" and suggests that in this dimension, "the encounter proceeds in terms of personal witness and example, sharing insights, confessing inadequacy. On the level of doctrine we seek to convey the content of what we believe in; on the level of faith we experience in one another the presence of a person radiant with reflections of a greater presence." Neither Jew nor Christian is required to surrender what is precious to them about faith, practice, worship, and community in such an encounter. When they stand together, bearing the image of God, in the very presence of God, something wonderful and powerful can occur. In spite of all the misunderstanding and misrepresentation, in spite of all the charges hurled and the blood spilt, in spite of the continuing fears and future failures, we can find ourselves together before the Holy One of Israel. I agree with Heschel's suggestion

> that the most significant basis for meeting of [people] of different religious traditions is the level of fear and trembling, of humility and contrition, where our individual moments of faith are mere waves in the endless ocean of [humankind's] reaching out for God, where all formulations and articulations appear as understatements, where our souls are swept away by the awareness of the urgency of answering God's commandment while stripped of pretension and conceit we sense the tragic insufficiency of human faith.[36]

QUESTIONS FOR DISCUSSION

1. How did/do Christian misunderstandings of their own texts contribute to anti-Semitism? Consider the "four dangerous anti-Jewish readings" discussed in the chapter.
2. Who were the Holocaust theologians and why is their work important?
3. What is the "replacement theory" or "supersessionism" and why is it a difficult and problematic issue?

36. Heschel, "No Religion," 239–40.

FURTHER READING

Fackenheim, Emil. *To Mend the World: Foundations of Post-Holocaust Jewish Thought*. Bloomington: University of Indiana Press, 1994.
Fleischner, Eva, ed. *Auschwitz: Beginnings of a New Era?* New York: Ktav, 1977.
Haynes, Stephen R. *Reluctant Witnesses: Jews and the Christian Imagination.* Louisville: Westminster John Knox, 1995.
Littell, Franklin. *The Crucifixion of the Jews: The Failure of Christians to Understand the Jewish Experience.* Macon, GA: Mercer University Press, 1986.

GLOSSARY

aliyah: to "go up"; used in the sense of going up to participate in the rituals of the synagogue or of immigrating to Israel.

Amidah: "standing"; referring to the central prayer of Jewish worship. It is also called the *Shemoneh-Esrei*, "Eighteen," in reference to the number of blessings or benedictions.

Ashkenazim: a term used to refer first to German Jews and then to Central and Eastern European Jews as a whole.

beit midrash: a house of study.

berakhah: "blessing" or praise, normally of God.

berith: "covenant"; used with reference to the agreements/commitments between God and his people, especially the covenants with Abraham, Moses, and David.

cohen/kohen: "priest"; a term used before the destruction of the Second Temple for the descendants of the house of Aaron who were responsible for the temple ritual. Jews still recognize certain families and individuals as *cohanim*. They are called upon for the first blessing of the Sabbath.

Diaspora: from the Greek word for "scatter," it is used to refer to Jews living outside of the land of Israel.

get: the official rabbinic document that sanctions a divorce.

haggadah or aggadah: a category of midrash (see below) that uses parable, legend, and creative, even playful, readings to interpret difficult texts and solve problems within the tradition.

halakah: from the Hebrew meaning "to walk," it refers to the corpus of Jewish law.

Hanukkah/*Chanukah*: "dedication"; a Jewish holiday celebrating the rededication of the temple after it was captured from the Seleucid Empire in the second century BCE.

haskelah: from the Hebrew word for "intellect"; it refers to the Jewish version of the European "Enlightenment" of the eighteenth century.

huppah: marriage canopy under which the ceremony takes place.

Kabbalah: "tradition"; especially the Jewish mystical tradition.

kaddish: a doxology, praise of God, said at the end of sections of Jewish worship; also used especially by mourners.

Ketuvah: the marriage contract describing the mutual obligations of husband and wife.

Kiddush HaShem: "sanctification of the name"; in medieval times especially, this referred to martyrdom.

kosher: "fit, proper"; anything appropriate for use by Jewish law.

matzah: unleavened bread, used on Passover.

menorah: a candelabrum with nine branches used in the ancient temple and in Hanukkah celebrations.

mezuzah: a case attached to the doorposts of Jewish homes that contains a parchment copy of the first two paragraphs of the Shema (see below).

midrash: "investigation," "inquiry"; used for exegesis or interpretation of Scripture, but it can also be used of collections of such exegesis.

mikveh: a ritual bath for the washing away of impurities.

Mishnah: "repeated study"; refers to the code of Jewish law produced by Rabbi Judah the Prince around 220 CE. Its origins are found in the "oral law" that traditional Jews trace back to Moses at Sinai. Contains both "religious" and "civil" law as well as stories, parables, and sayings of famous rabbis. It is the basis of the later discussion of the Talmud.

mitzvah: "commandment"; biblical or rabbinic injunctions. In common parlance it is used to refer to a good deed. Well known from the Bar Mitzvah when a Jewish boy becomes a full member of the Jewish community and responsible for the commandments. There is an equivalent service for girls in some traditions called a Bat Mitzvah.

mohel: a ritual circumciser.

Pesach: Passover; the Jewish festival commemorating the exodus from Israel.

piyyut: synagogue poetry and hymnody.

Purim: Jewish festival celebrating the rescue of the Jews from destruction during the Persian Empire as recorded in the biblical book of Esther.

Rosh Hashanah: "head of the year"; the Jewish New Year, which begins a series of holy days of repentance and hope culminating in Yom Kippur.

seder: "order"; the ritual meal and ceremony performed in the Jewish home on the first night of Passover (see above, *Pesach*). The ritual is described in a Passover prayer book called the *Haggadah* ("telling").

Sephardim: used from the Middle Ages to refer to Jews from Spain and North Africa.

Shavuot: "weeks"; the Feast of Weeks or Pentecost, which commemorates the giving of the Torah at Sinai.

Shema: "hear"; the core statement of Jewish belief recited at both the morning and evening prayers. It contains texts from Deuteronomy 6:4–9; 11:13–21; and Numbers 15:37–41.

shiva: "sitting"; a seven-day period of mourning following the death and burial of a loved one.

shofar: a horn, usually a ram's horn, sounded at certain occasions during the Jewish year.

Siddur: "order"; the Jewish prayer book.

Simchat Torah: a one-day celebration at the end of *Sukkot* (see below) that celebrates the end of the yearly cycle of Torah readings.

Sukkot: "huts" or "booths"; a Jewish harvest and pilgrimage festival that recalls the exodus wanderings.

synagogue: a Greek word for a place of gathering. A place of Jewish prayer, study, worship, and social activity.

tallit: the prayer shawl worn by adult Jewish males in the morning prayer service.

Talmud: contains the Mishnah plus the commentary and discussion (called Gemara) of the rabbinical schools in Palestine and Babylonia from 200 to 500 CE. It exists in two forms, the Palestinian and Babylonian traditions. The latter is considered the most authoritative.

Tanakh: the acronym for Torah, Nevi'im (Prophets), and Ketuvim (Writings)—the Hebrew Scriptures.

***tefillin* or phylacteries**: boxes containing small parchment scrolls worn by traditional Jewish males. These are attached to the body with leather straps and worn during morning prayer.

terefah: "torn"; usually refers to non-kosher foods.

Torah: "teaching"; a term used to refer specifically to the Pentateuch, the five books of Moses, but also used for the entire Hebrew Bible, the Oral Torah, the Talmud, and Midrash—all Jewish sacred texts can be called Torah.

tzedakah: an act of "righteousness," "justice," or, in common speech, "charity." Commonly refers to support for those less fortunate.

yeshiva: "session"; traditionally used to refer to a rabbinical academy offering the study of Jewish sacred texts as well as, in more recent years, secular studies.

Yom Kippur: Day of Atonement; a day of fasting, prayer, and repentance.

Zohar: the "Book of Splendor"; a medieval Jewish mystical text. Contains mystical commentary on biblical texts and stories of early Jewish mystics.

BIBLIOGRAPHY

Abrahams, Israel, ed. *Hebrew Ethical Wills.* Philadelphia: Jewish Publication Society of America, 1976.

Bader-Saye, Scott. *Church and Israel after Christendom.* Eugene, OR: Wipf and Stock, 1999.

Baeck, Leo. *Judaism and Christianity.* Translated by Walter Kaufmann. Philadelphia: Jewish Publication Society of America, 1958.

———. *The Pharisees and Other Essays.* Introduction by Krister Stendahl. New York: Schocken Books, 1966.

Baskin, Judith R., and Kenneth Seeskin, eds. *The Cambridge Guide to Jewish History, Religion, and Culture.* Cambridge: Cambridge University Press, 2010.

Becker, Adam A., and Anette Yoshiko Reed, eds. *The Ways That Never Parted: Jews and Christians in Late Antiquity and the Early Middle Ages.* Minneapolis: Fortress, 2007.

Bieringer, Reimund, and Didier Pollefeyt, eds. *Paul and Judaism: Crosscurrents in Pauline Exegesis and the Study of Jewish-Christian Relations.* London: Bloomsbury T & T Clark, 2012.

Bird, Michael F. *An Anomalous Jew: Paul among Jews, Greeks, and Romans.* Grand Rapids: Eerdmans, 2016.

Birnbaum, Philip, translation and introduction. *Mishnah Torah: Maimonides' Code of Law and Ethics.* New York: Hebrew Publishing Company, 1944.

Bleakney, Robert W. *Evangelical Interpretation After Auschwitz.* Atlanta: Hebraic Heritage Press, 2019.

Boccaccini, Gabriele, and Carlos A. Segovia, eds. *Paul the Jew: Rereading the Apostle as a Figure of Second Temple Judaism.* Minneapolis: Fortress, 2016.

Borowitz, Eugene B. *Liberal Judaism.* New York: Union of American Hebrew Congregations, 1984.

———. *Renewing the Covenant: A Theology for the Postmodern Jew.* Philadelphia: Jewish Publication Society, 1991.

Boyarin, Daniel. *Dying for God: Martyrdom and the Making of Judaism and Christianity.* Stanford, CA: Stanford University Press, 1999.

———. *The Jewish Gospels: The Story of the Jewish Christ.* New York: New Press, 2012.

———. *A Radical Jew: Paul and the Politics of Identity.* 3rd ed. Berkeley: University of California Press, 1997.

Bradshaw, Paul F., and Lawrence A. Hoffman. *The Making of Jewish and Christian Worship.* Notre Dame, IN: University of Notre Dame Press, 1991.

Braude, William G., and Israel J. Kapstein, trans. *Pesikta De-Rab Kahana.* Philadelphia: Jewish Publication Society of America, 2002.

———. *Tanna Debe Eliyyahu: The Lore of the School of Elijah.* Philadelphia: Jewish Publication Society of America, 1981.

Bruteau, Beatrice, ed. *Jesus through Jewish Eyes: Rabbis and Scholars Engage an Ancient Brother in a New Conversation.* Maryknoll, NY: Orbis Books, 2001.

Buber, Martin. *The Legend of the Baal-Shem.* Translated by Maurice Friedman. London: Horowitz, 1956.

———. *Moses: The Revelation of the Covenant.* New York: Harper & Row, 1958.

———. *On Judaism.* Edited by Norman Glatzer. The early addresses translated by Eva Jospe. New York: Schocken Books, 1967.

———. *Two Types of Faith.* Translated by Norman P. Goldhawk. Syracuse, NY: Syracuse University Press, 2003.

Cannon, Mae Elise, ed. *A Land Full of God: Christian Perspectives on the Holy Land.* Eugene, OR: Cascade Books, 2017.

Carroll, James. *Constantine's Sword: The Church and the Jews.* Boston: Houghton Mifflin, 2001.

Cohen, Abraham. *Everyman's Talmud: The Major Teachings of the Rabbinic Sages.* New York: Schocken Books, 1949.

Cohen, Shaye J. D. *From the Maccabees to the Mishnah.* 3rd ed. Louisville: Westminster John Knox, 2014.

Cohn-Sherbok, Dan. *Judaism: History, Belief and Practice.* London: Routledge, 2003.

Collins, John J., and Daniel C. Harlow, eds. *The Eerdmans Dictionary of Early Judaism.* Grand Rapids: Eerdmans, 2010.

Confino, Alon. *A World without Jews: The Nazi Imagination from Persecution to Genocide.* New Haven: Yale University Press, 2014.

Danby, Herbert, trans. and introduction. *The Mishnah.* Oxford: Oxford University Press, 1933.

Davies, Alan T. *Anti-Semitism and the Christian Mind: The Crisis of Conscience after Auschwitz.* New York: Herder and Herder, 1969.

———, ed. *AntiSemitism and the Foundations of Christianity.* New York: Paulist Press, 1979.

Davies, W. D. *Jewish and Pauline Studies.* London: SPCK, 1984.

———. *Paul and Rabbinic Judaism: Some Rabbinic Elements in Pauline Theology.* London: SCM, 1948.

Donin, Hayim Halevy. *To Be a Jew: A Guide to Jewish Observance in Contemporary Life.* New York: HarperCollins, 1991.

———. *To Pray as a Jew: A Guide to the Prayer Book and the Synagogue Service.* New York: Basic Books, 1980.

Dorff, Elliot N. *For the Love of God and People: A Philosophy of Jewish Law.* Philadelphia: Jewish Publication Society, 2007.

Dresner, Samuel H. *Heschel, Hasidim, and Halakha.* New York: Fordham University Press, 2002.

Efron, John, Steven Weitzman, and Matthias Lehmann. *The Jews: A History.* 2nd ed. Boston: Pearson, 2014.

Eisenbaum, Pamela. *Paul Was Not a Christian: The Original Message of a Misunderstood Apostle.* New York: HarperCollins, 2009.

Eklund, Rebekah A., and John E. Phelan Jr. *Doing Theology for the Church: Essays in Honor of Klyne Snodgrass.* Eugene, OR: Wipf and Stock, 2014.

Elazar, Daniel J., and Rela Mintz Geffen. *The Conservative Movement in Judaism: Dilemmas and Opportunities.* Albany: State University of New York, 2000.

Erickson, Robert P. *Complicity in the Holocaust: Churches and Universities in Nazi Germany.* Cambridge: Cambridge University Press, 2012.

———. *Theologians under Hitler: Gerhard Kittel, Paul Althaus, Emanuel Hirsch.* New Haven: Yale University Press, 1985.

Fackenheim, Emil L. *To Mend the World: Foundations of Post-Holocaust Jewish Thought.* Bloomington: Indiana University Press, 1994.

Fishbane, Michael. *Judaism: Revelations and Tradition.* New York: HarperCollins, 1987.

———. *Sacred Attunement: A Jewish Theology.* Chicago: University of Chicago Press, 2008.

Fishman, Hertzel. *American Protestantism and a Jewish State.* Detroit: Wayne State University Press, 1973.

Fleischner, Eva, ed. *Auschwitz: Beginning of a New Era?* New York: Ktav, 1974.

Flusser, David. *Jesus.* 3rd ed., corrected and augmented. Jerusalem: Hebrew University Press, 2001.

Frankel, Jonathan, and Ezra Mendelsohn. *The Protestant-Jewish Conundrum.* Oxford: Oxford University Press, 2010.

Fredriksen, Paula. *From Jesus to Christ.* 2nd ed. New Haven: Yale University Press, 2000.

Fredriksen, Paula, and Adele Reinhartz, eds. *Jesus, Judaism, and Christian Anti-Semitism: Reading the New Testament after the Holocaust.* Louisville: Westminster John Knox, 2002.

Fry, Helen P. *Christian Jewish Dialogue: A Reader.* Exeter: University of Exeter Press, 1996.

Frymer-Kensky, Tikva, et al. *Christianity in Jewish Terms.* Boulder, CO: Westview, 2000.

Gager, John G. *Who Made Early Christianity? The Jewish Lives of the Apostle Paul.* New York: Columbia University Press, 2015.

Gaston, Lloyd. *Paul and Torah.* Eugene, OR: Wipf and Stock, 2006.

Gilbert, Martin. *Israel: A History.* Revised and updated. New York: Harper Perennial, 2008.

Glatzer, Nahum N., ed. *The Essential Philo.* New York: Schocken Books, 1971.

Goldhagen, Daniel Johan. *A Moral Reckoning: The Role of the Catholic Church in the Holocaust and Its Unfulfilled Duty of Repair.* New York: Vitntage Books, 2003.

Goodman, Martin. *A History of Judaism.* Princeton: Princeton University Press, 2018.

Grabbe, Lester L. *Judaism from Cyrus to Hadrian.* Vol. 1, *The Persian and Greek Periods,* Philadelphia: Fortress, 1992.

———. *Judaism from Cyrus to Hadrian.* Vol. 2, *The Roman Period.* Philadelphia: Fortress, 1992.

Green, Arthur. *A Guide to the Zohar.* Stanford, CA: Stanford University Press, 2004.

Greenberg, Irving. *For the Sake of Heaven and Earth: The New Encounter between Judaism and Christianity.* Philadelphia: Jewish Publication Society, 2004.

Gushee, David P. *The Righteous Gentiles of the Holocaust: A Christian Interpretation.* Minneapolis: Fortress, 1994.

Guttman, Alexander. *Rabbinic Judaism in the Making: A Chapter in the History of the Halakhah from Ezra to Judah I.* Detroit: Wayne State University Press, 1970.

Hagner, Donald A. *The Jewish Reclamation of Jesus: An Analysis and Critique of the Modern Jewish Study of Jesus.* Eugene, OR: Wipf and Stock, 1997.

Halbertal, Moshe. *Maimonides: Life and Thought.* Translated by Joel Linsider. Princeton: Princeton University Press, 2014.

———. *On Sacrifice*. Princeton: Princeton University Press, 2012.

Halbertal, Moshe, and Donniel Hartman, eds. *Judaism and the Challenges of Modern Life*. London: Continuum, 2007.

Halevi, Yossi Klein. *At the Entrance of the Garden of Eden*. New York: HarperCollins, 2001.

———. *Letter to My Palestinian Neighbor*. New York: HarperCollins, 2018.

———. *Like Dreamers: The Story of the Israeli Paratroopers Who Reunited Jerusalem and Divided a Nation*. New York: HarperCollins, 2013.

Halkin, Abraham, trans. Discussions by David Hartman. *Crisis and Leadership: Epistles of Maimonides*. Philadelphia: Jewish Publication Society, 1985.

Hammer, Reuven, trans., introduction, and commentary. *The Classic Midrash: Tannaitic Commentaries on the Bible*. New York: Paulist Press, 1995.

Hartman, David. *Joy and Responsibility: Israel, Modernity, and the Renewal of Judaism*. Jerusalem: Ben-Zvi Publishers, 1978.

———. *A Living Covenant: The Innovative Spirit in Traditional Judaism*. Woodstock, VT: Jewish Lights, 1997.

Hartman, Donniel. *The Boundaries of Judaism*. London: Continuum, 2007.

———. *Putting God Second: How to Save Religion from Itself*. Boston: Beacon, 2016.

Hertzberg, Arthur. *Judaism: The Classic Introduction to One of the Great Religions of the Modern World*. Rev. ed. New York: Simon and Schuster, 1991.

———, ed. *The Zionist Idea: A Historical Analysis and Reader*. New York: Atheneum, 1972.

Hertzberg, Arthur, and Aron Hirt-Manheimer. *Jews: The Essence and Character of a People*. New York: HarperCollins, 1998.

Heschel, Abraham J. *Between God and Man: An Interpretation of Judaism*. New York: Free Press, 1997.

———. *God in Search of Man: A Philosophy of Judaism*. New York: Farrar, Straus, and Giroux, 1955.

———. *Maimonides*. Translated by Joachim Neugroschel. New York: Fall River Press, 2012.

———. *Man's Quest for God: Studies in Prayer and Symbolism*. New York: Charles Scribner's Sons, 1954.

———. *Moral Grandeur and Spiritual Audacity*. Edited by Susannah Heschel. New York: Farrar, Straus, and Giroux, 1996.

———. *Who Is Man?* Stanford, CA: Stanford University Press, 1963.

Heschel, Susannah. *Abraham Geiger and the Jewish Jesus*. Chicago: University of Chicago Press, 1998.

———. *The Aryan Jesus: Christian Theologians and the Bible in Nazi Germany.* Princeton: Princeton University Press, 2008.

Idel, Moshe. *Kabbalah: New Perspectives.* New Haven: Yale University Press, 1988.

Ilan, Tal. *Integrating Women into the Second Temple History.* Peabody, MA: Hendrickson, 2001.

Jacobs, Louis. *A Jewish Theology.* Springfield, NJ: Behrman House Publishers, 1973.

———. *Principles of the Jewish Faith: An Analytic Study.* New York: Basic Books, 1964.

Kaplan, Dana Evan. *American Reform Judaism: An Introduction.* New Brunswick, NJ: Rutgers University Press, 2003.

Karesh, Sara E., and Mitchell M. Hurvitz. *Encyclopedia of Judaism.* New York: Infobase Publishing, 2005.

Kessler, Edward, and Neil Wenborn, eds. *A Dictionary of Jewish-Christian Relations.* Cambridge: Cambridge University Press, 2005.

Klausner, Joseph. *Jesus of Nazareth: His Life, Times, and Teaching.* New York: Macmillan, 1926.

The Koren Siddur. Introduction, translation, and commentary by Jonathan Sacks. Jerusalem: Koren, 2006.

Kugel, James L. *How to Read the Bible: A Guide to Scripture Then and Now.* New York: Free Press, 2007.

Langton, Daniel. *The Apostle Paul in the Jewish Imagination.* Cambridge: Cambridge University Press, 2010.

Lau, Binyamin. *The Sages: Character, Context and Creativity.* Vol. 1, *The Second Temple Period.* Translated by Michael Prawer. Jerusalem: Maggid Books, 2010.

———. *The Sages: Character, Context and Creativity.* Vol. 2, *From Yavneh to the Bar Kokhba Revolt.* Translated by Ilana Kurshan. Jerusalem: Maggid Books, 2013.

Lederhendler, Eli, ed. *Jews, Catholics, and the Burden of History.* Oxford: Oxford University Press, 2005.

Levenson, Jon D. *The Death and Resurrection of the Beloved Son: The Transformation of Child Sacrifice in Judaism and Christianity.* New Haven: Yale University Press, 1993.

———. *Inheriting Abraham: The Legacy of the Patriarch in Judaism, Christianity and Islam.* Princeton: Princeton University Press, 2012.

———. *The Love of God: Divine Gift, Human Gratitude, and Mutual Faithfulness in Judaism.* Princeton: Princeton University Press, 2016.

Levine, Amy-Jill. *The Misunderstood Jew: The Church and the Scandal of the Jewish Jesus.* New York: HarperCollins, 2006.

Levine, Amy-Jill, and Marc Zvi Brettler, eds. *The Jewish Annotated New Testament: New Revised Standard Version.* Oxford: Oxford University Press, 2011.

Lewis, Bernard. *The Middle East: A Brief History of the Last 2,000 Years.* New York: Touchstone, 1995.

———. *Semites and Anti-Semites: An Inquiry into Conflict and Prejudice.* New York: W. W. Norton, 1986.

Lewy, Hans, Alexander Altmann, and Isaak Heinemann, eds. *Three Jewish Philosophers.* New York: Atheneum, 1973.

Littell, Franklin H. *The Crucifixion of the Jews: The Failure of Christians to Understand the Jewish Experience.* Macon, GA: Mercer University Press, 1986.

Lux, Richard C. *The Jewish People, the Holy Land, and the State of Israel: A Catholic View.* New York: Paulist Press, 2010.

MacCulloch, Diarmaid. *The Reformation: A History.* New York: Penguin Books, 2003.

Manuel, Frank A. *The Broken Staff: Judaism through Christian Eyes.* Cambridge, MA: Harvard University Press, 1992.

Matt, Daniel C. *The Essential Kabbalah: The Heart of Jewish Mysticism.* New York: HarperCollins, 1996.

———, trans. and introduction. *Zohar: The Book of Enlightenment.* Mahwah, NJ: Paulist Press, 1983.

McDermott, Gerald R. *Israel Matters: Why Christians Must Think Differently about the People and the Land.* Grand Rapids: Brazos, 2017.

———, ed. *The New Christian Zionism: Fresh Perspectives on Israel and the Land.* Downers Grove, IL: InterVarsity, 2016.

Mendes-Flohr, Paul. *Martin Buber: A Life of Faith and Dissent.* New Haven: Yale University Press, 2019.

Merkley, Paul Charles. *Christian Attitudes towards the State of Israel.* Montreal: McGill-Queen's University Press, 2001.

Montefiore, C. G. *Judaism and St. Paul: Two Essays.* London: Max Goschen, 1914.

———. *Some Elements of the Religious Teaching of Jesus according to the Synoptic Gospels.* London: Macmillan, 1910.

Montefiore, C. G., and H. Loewe, selection, arrangement, commentary, and introduction. *A Rabbinic Anthology.* Philadelphia: Jewish Publication Society of America, 1960.

Montefiore, Simon Sebag. *Jerusalem: The Biography.* New York: Alfred A. Knopf, 2011.

Munck, Johannes. *Christ and Israel: An Interpretation of Romans 9–11.* Translated by Ingeborg Nixon. Philadelphia: Fortress, 1967.

———. *Paul and the Salvation of Mankind.* Translated by Frank Clarke. Richmond: John Knox, 1959.

Nanos, Mark D., and Magnus Zetterholm, eds. *Paul within Judaism: Restoring the First-Century Context to the Apostle.* Minneapolis: Fortress, 2015.

Neusner, Jacob. *Introduction to American Judaism: What Books Say, What People Do.* Philadelphia: Fortress, 1994.

———. *Invitation to Midrash: A Teaching Book.* San Francisco: Harper & Row, 1989.

———. *Invitation to the Talmud: A Teaching Book.* Rev. and expanded ed. San Francisco: HarperSanFrancisco, 1984.

———. *Judaism and the Interpretation of Scripture: Introduction to the Rabbinic Midrash.* Peabody, MA: Hendrickson, 2004.

———. *A Rabbi Talks with Jesus.* Rev. ed. Montreal: McGill-Queen's University Press, 2000.

———. *Rabbinic Literature and the New Testament: What We Cannot Show, We Do Not Know.* Valley Forge, PA: Trinity Press International, 1994.

———. *The Way of Torah: An Introduction to Judaism.* Belmont, CA: Dickenson, 1970.

———, ed. *Understanding Rabbinic Judaism: From Talmudic to Modern Times.* New York: Ktav, 1974.

Neusner, Jacob, and Alan J. Avery-Peck, eds. *The Blackwell Reader in Judaism.* Malden, MA: Blackwell, 2001.

Nirenberg, David. *Anti-Judaism: The Western Tradition.* New York: W. W. Norton, 2013.

Peck, Abraham J., ed. *Jews and Christians after the Holocaust.* Philadelphia: Fortress, 1982.

Phelan, John E. Jr. *Essential Eschatology: Our Present and Future Hope.* Downers Grove, IL: InterVarsity, 2013.

Philo. *The Works of Philo.* New updated version. Translated by C. D. Yonge. Foreword by David M. Scholer. Peabody, MA: Hendrickson, 1993.

Poupko, Yehiel E. *Chana: A Life in Prayer.* Great Neck, NY: Arthur Kurzweil, 2017.

Raphael, Frederic. *A Jew among the Romans: The Life and Legacy of Flavius Josephus.* New York: Random House, 2013.

Raphael, Marc Lee. *Judaism in America.* New York: Columbia University Press, 2003.

Ravitzky, Aviezer. *Messianism, Zionism, and Jewish Religious Radicalism.* Translated by Michael Swirsky and Jonathan Chipman. Chicago: University of Chicago Press, 1996.

Reif, Stefan C. *Judaism and Hebrew Prayer: New Perspectives on Jewish Liturgical History*. Cambridge: Cambridge University Press, 1993.

Roper, Lyndal. *Martin Luther: Renegade and Prophet*. New York: Random House, 2016.

Rosenthal, Gilbert S. *What Can a Modern Jew Believe?* Eugene, OR: Wipf and Stock, 2007.

———, ed. *A Jubilee for All Time: The Copernican Revolution in Jewish Christian Relations*. Eugene, OR: Pickwick, 2014.

Ross, Robert W. *So It Was True: The American Protestant Press and the Nazi Persecution of the Jews*. Minneapolis: University of Minnesota Press, 1980.

Rudin, James. *Christians and Jews from Faith to Faith: Tragic History, Promising Present, Fragile Future*. Woodstock, VT: Jewish Lights Publishing, 2011.

Sacks, Jonathan. *The Dignity of Difference: How to Avoid the Clash of Civilizations*. London: Continuum, 2002.

———. *Future Tense: A Vision for Jews and Judaism in the Global Culture*. London: Hodder & Stoughton, 2009.

———. *A Letter in the Scroll: Understanding Our Jewish Identity and Exploring the Legacy of the World's Oldest Religion*. New York: Free Press, 2000.

———. *One People? Tradition, Modernity and Jewish Unity*. London: Littman Library of Jewish Civilization, 1993.

———. *To Heal a Fractured World: The Ethics of Responsibility*. New York: Schocken Books, 2005.

Sanders, E. P. *Jesus and Judaism*. Philadelphia: Fortress, 1985.

———. *Paul and Palestinian Judaism: A Comparison of Patterns of Religion*. Philadelphia: Fortress, 1977.

Sandmel, David Fox. "Into the Fray: Joseph Klausner's Approach to Judaism and Christianity in the Greco-Roman World." PhD diss., University of Pennsylvania, 2002.

Sandmel, Samuel. *Anti-Semitism in the New Testament?* Philadelphia: Fortress, 1978.

———. *The Genius of Paul: A Study in History*. Philadelphia: Fortress, 1979.

———. *We Jews and Jesus: Exploring Theological Differences for Mutual Understanding*. Preface by David Sandmel. Woodstock, VT: Jewish Lights, 2006.

Schafer, Peter. *Jesus in the Talmud*. Princeton: Princeton University Press, 2017.

———. *The Jewish Jesus: How Judaism and Christianity Shaped Each Other*. Princeton: Princeton University Press, 2012.

Schama, Simon. *The Story of the Jews.* Vol. 1, *Finding the Words, 1000 BC–1492 AD.* New York: HarperCollins, 2013.

———. *The Story of the Jews.* Vol. 2, *Belonging, 1492–1900.* New York: HarperCollins, 2017.

Schechter, Solomon. *Aspects of Rabbinic Theology: Major Concepts of the Talmud.* New ed. Introduction by Lewis Finkelstein. New York: Schocken Books, 1961.

Scherman, Nosson, ed., trans., anthologizing, and commentary. *The Expanded ArtScroll Siddur.* Meir Zlotowitz, coeditor. 3rd ed. Brooklyn, NY: Mesorah, 2016.

Schiffman, Lawrence H. *From Text to Tradition: A History of Second Temple and Rabbinic Judaism.* Hoboken, NJ: Ktav, 1991.

Schneer, Jonathan. *The Balfour Declaration: The Origins of the Arab-Israeli Conflict.* New York: Random House, 2010.

Schoeps, H. J. *Paul: The Theology of the Apostle in Light of Jewish Religious History.* Rev. ed. Translated by Harold Knight. Philadelphia: Westminster, 1961.

Scholem, Gershom. *Major Trends in Jewish Mysticism.* 2nd ed. Foreword by Robert Alter. New York: Schocken Books, 1995.

———. *On the Mystical Shape of the Godhead: Basic Concepts of the Kabbalah.* Edited and revised, according to the 1976 Hebrew edition by Jonathan Chipman. Translated by Joachim Neugroschel. New York: Schocken Books, 1991.

Segal, Alan F. *Paul the Convert: Apostolate and Apostasy of Saul the Pharisee.* New Haven: Yale University Press, 1990.

———. *Rebecca's Children: Judaism and Christianity in the Roman World.* Cambridge, MA: Harvard University Press, 1986.

———. *Two Powers in Heaven: Early Rabbinic Reports about Christianity and Gnosticism.* Waco, TX: Baylor University Press, 2012.

Seltzer, Robert M. *Jewish People, Jewish Thought: The Jewish Experience in History.* New York: Macmillan, 1980.

Small, Joseph D., and Gilbert S. Rosenthal. *Let Us Reason Together: Christians and Jews in Conversation.* Louisville: Witherspoon, 2010.

Solomon, Norman. *Judaism: A Very Short Introduction.* 2nd ed. Oxford: Oxford University Press, 2014.

———, ed., translation, and selection. *The Talmud: A Selection.* London: Penguin Books, 2009.

Soloveitchik, Joseph B. *Halakhic Man.* Translated by Lawrence Kaplan. Philadelphia: Jewish Publication Society, 1983.

———. *The Lonely Man of Faith.* Foreword by David Shatz. New York: Doubleday, 1992.

———. *On Repentance.* Adapted and edited by Pinchas H. Peli. Rev. ed. Jerusalem: Maggid Books, 2017.

———, and Abraham R. Besdin. *Reflections of the Rav: Lessons in Jewish Thought. Adapted from Lectures by Rabbi Joseph B. Soloveitchik.* Jerusalem: Department of Torah Education and Culture in the Diaspora of the World Zionist Organization Jerusalem, 1979.

Spinoza, Benedict. *A Theologico-Political Treatise* and *A Political Treatise.* Translated and introduced by R. H. M. Elwes. Mineola, NY: Dover, 2004.

Steinsaltz, Adin. *The Essential Talmud.* Thirtieth anniversary ed. with a new preface by the author and two new chapters. Translated by Chaya Galai. New York: Basic Books, 2006.

———. *A Guide to Jewish Prayer.* Translated by Rebecca Toueg. New York: Schocken Books, 2000.

———. *The Long Shorter Way: Discourses of Chasidic Thought.* Translated and edited by Yehuda Hanegbi. Jerusalem: Maggid Books, 2014.

———. *The Thirteen Petalled Rose: A Discourse on the Essence of Jewish Existence and Belief.* Rev. ed. translated by Yehuda Hanegbi. Jerusalem: Maggid Books, 2006.

Stendahl, Krister. *Paul among Jews and Gentiles.* Philadelphia: Fortress, 1976.

Sutton, Matthew Avery. *American Apocalypse: A History of Modern Evangelicalism.* Cambridge, MA: Belknap Press of Harvard University Press, 2014.

Talbert, Charles H., ed. *Reimarus: Fragments.* Philadelphia: Fortress, 1978.

Tanenbaum, Marc H., Marvin R. Wilson, and A. James Rudin, eds. *Evangelicals and Jews in an Age of Pluralism.* Grand Rapids: Baker, 1984.

———. *Evangelicals and Jews in Conversation on Scripture, Theology, and History.* Grand Rapids: Baker, 1978.

Twersky, Isadore. *Introduction to the Code of Maimonides.* New Haven: Yale University Press, 1980.

———, ed., introduction, and notes. *A Maimonides Reader.* New York: Behrman House, 1972.

Ullrich, Volker. *Hitler: Ascent 1889–1939.* Translated by Jefferson Chase. New York: Alfred A. Knopf, 2016.

Urbach, Ephraim E. *The Sages: The World and Wisdom of the Rabbis of the Talmud.* Translated by Israel Abrahams. Cambridge, MA: Harvard University Press, 1987.

Vermes, Geza. *Jesus the Jew: A Historian's Reading of the Gospels.* London: William G. Collins & Sons, 1973.

Weber, Timothy P. *The Road to Armageddon: How Evangelicals Became Israel's Best Friend.* Grand Rapids: Baker, 2004.

Wiesenthal, Simon. *The Sunflower: On the Possibilities and Limits of Forgiveness.* Rev. and expanded ed. New York: Schocken Books, 1997.

Wilson, Marvin R. *Exploring Our Hebraic Heritage: A Christian Theology of Roots and Renewal.* Grand Rapids: Eerdmans, 2014.

Wolski, Nathan. *A Journey into the Zohar: An Introduction to the Book of Radiance.* Albany: State University of New York Press, 2010.

Wright, N. T. *Paul and His Recent Interpreters.* Minneapolis: Fortress, 2015.

———. *Paul and the Faithfulness of God.* 2 vols. Minneapolis: Fortress, 2013.

Wyschogrod, Michael. *Abraham's Promise.* Edited and introduced by R. Kendall Soulen. Grand Rapids: Eerdmans, 2004.

———. *The Body of Faith: God in the People Israel.* New York: Seabury, 1983.

INDEX OF NAMES AND SUBJECTS

INDEX OF SCRIPTURE AND OTHER ANCIENT TEXTS